Employment and Development

IZA Prize in Labor Economics Series

Since 2002, the Institute for the Study of Labor (IZA) has awarded the IZA Prize in Labor Economics for outstanding contributions to policy-relevant labor market research and methodological progress in this sub-discipline of economic science. The IZA Prize is the only international science prize awarded exclusively to labor economists. This special focus acknowledges the global significance of high-quality basic research in labor economics and sound policy advice based on these research findings. As issues of employment and unemployment are among the most urgent challenges of our time, labor economists have an important task and responsibility. The IZA Prize in Labor Economics is today considered one of the most prestigious international awards in the field. It aims to stimulate further research on topics that have enormous implications for our future. All prize-winners contribute a volume to the IZA Prize in Labor Economics Series published by Oxford University Press, which has been established to provide an overview of the laureates' most significant findings.

The IZA Prize in Labor Economics has become an integral part of the institute's manifold activities to promote progress in labor market research. Based on nominations submitted by the IZA Research Fellows, a high-ranking IZA Prize Committee selects the prize-winner. In conjunction with the Award Ceremony the IZA Prize Conference brings together a number of renowned experts to discuss topical labor market issues.

It is not by coincidence that the IZA Prize in Labor Economics Series is published by Oxford University Press. This well-reputed publishing house has shown a great interest in the project from the very beginning as this exclusive series perfectly complements their range of publications. We gratefully acknowledge their excellent cooperation.

Winners of the IZA Prize in Labor Economics

Gary S. Fields
2014 IZA Prize Laureate

Employment and Development

How Work Can Lead From and Into Poverty

Gary S. Fields

Edited by
Janneke Pieters

OXFORD
UNIVERSITY PRESS

OXFORD
UNIVERSITY PRESS

Great Clarendon Street, Oxford, OX2 6DP,
United Kingdom

Oxford University Press is a department of the University of Oxford.
It furthers the University's objective of excellence in research, scholarship,
and education by publishing worldwide. Oxford is a registered trade mark of
Oxford University Press in the UK and in certain other countries

Published in the United States of America by Oxford University Press
198 Madison Avenue, New York, NY 10016, United States of America

British Library Cataloguing in Publication Data
Data available

Library of Congress Control Number: 2018950862

ISBN 978–0–19–881550–1

Award Statement
of the IZA Prize Committee

The 2014 IZA Prize in Labor Economics is awarded to U.S. economist Gary S. Fields for his outstanding contributions on the importance of efficient labor markets and stable employment for poverty reduction and the economic development in low- and middle-income countries. Fields established indicators such as poverty, inequality and income mobility as primary measures of economic development, revolutionizing traditional economic thinking about measuring development. He made fundamental contributions to our understanding of how labor markets function in developing countries.

Fields' groundbreaking book "Working Hard, Working Poor: A Global Journey" (2012) illustrates that the global poverty is a problem of the quality of employment; not, as widely believed, a matter of high unemployment rates, which are often lower in low- and middle-income countries than in high-income countries. A key problem is the lack of social insurance systems. Given that many jobs in developing countries are unstable and earnings are extremely low, people are unable to overcome the status of "working poor" and thus remain in poverty even when employed. Fields' policy recommendations aim at increasing the level and security of wages for employees and self-employed by incentivizing investments in the private sector, growth and international trade, and by providing the necessary skills and business know-how to stimulate labor demand. In this respect, Fields also shows the shortcomings of previous development aid, which had not sufficiently targeted labor market needs.

Gary Fields has worked on labor markets in developing economies since the beginning of his career and played a crucial role in renewing the then-established understanding of economic development. In his early studies ("Who Benefits from Economic Development?", American Economic Review,

1977; "Poverty, Inequality and Development", 1980), he already made the case for approaching economic development using earnings structures, the distribution of productive activities and other less aggregated factors. Fields formulated the core question for development economists as: who benefits how much from economic development and why? He emphasized the use of poverty and inequality measures as primary indicators of the progress of development. Fields' approach was challenging and novel at that time. The conventional approach in economic research had been to ask whether a specific type of distributional pattern promotes or hinders growth. Fields turned this approach upside down and called on economists to analyze how the rate and type of growth helps or hinders distributional goals.

In 2002 he published the equally successful book "Distribution and Development: A New Look at the Developing World". Given the extensive amount of data made available in the meantime, Fields was able to consider an additional factor next to poverty and inequality to measure economic development: income mobility.

In addition to development economics, Fields has worked on topics such as pensions, social insurance and welfare, and workplace organization. His contributions in these fields are also highly regarded and significant.

Gary Fields is Professor of Economics and the John P. Windmuller Professor of International and Comparative Labor at Cornell University, USA. He has been an Ivy League teacher and professor for more than forty years. After receiving his Ph.D. in economics from the University of Michigan, he became an assistant professor at Yale University at age 25 and an associate professor at age 29. Two years later, he took up a tenured professorship at Cornell University. He published more than 150 books and scientific articles mainly in the area of development economics. Fields also has extensive consulting experience for such organizations as the World Bank, the Inter-American Development Bank, the International Labor Organization (ILO), the United Nations and various national governments. Fields joined the IZA network as a Research Fellow in 2007 and has been cooperating closely with IZA ever since.

The 2014 IZA Prize in Labor Economics honors the outstanding contributions of a unique scholar, who has fundamentally shaped our understanding of labor markets in the developing world, helping policymakers tackle one of today's most pressing tasks – the reduction of global poverty and inequality.

George A. Akerlof, University of California, Berkeley; IZA
Rebecca M. Blank, University of Wisconsin-Madison; IZA
Corrado Giulietti, IZA
Richard Portes, London Business School; President CEPR
Klaus F. Zimmermann, IZA; University of Bonn

Contents

Contents

Part I
Introduction by the Editor

Global Poverty Is an Employment Problem

Janneke Pieters

> Most people derive most if not all of their income from the work they and other family members do. It follows that, to assure that economic development reaches the poor, development efforts must be targeted on improving employment and earnings of low-income households.
>
> *Gary Fields, IZA Newsroom Interview 2014*

The 2014 IZA Prize in Labor Economics was awarded to Gary Fields for his outstanding contributions on the importance of efficient labor markets and stable employment for poverty reduction in developing countries. According to the award statement of the IZA Prize Committee:

> Fields' groundbreaking book "Working Hard, Working Poor: A Global Journey" (2012) illustrates that global poverty is a problem of the quality of employment; not, as widely believed, a matter of high unemployment rates, which are often lower in low- and middle-income countries than in high-income countries. A key problem is the lack of social insurance systems. Given that many jobs in developing countries are unstable and earnings are extremely low, people are unable to overcome the status of "working poor" and thus remain in poverty even when employed. Fields' policy recommendations aim at increasing the level and security of wages for employees and self-employed by incentivizing investments in the private sector, growth and international trade, and by providing the necessary skills and business know-how to stimulate labor demand. In this respect, Fields also shows the shortcomings of previous development aid, which had not sufficiently targeted labor market needs.

Gary Fields has pioneered a welfare economic analysis of labor markets and development that focuses on employment and unemployment, labor market earnings, poverty, inequality, and income mobility. In his work, a chief contribution has been to incorporate the principal features of developing countries' labor markets, which often differ from labor markets in rich countries, into realistic theoretical labor market models. Quoting Ira N. Gang, former doctoral student of Gary Fields, in his laudation at the presentation of the 2014 IZA Prize (Gang, 2015):

> It is important to recognize that what Gary did in looking at labor and development was not to simply use straight labor economics in conjunction with data that happens to come from developing countries. What he did and pushed others to do brought about a fundamental shift in the questions asked and consideration of the institutions framing them, it is one in which the very different constraints agents face changes the entire nature of what we study and what we do. Quoting Gary [from my lecture notes, Fall 1979, Cornell University]:
>
>> "The essence of economic underdevelopment is the existence of severe constraints on people's behavior... The essence of economic development is the relaxation of such constraints... [We] need to learn how the constraints on individuals' choices are related to the nature and extent of government involvement in the economy, trade orientation, education and human resource policy and other aspects of development strategy and performance. These proximate explanations should be linked more closely to underlying causes, especially those that might be changed by public policy."

The 2014 prize marks the interest of IZA in fostering our understanding of the interactions between development and labor economics, and its support for the view that employment strategies need to be at the core of development policy. The 2013 World Development Report on Jobs (World Bank, 2012) has stressed the role of private sector-led growth in order to create jobs, where the role of governments is to ensure that the right conditions are in place. Similarly, a recent investigation into the link between development and productive employment (Scarpetta and Pierre, 2015) highlights the importance of policies and institutions directly and indirectly related to the labor market, including the investment climate and social protection schemes.

Work and Development

As described in the 2013 World Development Report (World Bank 2012, p.48), worldwide *"Some 1.65 billion [workers] have regular wages or salaries. Another 1.5 billion work in farming and small household enterprises, or in casual or seasonal day labor. The majority of workers in the poorest countries are engaged in these types of work, outside the scope of an employer-employee*

3

relationship." Hence, the key problem for developing countries is not so much unemployment, which is a major challenge for developed countries, especially since the onset of the global financial crisis in 2008. In developing countries, the main problem is the lack of decent work, providing a sufficient level of means for living.

The extent of the problem is captured well by estimates of working poverty, which measures the share of workers whose households live on less than US$2 per person per day. Projections by the International Labour Organization (Kapsos and Bourmpoula, 2013) estimate there will be 731 million working poor in 2017, with an additional 637 million workers near poverty (their families will live on US$2 to US$4 per person per day). Together, this means almost half of all workers in developing countries will be living on less than US$4 per day. Regional estimates show even more extreme numbers for South Asia and sub-Saharan Africa, where 87 percent and 79 percent of workers, respectively, will be poor or near poor in 2017.

Policies that target economic growth will not necessarily create jobs and achieve development goals. In fact, the 2013 World Development Report has argued that jobs are what drive development, and therefore a jobs strategy is central for successful development policies. "Efficient utilization of labor is essential for sustainable long-term economic growth" (Scarpetta and Pierre, 2015, p. 269), meaning that people need to increase productivity in their jobs and be able to move from low- to high-productivity jobs, while less productive jobs disappear from the economy. This requires investments in human capital, as well as in efficient allocation mechanisms to avoid serious mismatches and foster labor mobility in the face of changing economic and labor market conditions.

Changing conditions driven by market liberalization reforms have been a challenge in developing countries. Another major source of change is the rapid rate of urbanization many countries experience, as more and more people move from rural to urban areas. Globally, 54 percent of the population resided in urban areas in 2014. As Africa and Asia remain mostly rural, they are expected to urbanize faster than other regions over the coming decades. The UN estimates that by 2050, two thirds of the world's population, and 56 and 64 percent in Africa and Asia, respectively, will live in towns and cities (United Nations, 2014). Rural-urban labor migration has been considered to be a driver of development (Fields, 2004), but the transition also comes with large adjustment costs and many challenges for the wellbeing of migrants (as well as that of non-migrants left behind). These challenges will be concentrated in the lower-middle-income countries where urbanization is proceeding most rapidly.

While the adaptability of labor markets is important, labor market and social institutions are often not sufficiently developed to moderate the challenges, and often provide only limited access to social safety nets. Whereas labor market policies can regulate working conditions, work contracts, wage bargaining, and can provide other forms of protection for workers, in some cases they only aggravate existing imperfections – and not only because vast numbers of informal firms and workers are outside the reach of such policies. In several Latin American countries, for example, formal sector workers pay mandatory contributions to social insurance schemes, which increase the cost of formal labor, while informal workers are covered by social assistance programs, which effectively subsidize informal labor (Ferreira and Robalino, 2010). As an important role for labor policies and institutions is to provide mechanisms for voice and protection for the most vulnerable workers (e.g., youth, women, informal workers), doing so without obstructing efficiency and job creation is a major challenge.

Overall, the evidence for developing countries suggests that labor market policies have at most limited effects on efficiency and job creation (World Bank, 2012). While government policies play a central role in sustained job creation, it is ultimately the private sector that creates jobs. Governments should thus encourage the creation of good jobs by the private sector, including an enabling business environment, an effective judicial system, and a healthy and well-educated population. Fostering a friendly investment climate, for example, is known to bring higher wages and employment and better working conditions in the long run. Given the complex nature of developing countries' labor markets, and the diversity of income-generating activities that people undertake, employment challenges require policy action beyond labor markets, in areas such as education, credit markets, infrastructure, and business regulation.

Gary Fields' Contributions in this Volume

Gary Fields observed the central importance of labor markets for development early on and has contributed towards a better understanding of their functioning. In his work, Fields emphasizes that global poverty is an employment problem, not an unemployment problem. Many people in developing countries remain poor even when employed, and this is a much more pervasive problem than unemployment. As Fields describes in Chapter 1 of this volume, an estimated 900 million people were employed but earned too little to allow their families to live on more than US$2 per person per day in 2011. ILO estimates described above show that some improvement is expected, but still half of all workers in developing countries will live in poor or near-poor families in 2017.

5

Consequently, as Part III in this volume puts forward, the central question in development is how the poor can earn more for their labor. In Chapter 1, Fields describes a number of policy options for improving employment outcomes of poor people, including labor market policies and policies that are not labor market policies but which have an important bearing on labor markets such as liberalization of international trade and private sector development.

One consensus that has emerged is that helping the poor earn their way out of poverty entails creating new and more productive wage and salaried employment, but also increasing earnings from self-employment. There are not enough wage and salaried jobs available for all who want them. Self-employment, including own-account work and unpaid family work, is more prevalent than paid employment (see Chapter 3). Yet beyond the analysis of particular policies to increase employment and earnings, Fields' central contribution has been to develop a comprehensive framework for policy evaluation, which consists of two key parts – parts that constitute the principal themes in this volume.

The first is the modeling of developing country labor markets, which is the focus of the chapters in Part IV. Based on the central notion that labor market models for developing countries must incorporate the key empirical features observed in those countries, Fields has made fundamental contributions to the literature. One of his first journal publications (Chapter 4) extended the Harris-Todaro model of rural-urban migration by including the urban informal sector. This extension, as well as his work on modeling on-the-job search (Chapter 5), and the introduction of dualism within the informal sector (an "easy entry informal sector" and an "upper-tier informal sector" coexist, Chapter 7) have inspired and continue to inspire a large body of research on development.

This includes early work on the effects of trade liberalization on employment in developing countries (e.g., Krueger et al., 1981) and a large body of theoretical and empirical work on segmentation in urban labor markets (e.g., Rauch, 1991; Günther and Launov, 2011; Assaad, 2014). The coexistence of formal salaried jobs and informal wage work or own-account work remains a central feature of urban labor markets in the developing world and even increasingly so in developed countries. Dualism in labor market modeling is thus as relevant today as it was in the 1970s, and has also found its way into research on migration and development (Zenou, 2011; Clemens et al., 2014). Furthermore, the field has come to accept as a standard view that the informal sector consists of different types of employment, ranging from highly skilled professional entrepreneurship to low-productivity subsistence self-employment (e.g., Bosch and Maloney, 2010). How best to model these various segments of the informal sector is an area of research still in development, and one in which Fields remains an active contributor.

The second part of the framework assesses whether policy objectives have been met, by applying analytical tools to evaluate distributional changes: tools that force the researcher to be explicit about the welfare criteria that are applied. The five chapters in Part V are devoted to the assessment of changes in the distribution of income and earnings, including the measurement of poverty, inequality, and income mobility. Fields' work on the measurement of inequality and poverty, and on how to assess welfare when income distributions change (Chapters 9–12), has influenced research beyond the field of employment and development. His work is highly cited in the theoretical literature on inequality measurement and comparisons. As an example, six papers authored or co-authored by Fields are cited in the Handbook on Economic Inequality chapter on the measurement of inequality (Cowell, 2000). Applications of the theory span areas from the analysis of redistribution policies (e.g., Bargain et al., 2015) to the construction of multi-dimensional poverty indicators and measurement of inequalities in health.

The same holds for Fields' work in a relatively new area of research, which concerns the conceptualization and measurement of income mobility, and how mobility relates to inequality and poverty (Chapters 13–14). Eight papers authored or co-authored by Fields are cited in Jäntti and Jenkins' (2015) survey on income mobility. For empirical analysis, income mobility research requires longitudinal data that follow the same individuals or households over time. The increasing availability of panel surveys and administrative data have stimulated progress in this type of analysis. However, many conceptual issues have not yet been resolved. Fields shows that empirical analysis of income mobility and the analysis of cross-section income inequality can lead to qualitatively different conclusions (Chapter 14).

As illustrated by this volume, Fields' research on inequality and mobility is ultimately motivated by the global poverty problem and how to evaluate the effects of policies that aim to improve the well-being of the poor. In Part VI, the challenges of labor market modeling and assessment of welfare changes are brought together. One could argue that this combination is what is most distinct about Fields' work: not only has he made groundbreaking contributions to the fields of labor market modeling and income distribution, he has taken a further step to bring both parts together in the welfare economics of labor market policies. With this approach, Fields brings a level of rigor to labor market policy evaluation that few others do. He uses empirically grounded theoretical models of labor markets for market-level analysis of various labor market outcomes, and allows for empirical analysis of particular policy interventions in terms of social benefits and social costs, as distinct from individual level analysis. The question we should be asking, according to Fields, is what would happen in the economy and labor market as a whole, as opposed to what would happen to particular individuals. One point he emphasizes is the fundamental importance of improving the poor's access to markets, as this is the only way that increased productivity can translate into higher total earnings.

In Part VII Fields concludes with a discussion of three priority directions for future research, including further empirical analysis on the growth-employment-poverty nexus, more work on comparing cross-section and panel data approaches to income distribution analysis, and the development of more realistic labor market models for developing economies. As a perusal of his own current research shows, we can look forward to valuable new contributions by Gary Fields in each of these areas.

Public Reception of Gary Fields' Work

Google citations to Fields' work covered in this volume reached 2,135 by the end of July 2015. His most highly cited work ranges from early contributions in the 1970s (e.g., Chapter 10 on inequality, which was published in 1978) to very recent work such as his book Working Hard, Working Poor published in 2012; and includes both publications in top academic journals such Econometrica, the Quarterly Journal of Economics, and the Journal of Development Economics, as well as policy papers and book chapters. As Figure I.1 shows, a large share of these citations was made in the current decade, signaling the ongoing influence of Fields' work. In 2012, Fields was the second most highly cited economics professor at Cornell University.

Figure I.1. Google citations to Gary Fields' work collected in this volume.

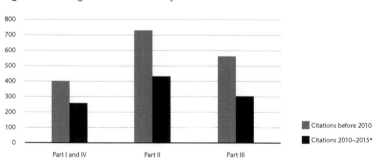

* Includes citations until the end of July 2015.

Among Fields' most widely cited work is his book Distribution and Development: A New Look at the Developing World (Fields, 2001), praised for its powerful combination of real-life examples, economic theory, and empirical evidence on whether and how growth improves people's standards of living. Through real-life examples, which also feature extensively in his most recent book Working Hard, Working Poor, Fields manages to make his readers understand the hardships faced by the working poor. He thus conveys a sense of urgency to the global poverty problem, as recognized by many of his peers, including Nobel Laureates Joseph E. Stiglitz and George Akerlof.

Gary Fields has not only contributed through his academic writings, but also by actively engaging in policy advisory work and consulting with governments and organizations such as the World Bank, Asian Development Bank, Inter-American Development Bank, and the International Labor Organization. Currently, he is engaged in projects funded by UNU-WIDER on the growth-employment-poverty nexus in Latin America and by the World Bank on the suitability of pseudo-panel data for economic mobility studies. Through visiting appointments, he has contributed to teaching and research in various countries, including Colombia, India, and Kenya.

Final Remark

The 2014 IZA Prize and this volume honor Gary Fields' outstanding work on the welfare economics of labor market policies. The research agenda he has advocated and continues to advocate is ambitious and challenging, but, as he put it: "It is better to answer the right questions approximately than the wrong questions exactly." We hope this volume will inspire all of us to put continued effort into the analysis of developing country labor markets, in order to inform policies for global poverty reduction.

IZA/World Bank Conference on Employment and Development

To launch the project and initiate research and fund raising for this purpose, IZA and the World Bank organized a launch-cum-research conference in Berlin in May 2006. Since then, the event has developed into an annual conference, and each conference since 2011 has had a special thematic focus:

- Berlin, Germany — May 25-27, 2006
- Bonn, Germany — June 8-9, 2007
- Rabat, Morocco — May 5-6, 2008
- Bonn, Germany — May 4-5, 2009
- Cape Town, South Africa — May 3-4, 2010

- Mexico City, Mexico — May 30-31, 2011:
  Social Insurance and Labor Markets
- New Delhi, India — November 4-6, 2012:
  Youth Employment and Entrepreneurship
- Bonn, Germany — August 22-23, 2013:
  The Political Economy of Labor Market Reforms
- Lima, Peru — June 25-25, 2015:
  Skills for Productive Employment
- Bonn, Germany — June 4-5, 2015:
  Technological Change and Jobs

Part II

Introduction by the Author

Getting Started on Two Big Problems

The world faces many economic problems. This is one reason that economics is often called "the dismal science". Of all the economic problems in the world, two form the basis for the collection of papers in this volume.

One is the extent of global poverty. According to the best estimates available (Chen and Ravallion, 2013), 1.3 billion people in the world live on less than $1.25 per day in Purchasing Power Parity-adjusted dollars and another 1.7 billion live on between $1.25 and $2.50. Three billion poor people are nearly half of humanity; the global poverty problem is huge.

The second problem highlighted here is the global employment problem. Although there are 200 million people in the world who are unemployed using standard international definitions, a much larger number of people in the world – 900 million – are working poor, defined as people who are working and yet they and their families live on less than $2 per person per day (ILO, 2015).

These, then are the two problems of overarching importance for this volume: the global poverty problem (note: not inequality) and the global employment problem (note: not unemployment). Given that these problems are concentrated overwhelmingly in the developing countries, this volume is primarily about those countries.[1,2]

I began working on these problems in a completely unplanned way. I was a Ph.D. student in Economics at the University of Michigan concentrating in labor economics as my major field and studying econometrics and public economics as my minor fields. Completely out of the blue, my dissertation advisor, George Johnson, said that the Rockefeller Foundation grant which was to take him to Kenya the next year provided funding for a graduate student as well. Would I and my wife Vivian like to go along? Vivian had the wisdom to tell me to say yes, and so we went.

When I got to the University of Nairobi's Institute for Development Studies, I started by reading some of the working papers and recent publications in their library. I found fascinating work by Joseph Stiglitz, John Harris and Michael Todaro, Peter Diamond, and Nick Stern, just to name a few. And Vivian and I drove around Kenya, first in our little Mini and then in our somewhat larger Volkswagen, seeing the country and talking to the people. Within weeks, I decided to set aside the dissertation I had brought along with me – "Returns to Quantity and Quality of Graduate Education in the United States" – thinking I would get back to it one day, but I never did. The problems I found around me were too compelling. As Nobel Prize-winning economist Robert Lucas wrote years later about development, "The consequences for human welfare involved in questions like these are simply staggering: Once one starts to think about them, it is hard to think about anything else" (Lucas, 1988, p. 5).

The "Big Questions"

As it turned out, I had discovered two tracks which have occupied most of my research, teaching, and policy attention ever since, first as I was finishing my Ph.D. at Michigan, then when I was an untenured professor at Yale, and then as a tenured professor at Cornell. I think of these as "the big questions":

1. Who benefits from economic growth and who is hurt by economic decline? Why? Two types of analysis are brought to bear. One is the analysis of changing distributional variables: inequality, poverty, income mobility, and economic well-being. The other is the analysis of changing employment conditions: employment and unemployment, employment composition, and labor market earnings.

2. How do developing countries' labor markets work? How would labor market conditions change if different policies were to be put into effect? What are the welfare consequences of these changes?

It is for my work on these two questions that I won the 2014 IZA Prize.

The relevance of the first question is that economic growth is featured more prominently in the literature than any other development intervention. Three notions need to be distinguished: "economic growth", which is an increase in the total amount of goods and services produced in an economy; "economic underdevelopment", which is when people's choice sets are severely constrained; and "economic development" which is the process of relaxing the constraints on choices, thereby increasing people's material standards of living. If economic growth does result in broad-based improvements in people's material standards of living, especially those of the poor, the case could be made that economic growth should be pursued as part of a development strategy. But it is possible that economic growth may not result in broad-based improvements in standards of living, and the recent experience of the United States all too clearly demonstrates that this possibility is a reality (e.g., Stiglitz, 2015). Rather, the gains may be concentrated among the few – in particular, those at the very top of the income distribution. Inequality may rise, poverty may not fall, inflation-adjusted labor market earnings may stagnate, and the median household may be worse off than before.

What is the usual pattern? Which countries are the exceptions? Why are distributional factors and labor market conditions changing for the better in some countries but not in others? Understanding how these factors have changed in the course of economic growth and decline and why is crucial to reaching a judgment about the most important development policy variable of all: to what extent the pursuit of economic growth serves as a means of achieving economic development.

The second big question concerns labor markets. Why concentrate on labor markets rather than capital markets, land markets, government taxes and transfers, or other markets and income sources? Three empirical facts are pertinent (Fields, 2012; World Bank, 2013). One is that throughout the world, labor income accounts for more of national income than do all other income sources combined. Second, most people derive most if not all of their income from the work they and other members of their households do. Whether they live well or badly is largely a function of how much they earn in the labor market. And third, to the extent that income inequality is of concern in its own right, we have learned from decomposition studies that labor income inequality accounts for a larger share of total income inequality than do the inequalities of all other income sources combined.

Look at it this way: what makes it probable that you, as a reader of this book, are in the top quintile of the world income distribution – perhaps near the top of the top quintile? (The top quintile of the world income distribution occurs at the income level of the U.S. lower-middle class (Milanovic, 2015)). The most likely answer is that your labor income is much higher than most others' – not your capital income or income from any other source. And, at the other end of the scale, why is it that three billion people in the world – nearly half of humanity – live on less than $2.50 per person per day, expressed in terms of purchasing power parity? The answer is that the main asset of the poor – often, their only asset - is their labor, and that asset earns pathetically low returns in the places where these workers are confined. And thus, concentrating on the poor and understanding how the labor markets for them work and how their labor market earnings might be raised if different policies were to be put into effect is a question of first-order importance for human well-being.

A Schematic Analytical Framework

The analytical framework can be visualized schematically in the following way. Consider a policy action of interest and an outcome variable by which the policy action is judged – for example, pursuing economic growth as a means for reducing poverty. For economic growth to contribute to poverty reduction, there must be at least one channel, maybe more, via which growth reduces poverty. Two such channels are often examined in the development literature: the employment channel and the social programs channel. For economic growth to reduce poverty via the employment channel, the growth must result in improved employment conditions (Channel A), and improved employment conditions must result in reduced poverty (Channel B). Similarly, economic growth reduces poverty if growth results in improved social programs (Channel C) and if the social programs reach the poor (Channel D). Figure II.1 displays a case in which all these channels are open, and consequently economic growth reduces poverty via both the employment channel and the social programs channel.

Figure II.1. Open Transmission Channels.

But what if these channels are blocked – for example, because employment is created but the wages and hours of work are such that workers cannot escape poverty or because the benefits of the social programs go to the haves but not to the have-nots. This second case is depicted in Figure II.2. In such a case, economic growth may take place, but employment conditions may improve only for those at the very top but not for those in the middle or bottom of the income distribution and the same may be true for socially-provided goods and services. Thus, although economic growth takes place, the poor may be left out.

Figure II.2. Blocked Transmission Channels.

Economic growth cannot be assumed to benefit everyone, nor can it be assumed to benefit just those at the top to the exclusion or even impoverishment of others further down in the income distribution. A fruitful way to proceed is to examine which channels are open, which are sluggish, and which are blocked. The essays in this volume focus on the channels involving employment.

Key Issues

Four key issues come to the fore:

1. How to summarize the empirical knowledge that is most relevant to understanding "the big questions".
2. How to bring together what we know into realistic, yet parsimonious, theoretical models of what is happening.
3. How to specify the policy evaluation criteria to be used in assessing the effects of actual or prospective policy interventions.
4. How to bring empirical knowledge, theoretical models, and policy evaluation criteria together to reach welfare economic judgments about what should or should not be done.

The four remaining sections of this volume are organized accordingly.

Before beginning your reading, you might find the following basic data about developing countries to be informative:

- *Most developing countries in the world have experienced real (i.e., inflation-adjusted) economic growth* (World Bank, 2015, Table 4.1). Economic growth is positive in every geographic region of the world. It is positive in every income group (high income, middle income, and low income). And it is positive in 98% of the countries of the world from 2000 to 2014.
- *Most developing countries in the world have experienced falling poverty* (World Bank, 2015, Table 2.8).
- *Economic growth and poverty reduction usually go together at the macro level* (Fields, 2001; Fosu, 2011, Table 5). Poverty has fallen in the great majority of country cases when economic growth has taken place. When poverty has not fallen, it typically is because economic growth has not taken place.
- *Human development indicators have risen in <u>every single</u> country of the world* (United Nations, 2014, Table 2).
- *In every country of the world, better-educated workers earn more on average than less-educated workers do* (Montenegro and Patrinos, 2014). *Consequently, countless poverty profiles from around the world show lower rates of poverty among households whose heads are better educated.*
- *An important reason why better-educated workers earn more is that they work in better job categories than less-educated workers do* (Schultz, 1988).
- *Unemployment is particularly prevalent among youth, defined by the ILO as persons between the ages of 15 and 24* (ILO, 2014, p. 36). *However, youth are only about 20% of the world's labor force* (ILO, 2012, p. 9).

Part III
Setting the Framework

This section is comprised of three essays that set the framework for my overall research program on Employment and Development. I have a straightforward reason for starting in this way: suitable policy formulation necessarily builds on suitable problem definition and solid empirical knowledge.

Chapter 1 ("Aid, Growth, and Jobs: A Five-Part Policy Framework") describes the overall policy analysis framework used not only by me but also by many others. In the first year of any university's Ph.D. program in economics, every student is required to master certain essentials - among them, how to maximize. The principles are known to all economists: Specify a maximand (or minimand). Write down a model of how things work. Specify the policy instrument or instruments under consideration. Using the model, determine what outcomes are predicted if a particular policy instrument were to be enacted. Specify a policy evaluation criterion or a number of policy evaluation criteria. Evaluate the predicted outcomes using the specified criterion/criteria.

What I discovered when I started my study of development economics was that many analysts had either forgotten or consciously set aside these lessons. Even today, when I read papers published or submitted for publication, when I teach development economics and labor economics to graduate students, and when I visit the hallowed halls of government buildings and international organizations, I find many of the same problems. Most egregious are the so-called "policy implications" which are not implications at all – that is, they are not implied by the analysis presented. Let us pursue sound policy-making for the real world – evidence-based policy, as it were.[1]

Let us not lament the bad but rather call attention to the good. Here are a few examples. Atkinson and Stiglitz's public economics textbook (1980) remains a model of clear, hard-headed thinking on public policy. One of my students, Debraj Ray, brought his considerable analytical skills to the teaching of development economics, both in the classroom and through his textbook (Ray, 1998). Our Cornell colleague Kaushik Basu's approach to analytical development economics exemplifies a master's approach to applied theory (Basu, 1997).[2] And I know of no one who blends quantitative and qualitative approaches to development economics better than does another Cornellian, Ravi Kanbur (e.g., Bali, Chen, and Kanbur, 2012).

The second essay in this section (Distribution and Development, pp. 1–9) introduces the question of how to think about the distributional consequences of economic growth, distinguishing inequality from poverty from income mobility from economic well-being. Early in my career, when I was still on the faculty at Yale, I put distributional concerns front and center in my graduate development economics course, and my students urged me to write up my class notes as a book.[3] The resultant book, my first (Fields, 1980), took stock of what was known analytically and empirically at the time, but nearly all of it has been supplanted by an enormous outpouring of research since. The parts that remain up-to-date and instructive even today are the alternative measurement approaches and numerical examples which reappeared in Fields (2001) and are included in this volume as Chapter 2.[4] We shall return to distribution and development in Part IV.

The third paper in this section ("How the Poor Are Working") introduces readers to the dimensions and nature of the employment problem in the world. Who are these people, how do they work if they work, how much do they earn for the work they do, and what are their consequent standards of living? My own introduction to the global employment problem came partly through what I saw with my own eyes, from countless conversations with working people first in Kenya and then in Colombia and in many other countries around the world, and from professional reading. Some excellent early contributions include books by David Turnham (1971, 1993) and Lyn Squire (1981). Also influential were the ILO books on Colombia, Ceylon (now Sri Lanka), Kenya, and Iran and the review essay on them by Erik Thorbecke (1973). Later works such as the World Bank's 2013 World Development Report on Jobs, the OECD Employment Outlook (annual), and the ILO's World Employment and Social Outlook (annual) convey a good sense of today's reality. And a fine source depicting the plight of working women around the world are the publications of WIEGO (www.wiego.org).

Finally, if you would like to view a few representative people and read their stories, take a look at their photos on the cover of my book *Working Hard, Working Poor* and read Chapter 3. Kalavati has become famous, and if you're humbled by it and moved to do something, that's great – that's why I wrote it.

1

Aid, Growth, and Jobs: A Five-Part Policy Framework

1.1 Introduction

It has been my distinct pleasure to teach literally hundreds of (Cornell Institute for Public Affairs) CIPA students in the last few years. In each course I teach, in the public policy work I do in the United States and around the world, and in my personal life, I use a five-part policy framework to decide what to do. In this article, I share that approach with you.

1.2 Picking the Policy Area to Work On

I work in the area of economic development, which I define as improving people's economic well-being. Various economic development objectives are worthy, but to my mind, one objective dominates all others: reducing the scourge of absolute economic misery in the world. In my teaching, research, and policy work, I focus on an important but relatively underemphasized approach to poverty reduction: helping the poor earn more in the labor market for the work they do, so that they can buy the goods and services they need to move up out of poverty.

The original version of this chapter was published as: Fields, Gary S. (2014). Aid, Growth, and Jobs: A Five-Part Policy Framework, in: The Cornell Policy Review, 4:7–15. © 2014 by Cornell Institute for Public Affairs.

1.3 Choosing the Most Promising Interventions

Assuming that a priority for economic development, though not necessarily *the* priority for economic development, is to improve labor market outcomes for the poor, how should country governments and aid organizations choose among policies aimed at this objective? Policy-makers face two broad policy decisions: choosing among broad policy areas and choosing *within* a broad policy area.

Choosing *among* broad policy areas means deciding whether to allocate more development resources to one area (stimulating economic growth, for example) or to another (e.g., increasing paid employment). Similarly, choosing *within* a policy area means, for example, deciding to try to raise the returns to self-employment by increasing the availability of affordable microcredit or by investing in education and training. The do's and don'ts presented in this section are equally applicable to both.

Before suggesting how to choose, let me suggest some ways not to choose. Consider the choice between helping the poor where they are and helping the poor get out of where they are:

- Line of argument 1: We want to help the poor. The poor work mainly on family farms and in family businesses. Therefore, we should invest our development resources in improving incomes where the poor are, on family farms and in family businesses.
- Line of argument 2: We want to help the poor. The poor will remain poor as long as they remain in poor sectors. Family farms and family businesses pay poorly relative to wage employment, particularly when the wage employment is in enterprises registered with the government (what is sometimes called 'formal sector). Therefore, we should invest our development resources in creating new wage employment in registered enterprises so that the poor can move to the parts of the economy where earnings are higher.
- Line of argument 3: We want to help the poor. It is good to help the poor where they are, and it is also good to help the poor get out of where they are. Therefore, we should invest our development resources by using some to help the poor where they are and using the rest to help the poor get out of where they are.

I hope you noticed that these three lines of argument led to precisely contradictory conclusions. Yet many so-called 'policy implications' offered in the literature are just like this: because a certain policy action would produce benefits if undertaken, it should be done. The problem is that none of the preceding arguments recognizes that to use more of the available resources for one purpose implies having less available for another. Economists use the term 'opportunity cost' to recognize the budgetary tradeoffs – in this case, the cost of using resources to help the poor where they are is to not have those resources available to help the poor get out of where they are. To decide that something is good to do without also weighing the value of what is not getting done is not a good way to choose.

Let us turn our attention to how to choose.

1.4 A Five-Part Policy Evaluation Framework

The following policy evaluation framework is one I have been using for a long time. I present it here for others who may also find it useful.

Figure 1.1. A Visualization of the Five-Part Policy Evaluation Framework.

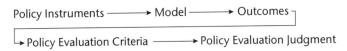

The first step in the framework is to specify the action or alternative actions under consideration. These could be a law that might be passed, a regulation that might be imposed or removed, a tax, or a public expenditure.

The second step is to specify an analytical model. The best ones involve an interplay between theory and empirics, capturing the essential aspects of reality while leaving aside the less essential ones.

The third step is to use the model to predict the likely outcomes. In a labor market model, these outcomes might be changes in the number of workers in each type of job and the amounts they get paid.

The fourth step is to specify the policy evaluation criterion or criteria to be used. An example of a single policy evaluation criterion would be to analyze a proposed policy solely in terms of its effect on reducing poverty. Alternatively, an evaluation might be conducted in terms of multiple policy evaluation criteria such as increasing both employment and earnings. Some evaluators are comfortable using efficiency and equity as their criteria.

The fifth and final step is to evaluate the outcomes in terms of the policy evaluation criterion or criteria and reach a judgment about whether the proposed policy would have positive, negative, or ambiguous consequences.

In practice, these steps are better thought of as being developed simultaneously rather than sequentially, with considerable back and forth movement between them. Let us examine some of these steps in more detail.

1.5 Specifying the Policy Evaluation Criteria

The best kind of policy analysis is one that starts with specifying an objective function: that which is to be maximized or minimized. The objective function sometimes has a single argument (e.g., minimize poverty as measured by the poverty headcount ratio) and sometimes multiple arguments (labor market well-being as a function of the number of jobs, how much workers earn in those jobs, the amount of social protection provided, and the honoring of core labor standards).[9] When the objective function has multiple components, none of the components is maximized; all components are optimized so that the objective function is maximized. Maximizing a multi-argument objective function therefore involves tradeoffs on the policy side. These policy tradeoffs are in addition to the budgetary tradeoffs described above, which always arise.

Many development recommendations I have seen are made without any explicit policy evaluation criteria at all. It is stunning that those who do this are often surprised to be asked to make their policy evaluation criteria explicit.

Other development recommendations are made on the basis of presumed goods – for example, it is presumably good to reduce a country's budget deficit, maintain a realistic exchange rate, or let supply and demand reign. Here too, it is worth asking those who make such recommendations what they think would be the effect on poverty of putting their recommendations into effect.

And still other policy recommendations are based on merit goods: education is socially meritorious, and therefore we should allocate more development resources to it. The problem with a merit goods argument is that many other things – health, housing, the arts, and many others – are also socially meritorious, which takes us right back to the point about budgetary tradeoffs: to use resources for one purpose means not to use them for another. What one gives up is as important to the decision as what one gets.

1.6 Specifying the Model

Policy interventions need to be analyzed using a model. Supply and demand is a model. 'Firms maximize profits' is a model. 'The poor have many needs' is not a model; it is a fact.

A good model involves the interplay of theory and data. It seems to me that the empirical reality of a developing country is that labor markets have multiple segments and multiple strata. By 'multiple segments', I mean that for workers of any given type, some jobs are better than others. And by 'multiple strata', I mean that workers differ in their type along some sort of hierarchy – for example, according to level of human capital or occupation.

A comprehensive labor market model would be one that recognizes multiple segments and multiple strata, models how each labor market segment and stratum works, and specifies how the various segments and strata link to one another via the migration of workers and the movement of firms.

Some features of a comprehensive labor market model are fairly generic. I would say that human capital plays an important role throughout the world in the sense that workers with more skills, often acquired through education and training, have the ability to perform certain jobs which those in the lower strata of the skills distribution lack. I would say too that a general feature of labor markets around the world is that they are segmented in the sense that (1) some jobs are better than others and (2) there are not enough of the good jobs for all who want them and are capable of performing them.

Beyond that, the right labor market model for a developing country might entail country-specific factors that vary from place to place. Examples are China's household registration system (in Chinese, *hukou*) and the essential differentiation of India's labor market between the peak and slack seasons in agriculture. It would be good to build such country-specific features into our analytical models.

Many development recommendations, including recommendations about employment and earnings in the developing world, suffer from one or another of these problems. I don't know which is worse: to have an *inapplicable* underlying model or to have *no* underlying model. It would be good if analysts could try to avoid them both.

1.7 Using Social Benefit-Cost Analysis in Formulating Policy

A unified way of bringing together the foregoing considerations is to aim for as comprehensive a social benefit-cost analysis as time and knowledge permit. Social benefit-cost analysis entails looking at the social benefits (as versus the private benefits) and comparing them with the social costs (as versus the private costs). Let me illustrate.

The economics columnist for The New Yorker, James Surowiecki, has written, 'Just fourteen per cent of Americans, for instance, are running (or trying to run) their own business. That percentage is much higher in developing countries – in Peru, it's almost forty per cent. That's not because Peruvians are more entrepreneurial. It's because they don't have other options. What poor countries need most, then, is not more microbusinesses ... To be sure, for some people the best route out of poverty will be a bank loan. But for most it's going to be something much simpler: a regular paycheck'.[1]

What Surowiecki leaves out is the fact that it is much more expensive to create a steady, regular paid job than it is to make a microloan to a microenterprise owner. Given the difference in costs, it is by no means clear that those who argue as Surowiecki does have necessarily reached the right conclusion (which does not imply that they have reached the wrong conclusion either).

Thinking in terms of social benefits and social costs could be done as follows. The easier question is to decide whether to do one single thing or not do it. In this case, we can ask three related questions:

1. What are the extra social benefits if the activity is undertaken?
2. What are the extra social costs of the activity?
3. How do the extra social benefits and extra social costs compare?

When more than one option is possible, similar questions can be asked:

1. What are the extra social benefits from each possible use of a development budget?
2. What are the extra social costs from each possible use?
3. For each possible use, how do the extra social benefits and extra social costs compare?
4. For which activity is the difference between benefits and costs the greatest?

(Note that I have used the word 'extra' rather than the word 'marginal', lest some readers understand 'marginal' in the sense of something that is unimportant. *Social* benefits and costs have been used throughout; many analysts neglect to distinguish social from private.)

The questions posed in the preceding paragraphs are not easy ones to answer. However, it is better to answer the right questions approximately than the wrong questions exactly.

Finally, we may not have a good sense of the sizes of the social benefits and/or the social costs of various policy interventions, and so research may be needed in order to find out. Some researchers favor statistical and econometric approaches[2,3,4] while others favor experimental approaches.[5,6] No researcher today can afford to ignore either approach.

1.8 Practical Questions to Be Asked

Imagine that you are a researcher or a country economist formulating a labor market policy proposal which you propose to take to a client country's government. Or imagine that you are a country government official formulating a policy proposal which you plan to take to a higher-level official in your organization. When you make such a proposal, it would be good to be prepared to answer the following three questions to the best of your ability:

- What specific labor market objective or objectives are you trying to achieve and by what welfare economic criterion or criteria will you decide if your objective(s) is/are being achieved?
- What theoretical labor market model are you using to analyze the effects of the proposed policy?
- What is the empirical evidence favoring one view of labor market functioning over another?

These three questions are the ideal. They define what we want to strive for. When you go out into the world, prepare the best answer you can to these three questions. The more skills you have and the more thoughtful your answers, the more valuable your advice will be.

Good luck.

2

The Distributional Effects of Economic Growth

2.1   An Introduction to the Issues

The world contains 1.3 billion desperately poor people who subsist on less than one U.S. dollar per person per day, and another 1.7 billion who live on between one and two U.S. dollars per person per day (United Nations 1997; World Bank 1999). With such low incomes, they are unable to attain a minimal standard of living, as gauged by access to adequate food, clothing, shelter, clean water, sanitation facilities, education, and health services. In the world's most populous country, China, the poverty-line income will buy a "basic food bundle" (in kg/person/year) consisting of grain (216.72), vegetables (112.49), pork (9.22), fruits (4.50), vegetable oil (2.56), eggs (1.87), sugar (1.62), fish (1.26), beef and mutton (.59), milk products (.25), and poultry (.06) (Ravallion 1996). The world's billions of poor live on the "margin of life" – their material well-being, their happiness, and even, in the most severe cases, their very existence hanging in the balance.[1]

Income inequality is endemic. In Brazil the income share of the richest 20 percent of the population is thirty-two times that of the poorest 20 percent – a figure that has hardly changed since 1960. This means that for every dollar of income gain received by the poor, the rich have gotten $32. Exactly the same ratio is found on Manhattan Island in New York City. Depending on where you live and what you have seen, this may help you visualize just how unequal a highly unequal economy is.[2]

The original version of this chapter was published as: Fields, Gary S. (2001). The Distributional Effects of Economic Growth, in: G. Fields: Distribution and Development: A New Look at the Developing World, 1–11. © 2001 by Russell Sage Foundation and the MIT Press.

Most of the world's poor live in the "underdeveloped" or "less developed" economies.[3] A country's economy may be said to be "underdeveloped" when its people face severely constrained choices. "Economic development" may then be thought of as the relaxation of the constraints on people's material standards of living, or alternatively, as the enlargement of people's choice sets and the expansion of their capabilities.[4] Improvements in material standards of living are not all there is to development, but that is the part of development that this chapter is about.

Economic development is sought primarily via economic growth. Economic growth rates in the world vary enormously. In the last twenty-five years, some countries (mostly in East Asia) achieved per capita GDP growth rates as high as +7.0 percent per annum, while others (mainly in Latin America and sub-Saharan Africa) declined at 5 percent annual rates.

To what extent and in what circumstances does economic growth bring broad-based improvements in the material standards of living of a country's people? For a long time, the development economics community simply assumed that the answer was that the larger the pie, the larger would be everybody's piece. But not everyone was so sanguine. Prime Minister Jawaharlal Nehru of India said in 1960: "National income over the First and Second Plans has gone up by 42 percent and the per capita income by 20 percent. A legitimate query is made, where has this gone?" (quoted in Parikh and Srinivasan 1993, p. 408). A heated debate was mounted on shaky statistical foundations. The evidence was read in diametrically opposed ways by the conflicting parties. The following two statements represent the range of thinking at the time:

> Development of the type experienced by the majority of Third World countries in the last quarter century has meant, for very large numbers of people, increased impoverishment. (Griffin and Khan 1978, p. 295)

> Rapid sustained growth has had positive effects on the living standards of all economic groups of those countries that experienced it ... Growth has not "failed"; there has simply not been enough of it in the great majority of less developed nations. (Galenson 1977, pp. 21–22)

The debate between "trickle-down" adherents on the one hand and "immiserizing growth" advocates on the other persisted for quite some time (Adelman and Morris 1973; Lewis 1976; Griffin 1989; Morley 1994; Rodgers and van der Hoeven 1995). Now, though, the two sides, though differing in emphasis, agree on two broad conclusions. One is that economic growth has raised the incomes of poor people and lowered the percentage in poverty. The other is that some particular groups have lost out because of changes accompanying economic growth. As the United

Nations now acknowledges, "Both are right" (United Nations 1997, p. 72).

How have we gotten to this point? What should be measured to see whether progress is being made? What does the evidence show? What policies and circumstances have caused some countries to do better than others? These are the major questions addressed in distributional analysis.

2.2 The Major Approaches to Distributional Analysis

Different ways of analyzing the distributional effects of economic growth may be illustrated by means of four examples.[5] First, consider two hypothetical countries A and B, which initially are identical. After a period of time, national income data reveal that Country A grew by 9 percent (in real terms, adjusting for inflation) while Country B grew by 18 percent. In the absence of distributional data, we might simply suppose that because Country B grew faster than Country A, the people in Country B came to be better off faster than those in Country A. This conclusion, however, assumes the answer to our question of whether the material standards of living of a country's people are improved by economic growth – it doesn't show it. Let us take income as our measure of economic well-being and collect data on the distribution of income in the population. (What to measure is discussed later in this chapter.) Suppose we find that the income share of the poorest 40 percent of income recipients in each country was .363, but that their share fell to .333 in Country A and to .307 in Country B. Suppose too that we calculate a commonly used measure of income inequality, the Gini coefficient, and find that it rose from .082 to .133 in Country A and from .082 to .162 in Country B.[6] Thus in this example there are two key facts: (1) Both economies grew, but Country B grew faster than Country A; (2) Income inequality increased in both economies, but it increased by more in Country B than in Country A. At this point, I invite you to decide whether economic development has taken place by asking yourself: Which do I prefer: the initial situation, the situation of Country A, or the situation of Country B?

Consider now a second example. Two hypothetical countries, C and D, initially start out with 10 percent of their people working in relatively high-wage jobs (paying a real wage of $2 to each worker) and with 90 percent of their people working in relatively low-wage jobs (paying a real wage of $1 to each).[7] After a certain period of time, we observe that 20 percent of the workers in Country C are in $2 jobs and 80 percent in $1 jobs, while in Country D, 30 percent are in the $2 jobs and 70 percent in the $1 jobs. Ask yourself again: Which do I prefer: the initial situation, the situation of Country C, or the situation of Country D?

The third example has two hypothetical countries, E and F, in both of which the poorest 40 percent of the people receive an average income of $40 each. We observe them later and find that the average income of the poorest 40 percent has remained at $40 in both countries. There is no point in asking which is preferable, E or F, because no progress appears to have been made.

Here now is our final example. In two hypothetical countries, G and H, we have data telling us not only people's current incomes but also their previous ones. Using these data, we find that in both countries, the nonpoor gained average income share while the poor lost. Furthermore, the difference between the average change in income share of the nonpoor and the poor was .044 in Country G and .047 in Country H. So in this example, the poor lost income share in both countries, but Country H exhibited a more disparate mobility experience than did Country G. Here too, you are invited to ask yourself which of these countries' experiences you would prefer, based on the available data.

We come now to the punch line: all of these examples come from the *same* underlying data. The initial situations were the same in all three examples; Countries A, C, E, and G are the same country, and Countries B, D, F, and H are the same country. Their respective income distributions are:

Initial: $(\underbrace{1, 1, 1, 1, 1, 1, 1, 1, 1,}_{9} \underbrace{2)}_{1}$

A-C-E-G: $(\underbrace{1, 1, 1, 1, 1, 1, 1, 1,}_{8} \underbrace{2, 2)}_{2}$

B-D-F-H: $(\underbrace{1, 1, 1, 1, 1, 1, 1,}_{7} \underbrace{2, 2, 2)}_{3}$

The growth figures are obtained by noting that the total income goes from $11 initially to $12 in A-C-E-G (a 9 percent increase) to $13 in B-D-F-H (an 18 percent increase). The income share of the poorest 40 percent is 4/11 = .363 initially, 4/12 = .333 in A-C-E-G, and 4/13 = .307 in B-D-F-H. The percentages in high- and low-wage jobs are apparent. The average incomes of the poorest 40 percent in example 3 are calculated assuming that $1 is an hourly wage and that each worker works a forty-hour work week.[8] The income mobility experiences of the currently poor and the currently nonpoor are detailed in the note.[9]

I have used the first three of these examples and asked these questions of literally thousands of students and colleagues in North America, South America, Europe, Africa, and Asia and have found very few who gave the same answer in each situation. The answers that have come back are the following: About half the respondents have said they prefer A to B. The justification commonly offered for this view is that A entails some growth (a good) and some increase in inequality (a bad) rather than the maximum amount of either one. Nearly everyone has expressed a preference for D over C. The only hesitation has been to question whether other things are equal – equal freedoms, for example – in the two cases. No one (except for a few jokesters) has favored E over F or the reverse. These examples show that one's view about economic growth – going so far as to question whether economic development takes place or not – depends on what one calculates.

I would now ask you to consider one last time which you prefer: the initial situation, the situation of Country A-C-E-G, or the situation of Country B-D-F-H? Oid your answer change depending on how the data were processed?

These examples illustrate the major approaches to income distribution analysis. The first is the *relative inequality approach*: the income share of the poorest 40 percent and the Gini coefficient measure how inequality in the distribution of income changes. The second example illustrates the *absolute income approach*: how many people receive how much income (in real terms). A special case of the absolute income approach is the *absolute poverty approach*, in which a poverty line is drawn and a poverty measure is calculated (e.g., the percentage of people with incomes below the poverty line). The third example illustrates the *relative poverty approach*, because a group that is relatively the poorest (the poorest 40 percent in this case) is defined and their average incomes calculated. The fourth example demonstrates the kind of *income mobility analysis* that might be conducted when data are available for the same people over time. Combining these and looking, say, at the change in absolute poverty and in relative inequality (with negative weights assigned to each) is one way of analyzing *economic well-being*.

The point is this: The same data, processed in different ways, can lead to conflicting, even opposite, conclusions. It is important to understand why these different ways of measuring changes in income distribution produce different results. It is *not* because they are alternative measures of the same underlying entity, but rather because they are gauging different things.

2.3   Income Distribution as a Multifaceted Concept

"Income distribution" is not a single phenomenon; it is a generic term including mean growth, relative inequality, absolute poverty, income mobility, and economic well-being. In much the same way that the raw data for any random variable can be processed to give information on distinct aspects of the distribution – location (mean, median, mode), dispersion (minimum, maximum, range, variance), shape (skewness, kurtosis, etc.) – the raw data on incomes can be processed to inform us about different aspects of the income distribution. In the examples of the preceding section, these different aspects change in different ways – the mean increases, inequality increases, poverty decreases, and mobility experiences become more disparate – in each case, according to the measures presented. In actual countries' experiences as well, we find not only that these different aspects *can* change in different directions but that in fact they *do* change in different directions quite often. If one is to use such data to help gauge how material conditions of living are changing, it is therefore of the utmost importance to understand what one is doing when one compares statistics such as Gini coefficients, poverty headcount ratios, and share mobility rates, or when one uses dominance methods such as Lorenz curve comparisons, Generalized Lorenz curve comparisons, and cumulative density functions. These are *not* alternative measures of the same underlying distributional phenomenon; in fact, they measure quite different aspects of the distribution.

The term "income distribution" will be reserved for an entire vector of incomes such as (1, 1, 1, 1, 1, 1, 1, 1, 1, 2). The phrase "income distribution improved (or worsened)" will be used to mean that a particular social welfare function $W(.)$ or a broad dass of such functions evaluates one vector of incomes more highly than another. Examples of such functions, are quasi-Pareto improvements, abbreviated social welfare functions, and direct dominance orderings. If using such functions, we find that $W(Y_1) > W(Y_2)$, then Y_1 may be said to be "better" than Y_2. It is in this sense, and only in this sense, that the phrase "income distribution improved" will be used here. It will never be used to mean "the income distribution became more equal" or "poverty decreased."

2.4   Some Important Methodological Preliminaries

2.4.1   *The Role of Theory*

Theory plays an important role in income distribution analysis. As the examples earlier in this chapter indicate, different distributional concepts can yield quite different pictures of the distributional effects of growth. It is essential therefore to take care in clarifying each of these underlying notions. Then, having done so, various indices (or synonymously, "measures") may be assessed to see whether they are "good" indicators of what they purport to measure. In this way, the empirical analysis is guided by careful theoretical work on what the underlying distributional concepts are and what are good measures of them.

Theory is often used in empirical economics in another way, and that is to formulate empirical predictions that are then "tested" in data. Take, for example, the case of the famed Kuznets hypothesis, according to which income inequality tends to increase in the early stages of economic development and then decrease. Many theoretical models have been formulated which generate the Kuznets curve; these are surveyed by Glomm and Ravikumar (1994, 1995) and Aghion, Caroli, and Garda-Pefialosa (1999). As these authors demonstrate, the Kuznets curve can be generated from short-run increasing returns to scale, capital market imperfections, human capital accumulation, occupational choice, migration, trade liberalization, technical change, or the emergence of new organizational forms. It is interesting that all of these models were formulated decades *after* Kuznets formulated the inverted-U hypothesis, and indeed these models are not needed for "testing" the shape of the relationship between economic growth and income inequality. Even if an inverted-U shape were to appear as a broad empirical regularity, such a finding would not establish the validity of any particular underlying model. Instead, we can test the Kuznets curve hypothesis as an empirical proposition and, upon finding that the data reject it empirically, we may then turn our attention to why inequality increases with economic growth in some countries and not in others. Inductive theory is likely to be much more promising than deductive theory at this point.

2.4.2 *From Growth to Distribution or from Distribution to Growth?*

There is ample reason to believe in dual causality, running from growth to distribution as well as from distribution to growth. The empirical literatures on the effect of growth on distribution and of distribution on growth are both vast. One point of intersection between them is in the literature on vicious and virtuous circles. Another is in the simultaneaus equations model formulated by Bourguignon (1994). For the most part, however, the two literatures have proceeded almost entirely independently of one another.

2.4.3 *The Distribution of What?*

No single variable can possibly serve as a fully satisfactory measure of economic well-being (or, as it is sometimes called, "standard of living"). The question then is, what would be the best thing or things to measure?

The literature offers two broad two types of answers. One is to choose certain goods and services and measure the distribution of each of those, singly or together. Basic human needs advocates have called for direct measures of people's access to food, clothing, shelter, health care, education, etc. (ILO 1976; Streeten 1981). Life expectancy, adult literacy, and real GDP per capita have been combined into a Human Development Index by the United Nations (1990 and subsequent).

The other answer is to use data on income or consumption to proxy the ability of persons to afford to be adequately nourished, clothed, and housed. The great bulk of the work on distribution by economists has used this latter approach. Consumption is regarded as the best available proxy for long-term standard of living, but consumption data are often not available, so income measures are used instead. In either case, it is desirable to have as comprehensive a measure as possible, including not only earned income or what can be consumed from it but also nonlabor income, goods and services provided by the state, and imputed values for food and other goods and services produced and consumed at home. The World Bank's Living Standards Measurement Surveys, which have been conducted in many countries, provide relatively comprehensive measures, but in other countries, the information is far from ideal: "What was your income in pesos last month?" is a common type of question, but it is subject to recall error, rounding, and other types of misstatement. In such cases, we have little choice but to utilize the limited data available.

Additional choices need to be made. Because of income pooling within families, the family (or household) would be the better recipient unit. Total income or consumption should be adjusted on a per capita or an adult-equivalent basis whenever possible. Systematic cost-of-living differences (rural/urban, for example) should be allowed for.

The literature on "distribution of what" is enormous. For more on these issues, see Anand and Ravallion 1993, Ravallion 1994, Fields 1994, Atkinson et al. 1995, Gottschalk and Smeeding 1997, and Sen 1997.

2.4.4 Data Concerns

The income distribution literature has walked a fine line between breadth of data coverage on the one hand and quality of data on the other. The compromise that has been reached in the literature is to use "minimally consistent data," that is, observations which are based on actual household surveys or censuses with national coverage and consistent definitions over time within a country (Fields 1991; Anand and Kanbur 1993a; Deininger and Squire 1996). Nonetheless, problems remain. It has been said, "There are many limitations to the data presented. They tell us nothing about expenditure, only about income; they omit important sources of income such as fringe benefits or capital gains or undisclosed earnings from the informal economy; they omit the benefits of government spending other than cash or near-cash transfers; they relate to the household and do not explore what happens within the family." These words come from the presidential address to the Royal Economic Society by A. B. Atkinson (1997, p. 299) who, for more than a quarter-century, has been one of the world's leading income distribution authorities and users of empirical data. Like Atkinson, I believe it is better to use what information we have than not to. Too much hinges on the answers to remain silent.

3

How the Poor Are Working

The people in developing countries are working, working hard, yet earning very little for the work they do.[1] How can we understand their situations? This chapter presents an analysis of the employment and unemployment outcomes facing them and people like them. As you will see, despite high-sounding pronouncements such as Article 23 of the United Nations' Universal Declaration of Human Rights, for billions of working persons around the world, the rights "to work, to free choice of employment, to just and favourable conditions of work ... to protection against unemployment ... and to just and favourable remuneration" are unattainable; they are not rights at all.[2]

3.1 The Poor Want to Work in Good Jobs

In May 2009, under the auspices of the UN's International Labor Organization (ILO), the leaders of many of the world's countries reached agreement on a Global Jobs Pact to combat the ill effects of the global economic crisis. In the words of Cristina Fernández de Kirchner, president of Argentina:

> When you listen to people saying that 50 million jobs have been lost this year, it is not enough just to agree how dreadful it is. It is not just the figure

The original version of this chapter was published as: Fields, Gary S. (2012). How the Poor Are Working, in: G. Fields: Working Hard, Working Poor: A Global Journey, 42–67. © 2012 by Oxford University Press.

that is important: it is the losses and destruction that have been caused to individuals and to families. It means 50 million people who are living on their wits and nothing else. These are the people we have to think about when we hear people talking pure economics or statistics.[3]

Work to gain a livelihood is a nearly universal aspiration among the poor. Money and the things that money can buy are mentioned repeatedly as reasons for working. A poor elderly man in Thompson Pen, Jamaica, says, "Work makes all the difference in the world. ... My wife, at 78, is still working. My dream is a little work to make ends meet." In Russia, the poor stress their desire for jobs that pay regular wages, reflecting their desire for productive work to provide an adequate and secure livelihood. In Bedsa, Egypt, another man says, "Lack of work worries me. My children are hungry and I tell them the rice is cooking, until they fall asleep from hunger."[4]

Like everybody else, the poor want to work in jobs that are steady and secure, pay well, offer benefits, meet labor standards, offer social protections, and so on. The problem in the developing world is that not enough good jobs are available for all who want them and who could do them.

Figure 3.1. Labor-intensive construction site, Ethiopia.

Figure 3.1 shows an Ethiopian construction site. The work is much more labor-intensive than is the case in the richer countries. And yet, employment opportunities are insufficient in number. Figure 3.2 shows a group of

would-be workers outside a marble factory in Ethiopia seeking a day's work. Some aspects of good jobs and bad jobs are detailed later in this chapter.

Figure 3.2. Unemployed seeking work, Ethiopia.

3.2 The Unemployment Rate Fails to Capture Labor Market Distress

Because the unemployment rate in developing countries is lower than it is in developed countries, the unemployment rate often does not reflect the labor market adequately. Economists and other labor market analysts use the terms "employment" and "unemployment" in quite specific ways that do not necessarily accord with their everyday usage. These terms are prescribed by the ILO, which is the specialized agency of the United Nations with responsibility for workplace issues around the world. They include the following:

- labor force (or synonymously, economically active population): Those people in the economy who either are working or who are actively looking for work – that is, those who are either employed or unemployed, as defined below.
- Employed: Any worker in paid employment (regardless of the number of hours), plus unpaid workers in a family business who worked

45

fifteen or more hours in the preceding week, plus persons temporarily laid off, ill, on vacation, or on strike.

- Unemployed: Persons of working age (in many countries, age sixteen or older, but age fourteen or even age twelve in many developing countries) who were not employed last week but who are actively looking for work, plus persons who are not temporarily laid off, on vacation, or on strike.
- Out of the labor force (or synonymously, economically inactive population): Those who were not employed last week and who were not actively looking for work, including the young, the old, the disabled, those who voluntarily were not seeking work, and those who were so discouraged by poor job prospects that they stopped looking.
- Unemployment rate: The employed as a percentage of the labor force.

For those who are not working at all and are therefore classified as unemployed, economists typically distinguish four categories:

- Deficient demand unemployment: This is the type of unemployment that arises because the economy does not generate a sufficient number of jobs for all who are seeking work. Often in the sectors of developing economies where earnings levels are high and working conditions good, the demand for labor is much smaller than the available supply.
- Structural unemployment: This is the type of unemployment that arises because of a mismatch between the types of jobs employers are trying to fill and the types of workers available. One type of structural unemployment arises when employers need skilled workers but only unskilled workers are available. Another arises when skilled workers are available but not in the geographic area where they are needed.
- Frictional unemployment: This is the type of unemployment that arises because workers don't know where jobs are available. An employer may post a job vacancy, but it may take time for workers to learn that that particular employer is hiring and to discover the terms and conditions of employment. Relative to deficient demand unemployment, frictional unemployment is believed to be of modest importance in developing countries.
- Seasonal unemployment: Especially in agricultural economies, demand for labor is very high during the planting and harvesting seasons and slack the rest of the year. Some economists regard seasonal unemployment as a particular kind of deficient demand unemployment rather than its own category.

According to statistics published by the ILO in 2011, the world unemployment rate was 6.2%. The developed economies and the European Union had above-average unemployment rates, 8.4%, while unemployment rates were below average in East Asia (4.4%) and South Asia (also 4.4%).[5] The median unemployment rate among twenty-four developed economies was more than one percentage point higher than among seventeen developing economies.[6]

The reason that unemployment rates are lower in developing countries than in richer countries is that few in the developing world can afford to spend an entire week doing no work at all, which is necessary to be counted as unemployed by the ILO definition.[7] Typically, would-be workers in a developing country live with family members or fellow migrants and for a short time are unemployed while searching full-time for jobs. Soon, however, the hosts expect the guests to contribute money or services in return for lodging. If they have not found a paid job in a reasonable time, they will have to create their own earning opportunities, whereupon they will be counted as employed.

Those who can afford to remain unemployed for longer periods of time are primarily well-educated individuals or young people in well-to-do families.[8] This view, termed "the luxury unemployment hypothesis," receives support from a variety of sources. One is the observation that unemployment rates in countries such as India and Brazil are lowest for the least educated people, not the better-educated ones. Another is the observation that in Africa, urban unemployment is found predominantly among those who belong to relatively high-income families. And in many countries of the world, unemployment is concentrated among the young, who frequently are dependents living in households in which other family members are employed, enabling them to rely on family support while searching for a job.[9]

The unemployment rates observed in the developing world – ranging from 4.4% in East Asia to 10.5% in North Africa – should not be interpreted to mean that 95.6% or 89.5% of the labor force are fully and gainfully employed. Many of the employed would like to work more hours in a week than employers want to hire them for. Many others have limited weeks of work, especially during the slack seasons in agriculture. Many of those who work full-time for a full year still earn so little that they are poor by the standards of their country or in terms of an internationally comparable poverty line. Taken together, those who work less than full-time in a day or less than a full number of days in a week or who earn less than a low earnings line are sometimes called "underemployed" or "disguised unemployed." But because these terms are not defined consistently, I prefer to stick to the international definitions of employment and unemployment.

This means that the unemployment rate is a flawed measure of distress in the labor market. Recognizing these deficiencies, the ILO has proposed a broader range of measures to better reflect developing countries' labor market conditions, giving equal weight to the unemployment rate, employment-to-population ratio, average earnings, percentage of working poor, government expenditures for social security, the number of key ILO conventions not ratified by the country, the percentage of children economically active, and the gender gap in labor force participation.[10] To my mind, the most important of these additional indicators is how much people earn when they work, to which we now turn.

3.3   Earnings Levels Are Very Low

Wage surveys show that for a wage worker in a typical unskilled occupation, daily wages in many countries of Asia, Latin America, and Africa are no more than one to two U.S. dollars per day. Laborers earn $145 a month in central China, $104 a month in Vietnam, and $87 a month in India.[11] In Sri Lanka, the hourly compensation cost in manufacturing is half a U.S. dollar per day.[12] It costs an employer 26% of what it does in the United States to hire a manufacturing worker for a day in Argentina, 23% in Brazil, 13% in Mexico, and 4% in the Philippines.[13] The ILO defines a "working poor household" as one in which at least one member is working but the household lives on less than $2 per person per day. The working poor constitute 39% of total employment in the world.[14] The rates of working poor range from about 15% of total employment in Central and Southeast Europe and the Commonwealth of Independent States (former Soviet republics) to more than 80% in South Asia and sub-Saharan Africa. (By this definition, the developed economies of Western Europe and North America have no working poor at all.) Thus, even by this very modest $2 a day standard, in the low-income regions of the world, the working poor constitute a majority of the poor.

Work hours in the developing world are long. In countries with the highest percentage of workers working more than 48 hours a week, Peru topped the list at 50.9% of workers, the Republic of Korea at 49.5%, Thailand at 46.7%, and Pakistan at 44.4%. By contrast, in developed countries, where working hours are typically shorter, the United Kingdom stood at 25.7%, Israel at 25.5%, Australia at 20.4%, Switzerland at 19.2%, and the United States at 18.1%.[15] What makes workers in the developing world poor is how little they earn per hour, not how many hours they work.

3.4   Incomes Are Also Uncertain

On a recent trip to South Africa, one man who looked to be in his forties told my colleague and me that both he and his wife were unemployed. They had no children nor any elderly person in their home, and so presumably they received no transfer income at all from the government. When we asked how they got by, he told us bit by bit about several activities. He is a bishop in his church, which has two hundred congregants. Some of them contribute to the work of the church. He is also a traditional healer. Sometimes, when a cure is successful, those who can afford to give him money. His wife does beadwork, which she sells in the African Arts Centre in the city. Yet, despite these various activities and modest sources of income, he insisted that they are unemployed. When we asked him what it means to be employed, he was crystal clear: "You are employed when you have a steady job that pays you every Friday."

A worker who has a steady job that pays the same amount every Friday has certainty about receiving an income, even if it is low. The great majority of the working poor not only have the problem of low incomes when they work, but they are also uncertain of whether they will have work the next day and, if they do, how much that work will yield. The poor have good days and bad days, great days and terrible days.

The ILO reports:[16] "The informal economy comprises half to three quarters of all non-agricultural employment in developing countries. ... Some of the characteristic features of informal employment are lack of protection in the event of non-payment of wages, compulsory overtime or extra shifts, lay-offs without notice or compensation, unsafe working conditions and the absence of social benefits such as pensions, sick pay and health insurance." Virtually all agricultural employment is also informal. One recent study tells us that "informal is normal," including more than 90% of nonagricultural and agricultural employment in the developing countries.[17] The informal economy has been written about widely.[18]

The poor face a "triple whammy": low incomes when they are working, irregular and unpredictable income flows, and a lack of suitable financial tools. Knowing that today's income might not be there tomorrow, even those who earn only a dollar a day do not live hand to mouth – they manage their money, as discussed in Portfolios of the Poor.[19]

3.5   Women Are Disadvantaged in Developing Country Labor Markets

Writing about India, one analyst has conveyed the general situation of women workers as follows:[20]

> Women work longer and harder than men, and their wage work is what is available when the tasks are done. They face discrimination in every conceivable respect. Over two-thirds of women have no money returns from their work, though the proportion of wage workers among those working is higher than it is for men. Female labour is heavily concentrated in rural sites, in agricultural work, on casual contracts and at wages bordering on starvation. Women's wages are practically everywhere lower than those of men, irrespective of the tightening effect of male migration or of the development of male jobs in the non-farm economy. In agriculture in the 1990s, women's wages were on average 71 per cent those of men. In nonfarm work, women are likely to be concentrated in the lowest grades and stages, on piece rate rather than time rate, and with earnings much lower than men.

What is true of India is true throughout the developing world: women's labor market outcomes are less favorable in a variety of ways.[21] Women are less likely to be working in the paid labor force and more likely to be segregated into low-paying occupations. They are more likely to suff er from labor market discrimination; less likely to have access to inputs such as land, credit, capital, and technology; more likely to be low earners if in self-employment; less likely to own land; and less likely to have secure land tenure rights. Women are no more likely than men to be rejected for loans or be subject to higher interest rates charged by lenders, but they are less likely to apply for loans in the first place. Female workers are more likely to be engaged in informal employment than are male workers, women are concentrated in the more precarious types of informal work, and the earnings levels in these types of employment are insufficient on their own to raise households out of poverty. Women in the labor market have many of the same needs that men do, but they have special needs besides.

Women also have special demands placed on them. Th roughout the developing world, fetching water is women's work. This task can take hours every day. One photo shows a Kenyan woman carrying a full water drum on her back while simultaneously weaving a Kikuyu basket. Another shows Indian women carrying full water jars at the crack of dawn. Another task reserved for women is fetching firewood. The loads are huge, far heavier than anything I could carry (Figures 3.3, 3.4, 3.5).

Figure 3.3. Woman at work, Kenya.

Figure 3.4. Women fetching water, India.

Figure 3.5. Woman carrying firewood, Ethiopia.

3.6 The Composition of Employment Is Different in Developing Countries

As compared with the developed countries, in the developing countries,

1. A smaller percentage of people work in offices and factories such as those found in countries like mine. We see a lot in the media about the information and communication technology (ICT) centers in cities such as Bangalore and Hyderabad in India and the garment and electronics industries in Shenzhen, Dongguan, Huizhou, and Zhongshan in coastal China. What should be understood is that these types of workplaces are the exceptions in the developing world, not the rule. Only one million of India's labor force of nearly half a billion people work in ICT. More typical workplaces are the fields, the streets, and people's homes.

2. A greater percentage of people work in agriculture. Of the world's workers, 35% worldwide are to be found in agriculture. Agriculture's share of total employment is 44% in Southeast Asia and the Pacific, 49% in South Asia, and 66% in sub-Saharan Africa. The share is 55% in India and 45% in China. By contrast, in the developed economies and European Union, only 4% of employment is

in agriculture.[22] Throughout the developing world – and in particular in low-income countries such as India, Indonesia, the Philippines, Thailand, and Vietnam and in most of sub-Saharan Africa – the concentration of employment in agriculture is problematic because wages in agriculture are lower even than the wages in these same countries' manufacturing sector.[23]

3. Self-employment, own-account work, and unpaid family work are more prevalent and paid employment is less prevalent. (The ILO defines an own-account worker as someone who is engaged in self-employment but has no employees.)[24] Figure 3.6 shows a mini-shopkeeper in Ethiopia. His shop could have been no larger than five feet by five feet – that is, one and half meters on a side.

Figure 3.6. Mini-shopkeeper, Ethiopia.

The poorer the country, the larger the share of people who earn their livelihoods in self-employment, own-account work, or unpaid family work: more than 80% of women and about 70% of men in South Asia and sub-Saharan Africa, more than 50% of men and women in East and Southeast Asia, and more than 30% of men and women in the Middle East and North Africa and in Latin America and the Caribbean.[25] Turning it around, wage and salaried employment is 13% of total employment in Ghana, less than 10% in Zambia, and less than 5% in Burkina Faso.[26]

The ILO combines own-account workers and unpaid family workers into a group they call "vulnerable employment." Vulnerable employment accounts for 51% of the world's employment, with rates of vulnerable employment ranging from 10% in the developed economies and the European Union to 32% in Latin America and the Middle East to 77% in South Asia and sub-Saharan Africa.[27] The reason that the rate of vulnerable employment is so much higher in the developing countries is the insufficient number of opportunities in wage and salaried employment relative to the number who would like such jobs.

Putting these pieces together for the case of Senegal, 59.3% of those employed are in agriculture, 30.0% are in nonagricultural non-wage employment, and 10.6% are in paid employment.[28] In India, of those employed, 15.3% are regular wage and salaried workers, 28.1% are casual wage and salaried workers, 32.3% are employers and own-account self-employed, and 23.8% are unpaid family workers.[29] The details differ but the overall picture is similar in all but the richest countries of the developing world: work in agriculture and in self-employment predominate.

3.7   Most Workers Work in the Private Sector

Nine out of ten workers in the developing world are to be found in the private sector.[30] In Latin America, 90% of the labor force is employed in the private sector (including both paid employment and self-employment), just 10% in the public sector. Kenya's private sector comprises 84% of registered employment and presumably all unregistered employment.In Ghana, the public sector is 6% of total employment. In China, 30% of formal sector employment in urban areas is in the public sector, which includes government and public institutions, state-owned enterprises, and collective-owned enterprises, and 28% of rural employment is in township and village enterprises. Government is a dominant employer in the formal sector, accounting for a two-thirds share in India, for example, but in the developing world most employment is not formal.

3.8 Most Workers Do Not Receive Job-Related Social Protections

Protective labor legislation is on the books of every country of the world, even the very poorest. These laws typically provide for job security, minimum wages, overtime pay, maximum hours, health and safety regulations, health insurance, unemployment benefits or severance payments, and/or old-age pensions. To receive them, however, workers must be registered with the government. But registering can be quite costly in time and money, so most workers and firms in the developing world do not register, and therefore the workers lack these protections.[31]

In Asia, only 20% of the unemployed and underemployed have access to labor market programs. The relative few who enjoy such benefits are often said to constitute a "labor aristocracy." It has also been said that in rural Bangladesh, "the 'labor aristocracy' is composed of those who have a job."[32]

In Mexico, 40% of workers are formal in the sense that they are in wage and salaried jobs where they are supposed to be registered and are registered with the Mexican Social Security Institute (Spanish acronym: IMSS). Then there is another 20% who are informal illegally in the sense that although they are working in wage and salaried jobs and are supposed to be registered with IMSS, they or their employers have chosen not to register, again for reason of monetary or time cost. The remaining 40% are self-employed persons and workers on commission who are not supposed to register with IMSS and do not. The formal workers in Mexico enjoy a variety of benefits including job protections, housing, health insurance, life insurance, workers' compensation, unemployment insurance, old-age pensions and others; the informal workers do not.[33] In Mexico, as in other Latin American countries, informal sector workers earn only about half of what formal sector workers do.[34]

In India, which is a much poorer country than Mexico, the lack of job-related social protections is even greater.[35] There, 86% of all workers are engaged in informal employment in the informal sector and another 7% in informal employment in the formal sector. Figures 3.7–3.10 show some of these workers: two bicycle rickshaw drivers, a construction crew, and an itinerant clothes ironer.

In a 2009 report, the Indian National Commission for Enterprises in the Unorganised Sector issued a detailed report calling for three pillars of a social floor which is now lacking in India: universal minimum social security, a national minimum wage, and minimum conditions of work. Such protections remain an unrealized dream for the vast majority of workers in India at present.

Figure 3.7. Bicycle rickshaw driver, India.

Figure 3.8. Bicycle rickshaw driver, India.

Figure 3.9. Construction crew, India.

Figure 3.10. Itinerant clothes ironer, India.

The ILO estimates that only one in five people in the world have adequate social security coverage. A variety of efforts, some headed by the ILO, are under way to remedy this situation.[36]

3.9   Wage Employment Versus Self-Employment

Typically, the better jobs are in wage employment, not self-employment. But within wage employment, regular wage jobs are better than casual wage jobs. In India, while self-employed households make up 34.5% of all urban households, they are 38.7% of poor urban households. Similarly, in Pakistan, the self-employed are estimated to be about 18.2% of the urban population, but this group accounts for 21.4% of the urban poor.[37] A study of thirteen developing countries concludes that what diff erentiates the middle class from the poor is who they are working for and on what terms: those who have a regular, well-paying, salaried job are much more likely to be middle class than those in self-employment.[38] In Bangladesh, nonfarm workers earn about twice what farm workers do, and salaried wage workers earn about twice what casual wage workers do.[39] In seven West African capital cities, employees in the private sector and informal sector employers have about the same earnings, but informal sector employees earn about 40% less and informal own-account workers earn about 50% less.[40]

Because wages and working conditions typically are better in wage jobs than in self-employment, "everybody" in developing countries wants a wage job. In India's Tata Steel Company, low-skilled workers earn more than they could elsewhere, have company-provided medical care, good-quality housing, drinkable tap water, and good schools for their children. These workers also benefit from job security and other measures provided under India's Industrial Disputes Act, explained later in this chapter. For these reasons, many of Tata's employees come from families that have worked there for generations.[41]

The Tata Steel Company jobs exemplify what is called regular employment. In regular employment, workers are hired for unlimited duration, often with a written wage contract. Such employment contrasts with what is called casual employment, in which workers are hired to perform a particular task; when the task is completed, the job ends. National data for rural India show that regular wage workers earn three times per day what casual wage workers do, with the self-employed earning an intermediate amount. Consequently, Indian workers seek wage jobs in the formal sector, but if they cannot get them, they tend to prefer self-employment.[42]

3.10 The Poor Create their Own Self-Employment Opportunities

The problem faced by the poor is that not enough regular wage employment is available for all who would like such jobs and are capable of performing them. Consequently, in most countries, the poor respond to insufficient wage employment opportunities by creating their own self-employment opportunities.

In 2002, the University of Cape Town in South Africa posted an advertisement for gardeners and cleaners. Thirty-nine thousand persons applied. As it turned out, the university wanted to hire only twenty new staff, which they did.[43]

In Mexico, I met Angela, a fireworks maker. Mari, her adult daughter, had spent two years in the United States, earning her living by cleaning rooms at a Motel 6 in California. When she returned to Mexico, she tried to obtain a job at a number of the local hotels including the one where our conference was held. Each time she tried, Mari was told "no." After a while, she gave up and turned to her own small business going door-to-door selling whatever clothing or other items she could.

In nearly all of the developing world, when wage jobs are not available, the poor respond by creating their own, often very small, businesses.[44] The year I lived in Kenya, I came to know a number of such people. One was a man who bought packs of cigarettes twenty at a time and sold them one cigarette at a time at a higher price to people who were too poor to buy a whole pack at once. Another was an old woman who sold newspapers at the entrance to the university; not only did I buy the paper from her whenever I could, but I was treated to a commentary about the news itself, which gave me a kind of insight into local people's thinking that I could never have gotten otherwise.[45] Another self-employed person I came to know was a man who sold whatever fresh vegetables were in season to drivers who stopped at a busy intersection near where we lived. Some of the merchandising was clever, such as his selling baggies full of podded peas which we could just pop into a pot of boiling water at home. He told me that he, like many urban dwellers, had a family farm in the countryside tended by his wife and other women and that the produce he sold was what he was able to bring with him from the farm whenever he had been able to accumulate enough money for a weekend visit to the family.[46]

Figure 3.11 shows a Mexican woman who contributes to the family income by walking a city neighborhood selling drinks to pedestrians and people who come out of their homes to buy from her. She doesn't earn much, but as she says, "Every little bit helps."

Figure 3.11. Drink vendor, Mexico.

An analysis of data for eighteen developing countries has led one research team to label such people "penniless entrepreneurs" in one context and "reluctant entrepreneurs" in another.[47] Their businesses are small and unprofitable. Few skills, little or no capital, and a shortage of wage jobs are the reasons for the prevalence of such activities. Later, these same authors continued: "Nothing seems more middle class than the fact of having a steady well-paying job. While there are many petty entrepreneurs among the middle class, most of them do not seem to be capitalists in waiting. They run businesses, but for the most part only because they are still relatively poor and every little bit helps. If they could only find the right salaried job, they might be quite content to shut their business down."[48]

3.11 Developing Country Labor Markets Are Usually Thought to Be Segmented

A segmented labor market has two defining features. First, for workers of any given skill level, some jobs are decidedly better than others. Second, access to the better jobs is rationed in the sense that not all who want those jobs and who are capable of performing them are able to get them.

The chief economist of the Inter-American Development Bank, Santiago Levy, stated it graphically for his native country, Mexico: "Of course, they all want to work for the telephone company." What Levy meant by this is that all workers, given their skills, would do better in terms of pay and/or working conditions if they were fortunate enough to be hired by the telephone company. The reason the telephone company pays so much better in Mexico is that labor unions are very powerful there. Some developing countries are like Mexico in having strong unions in some parts of the economy, but in most, labor unions are much less influential.

Of course, the telephone company does not want to hire all who would like to work there. Those workers not hired by the telephone company then have to do the best they can elsewhere. Often, the best alternative is to take paid employment in small enterprises, which typically pay less than larger enterprises do. Other times, it means entering self-employment, which also is lower-paying. In other countries, substantial pay differentials are found between the public sector and the private sector.

For a labor market to be segmented, comparable workers must be paid more in some parts of the labor market than in others. Using statistical techniques, researchers have tried to establish comparability by controlling for other wage-determining factors that can be observed in the data such as education, firm size, sector of employment, and so on. (Workers who are comparable in this way are said to be "observationally equivalent.") When such controlled studies have been done, wage differentials – often very large ones – have been found for observationally equivalent workers in various jobs in a developing country.[49]

Based on such evidence, most analysts including me regard developing countries' labor markets as being segmented. But such evidence is not accepted unanimously. Some argue that the differentials are found because workers who look comparable to researchers have unobservable characteristics that make them different from one another in fact.[50]

There are alternatives to thinking of labor markets as being segmented. One is to regard conditions as essentially the same in the different sectors of the economy for workers of comparable skill. Another is to suppose that the various sectors are open to all who would like to work in them but workers differ in terms of their relative abilities in one sector versus another, and therefore some workers willingly choose one sector while other workers choose the other.

In summary, there is widespread but not universal agreement among labor economists that the segmented labor market model – which assumes that some jobs are demonstrably better than others for workers of a given skill level and that not enough of the better jobs are available for all who want them and who could perform them satisfactorily – is the best way to understand developing countries' labor markets.

3.12   Some Choose Not to Be Wage Employees

Not all microenterprise operators and family workers are doing such work involuntarily, however. Some could be working as wage employees but choose not to. One such person is a man interviewed by my research team in San José, Costa Rica. For thirty-seven years, he had been selling a peanut-sugar-butter candy called "melcochas" in the city center, as his father had done before him. He was very insistent that he was there voluntarily, doing what he likes to do, and that it pays better than any wage job he might have gotten. He also reported that his brother had at one time started up a melcocha factory, but that he later gave up melcocha making because he realized he could make more money selling in the streets himself.

Figure 3.12. Backyard auto mechanic, Mexico.

I have met many working people who reported that they had left wage employment voluntarily to set up their own small enterprises. Among them were one of Angela's brothers, who voluntarily left a job in a Ford garage to set up his own backyard auto mechanic shop in Oaxaca, Mexico (Figure 3.12); a noodle vendor outside a factory gate in Jakarta, Indonesia, who previously had cooked in a hotel restaurant; and a free-lance tourist guide in Chennai, India, who could have remained as an employee with a local travel company but chose to set up operations on her own.

There can be no doubt that some of the people working in self-employment are doing so by choice. What is unsettled is how large the proportion is. On the one hand, World Bank economist William Maloney and the World Bank as an institution both maintain that the proportion is quite large, particularly in Mexico but also in Latin America more generally.[51] This view is a minority one, and the "penniless entrepreneur" view reported earlier dominates the literature. New research, as yet unpublished, estimated for Côte d'Ivoire that 55% of those working informally have a comparative advantage in informal employment and so work informally by choice, while 45% of informal employment is involuntary.[52] More such work is needed.

3.13 Many Jobs Are Miserable

Apart from low earnings and lack of social protections, a large number of jobs are really awful. On April 4, 2008, my hometown newspaper, the Ithaca Journal ran the following story from the Associated Press datelined Gorakhpur, India: "When Durga Prasad heard of the mysterious job with the hefty paycheck, he jumped at it, no questions asked. The work could be risky – Prasad figured he'd be asked to smuggle drugs into Nepal – but for the itinerant laborer from Uttar Pradesh, one of the poorest states in India, the money was worth it: 250 rupees a day, about $6. 'I knew it must be some illegal work because no one pays so much money to an illiterate person like me,' Prasad said. The salary turned out to be part of a trap that ensnared Prasad and 14 other poor laborers, who were held captive while their blood was drained for sale to private medical clinics."[53]

Some of the jobs in which the poor in the developing world work are outrageous. Sex workers are found all over the world, of course. In Kenya, a female sex worker earns more money if the client does not use a condom than if he does. Sex workers in developing countries do not engage in unsafe sex out of ignorance. They do so because they are so poor that the risk of AIDS is worth the extra money they can get from unsafe sex. A seventeen-year-old Kenyan sex worker named Alice said, "I try to use condoms every time, but sometimes they refuse or offer much more money if we don't. If I am offered 200 (shillings) for sex with a condom or 1,000 (shillings) for sex without, then I don't use condoms. I have to feed my baby."[54]

Worse than the fact that economic conditions force women like Alice to engage in unsafe sex by choice is the sex slavery found throughout the world. Women (and a lesser number of men and children) are kidnapped, trafficked (that is, forcibly moved to another location), locked in rooms or buildings from which they cannot escape, and forced to perform sex without payment.[55]

Figure 3.13. Child labor, Turkey.

Figure 3.14. Child laborer, Turkey.

Figure 3.15. Child laborers, India.

Figure 3.16. Boy plowing fields with oxen, Ethiopia.

Yet another outrage is the phenomenon of child labor. According to the ILO, some 218 million children in the world are working at any given time.[56] Figures 3.13 and 3.14 show two young boys working in Turkey's garment industry. Figure 3.15 shows an incense stick workshop in India. The overseer swore that all of the girls working there had papers certifying that they are at least fourteen years of age. My wife and I had our doubts about the veracity of these work papers. Figure 3.16 shows a young Ethiopian boy in the family field holding a plow pulled by two oxen – this, at an hour of the day when he should have been in school.

All child labor is bad, but even worse than the fact that hundreds of millions of children are working is that millions of children are engaged in the worst forms of child labor. The ILO defines the worst types as (1) all forms of slavery or practices similar to slavery, such as the sale and trafficking of children, debt bondage and serfdom, and forced or compulsory labor, including forced or compulsory recruitment of children for use in armed conflict; (2) the use, procuring, or offering of a child for prostitution, for the production of pornography, or for pornographic performances; (3) the use, procuring, or offering of a child for illicit activities, in particular for the production and trafficking of drugs as defined in the relevant international treaties; (4) work which, by its nature or the circumstances in which it is carried out, is likely to harm the health, safety, or morals of children.[57] India alone is reported to have some 1.2 million child prostitutes.[58]

I have seen and read a lot about outrages in the labor market, but I will tell you about one particularly reprehensible incident. When my wife and I visited a textile museum in Ahmedabad, India, we were shown a dazzling display of truly beautiful works of art. At the end of our tour, the museum official encouraged us and the other guests to stop at the museum shop and buy the products on offer. What amazed and appalled me was the reason she gave for why we should purchase these products. The textiles on display in the museum, she said, had been woven by children as young as age eight who, by the time they were fourteen, had become blind from the fine handwork they had been performing in low-light conditions over a number of years. A portion of the proceeds from our purchases, she continued, would be used to support these teenagers who would never be able to work again. We left at once. I regret that I did not say what was on my mind: that if blinding children is what it takes to produce such textiles, then the world would be better off if we did not have the textiles and the museum and the industry that supports it were closed down.

3.14 Developing Countries Have an Employment – Not an Unemployment – Problem

In developing countries, poverty among those who work is a more serious problem than is unemployment.[59] According to the latest ILO statistics, more than 200 million people in the world are unemployed. By contrast, some 1,300 million people (i.e., 1.3 billion) belong to the working poor, defined as workers who lived in families earning less than the $2 per person per day poverty line. That is, six-and-a-half times as many people in the world are working poor as are unemployed (and indeed many of the unemployed live in well-to-do families). In other words, 85% of the poor are working. In the 2009 recession, conditions got worse according to three measures of labor market outcomes – unemployment, vulnerable employment (defined as own-account workers plus contributing family workers), and working poverty[60] – because working poverty is so much larger than unemployment, unemployment is the tip of the proverbial iceberg. By far the greatest part of the world's employment problem is low earnings among the employed, not zero earnings among the unemployed.

There is one important exception to this generalization, and that is South Africa. South Africa has a frightful unemployment problem. Using the standard ILO definition, that country's unemployment rate is 25.2%. When discouraged workers are included – those who are not working, who are not actively looking for work, but who report that they would take a job if one became available – the so-called broad unemployment rate reaches 32.5%. An estimated 46% of the labor force – about seven million people – earned less than a South Africa-specific low-earnings line. The unemployed, defined broadly, make up about half this group, and the working poor make up the other half. South Africa's one-to-one ratio of working poor to unemployed is of an entirely different magnitude from the six-and-a-half-to-one ratio in the world as a whole. This country is so different from the rest of the world because of the enduring effects of apartheid.[61]

3.15 In Summary: Correcting Some Misimpressions

I hope that the evidence presented in this chapter has cleared up some common misimpressions about whether the poor in developing countries work and how they work:

Misimpression: Poor people do not want to work.
Fact: Poor people want very much to work.

Misimpression: Poor households are poor because nobody in the household works.
Fact: The great majority of poor households have workers who despite working long hours do not earn enough to raise the household out of poverty.

Misimpression: What most developing countries have is an unemployment problem.
Fact: What most developing countries have is an employment problem.

Misimpression: Most workers making less than $2 per day or some other low earnings line are unemployed, earning nothing.
Fact: Most low earners are employed, but they have too little work and/or very low hourly earnings to be able to reach $2 or some other low earnings line.

Misimpression: Most low earners work as paid employees.
Fact: Most low earners are self-employed.

Part IV

Modeling Labor Markets and the Effects of Labor Market Policies

When I got to Kenya as a graduate student, what stared me in the face was the huge chasm in living standards between the well-to-do minority and the poor majority. Not only did the two groups live differently but they worked differently. My graduate training had not prepared me for multi-sector analysis, and at first I wasn't sure how to handle it, so I started reading. I found four outstanding contributions to the literature on dualistic development.[1]

One was the work for which W. Arthur Lewis won the Nobel Prize in Economics: the Lewis (1954) paper and Fei and Ranis's (1964) book-length amplification of it. In Lewis's terminology, there was a small capitalist sector, a large subsistence sector, and wage dualism in that a job in the capitalist sector paid a worker better and offered higher utility than that worker could get in the subsistence sector. Lewis explained the workings of the capitalist sector, the subsistence sector, and inter-sectoral links: capitalist sector employers hired a fraction of the economy's labor supply, and any worker who did not succeed in getting hired for a capitalist sector job immediately crowded into the subsistence sector and earned a share of subsistence sector output. Subsistence sector workers remained available to work in the higher-paying capitalist sector if more jobs became available there. In this sense, in the first phase of dualistic economic development, the capitalist sector faced an unlimited supply of labor: hence, the use of that phrase in Lewis's title. And yet nobody was unemployed, because they could not afford to be.

A second outstanding contribution was Simon Kuznets's 1954 presidential address to the American Economic Association, published as Kuznets (1955). Kuznets also had two sectors – he called them urban and rural – each having its own within-sector income inequality, with the urban sector paying higher incomes on average than the rural sector. Economic development for Kuznets involved a process of inter-sectoral shifts: specifically, the urban sector enlarging and the rural sector shrinking. Kuznets won the Nobel Prize "for his empirically founded interpretation of economic growth which has led to new and deepened insight into the economic and social structure and process of development."

Third was the two-sector labor market model of Harris and Todaro (1970), which had been formulated specifically with the Kenyan labor market in mind. Their two sectors were an urban manufacturing sector and a rural agricultural sector. Because of the spatial differentiation in their model, workers would have to migrate to try to find jobs. The resultant equilibrium had some workers employed in the relatively high-paying manufacturing sector, other workers employed in the relatively low-paying agricultural sector, and some workers unemployed because they had tried to find high-paying urban manufacturing jobs but were unsuccessful. Harris and Todaro's analysis led them to two policy conclusions: 1) A policy of urban employment creation would *increase* urban unemployment, and 2) The solution to urban unemployment is *rural* development. I found these policy conclusions amazingly insightful and still do. Years later, a committee of distinguished luminaries (Arrow et al., 2011) selected the twenty most important papers published in the American Economic Review during its first 100 years of existence, and the Harris-Todaro paper was one of them.

Fourth was the theoretical work of Nobel laureate Joseph Stiglitz, which I continue to hold in the highest esteem. Stiglitz had written a working paper in Kenya the year before I got there developing efficiency wage theory, which is the idea that it might be in some firms' profit-maximizing interests to pay higher-than-market-clearing wages in order to incentivize existing workers to work harder or better and/or to attract more productive individuals (Stiglitz, 1969). When Stiglitz and I met in Nairobi in 1971, we found that we both were working on models in which firms did not know the productivity of would-be workers, so they used education as a screening device to select individuals whom they believed would be more productive on average. I published my analysis as Fields (1972, 1974) and he published his as Stiglitz (1975). Stiglitz found that early work of mine important enough that he made substantial mention of it in his Nobel speech (Stiglitz, 2002).

The Lewis, Kuznets, Harris-Todaro, and Stiglitz papers contributed enormously to my understanding of what the best applied economic theory could do to elucidate important social and economic issues. And yet, I saw gaps and the opportunity to fill in some of them, and so I set to work on a Ph.D. dissertation with the title "A Theory of Education and Labor Markets in Less Developed Countries." I thought of that research as something that would earn me a Ph.D. and a job as an economist, which it did. But as it turned out, research on how developing country labor markets work and how labor market conditions change in response to policy interventions became one of my two lifelong streams of work; see Chapters 4, 5, and 15 for some of the papers which came out of my dissertation research.

My most-cited paper is one emanating from my dissertation "Rural-Urban Migration, Urban Unemployment and Underemployment, and Job Search Activity in LDCs" (Chapter 4). This paper built on the key features of the Harris-Todaro model – a high-wage sector and a low-wage sector plus unemployment – but extended the analysis to bring in some features not in the Harris-Todaro model: on-the-job search from agriculture, the existence of an urban informal sector, educational differences among workers and preferential hiring of the better educated, and the fixity of some workers in some jobs. (Subsequent work by others added countless other extensions.) The policy analysis in "Rural Urban Migration ..." was conducted in terms of the welfare criterion used at the time: the rate of unemployment. Extending the welfare analysis beyond unemployment came later; see Chapter 18 of this volume.

The on-the-job search analysis in "Rural-Urban Migration ..." was later modified to distinguish between search strategies and subsequent outcomes. The result is "On-the-Job Search in a Labor Market Model: Ex Ante Choices and Ex Post Outcomes" (Chapter 5). The two should be viewed together as a package.

Dualistic development fascinated me and still does. My paper "A Welfare Economic Approach to Growth and Distribution in the Dual Economy" (Chapter 6) extends the Lewis and Kuznets lines of work to ask what happens to the entire income distribution under three types of dualistic growth, which I termed traditional sector enrichment, modern sector enrichment, and modern sector enlargement. Under each of these policy interventions, how many people would be employed in each sector earning how much money? This paper has both positive economics and normative economics elements. I have placed it in this section to highlight its positive economics features.

"Rural-Urban Migration ..." introduced a model which included an urban informal sector offering worse jobs than the urban formal sector, which is how the informal sector was conceptualized for a long time. Later, it became clear that some informal sector employment was *better* than employment in the formal sector and that some workers choose to work informally, not because they *have to* but because they *want to*. I continue to believe that *some but not all* people who work informally could have worked in formal jobs but chose not to, but I see this as a minority. Most who work informally, I think, choose informal work over an even worse alternative: open unemployment which, in the absence of unemployment insurance in the poor countries where they live, results in zero income. It appears to me that for most of those in informal employment, working formally is not an option. The essential duality of the informal sector – parts of it being *better* than formal employment and parts *worse* – was introduced in "Labor Market Modeling and the Urban Informal Sector," an excerpt from which is included here as Chapter 7. It is an idea that very much lives on (e.g., Perry et al., 2007; Günther and Launov, 2012).

One last question remains to be considered in this section: How have labor market conditions changed within countries in the course of their economic growth? The extant literature as of 2012 is summarized in the excerpt from "Challenges and Policy Lessons for the Growth-Employment-Poverty Nexus in Developing Countries" (Chapter 8).

4

Rural-Urban Migration, Urban Unemployment and Underemployment, and Job Search Activity in LDCs

4.1   The Received Theory of Rural-Urban Migration

The received theory of rural-urban migration, first set forth in Todaro (1968), has been revised and augmented by Todaro (1969), Harris and Todaro (1970), again by Todaro (1971), and by Johnson (1971). The Rarris-Todaro version is best known and we shall consider it in that form.

The model treats rural-urban migration primarily as an economic phenomenon. In essence, the theory postulates that workers compare the *expected* incomes in the urban sector with agricultural wage rates and migrate if the former exceeds the latter. The reason workers compare expected wages is that the urban wage is set institutionally above the market-clearing level and urban unemployment results. It is assumed that there is always full employment in agriculture. Rural-urban migration is thus the equilibrating force which equates rural and urban expected incomes and as such is a disequilibrium phenomenon.

The four basic characteristics of their model – that migration occurs largely for economic reasons, that urban wages are rigid and set too high for there to be full employment, that the migration decision depends on *expected* rather than nominal wage differentials, and that migration takes place in disequilibrium – suggest that rural-urban migration be given a new emphasis. Rather than considering it as a key phenomenon in its own right, migration could better be regarded as the adjustment mechanism

The original version of this chapter was published as: Fields, Gary S. (1975). Rural-Urban Migration, Urban Unemployment and Underemployment, and Job Search Activity in LDCs, in: Journal of Development Economics, 2(2):165–187. © 1975 by Elsevier B.V.

by which workers allocate themselves between different labor markets, some of which are located in urban areas and some in rural areas, while attempting to maximize their expected incomes.

Harris and Todaro formulate the problem in the following way. Let W_a and W_u respectively denote the nominal agricultural and urban wage rates, E_u be the number of urban jobs, and L_u be the urban labor force. The expected urban income $(E(W_u))$ is

(1) $$E(W_u) = W_u \, (E_u/L_u).$$

Expected rural income $(E(W_a))$ is simply W_a. The amount of rural-urban migration $(\dot{L}_u)$ is a function of the urban-rural expected wage differential,

(2) $$\dot{L}_u = \Psi(E(W_u) - E(W_a)).$$

The rural-urban equilibrium condition

(3) $$E(W_u) = E(W_a)$$

becomes

(4) $$W_u \, (E_u/L_u) = W_a,$$

and the equilibrium employment rate is

(5) $$(E_u/L_u) = (W_a/W_u).[1]$$

How does this prediction square with available empirical evidence? Not well. Per capita incomes in urban areas are anywhere from two to eight times as high as in rural areas.[2] Thus, Harris-Todaro would predict urban employment rates of 1/2 to 1/8. Yet the highest *unemployment* rate observed in seventeen less developed countries is 20 percent.[3] While it might be argued that equilibrium has not yet been reached, it seems much more likely in light of the size of the gap between actual and predicted unemployment rates that the theory as stated needs to be amended to conform more closely to the observed facts. This is our task in the remaining sections.

4.2 A More Generalized Formulation of the Job Search Process

In the Harris-Todaro model, the probability of obtaining an urban job is defined as the number of urban jobs divided by the urban labor force. Implicitly, this specification assumes that persons living in rural areas have no chance whatever of finding urban jobs. In this section, we shall show that the Harris-Todaro specification implies a higher equilibrium unemployment rate than would be predicted by a more generalized formulation of the job search process.

There are several reasons why rural residents would be expected to have a positive chance of obtaining urban jobs. Much urban hiring is done through channels which do not exclude rural residents. Some jobs are 'advertised' and filled informally by word of mouth. An urban resident may locate a job for a friend or relative and then send word (and money) for him to come to the city. Other jobs are filled by a central labor exchange with which rural residents are able to register. Finally, those persons in rural areas proximate to cities may on occasion be able to look actively for an urban job.

However, a number of factors make it probable that locating in the cities and searching for a job would still have a positive payoff. These include delays in conveying information to persons in rural areas, the preference of employers for personal contact with prospective employees, the costs of repeated visits to cities in search of work, and the simple fact that many jobs are found by happening to be at the right place at the right time.

All these considerations may be summarized by a single parameter. Should an urban job become available, each urban resident would have some particular chance of being selected for it and each rural resident would have some lesser chance. Let the relative chance of any given rural worker obtaining the job relative to any given urban worker be denoted by n. We shall call this number n the relative rural-urban job search-parameter. It is an (inverse) index of the payoff to job search; when job search is profitable, n is low, and vice versa.

To give an example, suppose $n = 1/2$ and let the probfibility that a worker who resides in the urban sector will obtain an urban job in the current period be 0.8. Then, the probability that a comparable worker who lives in the rural sector will obtain an urban job is 0.4. Similarly, if n were equal to $1/4$, the probability of a rural worker securing an urban job would be 0.2.

The value of the rural-urban job-search parameter n in a given country may be presumed to depend on a number of economic and cultural variables including the length of the work week in agriculture, the extent of favoritism, nepotism, and discrimination in the labor market, and the efficiency of the labor exchange.

We would expect that other things equal, the longer the work week, the smaller the job-search parameter n. This is because a longer work week leaves fewer hours for other activities including job search. Thus, the longer the work week, the poorer the relative chance of rural workers obtaining urban employment and so the lower the rural-urban job-search parameter.

The greater the degree of nepotism, favoritism, and discrimination in an economy, the greater the expected job-search parameter. When these factors are important, one's contacts, skin color, tribal origin, or other personal characteristics have a greater bearing on his employment status than the extent of his job search. Members of the favored group could remain on the farm and just wait to be called; their prospects would be little improved by migrating to the city and searching full-time. Persons not in the favored group would have almost as poor a chance of obtaining a job from the farm as they would in the city where they are discriminated against; their prospects also would be little improved by full-time job-search in the city. Consequently, a high job-search parameter would be expected where favoritism and discrimination are prevalent.

Finally, an efficient labor exchange, in which most urban job openings are filled by lotteries conducted by the labor exchange, would cause there to be little payoff to job search and raise the job search coefficient to near unity. For instance, this was the case in Kenya during the Tripartite Agreement of 1970, at which time all employers were required to increase employment by ten percent, workers were required to register with the labor exchange and the lottery results were published in the daily press.

Let us now incorporate the generalized job-search formulation into the Harris-Todaro model and determine the resulting effect of the equilibrium unemployment rate. We shall denote the probability of a given urban resident becoming employed in an urban job by P_u. Assuming that all jobs are available to all persons equally,[4]

$$(6) \qquad P_u = (E_u/J_u),$$

where E_u is urban employment and J_u is the number of job-seeker equivalants, defined as follows. J_u is a weighted sum of the urban and rural labor forces, the weights reflecting the relative chances of being hired. Since each rural resident has only an n'th as great a chance of being hired, a weight of one is assigned to each urban resident and a weight of n to each rural resident. Letting L_u and L_a be the number of residents in the urban and rural areas respectively, we therefore have, by definition,

$$(7) \qquad J_u = L_u + nL_a.$$

J_u is called the number of job-seeker equivalents because the same number of urban residents as J_u and no rural residents would leave each with an equivalent probability of finding urban employment.

The labor market just described may be thought of as functioning like a lottery in which each urban resident (L_u) has one ticket, each rural resident (L_a) has an n'th of a ticket, each ticket is identical, each prize is equally valuable, and the total number of prizes is E_u.

The expected wage of a member of the urban labor force $(E(W_u))$ is simply the urban wage W_u times the probability of employment P_u,

(8) $$E(W_u) = W_u P_u = W_u (E_u/J_u).$$

The expected income of a rural resident is slightly more involved, since it depends on whether or not he is hired for an urban job. If he does obtain an urban job, he will earn the urban wage W_u; otherwise he earns the rural wage W_a; The respective probabilities are $n(E_u/J_u)$ and $1 - n(E_u/J_u)$. Therefore, the expected income of a member of the rural labor force is

(9) $$E(W_a) = W_u n (E_u/J_u) + W_a[1-n(E_u/J_u)].$$

The rural-urban migration equilibrium condition $E(W_u) = E(W_a)$ becomes

(10) $$W_u (E_u/J_u) = W_u n (E_u/J_u) + W_a[1-n(E_u/J_u)].$$

The situation described by the Harris-Todaro model is easily seen to be the case where $n = 0$.

In order to determine the equilibrium employment rate, we solve the equilibrium condition (10) for E_u/L_u. Substituting (7) for J_u and $(L - L_u)$ for L_a, where L is the total labor force, we find

(11) $$(E_u/L_u) = \frac{1 + n[(L/L_u - 1)]}{(W_u/W_a) - n[(W_u/W_a) - 1]}.$$

In the Harris-Todaro case where $n = 0$, $(E_u/L_u) = 1/(W_u/W_a)$. However, when agricultural workers have some chance of obtaining urban employment and $n = 0$, $E_u/L_u > 1/(W_u/W_a)$. Furthermore, by differentiating (11) with respect to n, one can easily see that the larger is n, the larger is the urban employment rate (E_u/L_u). Thus we find that there is a lower equilibrium unemployment rate in general than would be predicted by the Harris-Todaro model and the greater the relative chance of rural workers finding urban jobs, the greater the discrepancy between the general result and the Harris-Todaro result.

4.3 The Introduction of a Murky Sector[5]

The nature of the migration process and the resulting urban growth are perhaps best described impressionistically by a typical scenario. New arrivals in the cities ordinarily stay with friends or relatives who help house and feed them while they look for work. A dozen or more people crowded into one room is not uncommon. They need not blive in housing which is rented or provided as part of job compensation. Squatter settlements and shanty towns house a substantial portion of urban populations, particularly in Africa.

Open unemployment is not very common. Additional household members are expected to contribute to their support. Frequently, they assist with the household chores by preparing meals, washing clothes, or caring for children. Simultaneously, they search for work (albeit on an irregular basis) and are classified as unemployed.

The most fortunate new migrants obtain a permanent modern sector job as a clerk, messenger, or whatever. However, these are the best jobs and the typical migrant is forced to find some lesser means of earning a cash income. He may secure one or more typically a succession of wage jobs (e.g., house-servant, cook in a small lunch kiosk, assistant in a family shop) or engage In self-employment (e.g., selling produce, newspapers, curios, or shoe shines on the street corner). These activities have been given several names including petty capitalism, the traditional sector, the service sector, and the grey area. A particularly graphic term, and the one we shall use to denote this whole range of activities, is the 'murky sector.'

The defining characteristics of the murky sector are ease of entry and the lack of a stable employer–employee relationship. The urban areas of less developed countries typically have a wide variety of such open entry, casual employment types of jobs. For instance, a person can get started by buying some peas in the market, removing the pods at the side of the road, and selling podded peas to passers-by at a higher price. Prostitution is another occupation which has notoriously easy entry.

Workers in the murky sector are ordinarily classified as employed[6] although they themselves and the statisticians who measure those things would be inclined to consider them underemployed. An examination of available time series evidence suggests that unemployment rates have not in general worsened substantially over time. Of ten countries which permit analysis, unemployment rates have risen in three (Korea, Colombia, and Panamu), fallen in five (UAR, Taiwan, Argentina, Chile, and Puerto Rico), and remained unchanged in two (Philippines and Trinidad-Tobago).[7] The tentative conclusion to be drawn is that most migrants have encountered limited success and are engaged in some sort of murky-sector employment.

The existence of opportunities for paid employment in the murky sector gives each member of the labor force a new option. Not only can he choose between staying in (or returning to) agriculture or being either employed or unemployed in the cities, but he can also voluntarily choose to be under-employed in the urban murky sector while looking for a better job.

Why don't all workers enter the murky sector? While underemployment in the murky sector yields a positive wage and unemployment pays no wage, the murky sector income is earned at the cost of reduced job search opportunities. This may be simply because murky sector workers have less time to look for modern sector jobs or for some other reason.

In the remainder of this section, we shall examine these effects and show that introduction of the murky sector leads to a lower equilibrium unemployment rate than the Harris-Todaro result.

The murky sector may be introduced in a manner similar to the development of the agricultural sector in the last section. In order to keep the effects of recognizing the murky sector separate, we return to the original model (equations (1) – (5)) and assume that agricultural workers have no chance of obtaining modern sector jobs.

We now have two kinds of urban jobs, modern sector and murky sector, with wage rates W_u and W_m respectively. While we will hold W_u constant as before, we will regard W_m as an endogenous variable to be determined by the model.

Let the relative job search parameter between murky and mcdern sector jobs he denoted by h. The parameter h is the probability that any given person in the murky sector labor force would be hired for a modern sector job relative to the probability of any given member of the modern sector labor force being hired.

Since we are now assuming that rural residents have no chance of obtaining urban jobs, the number of job-seeker equivalents for modern sector urban jobs is

(12) $$J_u = L_u + hL_m,$$

where L_u and L_m are the modern sector and murky sector labor forces respectively.

Equilibrium between the murky and modern sectors requires that the expected wage in the modern sector $(E(W_u))$ equal the expected wage in the murky sector $(E(W_m))$. By analogy with the expected agricultural wage under general job search conditions,

(13) $$E(W_m) = W_u\, h(E_u/J_u) + [1 - h(E_u/J_u)]\, W_m.$$

As before,

(14) $$E(W_u) = W_u\, (E_u/J_u).$$

Equilibrium between the rural and urban sectors requires that these, in turn, equal the expected agricultural wage $(E(W_a))$,

(15) $$E(W_a) = W_a,$$

since we are once again assuming that agricultural workers have no opportunity of obtaining an urban job. Therefore, the rural-urban and intra-urban equilibrium conditions may be combined as

(16) $$W_a = W_u\, h(E_u/J_u) + [1 - h(E_u/J_u)]\, W_m = W_u(E_u/J_u).$$

We now wish to solve for the equilibrium labor force allocation, urban unemployment rate, and murky sector wage rate. From the equality between the first and third members of (16), in equilibrium,

$$(17) \qquad J_u = (W_u/W_a)E_u.$$

Substituting this into the equality between the second and third members and solving for W_m, we obtain for the equilibrium murky-sector wage

$$(18) \qquad W_m = W_a (1 - h)/[1 - h(W_a/W_u)]$$

To determine the murky sector labor force, let us assume that the demand for murky-sector output (Q_m) is the sum of the demand by employed modern sector workers $f(E_u)$ plus the demand by murky-sector workers $g(L_m)$:

$$(19) \qquad Q_m = f(E_u) + g(L_m), f' > 0, g' > 0.$$

We further assume that since murky sector workers are underemployed, the demand is supplied and the resultant income is shared equally among murky sector workers, i.e.,

$$(20) \qquad W_m = (Q_m/L_m)$$

Substituting (18) and (19) into (20), we obtain an implicit expression for the murky sector labor force as

$$(21) \qquad [f(E_u) + g(L_m)]/L_m = W_a(1 - h)/[1 - h(W_a/W_u)].$$

In this general form, we cannot solve explicitly for L_m. However, if we adopt the simplifying assumption that the amount of murky sector output demanded by murky sector workers is fixed, this along with the assumed constancy of E_u implies that the total murky sector output is fixed at some level $\bar{Q}_m$. Substituting $\bar{Q}_m$ for $[f(E_u) + g(L_m)]$ in (21) and rearranging, we derive the murky sector labor force as

$$(22) \qquad L_m = \bar{Q}_m [(1 - h \frac{W_a}{W_u})]/W_a (1 - h)$$

Substituting (22) and (17) into (12) and rearranging, we find that the total urban labor force (L_{urb}) is

$$(23) \qquad L_{urb} = [W_u E_u + \bar{Q}_m (1 - h (W_a/W_u)]/W_a.$$

The urban employment rate is modern sector employment plus murky sector employment divided by the total urban population:

$$(24) \qquad (E_u + L_m/)L_{urb}.$$

Substituting (22) and (23) into (24), we find that the urban employment rate is

(25) $$[E_u + (\Omega/W_a (1 - h))]/[(W_u E_u + \Omega)/W_a],$$

where $\Omega = \bar{Q}_m[(1 - h\ W_a/W_u)]$. This may readily be shown to be greater than Harris-Todaro equilibrium unemployment rate (W_a/W_u) by subtracting (5) from (25) and observing that the result is unambiguously positive. We have therefore demonstrated the validity of the proposition that introduction of the murky sector leads to a lower equilibrium unemployment rate than predicted by the Harris-Todaro model.

What is the effect of the size of the murky-modern relative job search parameter on the equilibrium urban employment rate and other labor market variables? Our model suggests that the greater the chance of a worker employed in the murky sector of obtaining a modern sector job relative to an unemployed worker who searches full-time (i.e., the larger is h):

a) the smaller the equilibrium murky sector wage rate,

b) the larger the equilibrium murky sector labor force,

c) the smaller the modern sector labor force in equilibrium,

d) the smaller the total urban labor force in equilibrium,

e) the larger the equilibrium urlan employment rate.

Point a) may be demonstrated by partially differentiating (18) with respect to h and noting that since $W_U > W_a$ the result is negative. To show b), differentiate (22) and observe that the result is positive for $W_U > W_a$. For c), (12) and (17) give

(26) $$L_u = (W_u E_u/W_a) - hL_m$$

which clearly varies inversely with h. Point d) is easily seen from the expression for the equilibrium urban labor force in (23). Finally, differentiating (16) with respect to h, gives a constant J_u and

(27) $$\partial W_m/\partial h < 0.$$

(20) and (27) imply $\partial L_m/\partial h > 0$, which along with the constancy of J_u implies that $\partial L_u/\partial h < 0$. We now have more urban residents employed in the murky sector and fewer unemployed seeking modern sector unskilled jobs and therefore an unambiguously higher urban employment rate for a larger value of h.

A priori considerations suggest that the murky sector relative job search parameter h would be fairly large, i.e., worker' job search activity would not be seriously impeded by taking a murky sector job rather than remaining unemployed in search of work in the modern sector. This would seem so for two reasons. First, the nature of the murky sector is such that self-employment, flexible hours, and part-time work are common. Thus, it is often possible to adapt one's work week and the specific work hours so as to be relatively free to search for modern sector jobs. Second, many modern sector jobs are obtained by contacts from employed friends or relatives. Consequently, workers would have relatively little to gain by searching full-time and they would be more likely to take up employment in the murky sector in order to earn a cash income. To the extent that these two considerations hold, urban unemployment rates are likely to be fairly low in absolute terms as well as relative to the prediction of the Harris-Todaro model. However, it should not be forgotten that these low unemployment rates conceal a considerable volume of underemployment in the murky sector.

As long as the murky sector labor force has some positive chance of becoming employed in the modern sector, the equilibrium murky sector wage would be less than the agricultural wage.[8] This would be expected because the lower wage is the price workers must pay in equilibrium in order to have a better chance of obtaining a relatively high-paying modern-sector job.

This gives an additional reason for the existence of an impoverished urban class. Not only are some people willing to be unemployed much of the time in order to earn high wages when they are employed in the modern sector, but others are willing to be underemployed by working for very low wages (less even than they could earn in agriculture) in order to have a better chance of being hired for those same modern sector jobs.

4.4 Preferential Treatment by Employers of the Better Educated

A number of observers of less developed countries report employers using educational attainment as a criterion for hiring and selecting the better educated in preference to those with less education.[9] What effect does this have on the equilibrium employment rate?

Let us once again return to the original model and neglect the possibility of employment in the murky sector. Now suppose there are two categories of workers: the educated (L_e) and uneducated (L_u), of whom L_{uu} live in urban areas e and L_{ua} in agriculture. Suppose further that because of this systematic preference by employers the available supply of educated workers are hired immediately without unemployment and uneducated workers must divide the remaining jobs.

The expected income of an uneducated worker who enters the urban labor force $(E(W_u \mid u))$ is

(28) $E(W_u \mid u) = W_u \left[(E_u - L_e)/L_{uu} \right],$

and the expected income of an uneducated worker who enters the agricultural labor force $(E(W_u \mid a))$ is

(29) $E(W_u \mid a) = W_a.$

Equilibrium between the two labor markets for uneducated workers requires that $E(W_u \mid u) = E(W_u \mid a)$ or

(30) $W_u[(E_u - L_e)/L_{uu}] = W_a.$

The equilibrium employment rate for uneducated workers is

(31) $(E_u - L_e)/L_{uu} = W_a/W_u,$

and the equilibrium employment rate for educated workers is one. The total employment rate is a weighted average of these two rates, the weights given by the percentage of uneducated and educated workers, respectively. Therefore, the total urban employment rate in equilibrium is

(32) $(L_{uu}/L_{urb})(W_a/W_u) + (L_e/L_{urb}),$

which is clearly greater than the Harris-Todaro result (W_a/W_u) except when $L_e = 0$.

The reason for this greater employment rate is inherent in the job search mechanism itself. When an educated worker is hired, he fills a position which some greater number of uneducated workers had been seeking. For example, if $W_a = \frac{1}{3} W_u$, the equilibrium employment rate for uneducated workers is $\frac{1}{3}$, as given by (31). For each educated worker who is hired preferentially, there is one less urban job available to uneducated workers and in equilibrium there would be three fewer job-seekers.

4.5   Present Values and Labor Turnover

In the paper by Harris and Todaro (1970), rural-urban migration was taken to be a response to expected income differentials between rural and urban areas, the urban employment probability being the ratio of urban jobs to the urban labor force. The assumptions implicit in this formulation are that migration is a function of *current* expected values rather than *present discounted* values of expected future income, and the employment probability is the ratio of *all* jobs to the *entire* urban labor force rather than *job hiring* (newly-created employment plus replacement demand) in relation to those *not already employed* in such jobs.[10]

The Harris-Todaro specification is equivalent to a situation where all jobs turn over every period,[11] while the earlier Todaro specification had no job turnover at all (i.e., once a worker gets a job, he is assumed to keep it for life). Johnson (1971) has worked out the relationship between the labor turnover rate and the equilibrium unemployment rate and has shown that they vary directly. Because the Harris-Todaro model has the maximum possible turnover rate, it therefore predicts a higher unemployment rate in equilibrium than would be expected for any finite rate of labor turnover. Since involuntary turnover rates are apparently quite low,[12] the overstatement is apt to be substantial.

4.6 A Generalized Model of Migration, Unemployment, and Underemployment

In this section, we consider simultaneously the four extensions of the Harris-Todaro model presented in Sections 4.2–4.5. The results here build on the work of Fields and Hosek (1973).

Consider an economy with three sectors; (1) a modern urban sector paying a high-wage W_u; (2) a 'murky' urban sector paying a lower wage W_n; and (3) an agricultural sector paying wage W_a. Assume there is no unemployment compensation. Suppose there is a shortage of modern-sector urban jobs relative to the number of workers seeking those jobs, but that entry to the murky sector and agriculture are open. Potential migrants may then choose among three alternative labor market search strategies:

a) Work in agriculture at W_a; seek a modern-sector job with a reduced chance n.

b) Work in the murky sector at W_m; seek a modern-sector job with a reduced chance h.

c) Be unemployed while seeking a modern-sector job full-time.

Let us suppose that workers choose among available labor market alternatives according to the present discounted value of expected future income in each,

$$(33) \qquad v^i = \sum_{n=0}^{t} \{[W_u(t)E_u^i(t)+W_m(t)E_m^i(t)+W_a(t)E_a^i(t)]\}/[1/1+r)]^t,$$

where

$W_j(t)$ = wage rate of job j at time t,
$E_j^i(t)$ = probability of being employed at job j at time t if search strategy i is adopted,

r   = discount rate,

τ = time horizon.

While r and τ have clear interpretations, the appropriate future values of W_u and E_u are subjective; in this sense there are as many different expected present values as there are workers with different notions about future wages and employment probabilities. Perhaps the simplest, yet most economically meaningful, way of standardizing workers behavior is to suppose that all workers behave as if today's wage structure and probabilities of becoming employed and losing one's job in the various labor markets will prevail forever. These assumptions enable us to use the results from Markov chains to derive expressions for the present values of expected incomes under the various search strategies and to determine the equilibrium allocation of the labor force among alternative labor markets.[13]

Consider first what a potential migrant would expect to find in the city. Denote the rate of flow of modern-sector urban job offers by f_u. If such a job is offered, he will accept it, since it is the best thing available. However, if a modern-sector job offer is not forthcoming, he *may* engage in murky-sector activity. Whether he does or does not is conditional on the simultaneous occurrence of three (presumably independent) events and is therefore the mathematical product of the three: f_m, the rate of flow of murky-sector job opportunities, which we shall assume is equal to one; $1-f_u$, the probability of not receiving a modern-sector job offer; and π, a categorical variable taking on the value one if the individual decides to accept murky-sector employment and zero if he rejects it. Since the conditional transition probabilities must sum to one, it follows that an unemployed migrant will remain unemployed with probability $(1-f_u)(1-\pi)$.

Suppose the potential migrant were to take a murky-sector job. He would have probability nf_u, of obtaining a modern-sector job, zero of an involuntary return to unemployment, and hence $1-nf_u$, of remaining in the murky sector.

Should the potential migrant find a modern-sector job, there is some chance that he will subsequently be disemployed for reasons such as the bankruptcy of his employer or dismissal due to conflicts with his supervisors or coworkers. Denoting this turnover rate in urban jobs by t_u, and assuming that workers are not demoted, the (conditional) probability of remaining employed in a modern-sector urban job is $1-t_u$.

For a potential migrant in agriculture, everything is the same, with one exception: if he takes the agricultural job, his probability of securing a modern-sector job is hf_u rather than nf_u, as in the case of a murky-sector worker.

The transition probabilities based on these assumptions for potential migrants under each of the three alternative search strategies are presented in Table 4.1.

The present value of expected future income under the ith search strategy may, following Fields and Hosek (1973), be expressed in terms of the transition probabilities as

(34) $\qquad V^i = (1/\Delta^i)(W_1^i C_1^i + W_2^i C_2^i),$ $\qquad\qquad$ where

$C_1^i \quad = \delta^2 P_{32}^i P_{21}^i + \delta P_{31}^i (1-\delta P_{22}^i),$

$C_2^i \quad = \delta P_{32}^i (1-\delta P_{11}^i) + \delta^2 P_{32}^i P_{12}^i,$

$\Delta^i \quad = -\delta P_{31}^i [\delta^2 P_{12}^i P_{23}^i + \delta P_{13}^i (1-\delta P_{22}^i)]$

$\qquad\qquad +\delta P_{32}^i [(1-\delta P_{11}^i)(-\delta P_{23}^i) - \delta^2 P_{13}^i P_{21}^i]$

$\qquad\qquad +(1-\delta P_{33}^i)[(1-\delta P_{11}^i)(1-\delta P_{22}^i) - \delta^2 P_{12}^i P_{21}^i],$

$\delta \quad = 1/(1+r),$

$W_1 \quad$ = wage in higher-paying alternative,

$W_2 \quad$ = wage in lower-paying alternative,

$P_{mn} \quad$ = probability of moving to state n conditional on being in state m.

The essence of the Harris-Todaro model is that workers would be expected to choose among labor markets on the basis of the present value of expected lifetime income in each. Following this logic, equilibrium would be realized in our model when

(35) $\qquad\qquad\qquad\qquad V^{(a)} = V^{(b)} = V^{(c)}.$

We now turn to a numerical example showing that for plausible parameter values the predicted urban unemployment rate accords quite well with the range of values observed in LDCs.

4.7 Numerical Illustration

To see the effects of taking into account the various modifications considered in this paper, let us derive the equilibrium unemployment rate in an illustrative example. This should be thought of as suggestive of the approximate order of magnitude, and the interested reader is invited to substitute his own parameter values.

Suppose that in a hypothetical economy, modern-sector employment (E_u) is available to 30 percent of the labor force (L). The number of such jobs is growing at the rate of 3 percent per year (g_u), 1 percent of current workers are dismissed and replaced (t_u), and another 1/2 percent die or retire and are also replaced (d_u). Let the real modern-sector urban wage (W_u) be three times the annual agricultural wage. The total modern-sector urban labor force, including the openly unemployed, is L_u.

Table 4.1. Transition probabilities for potential migrants pursuing alternative job-search strategies

P_{mn} = probability of moving to state n conditional on being in state m	Transition probabilities for an unskilled worker		
	Working in agriculture	Unemployed in urban area searching full-time for modern-sector job ($\pi = 0$)	Engaged in murky-sector activity, searching part-time for modern-sector job ($\pi = 1$)
	Search strategy (a)	Search Strategy (b)	Search Strategy (c)
P_{11}	$1 - t_u$	$1 - t_u$	$1 - t_u$
P_{12}	0	0	0
P_{13}	t_u	t_u	t_u
P_{21}	hf_u	nf_u	nf_u
P_{22}	$1 - hf_u$	$1 - nf_u$	$1 - nf_u$
P_{23}	0	0	0
P_{31}	f_u	f_u	f_u
P_{32}	$1 - f_u$	$(1 - f_u)\pi = 0$	$(1 - f_u)\pi = 1 - f_u$
P_{33}	0	$(1 - \pi)(1 - f_u) = 1 - f_u$	$(1 - \pi)(1 - f_u) = 0$
	State 1 = Employed in urban modern-sector job	State 1 = Employed in urban modern-sector job	State 1 = Employed in urban modern-sector job
	State 2 = Employed in agriculture	State 2 = Engaged in murky-sector activity	State 2 = Engaged in murky-sector activity
	State 3 = Unemployed	State 3 = Unemployed	State 3 = Unemployed

Modern-sector employees are assumed to spend 20 percent of their incomes on goods and services produced in the murky sector. Murky-sector output (Q_m) is assumed to be divided equally among members of the murky-sector labor force (L_m). A murky-sector worker has only half as great a chance (n) as an unemployed person in the modern-sector of being hired for any given modern-sector job opening.

Agricultural jobs are assumed to be freely available; the agricultural wage (W_a) is chosen as numeraire. An agricultural worker is assumed to have only one-fourth as great a chance (h) as an unemployed person in the modern sector of being hired for any given modern-sector job opening.

Workers are assumed to discount future benefits at the rate of 5 percent per year (r). All other magnitudes, in particular the murky-sector wage rate and urban unemployment rate, are determined endogenously.

Substituting the above values and the probabilities from Table 4.1 into the present value expression (34) we have:

(36) $V^{(a)} = (0.0544 + 0.7619\ f_u)/(0.0027 + 0.0110\ f_u),$

$V^{(b)} = (0.1361\ f_u + 1.3605\ f_u^2)/(0.00013 + 0.0035\ f_u + 0.0216\ f_u^2),$

$V^{(c)} = [1.4966\ f_u + W_m(0.0544 - 0.0544\ f_u)]/(0.0027 + 0.0225\ f_u).$

Equating $V^{(a)}$ and $V^{(b)}$ we find $f_u = 0.0478$, i.e., an urban worker who remains unemployed for a year would have only a 4.8 percent chance of obtaining a modern-sector job during that time.

The equilibrium murky-sector wage rate (W_m) may be found by substituting for f_u, in $V^{(c)}$ and equating the present values under the alternative search strategies. This yields a murky-sector wage rate of 0.6674, i.e., murky-sector workers earn only two-thirds of the agricultural wage and two-ninths of the modern-sector wage. As was noted in Section 4.3, this low wage is the price urban workers must pay in order to have a better chance (relative to agricultural workers) of obtaining the high-paying, modern-sector jobs.

The equilibrium urban unemployment rate is found by deriving that labor force allocation which gives the appropriate values of W_m and f_u. Total murky-sector income is

(37) $Q_m = 0.2(W_u E_u) = 0.6E_u = 0.18L.$

Since murky-sector income is shared equally among murky-sector workers, i.e., $W_m = Q_m/L_m$, and $W_m = 0.6674$, we derive the murky-sector labor force,

(38) $L_m = 0.18L/0.6674 = 0.2696L,$

and we see that 27 percent of the labor force will be in the murky sector.

The number of (openly) unemployed is found by substituting into f_u the ratio of modern-sector hires to job-seeker equivalents (cf. eqs. (7) and (12)),

(39) $f_u = E_u(g_u + t_u + d_u)/(L_u - E_u + hL_a + nL_m)$

             $= 0.045E_u/(L_u - E_u + 0.25L_a + 0.5L_m).$

Substituting (38), $L = L_u + L_m + L_a$, and $E_u = 0.3L$ into (39), we find $L_u/L = 0.3765$. Thus, the equilibrium allocation of the labor force is: 30 percent employed in modern sector, 8 percent unemployed, 27 percent employed in murky sector, 35 percent employed in agriculture. The equilibrium urban unemployment rate is

$$1-(E_u + E_m)/(L_u + L_m) = 1-(30\% + 27\%)/(38\% + 27\%) = 12\%.$$

What if the better-educated members of the urban labor force are hired preferentially? Suppose, for example, that 5 percent of the modern-sector jobs go to highly-educated workers who, being hired preferentially, experience no unemployment. Then modern-sector jobs are available to 28.5 percent of the uneducated workers, and the relations summarized in eq. (39) apply to uneducated workers only. Substituting $E_u = 0.285L$ into (39), we find $L_u/L = 0.3204$, meaning that 32 percent of the *unskilled* labor force is in the urban sector.

The equilibrium labor force allocation is then as follows,

Uneducated	Educated
28.5%	100% Employed in modern sector
3.5%	0% Unemployed
27.0%	0% Employed in murky sector
41.0%	0% Employed in agriculture

and the equilibrium urban unemployment rate is 6 percent.[14]

Finally, suppose this hypothetical economy were to increase the size of its modern sector by 1 percent (i.e., from 30.0 percent of the labor force to 30.3 percent), thereby increasing the growth rate of the modern sector by 10 percent (from 3.0 percent to 3.3 percent). Workers would migrate to urban areas in larger numbers because (1) the absorption of additional labor reduces the pool of job-seekers, thus increasing the probability of finding a job, and (2) the increased growth rate of employment raises the hiring rate, also increasing the probability of finding a job. The first effect is not inconsiderable: in the absence of preferential hiring, and neglecting for the moment the increased rate of job creation, the enlargement of the modern sector by only one percent increases the modern-sector labor force by three percent (from 38 percent to 39 percent of the total labor force). Yet even more substantial is the effect on migration of the increased hiring rate (from 4.5 percent to 4.8 percent). The two effects together yield a modern-sector labor force of 43 percent (as opposed to 38 percent previously) and an urban unemployment rate of 18 percent (as versus 12 percent previously).[15] The reason for both of these magnified effects is that when E_u/L and g_u are increased, the agricultural labor force must contract so as to increase the number of job-seeker equivalents (the denominator of (39)) by enough to keep f_u unchanged.[16] Thus we see from this example that small changes in the size of the modern sector may induce much larger changes in migration and urban unemployment.

Three results emerge from these examples. First and most important is the fact that the urban unemployment rates derived fall well within the range of values found by Turnham (1971) and others. Although both the expectation formation process and the specific numerical values are only hypothetical, the results suggest that the theory developed here conforms more closely to observed urban unemployment rates than does the Harris-Todaro model. These extensions permit us to retain the quite plausible notion, as set forth by Harris and Todaro, that the voluntary movement of workers between geographical areas is the primary equilibrating force in the labor markets of LDCs, while at the same time having a theory which is not contradicted by the facts.

Second, if highly-educated workers are hired preferentially for modern-sector jobs, the urban unemployment rate will be lower than if workers were hired randomly without regard to educational attainment. This is because preferential hiring reduces the number of jobs available to the uneducated, thereby lowering the probability of finding an urban job and inducing large numbers of them to remain in or move back to agriculture.

Third, both the urban unemployment rate and the number of urban unemployed respond positively and within great sensitivity to additions in the number of modern-sector jobs. This results from an acceleration-like process whereby small increments in the availability of modern-sector jobs lead to large increases in the rate of modern-sector job hiring, to which present-value-maximizing migrants presumably respond.

The policy implications of these findings are discussed in the concluding section.

4.8   Policy Implications

In their original discussion, Harris and Todaro concluded that a combination of a wage subsidy in the modern sector, along with physical restriction of migration, would be necessary to achieve a first-best state lying on the economy's production-possibility frontier. They have since been taken to task by Bhagwati and Srinivasan (1974), who have demonstrated that a first-best solution can be achieved by means of a variety of alternative tax or subsidy schemes, none of which require migration restriction.

The analysis presented in this chapter suggests three additional policy variables, beyond those considered by either pair, which might be expected to have an important effect on the volume of unemployment and underemployment in less developed countries. The first, suggested by the models of Sections 4.2 and 4.3, has to do with the operation of labor markets. We saw that the amount of unemployment depends inversely on the efficiency of the labor exchange (among other things). This is because a smoothly functioning labor exchange would reduce the incentive to remain unemployed while searching for a superior job. Workers could thus remain on the farm or in the murky sector and wait to be notified that their numbers had come up. To the extent that they create additional product in the meantime, national income is increased and open unemployment lessened.

Secondly, the model of Section 4.4 suggests that the size of the educational system would also influence the amount of unemployment.[17] As we have seen, if employers hire better-educated workers preferentially, the education of an additional worker will lower the number of urban jobs available to uneducated workers by one, reduce the uneducated urban labor force by something more than one, and thereby lower the total number of urban unemployed. These workers will return to agriculture and add to national output there, while the educated workers might be more productive in the urban sector than their uneducated counterparts and further contribute to national output. Hence, we derive the somewhat paradoxical result that overeducation of the labor force might have the beneficial effect of both lessening urban unemployment and increasing national income in both the rural and the urban sectors.

Lastly, the model of Section 4.6 and the illustrative example of Section 4.7 suggest that it is job hiring in the modern sector, more than the number of jobs, which primarily influences workers' locational decisions. We have seen that a small increase in the number of jobs has a much larger proportional effect on job hiring and induces substantial rural-urban migration and increases the rate of urban unemployment. Thus migration can be stemmed simply by not growing so fast. For countries which need or choose to develop by enlarging their modern sectors rather than by improving the well-being of those in the traditional sectors, this creates a harsh dilemma: the cost of more rapid growth is the enrichment of some (the fortunate few who are hired for the newly-created jobs), the impoverishment of others (those who respond to the new incentives by choosing a high unemployment labor market search strategy), and greater inequality in the distribution of income. Hopefully, this conflict between growth and distributional objectives might be moderated by improving the functioning of labor markets as suggested above or by designing a tax-transfer system following Bhagwati and Srinivasan's guidelines. Thus, Harris and Todaro's pessimistic conclusion about the undesirability of modern-sector job creation may not be fully justified.

In interpreting these results, one should not jump to the conclusion that things are not (or will not become) as bad as the Harris-Todaro model might have led us to believe. It is important that we remember that open unemployment rates fail to take into account employment at very low wages or the plight of the working poor. Poverty is no less real when people eke out an existence in agriculture or earn less than a living wage while underemployed in the murky sectors of the cities. In fact, the social consequences of a low unemployment rate may be severe; for if planners and policy-makers mistakenly regard unemployment rates of 10–20 percent as indicating that 80–90 percent of the urban population are fully and gainfully employed, they may fail to act to increase earning opportunities.

5

On-the-Job Search in a Labor Market Model: Ex Ante Choices and Ex Post Outcomes

5.1   Introduction

The purposes of this paper are to formulate a theoretical model of some of the pertinent features of labor markets and to indicate how this model might be used to analyze patterns of employment, unemployment, and underemployment and policies to affect them. The model is set in the context of a multisector economy, the sectors being defined by product, location, or method of wage determination. The model builds on previous contributions by Harris and Todaro (1970), Fields (1975), and McDonald and Solow (1985). The most important new feature is the distinction between the ex ante allocation of the labor force among search strategies on the one hand and, on the other, the ex post allocation of the labor force among employment in different sectors and unemployment.

This model is motivated by a number of empirical observations about employment and wages in various countries' labor markets. One is that certain geographical areas tend to have persistently higher real wages than others (Hanushek, 1983; Squire, 1981). This suggests that wage rigidity rather than market-clearing wages may typify certain segments of the labor market. Another is the finding that high-wage labor markets are characterized by high unemployment rates (Hall, 1970; Harris and Todaro, 1970). This may be interpreted as reflecting the influx of job-seekers in pursuit of jobs in high-paying industries or localities.

The original version of this chapter was published as: Fields, Gary S. (1989). On-the-job search in a Labor Market Model: Ex ante choices and ex post outcomes, in: Journal of Development Economics, 30(1):159–178. © 1989 by Elsevier B.V.

Another is the observation (Fields, 1976; Todaro, 1976) that patterns of labor force migration can be substantially explained by the rates of hiring, quits, and layoffs prevailing in different labor markets. One may infer from this that workers on the margin will indeed seek to reallocate themselves toward areas where job opportunities are more plentiful. And finally, an important feature of labor markets is the fact that many workers take up low-paying jobs from which they search (not necessarily successfully) for better ones (Tobin, 1972; Matilla, 1974; Merrick, 1976; Banerjee, 1983).

We need a model which captures these features. The textbook characterization of labor markets does not suffice. In that model, different firms pay the same wage to comparable workers, the wage being set by supply and demand to clear the market. No unemployment emerges, save possibly for frictional unemployment. As a general characterization of labor markets, the textbook model is at odds with two observed facts: the existence of unemployment, apparently above frictional levels; and wage diversity for observationally-equivalent workers. Other models also assume away these facts - among them, international trade models, dualistic economic development models, and even some minimum wage models.

Some existing models incorporate both unemployment and wage diversity. Foremost among these are the works of Harris and Todaro (1970), Harberger (1971), Gramlich (1976), Mincer (1976), Stiglitz (1982), and McDonald and Solow (1985). Wage diversity arises in these and kindred models due to partial applicability of minimum wage laws and limited enforcement of them, strong trade unions in some sectors of the economy but not others, etc. and/or efficiency wages being paid in some economic sectors but not in others. Open unemployment results from the purposeful movement of labor between sectors on the basis of the expected wages (or utility) in each. In these models, the equilibrium tendency is toward equalization of wages or utility adjusted for probability of employment; it is an increase in unemployment in the high-wage sectors rather than a fall in wages there that ultimately brings the supply side of the labor market into balance.

The model developed below incorporates wage dualism, open unemployment, underemployment, on-the-job search, and expected wage equalization among search strategies. By 'wage dualism', I mean that a wage floor above market-clearing levels applies to one economic sector but not others. 'Open unemployment' is distinguished from 'underemployment', whereby workers are engaged in labor market activity and thus classified as employed, yet because this activity pays wages below what they might earn elsewhere in the economy, the workers may be said to be underemployed. 'On-the-job search' means that workers employed in the lower-paying economic sectors devote some fraction of their time to obtaining better positions elsewhere in the economy and have some non-zero probability of obtaining such positions. 'Expected wage equalization' is the rule by which the labor force allocates itself among jobs and search opportunities.

Some of the components for this model were first presented in Fields (1975) and later appeared, apparently independently, in the work of McDonald and Solow (1985). The model formulated here moves beyond those earlier works, both by drawing the distinction between the ex ante allocation of the labor force among job search strategies and the ex post allocation of the labor force among employment in the various sectors and unemployment and by deriving new results based on that distinction.

Why does the ex ante/ex post distinction matter? Consider first a multisector model without on-the-job search, such as Harris-Todaro (1970) or Mincer (1976). In such a model, all workers end up in the same sector in which they began. Think about the number who choose a search strategy ex ante (e.g., those who migrate to the urban economy and seek a job there). Then consider that sector's labor force ex post (e.g., those who are in the urban economy, employed or unemployed) after the jobs are allocated. Without on-the-job search, it is not necessary to distinguish between the number of ex ante searchers and the ex post labor force – the two numbers are the same, because people get jobs only in the sectors where they are located. But with the possibility of searching on-the-job and getting a job in one sector while living in another, the two numbers will differ. Take the example where wages are higher in the urban economy than in the rural economy and rural residents have a positive (i.e., strictly non-zero) probability of obtaining a high-paying urban job. In this case, some urban jobgetters will be rural residents. Consequently, the rural labor force ex post will be smaller than the number of rural searchers ex ante; and likewise, the urban labor force ex post will be larger than the number of urban searchers ex ante. Unemployment rates will be affected as a result.

It bears mention that this model is characterized by rational expectations. That is, workers allocate themselves among search strategies ex ante knowing what those decisions imply about ex post outcomes, and those ex post outcomes are in fact realized. The ex ante/ex post distinction is made here to reflect the predictable movement of workers across sectors when some get jobs and some do not. It does not reflect intervening shocks, because there are no intervening shocks in the model; the only stochastic element is which individuals will get jobs and which will not.

The model is presented in Section 5.2. Four results using this model are developed in Section 5.3. Conclusions appear in Section 5.4.

5.2 Modeling Workers' Choices of Ex Ante Search Strategies and the Ex Post Rate of Employment, Unemployment, and Underemployment with On-the-Job Search

5.2.1 *Overview of the Model*

The economy I am modeling is atemporal and consists of a large number of homogeneous, risk-neutral individuals and a small number of economic sectors.[1] Following the familiar terminology of development economics, these three sectors are termed modern, traditional, and agriculture, though they might equally well be called high-wage, free-entry, and low-wage, respectively. Primary attention is given to the supply side of the labor market. The production side of the model is specified only to the extent that it is necessary for the formulation of the labor market model. The various sectors differ from one another in two major respects: wages and job search opportunities.

The highest-paying sector is named 'the urban modern sector' and is denoted by M. The wage in this sector, W_M, is set by some combination of market and/or institutional forces, above market-clearing levels and higher than the wage elsewhere in the economy. All workers, being risk-neutral income-maximizers, aspire to jobs in the modern sector. They may elect to search for these jobs by being openly unemployed and searching full-time (assuming for simplicity that there is no unemployment compensation) or by accepting low-wage employment elsewhere in the economy at a positive wage and searching part-time. Two such low-wage sectors are assumed to exist. One of them, termed 'rural agriculture', is assumed to be located some distance from the modern sector. Because of this distance, and because workers in the agricultural sector are occupied with their jobs for some number of hours each day, agricultural workers would probably face reduced job search prospects compared to their search chances if searching full-time in the urban economy. However, the wage in agriculture, W_A, exceeds the wage if unemployed (zero).[2] The other economic sector, termed the 'urban traditional sector', is assumed to be located in the same place as the modern sector. The wage paid there is W_T.

5.2.2 *Search Strategies*

To search for modern sector jobs, three search strategies are possible.

Search Strategy I: The Strategy of Open Unemployment
This is the search strategy specified in the models of Harris and Todaro (1970), Harberger (1971), Mincer (1976), Gramlich (1976), and Stiglitz

(1982) and one of the search strategies allowed for by McDonald and Solow (1985). Those who adopt Search Strategy I begin unemployed and search full-time. Each such worker faces the same probability n of obtaining a job in the modern sector; n is endogenous and is specified further below. Those who are successful become employed at wage W_M, while those who are unsuccessful end up unemployed and earn zero.

Search Strategy II: The Strategy of Remaining in Agriculture
This is the other option offered in the models of Harris and Todaro (1970), Harberger (1971), and Stiglitz (1982).[3] In their models, those who elect to remain in agriculture give up any chance of obtaining a job in the modern sector. They then settle for the agricultural wage W_A.

This formulation is unduly restrictive. In practice, it is quite common for those working in low-paying sectors of the economy to have a non-zero chance of finding jobs in the modern sectors of their economies. For instance, they may search for jobs at night and on weekends, hear of jobs through friends and relatives already at work, or secure a position through an employment agency or labor exchange.

To allow for the possibility of on-the-job search by workers in agriculture, I formulate a model in which each person not in the modern sector has a positive but reduced chance of finding a job in the modern sector. But unlike those job search models such as Burdett and Mortensen (1978) in which searchers have discretion over the amount of search they will engage in, and hence the margin of interest is the intensive margin (how intensively to search on the job), the formulation here treats the amount of on-the-job search as parametric, so the action takes place on the extensive margin (i.e., how many workers engage in on-the-job search rather than search while unemployed).[4]

Denote the relative efficiency of on-the-job search while in the agricultural sector as compared with search while unemployed by θ, which is best thought of as a relative job search parameter. For instance, suppose θ were equal to 1/2. This would mean that any given job searcher has only half as good a chance of obtaining a modern sector job if he or she is working in agriculture compared to the chance he or she would have were (s)he searching full-time.

Search Strategy III: Searching while Employed in the Urban Traditional Sector
This is defined analogously to the situation facing those searching while in agriculture. On-the-job search while working in the urban traditional sector is possible but it is less efficient than full-time search. Analogously, therefore, denote the relative job search parameter while working in the urban traditional sector by φ. On-the-job search prospects are assumed

to be better for workers in the urban traditional sector than for workers in rural agriculture, because the urban traditional sector workers are in closer proximity to the modern sector jobs than are rural agricultural workers. Therefore, the model is restricted so that $\theta < \varphi$.[5]

5.2.3 Formulation of the Model

Workers are assumed to choose among alternative search strategies on the basis of the expected wage associated with each.[6] These expected values are denoted by V_i. The respective values are:

(1) $V_I = W_{M^*}$

(2) $V_{II} = W_M \theta \pi + W_A(1 - \theta \pi)$, *and*

(3) $V_{III} = W_M \varphi \pi + W_T(1 - \varphi \pi)$.

The expression for V_I requires no explanation. The expressions for V_{II} and V_{III} each consist of two terms. Take the expression for V_{II}. The first term, $W_M \theta \pi$, is the wage in the modern sector multiplied by the probability of obtaining a job at that wage given that the individual has elected Search Strategy II. That probability is the probability π associated with full-time search multiplied by the relative search parameter θ applicable to an individual who accepts a reduced search opportunity while working in agriculture. The product $\theta \pi$ is then the probability of successfully obtaining a modern sector job while working in agriculture. In the event that this search is unsuccessful, which occurs with probability $(1 - \theta \pi)$, those who adopt this search strategy end up remaining in agriculture and earning W_A. V_{II} then consists of the wages in the two sectors weighted by the respective probabilities of receiving them under Search Strategy II. The expression for V_{III} in eq. (5.3) is derived analogously.

Let us turn our attention now to the probability of employment, π, defined as the ratio of modern sector jobs E_M to job-seeker equivalents (defined below) J_M:

(4) $$\pi = E_M/J_M.$$

Of course, the amount of employment in the modern sector, E_M, is a function of the wage in the modern sector and perhaps of other things as well; it may be written as

(5) $$E_M = h(W_M) + \xi$$

where $h(W_M)$ is the usual labor demand function and ξ is a shifter reflecting the possibility of resources being made available to modern sector employers (say, by the government or an external aid agency) for purposes of job creation.

J_M is the number of 'job-seeker equivalents' and has the following interpretation. A worker searching from the agricultural sector has only θ as great a chance for getting a job as does an unemployed worker who is searching full-time; the relative chance for a worker searching from the urban traditional sector is φ. Denoting the number of workers electing each search strategy by L_i, $i =I, II, III$, each of the L_I workers has a full chance of obtaining any given job, each of the L_{II} workers has θ of a chance, and each of the L_{III} workers has φ of a chance. If each job-seeker is weighted according to the relative chance of obtaining a job, then the number of job-seeker equivalents is

(6) $$J_M = L_I + \theta L_{II} + \varphi L_{III}.$$

Note that it is the number initially choosing the three search strategies $i = I, II, III$ and *not* the number ending up in the three employment sectors $j = M, A, T$ that enters into the expression for job-seeker equivalents. By distinguishing between the ex ante allocation of searchers in (6) and the ex post allocations between employment in the various sectors and unemployment in (7H 1 0), the formulation presented here improves upon that of Fields (1975) and McDonald and Solow (1985), who did not draw this distinction. On the assumption that modern sector jobs are filled in exact proportion to the number of job-seeker equivalents, it is easily verified that the formulation given by (6) indeed yields just the right amount of modern sector employment.[7]

The wage determination process must be specified. As already stated, the wage in the modern sector W_M is determined exogenously above market-clearing levels. This may occur for a number of possible reasons including minimum wages, trade unions, or firms deliberately setting the wage above market-clearing levels for efficiency wage reasons. But whatever those reasons may be, they do not carry over to agriculture and the urban traditional sector. In those sectors, wages are market-clearing, determined as functions of their respective labor forces. Certainly, we wish these functions to be nonincreasing. They may either be constant or decreasing. The wage being invariant with respect to the size of the agricultural sector's labor force would be relevant, for example, in a land abundant economy in which anyone who wishes to enter the agricultural sector can take up self-employment and earn a wage W_A. A decreasing wage as a function of the size of the labor force would be consistent with the wage equaling a diminishing marginal product of labor or even with a situation of zero marginal product of labor and income-sharing among all those working in that sector. Some special cases will be dealt with below. But at this point, it is useful to stick to the general wage functions

(7) $W_A = f(L_A),$ $f' \leqq 0,$ and

(8) $W_T = g(L_T),$ $g' \leqq 0.$

A bit of explanation may be in order regarding the sizes of the labor forces in the different sectors, from which W_A and W_T are derived. L_A and L_T in eqs. (7) and (8) are the numbers of workers who ultimately end up in the agricultural and traditional sectors, respectively. These numbers are not the same as the numbers electing Search Strategies II and III. Take, for instance, those who elect on-the-job search from the agricultural sector. Of those persons (L_{II} in number), the fraction who successfully obtain modern sector employment is $\theta\pi$: only *(1 - $\theta\pi$)%* are left in agriculture. Hence,

(9) $L_A = L_{II}(1 - \theta\pi).$

By identical reasoning,

(10) $L_T = L_{III}(1 - \varphi\pi).$

The adding-up conditions for the labor force are, ex ante,

(11) $L = L_I + L_{II} + L_{III},$

and ex post

(12) $L = L_M + L_A + L_T.$

Finally, we must have the rule specifying the allocation of the labor force between search strategies and sectors. The rule is expected wage maximization. If the solution is interior, meaning that all three search strategies have the same expected value, for some allocation of the labor force among search strategies, then

(13) $V_I = V_{II} = V_{III}.$

For the solution to in fact lie in the interior, the parameters of the model are restricted to take on certain values. In the three-sector model below, it is assumed that they do.

5.2.4   *A Note on Non-Interior Solutions and Two-Sector Models*

Some of the results derived below do not require three sectors, though they are indeed valid in the three-sector case. In the derivation of these results, a two-sector model is used. The two-sector model may be thought of as a non-interior solution to the three-sector model.

A non-interior solution might arise for either of two reasons. One is that in a particular country, one of the three sectors might simply not exist. Examples might be the absence of agriculture in a city-state or the absence of a free-entry traditional sector in a relatively advanced economy. The other reason for a non-interior solution is that one search strategy may be dominated by others. For example, if opportunities for on-the-job search from agriculture are sufficiently high and income opportunities in the urban traditional sector sufficiently low, it may pay nobody to enter the urban traditional sector.

Whether a non-interior solution arises because of non-existence of a sector or domination of one search strategy by others, the model reverts to a two-sector model. Some of the results below are proved for the case L_{III} and L_T identically zero and V_{III} irrelevant.

5.2.5 A Special Case

If the solution to the model given in this section is interior (which must, of course, be verified), the equilibrium allocation is given by the condition that alternative search strategies have the same expected values; this is eq. (13). The solution would be found by substituting the remaining equations of the system into (13) and solving for the ex ante distribution of search strategies. From this, we may then derive the ex post allocation of the labor force between employment in various sectors and unemployment.

With the general wage-determination functions (7) and (8), it is not possible to obtain explicit expressions for the allocations of the labor force among ex ante search strategies and ex post labor market outcomes. This is because the wage functions $W_A = f(L_A)$ and $W_T = g(L_T)$ enter into the equilibrium conditions (13), and until we know those functions and can invert them, we cannot proceed. However, if specific functional forms are assumed, closed-form solutions can be obtained. This is the strategy followed when needed below.

The restricted functions are the following. Suppose, as in Fields (1975), Anand and Joshi (1979), and Stiglitz (1982), that the agricultural wage is invariant with respect to the size of that sector's labor force. This would be meaningful if either (a) the economy is land-abundant, so that any worker who wishes to work in agriculture can obtain a plot of land and earn the same self-employment income as others already in that sector, or (b) within the range of variation, the size of the agricultural sector labor force varies only negligibly in response to other changes in the economy. In either case, the agricultural sector wage function is restricted such that

$$(7') \qquad\qquad W_A = \text{constant}.$$

As for the urban traditional sector, suppose (a) whatever income is generated in the urban traditional sector is divided equally among the workers in that sector (e.g., each street vendor earns the same as any other), and (b) the total demand for traditional sector output is fixed in amount (e.g., because all of the demand comes from those employed in the modern sector, the number and wage of whom is constant). Under these conditions, the urban traditional sector wage function takes the form

(8') $$W_T = Q_T/L_T,$$

Q_T denoting the amount of income to be shared.

In what follows, eq. (7') is used in Propositions 1 and 2 and eq. (8') in Proposition 2. The general forms are used in Propositions 3 and 4.

5.3 Results

This section proves four propositions. Some are for two-sector models, the reason being that only two sectors are needed to prove them and the presence of a third sector obfuscates the issue. Others are for three-sector models, the third sector being included because it is needed.

5.3.1 On-the-Job Search from Agriculture and the Urban Unemployment Rate in the Two-Sector Model

In Fields (1975), I introduced on-the-job search from agriculture into what was otherwise a two-sector Harris-Todaro model with a constant agricultural wage. I claimed (p. 171): "... there is a lower equilibrium [urban] unemployment rate in general than would be predicted by the BarrisTodaro model; and the greater the relative chance of rural workers finding urban jobs, the greater the discrepancy between the general result and the Harris-Todaro result". In that paper (eq. 11), no ex ante/ex post distinction was made. Unemployment was calculated on the basis of what we are here calling L_I, the number who choose Search Strategy I (search full-time for a modern sector job, accept unemployment otherwise). While that is not wrong, it is also not the most interesting. A more appropriate unemployment rate is that using the ex post urban labor force, denoted here by L_M in the two-sector model. If we calculate urban unemployment (U) as a proportion of the urban ex post labor force (L_M), the claim that more efficient on-the-job search from agriculture lowers the urban unemployment rate must be verified. Indeed, it continues to hold.

Begin with the two-sector version of the model of Section 5.2, i.e., only the modern and agricultural sectors but no traditional sector. Fix the agricultural wage. The model may be manipulated to yield

(14a) $$U = L + E_M \left(\frac{W_M}{W_A} - 1\right) + \frac{W_M L}{(W_M + W_A)\theta - W_M},$$

(14b) $$L_M = L + E_M \frac{W_M}{W_A} + \frac{W_M L}{(W_M - W_A)\theta - W_M}.$$

By (14a), since an increase in θ increases the denominator, it follows that more efficient on-the-job search implies that fewer persons will be unemployed. But by (14b), a higher θ also implies that the ex post urban labor force, LM, will be smaller. Thus, to determine what happens to the urban unemployment *rate*, U/L_M, we must do more work.

The only difference between U in (14a) and L_M in (14b) is the second term on the right-hand side. This is as it should be: the numerator is less than the denominator, so the urban unemployment rate is a positive fraction. To show how the urban unemployment rate changes with θ, note that in (14a) and (14b) the denominator of the last term is negative. When θ increases, the denominator is less negative, and therefore the third term is more negative as e increases. When larger equal amounts are subtracted from a fraction less than one, the value of the fraction falls. This confirms my earlier claim, though now for an unemployment rate expressed as a fraction of the ex post rather than ex ante labor force.

Proposition 1. In the two-sector model with a constant agricultural wage, more efficient on-the-job search from agriculture lowers the urban unemployment rate in equilibrium.

5.3.2 On-the-Job Search from the Urban Traditional Sector and the Urban Unemployment Rate in a Specialized Three-Sector Model

In Fields (1975), in another extension of the Harris-Todaro model, I introduced an urban traditional sector, from which on-the-job search for high-paying modern sector jobs was possible. The relative job search parameter from that sector (φ in present notation) was assumed to be greater than the corresponding parameter from agriculture (θ) but less than the search parameter if unemployed in the urban area (normalized at 1). I claimed (p. 175) that in a specialized three-sector model with wage functions given by

(7′) $$W_A = \text{constant.}$$

and

(8′) $$W_T = Q_T/L_T,$$

and with $\theta = 0$, the larger is φ, the larger is the equilibrium urban employment rate. Again, it must be verified that an earlier claim holds once due account is taken of the ex ante/ex post distinction. Once again, it does.

The model given by (1)–(6), (7'), (8'), and (9)–(13) and with $\theta \geqq 0$ may be solved to give the following results:

Ex Ante Allocations

(15a) $\quad L_I = -\dfrac{\theta L}{1 - \theta} + \dfrac{E_M W_M}{W_A} + \dfrac{E_M \theta}{1 - \theta} - \dfrac{Q_T(\varphi - \theta)}{W_A(1 - \varphi)} - \dfrac{Q_T \theta(\varphi - \theta)}{W_M(1 - \varphi)(1 - \theta)}$,

(15b) $\quad L_{II} = \dfrac{L}{1 - \theta} - \dfrac{E_M W_M}{W_A} - \dfrac{E_M \theta}{1 - \theta} - \dfrac{Q_T}{W_A} - \dfrac{Q_T \theta}{W_M(1 - \theta)}$,

(15c) $\quad L_{III} = \dfrac{Q_T\{W_M(1 - \theta) + W_A \theta\}}{W_A W_M(1 - \varphi)}$,

Ex Post Allocations

(15d) $\quad L_T = \dfrac{Q_T(1 - \theta)}{W_A(1 - \varphi)} - \dfrac{Q_T(\varphi - \theta)}{W_M(1 - \varphi)}$,

(15e) $\quad L_A = \dfrac{L}{1 - \theta} - \dfrac{E_M W_M}{W_A} - \dfrac{Q_T}{W_A} - \dfrac{\theta W_A L}{\{W_M(1 - \theta) + W_A \theta\}(1 - \theta)}$,

(15f) $\quad E_M$ is given,

(15g) $\quad U = L - L_T - L_A - E_M$,

Now let $\theta = 0$, as in my earlier paper. From expressions (15a)–(15g), we may derive the equilibrium urban unemployment rate based on the ex post urban labor force $L_M + L_T = L - L_A$ as

$$\text{Urban Unem Rate} = \frac{L - L_T - L_A - E_M}{L - L_A} = 1 - \frac{L_T + E_M}{L - L_A}$$

$$= 1 - \{W_A[(Q_T/W_A(1 - \varphi)) - (Q_T \varphi/W_M(1 - \varphi) + E_M]$$

$$/[E_M W_M + Q_T]\}.$$

The only term that changes with φ is the bracketed term, and the urban unemployment rate varies inversely with it. To see how the bracketed term varies with φ, differentiate and simplify to obtain

$$\frac{\partial [\,\cdot\,]}{\partial \varphi} = \frac{Q_T}{(1 - \varphi)^2} \left(\frac{1}{W_A} - \frac{1}{W_M} \right),$$

which is positive since $W_M > W_A$. Hence, the equilibrium urban unemployment rate *falls* with φ. Thus, we have proved

Proposition 2. In the specialized three-sector model given by (1)–(6), (7'), (8'), and (9)–(13) and with $\theta = 0$, more efficient on-the-job search from the urban

traditional sector lowers the equilibrium rate of urban unemployment.

The earlier result is confirmed even after the ex ante/ex post distinction is made and the ex post labor force is used instead as the base.

5.3.3 *Intersectoral Wage Differentials Ex Ante and Ex Post in the Two- and Three-Sector Models*

This subsection shows that the pattern of wage differentials in the economy is affected fundamentally by the distinction between the ex ante distribution of workers among job search strategies on the one hand and, on the other, the ex post allocation of the labor force between work in the different sectors and unemployment. Begin with the familiar models of intersectoral labor force allocation with search while unemployed only, i.e., no on-the-job search. The Harris-Todaro model is probably the most famous of these. The equilibrium in their model is characterized by equality of expected wages for alternative search strategies. (Of course, in their model, one of the search strategies is to remain in agriculture which, in the absence of on-the-job search, is tantamount to not searching at all for a modern sector urban job.) Thus, in the Harris-Todaro model, the labor force allocates itself such that expected wages are equalized across alternatives ex ante.

For present purposes, it should be noted that in addition to ex ante wage equalization, in a Harris-Todaro world, another type of wage equalization occurs: the average wages in the urban and rural sectors are also equalized ex post. That is, in a Harris-Todaro economy, a researcher looking at the data would find that the average wage received in the urban economy (remembering to include zeroes for the unemployed) would exactly equal the average rural wage.

With on-the-job search, this is no longer so. Workers would still allocate themselves between search strategies so that the expected returns from alternative search strategies are equalized ex ante (if in fact parameter values are such that they can be equalized). But unlike the case analyzed by Harris and Todaro, in which on-the-job search is absent, when there *is* on-the-job search, average wages are *not* equalized across sectors ex post. This holds even under the rational expectations assumed here; that is, even though every worker knows that the average wages will not turn out to be equal in the urban and rural sectors, no worker has an incentive to alter his/her search behavior. This may be stated formally as

Proposition 3. Denote the average urban wage by W_U, the average rural wage by W_R, and the relative search parameter associated with the agricultural sector by

θ. *Then in both the general two-sector model and the general three-sector model:*

(a) $\qquad \theta = 0 \Rightarrow W_U = W_R,$

(b) $\qquad \theta = 0 \Rightarrow W_U > W_R,$

Proof. See Appendix at the end of this chapter.

It should be noted that the discrepancy between average urban and average rural wages ex post is *not* attributable to the existence of a third sector per se; the same discrepancy is shown to arise even in a two-sector model with on-the-job search. It should also be noted that the discrepancy between the average wages in urban and rural areas arises apart from other reasons such as higher cost-of-living in urban as opposed to rural areas, risk aversion in the part of workers, a greater concentration of better skilled workers in the urban economy, and multi-period decision-making – all of which might be considered in more general models.

In sum, in an economy with on-the-job search from the rural sector, a researcher looking at the data might observe a difference between the average urban and rural wages and conclude that expected wage equalization had not yet taken place. Proposition 3 implies that such a conclusion would be erroneous.

5.3.4   *Effects of Modern Sector Enlargement*

By 'modern sector enlargement' in this context. I mean that the government or some other body creates additional modern sector jobs beyond those that would otherwise exist. This possibility is accommodated by the term ξ in eq. (5) above.

For policy purposes, the most significant implication of the Harris-Todaro model is that modern sector enlargement creates additional unemployment under fairly general conditions. This is because each additional high wage job attracts more than one job-seeker from the rural area, adding to unemployment. It is because of this that Harris and Todaro reached their famed conclusion that 'the solution to urban unemployment is rural development'.

The question may then be asked: In a three-sector model, in which underemployment in the urban traditional sector is an additional option, are the adverse effects of modern sector enlargement mitigated? The answer hinges on whether the urban traditional sector absorbs any of the impact which would otherwise fall on unemployment. The following, possibly surprising, result emerges:

Proposition 4. Consider the effects of modern sector enlargement in the threesector model given by eqs. (1)–(13). Suppose that the wage rate in one of the other sectors is invariant with respect to the size of that sector's labor force. Then, in the third sector, the wage, the number of ex ante searchers, and ex post employment will all be constant. Specifically:

(a) *Suppose* $W_A = f(L_A)$, $f' = 0$ *and* $W_T = g(L_T)$, $g' < 0$. *Then the effect of modern sector enlargement is to leave* W_T, L_T, *and* L_{III} *unchanged.*

(b) *Suppose* $W_A = f(L_A)$, $f' < 0$ *and* $W_T = g(L_T)$, $g' = 0$. *Then the effect of modern sector enlargement is to leave* W_A, L_A, *and* L_{II} *unchanged.*

The proofs are straightforward. Take (a) first. From (13), we have $W_M \pi = W_M \theta \pi + W_A(1 - \theta \pi)$. W_M and θ have been assumed constant throughout. With W_A constant by assumption in this special case, the only other variable, n, cannot change. Now consider $W_M \theta \pi + W_A (1 - \theta \pi) = W_M \varphi \pi + W_T(1 - \varphi \pi)$. With W_M, W_A, θ, φ, and π all constant, a unique value of W_T is determined. Given $W_T = g(L_T)$, $g' < 0$, a unique value of L_T is determined. And from $L_T = L_{III}(1 - \varphi \pi)$, a unique value of L_{III} is determined. This confirms that when the wage in the agricultural sector is invariant with respect to the size of that sector's labor force, then nothing in the traditional sector changes in response to modern sector enlargement. The proof of (b) goes through in precisely analogous fashion, starting with $W_M \pi = W_M \varphi \pi + W_T(1 - \varphi \pi)$. This means that *all* of the adjustment will be felt in the sector with the constant wage or in unemployment, but not in the sector with the variable wage. This results from the need to preserve a three-way equality among expected wages when one of the wage functions, $W_A = f(L_A, f' < 0$ or $W_T = g(L_T)$, $g' < 0$, is monotonically decreasing.[8]

This shows that the adverse effects of modern sector enlargement on unemployment are *not* mitigated by the existence of a low-wage, free-entry urban traditional sector. If modern sector enlargement draws additional unemployed into the urban economy when work in the urban traditional sector is not a possibility, it will continue to do so when that possibility exists.

5.4 Conclusion

I began in Section 5. by claiming that the desirable features of a multi-sector labor market model include wage dualism, open unemployment, underemployment, on-the-job search, and expected wage equalization and noting that previous models had not taken adequate account of the distinction between the ex ante allocation of the labor force among search strategies and the ex post allocation of the labor force among labor market outcomes. A three-sector model containing the desired features was developed in Section 5.2. Section 5.3 derived four results showing how on-the-job search matters using this model:

Proposition 1. In the two-sector model with a constant agricultural wage, more efficient on-the-job search from agriculture lowers the urban unemployment rate in equilibrium.

Proposition 2. In the specialized three-sector model given by (1)–(6), (7'), (8'), and (9)–(13) and with θ = 0, more efficient on-the-job search from the urban traditional sector lowers the equilibrium rate of urban unemployment.

Proposition 3. Denote the average urban wage by W_U, the average rural wage by W_R, and the relative search parameter associated with the agricultural sector by θ. Then in both the general two-sector model and the general three-sector model:

(a) $\quad \theta = 0 \Rightarrow W_U = W_R$,

(b) $\quad \theta = 0 \Rightarrow W_U > W_R$.

Proposition 4. Consider the effects of modern sector enlargement in the threesector model given by eqs. (1)–(13). Suppose that the wage rate in one of the other sectors is invariant with respect to the size of that sector's labor force. Then, in the third sector, the wage, the number of ex ante searchers, and ex post employment will all be constant. Specifically:

(a) *Suppose $W_A = f(L_A)$, $f' = 0$ and $W_T = g(L_T)$, $g' < 0$. Then the effect of modern sector enlargement is to leave W_T, L_T, and L_{III} unchanged.*

(b) *Suppose $W_A = f(L_A)$, $f' < 0$ and $W_T = g(L_T)$, $g' = 0$. Then the effect of modern sector enlargement is to leave W_A, L_A, and L_{II} unchanged.*

Development policy-makers and analysts are concerned with such ex post outcomes as unemployment, poverty, and inequality. However, they cannot affect these directly. They must work instead on factors which influence workers' ex ante choices and determine the ex post effects of these choices. Among those factors which have been considered here are the relative efficiency of on-the-job search compared with search while unemployed and modern sector job creation.

The call has gone out for development economists to develop more realistic models of labor markets. The present paper is a step in that direction. Other applications and extensions will be considered in future work.

APPENDIX: PROOF OF PROPOSITION 3

Proposition 3. Denote the average urban wage by W_U, the average rural wage by W_R, and the relative search parameter associated with the agricultural sector by θ. Then in both the general two-sector model and the general three-sector model:

(a) $\theta = 0 \Rightarrow W_U = W_R$,

(b) $\theta = 0 \Rightarrow W_U > W_R$.

Proof in the three-sector case

Proof of (a)
By definition, the average urban wage equals

(A.1) $W_U = W_M E_M + W_T L_T / L_M + L_T$,

and the average rural wage equals

(A.2) $W_R = W_A$.

Note that

(A.3) $L_M + L_T = L - L_A$

and

(A.4) $E_M = \pi J_M$.

When $\theta = 0$, the model simplifies to

$$W_M \pi = W_A = W_M \varphi \pi + W_T (1 - \varphi \pi),$$
$$L_A = L_{II},$$
$$L_T = L_{III}(1 - \varphi \pi),$$
$$J_M = L_I + \varphi L_{III}.$$

Substitute these into (A.1) as follows:

$$\begin{aligned}
W_U &= \frac{W_M \pi J_M + W_T L_T}{L - L_{II}} \\
&= \frac{W_M \pi (L_I + \varphi L_{III}) + W_T (1 - \varphi \pi) L_{III}}{L - L_{II}} \\
&= \frac{[W_M \varphi \pi + W_T (1 - \varphi \pi)] L_{III} + W_M \pi L_I}{L_I + L_{III}} \\
&= \frac{W_A L_{III} + W_A L_I}{L_I + L_{III}} = W_A.
\end{aligned}$$

Given $W_U = W_A$ when $\theta = 0$ and $W_A = W_R$, it follows that $W_U = W_R$ when $\theta = 0$. This completes the proof of (a).

Proof of (b)

When $\theta > 0$, (A.1)–(A.4) hold as before. Now, however,

(A.5) $\quad W_M\pi = W_M\theta\pi + W_A(1 - \theta\pi) = W_M\varphi\pi + W_T(1 - \varphi\pi) = V$

Substitute into (A.1) as follows:

(A.6) $\quad W_U = \dfrac{W_M\pi J_M + W_T L_T}{L - L_A}$

$$= \frac{W_M\pi(L_I + \theta L_{II} + \varphi L_{III}) + W_T L_{III}(1 - \varphi\pi)}{L_I + L_{II} + L_{III} - L_{II}(1 - \theta\pi)}$$

$$= \frac{V L_{III} + V L_I + V\theta L_{II}}{L_I + L_{III} + \theta\pi L_{II}}$$

$$= V\left\{ \frac{[L - (1 - \theta)L_{II}]}{[L - (1 - \theta\pi)L_{II}]} \right\}.$$

Now,

$$\theta > 0, \pi < 1 \Rightarrow \theta\pi < \theta \Rightarrow -\theta\pi > -\theta \Rightarrow (1 - \theta\pi) > (1 - \theta) \Rightarrow$$
$$-(1 - \theta\pi) < -(1 - \theta) \Rightarrow L - (1 - \theta\pi)L_{II} < L - (1 - \theta)L_{II}.$$

Hence,

(A.7) $\quad \{\cdot\} > 1 \quad$ if $\quad \theta > 0$.

Eqs. (A.6) and (A.7) establish

Lemma 1. $\quad \theta > 0 \Rightarrow W_U > V$.

Given $\pi, \theta > 0$ and (A.5), we obtain

Lemma 1. $\quad \theta > 0 \Rightarrow V > W_A$.

From Lemmas 1 and 2 and $W_A = W_R$, we have

$$\theta > 0 \Rightarrow W_U > W_R.$$

This completes the proof of (b).

Having shown (a) and (b), the theorem is now proved for the three-sector case. Observe that these results are completely general: they are valid for any wage eqs. (7) and (8).

Proof in the two-sector case

In the preceding proof, set L_T and L_{III} and identically equal to zero, drop $V_{III} = W_M\varphi\pi + W_T(1 = \varphi\pi)$, and proceed as before.

6

A Welfare Economic Approach to Growth and Distribution in the Dual Economy

6.1   Introduction

This chapter presents a welfare economic analysis of the distributional consequences of growth, a problem that has attracted much attention from development economists of late. We shall explore the similarities and differences between the absolute income and poverty and relative inequality approaches for a general dualistic development model and for three stylized special cases. It will be shown that these approaches are not always in agreement and, more disturbingly, that the most notable discrepancy is found in the most relevant stylized model-growth via the transfer of population from a backward to an enlarging advanced sector. The fact of these discrepancies raises the important question of how to measure changing income distribution in a manner consistent with the judgments we wish to make about the alleviation of absolute poverty and changes in relative income inequality. A general welfare function is formulated to address these issues. Recent controversies over who received the benefits of growth in two less developed countries – Brazil and India – are examined in these terms.

A review of the literature reveals that the poor in less developed countries are generally at least as well off in absolute income terms; in many countries, their absolute economic position is demonstrably improved.[1] Still the pace of improvement in economic position of the poor is

The original version of this chapter was published as: Fields, Gary S. (1979). A Welfare Economic Approach to Growth and Distribution in the Dual Economy, in: The Quarterly Journal of Economics, 93(3):325–353. © 1979 by Oxford University Press.

disappointingly slow, even in the rapidly growing countries.[2] This may be because the rules of distribution channel development resources to the middle and upper income groups. Nearly everywhere, the wages received by upper level workers (the skilled, government employees, etc.) have risen in real terms. These wage increases are larger in absolute terms than those received by lower-level workers (the unskilled, self-employed, etc.).[3]

How are we to evaluate these various events? We turn now to an analysis of some of the approaches that have been suggested.

6.2 Absolute and Relative Approaches for Evaluating Growth and Distribution

Economists are used to regarding social welfare as a positive function of the income levels of the n individuals or families in society before and after development takes place. In empirical studies the general social welfare function,

(1) $W = W(Y_1, Y_2, ..., Y_n),$ $W_1, W_2, ..., W_n > 0,$

is too general to be useful, and the Pareto criterion,

(2) $W^A(Y_1^A, Y_2^A, ..., Y_n^A) > W^B (Y_1^B, Y_2^B, ..., Y_n^B)$

if $Y_i^A \geq Y_i^B$ for all i and $Y_i^A > Y_i^B$ for some i is too stringent.

For analytical ease the information contained in the income vector $(Y_1, Y_2, ..., Y_n)$ is usually collapsed into one or more aggregative measures. The three classes of measures in most common use are total income (Y) or its per capita equivalent, indices of relative inequality (I), and measures of absolute poverty (P).

The customary approach to studies of distribution and development is to posit (explicitly or implicitly) a social welfare function containing an index of relative inequality as one of its arguments:

(3) $W = f(Y,I),$ $f_1 > 0, f_2 < 0,$

where Y is total income and I is an indicator of inequality in its distribution. In what follows, this type of welfare judgment will be termed the "relative inequality approach." Theoretical support for this approach may be found in the welfare economics literature in the writings of Sheshinski (1972) and Sen (1976B). In the study of distribution and development, the relative inequality approach is best exemplified in the Nobel Prize winning work of Professor Kuznets (1955, 1963). Income distribution is said to have "improved" or "worsened" according to Lorenz domination (i.e., whether one Lorenz curve lies wholly above or below a previous one (L)) or according to one or more measures of relative inequality, such as the income share of the poorest 40 percent (S) or the Gini coefficient (G). Thus, relative inequality studies typically make one or more of the following judgments:

$$(4) \qquad \text{(a) } W = f(Y,L), \qquad f_1 > 0, f_2 > 0,$$
$$\text{(a) } W = f(Y,S), \qquad f_1 > 0, f_2 > 0,$$
$$\text{(a) } W = f(Y,G), \qquad f_1 > 0, f_2 < 0.$$

A great many studies have made use of this framework. Some of the most influential recent contributions, which include extensive surveys and bibliographies of prior research studies, are those of Cline (1975), Chenery et al. (1974), and Adelman and Morris (1973).

As an alternative to the relative inequality approach, some writers have examined the income distribution itself, assigning a lower social welfare weight to income gains of the relatively well-off as compared with those of the poor. With no loss of generality we may order the n income recipient units from lowest to highest. The general class of studies that treats social welfare in the form,

$$(5) \qquad W = g(Y_1, Y_2, ..., Y_n), \ g_i > g_j \ \forall \ i < j,$$

shall be termed the "absolute income approach." In the development literature, the studies of Little and Mirrlees (1969), Atkinson (1970), and Stern (1972) are notable examples. As an extreme version of (5), Rawls (1971) has proposed the maximin principle, i.e., maximizing the income of the worst-off person in the economy:

$$(5') \qquad W = g(Y_1), \qquad g' > 0.$$

Finally, for some purposes, we may wish to define a poverty line P^* and concentrate our attention on the group in poverty to the exclusion of the rest of the income distribution. This practice, termed the "absolute poverty approach," is common in studies of growth in the United States; see, for example, Bowman (1973) or Perlman (1976). Denoting the extent of poverty by P, absolute poverty studies hold that

$$(6) \qquad W = h(P), \qquad h' < 0.$$

Usual measures of poverty are the number of individuals or families whose incomes are below that line or the gap between the poverty line and the average among the poor. In a recent paper Sen (1976A) combines these and argues elegantly for the use of an index $\pi = H[\bar{I} + (1 - \bar{I})Gp]$, where H is the headcount of the poor, $\bar{I}$ is the average income shortfall of the poor, and G_p is the Gini coefficient of income inequality among the poor. Thus, alternative forms of the absolute poverty approach are given by

(7)   (a) W = h(H),   h' < 0,
       (b) W = h($\bar{I}$),   h' < 0,
       (c) W = h(π) = h[H[$\bar{I}$ + (1 - $\bar{I}$)G$_p$]]   h' < 0.

It is not necessary that the relative and absolute approaches be regarded as mutually exclusive. In the following section we formulate a more general welfare function combining these various approaches.

6.3   A General Welfare Approach for Assessing Dualistic Development

The various welfare approaches of Section 6.2 were originated largely in a static context. However, since the distribution of benefits in the course of economic development refers to a phenomenon that takes place over time, it is appropriately measured by a dynamic index. It is important, therefore, to establish a suitably dynamic measure. We now posit a dualistic development model, a general welfare function, and a number of properties of this welfare function that are desirable for the purpose of evaluating economic development in the dual economy.

At the forefront of studies of modern economic growth are the dualistic development models of Lewis (1954), Fei and Ranis (1964), and Jorgenson (1961). While these models differ one from another in a number of important respects, they have in common the division of the economy into a relatively advanced sector and a relatively backward sector, which we shall call "modern" and "traditional," respectively. As with all dualistic models the working assumption is that the members of each sector are relatively similar to others in that sector and relatively different from those in the other sector. We shall regard the modern sector as synonymous with high wages and the traditional sector as synonymous with low wages. "Wage" and "income" will be used interchangeably.[4]

In the two sectors workers receive wage rates W^m and W^t, respectively.[5] $W^m > P^* > W^t$, where P^* is an agreed-upon absolute poverty line that is constant over time (except for allowing for price changes). The shares of the labor force in the two sectors are f^m and f^t, respectively; the total economically active population $f^m + f^t$ is normalized at 1. Economic development consists of changes in W^m, W^t, f^m, and f^t.

Suppose that we now want to implement a welfare function of the form,

(8)   W = W(Y,I,P),

which includes both absolute and relative considerations in the dualistic development model. Total income (Y) is given by

(9) $Y = Y^m + Y^t = W^m f^m + W^t f^t.$

Whichever measure of relative inequality (I) one chooses is functionally related to the distribution of the labor force between the two sectors and to the intersectoral wage structure:

(10) $I = I(W^m, f^m, W^t, f^t).$

The poverty index (P) depends on the wage in the traditional sector and the share of the population in that sector:

(11) $P = P(W^t, f^t).$

Substituting (9)–(11) into (8), we have

(12) $W = W(W^m f^m + W^t f^t, I(W^m, f^m, W^t, f^t), P(W^t, f^t)),$

which we term the "general welfare approach."

We must now specify the relationship between W and its various arguments. In line with the considerations discussed in Section 6.2, it is desirable to posit

(A) $\frac{\partial W}{\partial Y} > 0,$

(B) $\frac{\partial W}{\partial I} < 0,$

(C) $\frac{\partial W}{\partial P} < 0.$

Condition (A) relies for its validity on the assumption that the basic goal of an economic system is to maximize the output of goods and services received by each of its members. We should be clear that acceptance of the judgment $\partial W/\partial Y > 0$ does *not* require us to accept the stronger quasi-Pareto conditions $\partial W/\partial Y_i > 0 \ \forall \ i$, which in our dualistic development models becomes $\partial W/\partial Y_k > 0, \ k = m, t$. (This is quasi because it is formulated in terms of incomes rather than utilities). The judgment $\partial W/\partial Y_m > 0$ is one that many observers would not want to make, since it implies that even if the richest were the sole beneficiaries of economic growth, society would be deemed better off. No such judgment is imposed in what follows.

Condition (B) requires us first to define what we mean by a more equal relative distribution of income. A generally accepted (although incomplete) criterion is that one distribution A is more equal than another B if A Lorenz-dominates B, i.e., if A's Lorenz curve lies above B's at at least one point and never lies below it. If A Lorenz-dominates B for the same level of income, it means distribution A can be obtained from distribution B by transferring positive amounts of income from the relatively rich to the relatively poor.[6]

The judgment that such transfers improve social welfare dates back at least to Dalton (1920). One possible justification for this principle is diminishing marginal utility of income, coupled with independent and homothetic individual utility functions and an additively separable social welfare function.[7] But these assumptions are not necessary for the affirmation of the axiomatic judgment $\partial W/\partial I < 0$.

The difficulty with Lorenz-domination as a defining criterion for judgments concerning relative inequality is its incompleteness. When Lorenz curves cross, there is nothing to say. We therefore require a more complete relative inequality measure in order to rank various income distributions when Lorenz curves intersect. For this purpose, many indices of relative income inequality that provide complete orderings have been constructed.

The properties of various inequality indices have been examined by a number of writers (e.g, Champernowne, 1974; Kondor, 1975; Szal and Robinson, 1977; and Fields and Fei, 1978). It is agreed that a "good" inequality index should have the following properties: *scale irrelevance* (if one distribution is a scalar multiple of another, then they have the same relative inequality), *symmetry* (if one distribution is a permutation of another, then relative inequality in the two cases is the same), and the *Daltonian condition* (if one distribution is obtained from another by one or more income transfers from a relatively rich person to a relatively poor one, then the first distribution is more equal than the second).

Three other properties of relative inequality measures are desirable for analyzing the growth of a dualistic economy. These are

(D) $$\frac{\partial I}{\partial W^t} < 0,$$

(E) $$\frac{\partial I}{\partial W^m} > 0.$$

These accord with our intuitive notions about relative inequality (in terms of $W^m - W^t$ or W^m/W^t) and will probably not strike the reader as unusual. Then, we have

(F) $$\frac{\partial I}{\partial f^t} = -\frac{\partial I}{\partial f^m} \geq 0.$$

This condition holds that when an increasing fraction of the economically active population is drawn into an enlarged modern sector, then other things being equal, relative inequality should be no greater than before. Since the wage differential between modern and traditional sector workers is being held constant, this is hardly an unreasonable property. Many would wish to go one step further and replace (F) by

(F') $$\frac{\partial I}{\partial f^t} = -\frac{\partial I}{\partial f^m} = 0,$$

which I myself prefer. The choice between (F) and (F') has no bearing on any of the results that follow; what is important is the exclusion of $\partial I/\partial f^t = -\partial I/\partial f^m < 0$. Note that conditions (F) and (F') describe how *the inequality index itself* varies with the level of development. This does *not* mean that our *feelings* about inequality are invariant to income level. For a perceptive analysis of changing tolerance for inequality in the course of economic development, see Hirschman and Rothschild (1973).

Finally, we turn to condition (C), which holds that social welfare (W) is increased the less absolute poverty (P) there is. Whatever poverty measure(s) we employ should satisfy the properties,

(G) $$\frac{\partial P}{\partial f^t} > 0,$$

and

(H) $$\frac{\partial P}{\partial W^t} < 0,$$

These conditions state that absolute poverty P is reduced if there are fewer people in the low-income traditional sector or if the wage received by those in the traditional sector is increased, i.e., they become less poor. These concepts are equivalent to the "poverty population" and "poverty gap" notions used in studies of the United States and the "headcount" and "income shortfall" components of the poverty measure proposed by Sen (1976A). The appeal of these properties is intuitive and requires no further elaboration.

Function (12) and conditions (A)–(H) constitute the "general welfare approach." Condition (B) may be modified to

(B') $$\frac{\partial W}{\partial I} = 0,$$

for observers interested only in absolute poverty, while (C) might be replaced by

(C') $$\frac{\partial W}{\partial P} = 0,$$

for those concerned only about relative inequality. The various approaches for analyzing growth and distribution in the dual economy are summarized in Table 6.1.

As they stand, the welfare functions, (4), (5), (7), and (12), are purely static. They are, however, easily made dynamic by differentiating (or differencing) them with respect to time or to their underlying arguments. Changes in W^m, W^t, f^m, and f^t enter directly into (12), indirectly into the others.

The questions that then arise are how the various approaches evaluate distributional change in dualistic economic development and under what circumstances the judgments agree or differ. We address these questions in Sections 6.4 and 6.5.

Table 6.1. Various Welfare Economic Approaches for analyzing dualistic economic development

---

Relative inequality approach

General form:

(3)	$W = f(Y,I)$,	$f_1 > 0$, $\quad f_2 < 0$	... Inequality index

Specific applications:

(4) (a)	$W = f(Y,L)$,	$f_1 > 0$, $\quad f_2 > 0$	... Lorenz criterion
(b)	$W = f(Y,S)$,	$f_1 > 0$, $\quad f_2 > 0$	... Income share of poorest
(c)	$W = f(Y,G)$,	$f_1 > 0$, $\quad f_2 < 0$	... Gini coefficient

---

Absolute income approach

General form:

(5)	$W = g(Y_1,Y_2,...,Y_n)$,	$g_i > g_j \; \forall \, i < j$	... Absolute income

Specific application:

(5')	$W = g(Y_1)$,	$g' > 0$	... Rawlsian maximum criterion

Absolute poverty approach

General form:

(6)	$W = h(P)$,	$h' < 0$	... Poverty index

Specific applications:

(7) (a)	$W = h(H)$,	$h' < 0$	... Headcount of poor
(b)	$W = h(I)$,	$h' < 0$	... Income shortfall
(c)	$W = h(\pi)$,	$h' < 0$	... Sen index
	$\pi = H[I + (1 - I)G_p]$		

General social welfare approach

General form:

(8) $\quad W = W(Y,I,P)$, $\qquad \frac{\partial W}{\partial Y} > 0$,

$\frac{\partial W}{\partial I} < 0$, $\; \frac{\partial W}{\partial P} < 0$ $\qquad$ ... General welfare

Specific application:

(12) $\quad W = W(W^m f^m + W^t f^t, \; I(W^m,W^t,f^m,f^t), P(W^t,f^t))$,

$\frac{\partial W}{\partial Y} > 0$, $\; \frac{\partial W}{\partial I} > 0$, $\; \frac{\partial W}{\partial P} > 0$, $\qquad$ ... General welfare, dualistic

$\frac{\partial Y}{\partial W^m}$, $\frac{\partial Y}{\partial W^t}$, $\frac{\partial Y}{\partial f^m}$, $\frac{\partial Y}{\partial f^t} > 0$,

$\frac{\partial I}{\partial W^m} > 0$, $\; \frac{\partial I}{\partial W^t} < 0$, $\; \frac{\partial I}{\partial f^m} = -\frac{\partial I}{\partial f^t} \leq 0$,

$\frac{\partial P}{\partial W^t} < 0$, $\; \frac{\partial P}{\partial f^t} > 0$.

6.4 Welfare Economic Analysis of Dualistic Development: The General Case

The overall growth of the dualistic economy is the sum of growth in the two sectors as given by (9). In turn, each sector's growth (or lack thereof) may be partitioned into two components: one attributable to the *enlargement* (or contraction) of the sector to include a greater (or lesser) percentage of the economically active population, the other attributable to the *enrichment* of persons engaged in that sector. If a dualistic economy is growing successfully, one or more of the following must be happening: (i) the fraction of workers in the modern sector is increasing; (ii) those in the modern sector receive higher average incomes than before; or (iii) the incomes of those who remain in the traditional sector may rise. While every successfully developing country experiences some or all of these phenomena to varying degrees, some pursue more broadly based or more egalitarian courses than do others.

A useful way of examining how different groups benefit from economic growth is to take the first difference of (9), year 1 being the base year and year 2 the terminal year, and to decompose the change in income in the following way:

$$(13) \quad \Delta Y = \underbrace{(f_2^m - f_1^m)(W_1^m - W_1^t)}_{\substack{\text{Modern sector} \\ \text{enlargement effect } (\alpha)}} + \underbrace{(W_2^m - W_1^m)f_1^m}_{\substack{\text{Modern sector} \\ \text{enrichment effect } (\beta)}}$$

$$+ \underbrace{(W_2^m - W_1^m)(f_2^m - f_1^m)}_{\substack{\text{Interaction between} \\ \text{modern sector enlargement} \\ \text{and enrichment effects } (\gamma)}} + \underbrace{(W_2^t - W_1^t)f_2^t}_{\substack{\text{Traditional sector} \\ \text{enrichment effect } (\delta)}}$$

where

α = enlargement of the high-income sector,
  = change in the number of persons in the high-income sector, multiplied by the income differential between the high-income and low-income sectors in the base year;
β = enrichment of the high-income sector,
  = change in income within the high-income sector, multiplied by the number of persons who were originally in that sector in the base year;
γ = interaction between enlargement and enrichment of the high-income sector,
  = change in income within the high-income sector, multiplied by the change in the number of persons in that sector;

δ = enrichment of the low-income sector,

= change in income within the low-income sector, multiplied by the number of persons who remained in that sector in the terminal year.

In the general case, a comparative static analysis of (1) reveals the following:

a) *The modern sector enlargement effect* (α) is greater: (i) The greater the increase in modern sector employment; and (ii) the greater the difference between modern sector and traditional sector wage rates.

b) *The modern sector enrichment effect* (β) is greater: (i) The greater the rate of increase of modern sector wages; and (ii) the more important the modern sector in total employment.

c) *The traditional sector enrichment effect* (δ) is greater: (i) The greater the rate of increase of traditional sector wages; and (ii) the more important the traditional sector in total employment.

Note that negative enlargement and enrichment effects are both possible. Negative enlargement would occur when a sector shrinks in size, while negative enrichment would result when real incomes in that sector fall.

Total income growth can be positive, while either of these effects is negative. For example, a 10 percent growth rate in a sector might result from either (i) a 20 percent rise in the size of the sector, coupled with a 10 percent fall in average wages, or (ii) a 20 percent rise in average wages, accompanied by a 10 percent decline in the number of persons in that sector. This example should make clear that *our qualitative judgments about the desirability of any particular sector growth rate depend crucially on the enlargement and enrichment components of that growth;* examination of the sector growth rate is not enough.[8]

One immediate application of the decomposition in (13) is to poverty gap analysis. The poverty gap is the total income shortfall of the poor, i.e., the sum of the differences between each poor person's (or family's) income and the poverty line, which may be denoted by *IS*. The poor may benefit from economic growth in two ways: by more of them (Δf^m) being drawn into an enlarged modern sector (α) or by those remaining receiving higher incomes (ΔW^t) within the traditional sector (δ). The sum $\alpha + \delta$ is then the ex post income gain of the poor and $(\alpha + \delta)/IS$ is an index of an economy's progress toward alleviating absolute poverty. This is one way in which the welfare judgments in (6) and (7) might be implemented. In addition, if the β component is also taken into account, we are able to gauge success in raising incomes more generally, which is what the absolute income approach (5) requires.

Relative inequality judgments may also be made using the decomposition in (13). It would seem natural to compare the share of income growth accruing to the poor $(\alpha + \delta)$ and to the nonpoor (β), but I would be wary of such calculations, because $\alpha + \delta$ will almost inevitably be less than β, for much the same reason that the income share of the poorest X percent must always be less than the income share of the richest Y percent.[9] A more meaningful measure, one that is more sensitive to relative income differentials to begin with, is one that normalizes for the amount of initial income. Then, the percentage gains in the two sectors may be calculated as β/Y_1^m and $(\alpha + \delta)/Y_1^t$ or the equivalent per capita form.

Finally, the general welfare function (12) may be related to the enrichment and enlargement components of growth as follows:

$$\text{(14a)} \qquad\qquad \frac{\partial W}{\partial \alpha} > 0;$$

$$\text{(14b)} \qquad\qquad \frac{\partial W}{\partial \beta} \gtrless 0;$$

$$\text{(14c)} \qquad\qquad \frac{\partial W}{\partial \delta} > 0.$$

The ambiguity in (14b) reflects the fact that by itself greater modern sector enrichment increases both total income and income inequality. These changes receive positive and negative weights, respectively, in welfare judgments according to conditions (A) and (B) of Section 6.3, at least among observers who wish to take account of relative inequality changes. Observers interested only in absolute incomes and absolute poverty face no such difficulty.

It would be most interesting in future research to analyze different countries' growth experiences from these alternative welfare approaches. At present, suitable data are scarce.

6.5   Welfare Economic Analysis of Dualistic Development: Special Cases

It is of interest to examine the three limiting cases of dualistic development. We might distinguish between three stylized development typologies. In the *Modern Sector Enlargement Growth* model, an economy develops by enlarging the size of its modern sector, the wages in the two sectors remaining the same. *Modern Sector Enrichment Growth* occurs when the growth accrues only to a fixed number of persons in the modern sector, the number in the traditional sector and their wages remaining unchanged. Finally, we have *Traditional Sector Enrichment Growth* when all of the proceeds of growth are divided evenly among those in the traditional sector.

Table 6.2. Summary of distribution and welfare effects in three models of dualistic development

	Traditional sector enrichment growth	Modern sector enrichment growth	Modern sector enlargement growth		
			Phase 1 $0 \leq f^m < \frac{\sqrt{W^{mt} - W^t}}{W^m - W^t}$	Phase 2 $\frac{\sqrt{W^m W^t} - W^t}{W^m - W^t} \leq f^m \leq 60$ percent	Phase 3 $f^m > 60$ percent
Growth and distributional effects					
f^m	Unchanged	Unchanged	Rises	Rises	Rises
f^t	Unchanged	Unchanged	Falls	Falls	Falls
W^m	Unchanged	Rises	Unchanged	Unchanged	Unchanged
W^t	Rises	Unchanged	Unchanged	Unchanged	Unchanged
Y	Rises	Rises	Rises	Rises	Rises
π	Falls	Unchanged	Falls	Falls	Falls
L	Lorenz-superior	Lorenz-inferior	Lorenz-crossing	Lorenz-crossing	Lorenz-crossing
G	Falls	Rises	Rises	Falls	Falls
S	Rises	Falls	Falls	Falls	Rises
Y_{min}	Rises	Unchanged	Unchanged	Unchanged	Unchanged

Welfare effects according to:					
Absolute income approach	Unambiguous improvement	Unambiguous improvement	Unambiguous improvement	Unambiguous improvement	Unambiguous improvement
Rawlsian maximin approach	Unambiguous improvement	Unchanged	Unchanged	Unchanged	Unchanged
Absolute poverty approach	Unambiguous improvement	Unchanged	Unambiguous improvement	Unambiguous improvement	Unambiguous improvement
Relative inequality approach:					
L	Unambiguous improvement	Lorenz-inferior	Lorenz-crossing	Lorenz-crossing	Lorenz-crossing
G	Unambiguous improvement	Ambiguous	Ambiguous	Unambiguous improvement	Unambiguous improvement
S	Unambiguous improvement	Ambiguous	Ambiguous	Ambiguous	Unambiguous improvement
Eq. (12) and condition (C')	Unambiguous improvement	Ambiguous	Unambiguous improvement	Unambiguous improvement	Unambiguous improvement
General welfare approach	Unambiguous improvement	Ambiguous	Unambiguous improvement	Unambiguous improvement	Unambiguous improvement

In relation to existing literature the modern sector enlargement growth model most closely reflects the essential nature of economic development as conceived by a number of writers. Fei and Ranis (1964), for example, have written: "... the heart of the development problem may be said to lie in the gradual shifting of the center of gravity of the economy from the agricultural to the industrial sector ... gauged in terms of the reallocation of the population between the two sectors in order to promote a gradual expansion of industrial employment and output," and this is echoed by Kuznets (1966). Empirical studies of many countries have quantified the absorption of an increasing share of the population into the modern sector; see, for instance, Turnham (1971). Thus, modern sector enlargement comprises a large and perhaps even predominant component of the growth of currently developing countries.

Let us now analyze the growth and distributional patterns that arise in each of the three stylized models of dualistic development according to the various welfare economic approaches previously discussed. The principal results are summarized in Table 6.2.

Figure 6.1.

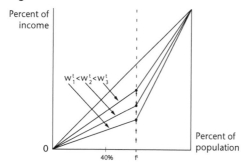

6.5.1 *Traditional Sector Enrichment Growth*

In the traditional sector enrichment growth model, incomes in the traditional sector are assumed to rise; incomes in the modern sector remain the same; and the allocation of the labor force between the two sectors also remains the same. The following proposition is easily established:

Proposition 1. Traditional sector enrichment growth results in higher income, a more equal relative distribution of income, and less poverty.

The increase in income and the alleviation of poverty (since each of the poor becomes less poor) are evident. Regarding the relative income distribution, we need observe only that traditional sector enrichment growth has the effect of shifting the kink point on the Lorenz curve vertically as in Figure 6.1, which establishes Lorenz domination. By inspection, it is apparent that the income share of the poorest 40 percent (S) increases and the Gini coefficient (G) (the ratio of the area above the Lorenz curve to the entire triangle) decreases. Hence, relative income inequality declines, as was to be shown. By all of the social welfare criteria presented above, this type of growth therefore results in an unambiguous welfare improvement.

Figure 6.2.

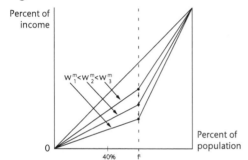

6.5.2 *Modern Sector Enrichment Growth*

In modern sector enrichment growth, incomes in the modern sector rise, while incomes in the traditional sector and the allocation of the labor force between the modern sector and the traditional sector remain the same. In this case we have the following proposition:

Proposition 2. Modern sector enrichment growth results in higher income, a less equal relative distribution of income, and no change in poverty.

Adherents of the more general form of the absolute income approach would regard this type of growth as an unambiguous improvement, although they would have preferred a pattern where less of the benefit accrued to the well-to-do. However, Rawlsians and persons who adopt the absolute poverty criterion would be indifferent to this type of growth, since no poverty is being alleviated.

With respect to relative inequality the gap between the modern sector wage and the traditional sector wage increases. The kink point on the Lorenz curve shifts vertically downward, which is shown in Figure 6.2. In Figure 6.2 we see clearly the Lorenz-inferiority of the new situation compared with the old. The Gini coefficient rises, and the share of the poorest 40 percent falls. Those concerned with relative inequality would give positive weight to the growth in income but negative weight to the rising relative inequality. Thus, the judgments rendered by the various welfare economic approaches are in disagreement. The observed discrepancy is not entirely undesirable. It is quite plausible that some observers may wish to regard the rising gap between the rich and poor unfavorably, not because the poor have lower incomes, but rather because the growing income differential might make the poor *feel* worse off. Some might even wish to allow envy of the rich by the poor to more than offset the gain in utility of the income recipients themselves. This is a defensible position – that income growth concentrated exclusively in the hands of the rich might be interpreted as a socially inferior situation as compared with the rich having less and the poor the same amount – but certainly an extreme one based on the primacy of relative income considerations. In the case of modern sector enrichment growth, therefore, the differing judgments according to the welfare functions, (4), (5), (7), and (12), reflect a true difference of opinion.

This is not so in the case of modern sector enlargement growth, to which we now turn.

Figure 6.3.

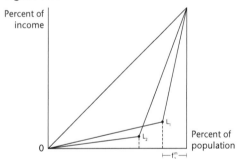

6.5.3 *Modern Sector Enlargement Growth*

As observed earlier, many leading writers in the field hold that countries develop principally by absorbing an increasing share of their labor forces into an ever-enlarging modern sector. As a stylized version of this, in the modern sector enlargement growth model, incomes in both the modern and the traditional sectors remain the same but the modern sector gets bigger. In this case we may derive the following results:

Proposition 3. In modern sector enlargement growth: (a) Absolute incomes rise, and absolute poverty is reduced. (b) The Rawlsian criterion shows no change. (c) Lorenz curves always cross, so relative inequality effects are ambiguous. (d) Relative inequality indices first increase and subsequently decline.

PROOFS

a) The proofs of the absolute income and absolute poverty effects are immediate. Clearly, absolute incomes are higher, and since there are fewer poor, poverty is alleviated.

b) In modern sector enlargement growth there are fewer poor, but those who remain poor continue to be just as poor as before. Until poverty is totally eliminated, the Rawlsian criterion is completely insensitive to modern sector enlargement growth.

c) The crossing of Lorenz curves is demonstrated in Figure 6.3 The explanation is the following: (i) Those among the poor who are left behind due to the incapacity of the modern sector to absorb everyone have the same incomes, but these incomes are now a smaller fraction of a larger total, so the new Lorenz curve lies below the old Lorenz curve at the lower end of the income distribution; (ii) each person in the modern sector receives the same absolute income as before, but the share going to the richest f_I^m percent is now smaller, and hence the new Lorenz curve lies above the old one at the upper end of the income distribution; (iii) therefore, the two curves necessarily cross somewhere in the middle. Of course, when Lorenz curves cross, welfare judgments based on relative inequality considerations are ambiguous.

d) We shall now demonstrate the inevitability of an initial increase in relative inequality in the early stages of development followed by a subsequent decline for the income share of the poorest 40 percent (S) and the Gini coefficient (G). This is the inverted-U pattern made famous by Kuznets.

Considering S first, it is evident that in the early stages of modern sector enlargement growth, the poorest 40 percent receive the same absolute amount from a larger whole, and therefore their share falls. However, in the later stages (i.e., for $f^t < 40$ percent), they receive all of the income growth, and hence their share rises. This result may be generalized as follows: If our measure of inequality is the share of income accruing to the poorest X percent, that share falls continuously in modern sector enlargement growth until the modern sector has grown to include $(1 - X)$ percent of the population.

Turning now to the Gini coefficient, the proof is given in note 10.[10]

While both measures exhibit the inverted-U pattern in modern sector enlargement growth, the turning points do not coincide. There are three phases: (1) Initially, both G and S show rising relative inequality; (2) Then, G turns down while S continues to fall; (3) Finally, S rises while G continues to fall. To indicate the importance of this discrepancy for just these two measures, it is thought that in real terms the modern-sector-traditional-sector wage gap is something like 3:1. This implies that Phase 2 ranges from 37 percent to 60 percent of the population in the traditional sector. This range is substantial and may well include many LDC's.

Kuznets (1955) demonstrated this pattern in the historical experiences of a number of then developed economies. Kuznets' explanation was that the inverted-U pattern was caused by the transfer of workers from the rural sector, where incomes were relatively equally distributed at low levels, to the urban sector, where there was greater income dispersion, owing to the presence of a skilled professional class at the top and poor recent migrants at the bottom. In terms of the development typologies analyzed above, Kuznets' model is basically one of *modern sector enlargement growth with within-sector inequality*.

In an unpublished Appendix, I extend the dualistic models of this chapter to allow for within-sector inequality. There, I prove that the inverted-U pattern *always* arises in modern sector enlargement growth, even if the *traditional sector has a more unequal distribution of income within it*. This result has been observed by previous researchers, although not for the Gini coefficient.[11] Where I differ from the others is over the welfare interpretation of these patterns.

Proposition 4. The various welfare approaches give different evaluations of the desirability of modern sector enlargement growth. (a) The absolute income and absolute poverty approaches rate this type of growth as an unambiguous welfare improvement. (b) Rawlsians would be indifferent to this type of growth. (c) The relative inequality approach regards this type of growth ambiguously in the early stages but once the turning point is reached, it is a good thing. (d) The general welfare approach (12) considers modern sector enlargement growth as an unambiguous improvement regardless of the stage of development.

The proofs of (a)–(c) are immediate given the respective welfare functions and the patterns established in Proposition 3. Point (d) follows from (12) and conditions (A), (C), (F), and (G). The lack of correspondence between (c) and (d) warrants further attention.

Kuznets (1955, 1963, 1966), Swamy (1962), Robinson (1976), and many others have interpreted the inverted-U pattern as signifying that in a true economic sense "the distribution of income must get worse before it gets better." It would seem at first that a falling share going to the poor (S) or a rising Gini coefficient (G) should receive negative weight in a social welfare judgment, possibly negative enough to outweigh the rising level of income. But why? There are at least two possible answers.

Implicitly, we may have in mind that a falling S or rising G implies that the poor are getting *absolutely* poorer while the rich are getting absolutely richer, and many of us would regard this as a bad thing indeed. The problem with this notion is that it confuses cause and effect, that is to say, absolute emiseration of the poor would definitely imply falling S and rising G, but as we have just seen, G rises and S falls in the early stages of modern sector enlargement growth without the poor becoming worse off in absolute terms.

Ruling out the necessity of absolute emiseration of the poor as a reason for reacting adversely to a falling S or rising G in modern sector enlargement growth, we may instead have in mind *relative* income comparisons – that a growing income differential between rich and poor reduces poor people's utilities. Yet, in the early stages of modern sector enlargement growth, despite the rising Gini coefficient and the falling share of the poorest 40 percent, *the income differential between rich and poor is not changing*. Hence:

Proposition 5. For modern sector enlargement growth the conventional relative inequality measures do not "correctly" measure relative inequality, if the "correct" definition of relative inequality in dualistic development is the intersectoral wage difference or ratio (or a monotonic transformation thereof).

In the early stages of modern sector enlargement growth, we may be misled into thinking that relative inequality is "worsening" when in fact the wage structure is not changing. This same point holds in reverse for relative inequality "improvements" in the later stages of modern sector enlargement growth. This is because condition (F) is violated.

Proposition 5 implies that rising relative inequality *as measured by conventional indices* may be a perfectly *natural*, and even highly desirable, outcome for this type of development. Put differently, the falling share of the lowest 40 percent and rising Gini coefficient that arise in this case are *statistical artifacts without social welfare content*. For this type of growth, the specification of social welfare functions like (4) *conflicts* with our ideas of social well-being as given by (12). This conflict is particularly acute for persons who wish to give heavy weight to relative income considerations. If relative-inequality- averse persons compare Gini coefficients or income shares of the poorest 40 percent at two points in time when modern sector enlargement growth is taking place, they will be led to social welfare judgments which *they themselves would not wish to make*. Unfortunately, functions like (4) based on G or S are being used with increasing frequency in current empirical studies of economic development. The use of functions like (12), based on the enlargement and enrichment components of various sectors' growth experiences, would avoid such difficulties.

137

6.6   Extensions of the Methodology

6.6.1   *Extension to n Sectors*

In practical applications the strict division of an economy into a modern sector and a traditional sector may be unsatisfactory, and a finer breakdown may be more desirable, for instance, into a modern urban sector, traditional urban sector, and a traditional agricultural sector. In general, with n sectors national income *(Y)* is

$$(15) \qquad\qquad Y = \sum_{i=1}^{n} W^i f^i.$$

The change in national income is

$$(16) \qquad\qquad \Delta Y = Y_2 - Y_1 = \sum_{i=1}^{n} W_2^i f_2^i - \sum_{i=1}^{n} W_1^i f_1^i,$$

which, when rewritten as

$$(17) \qquad\qquad \Delta Y = \sum_{i=1}^{n} (W_2^i f_2^i - W_1^i f_1^i),$$

enables us to measure the contribution of the ith sector to total growth. To distinguish each sector's enlargement and enrichment effects and the interaction between them, (17) may be manipulated to yield

$$(18) \qquad \Delta Y = \sum_{i=1}^{n}$$

$$[\underbrace{W_1^i (f_2^i - f_1^i)}_{} \quad + \quad \underbrace{(W_2^i - W_1^i) f_1^i}_{} \quad + \quad \underbrace{(W_2^i - W_1^i)(f_2^i - f_1^i)}_{}]$$

| Sector *i* enlargement effect | Sector *i* enrichment effect | Interaction of sector *i* enlargement and enrichment effects. |

The results of the comparative static analysis of the two-sector case carry over to the n-sector case in an analogous manner.

Besides extensions to more than two *sectors*, the methodology may be carried over as well to more than two *income sources*, or to a hybrid classification of *sectors and sources*. For example, it might be useful to measure income growth in the following six groups:

   (i) Labor income among modern sector workers in urban areas
   (ii) Labor income among traditional sector workers in urban areas
  (iii) Labor income among traditional sector workers in agriculture
  (iv) Capital income in urban areas
   (v) Capital income in rural areas
  (vi) Other income.

With such an extended methodology we are limited only by restrictions of our data and our own ingenuity.

6.6.2 *Explicit Allowance for Population Growth*

It is a straightforward matter to give explicit recognition to population growth. Total income growth (ΔY) may be thought to have two components: (i) A *population growth effect (P)*, defined as the expansion of the economy to absorb a growing population at the initial occupational and wage structure, and (ii) A *net growth effect (N)*, which results from higher wages and a higher proportion of the population employed in high paying activities. Let f^i be the *number* of persons in sector i and p the rate of growth of population between years 1 and 2. Then *net growth* (income growth net of population) is given by

(19) $N = \Delta Y - P$

$$= \sum_{i=1}^{n} (W_2^i f_2^i - W_1^i f_1^i) - \sum_{i=1}^{n} W_1^i f_1^i p.$$

This can be decomposed into the various net effects as

(20) $N = \sum_{i=1}^{n} [W_2^i f_2^i - W_1^i f_1^i (1 + p)]$

$$= \sum_{i=1}^{n} [W_1^i [f_2^i - f_1^i (1 + p)]] + \sum_{i=1}^{n} [(W_2^i - W_1^i) f_1^i (1 + p)]$$

$\qquad\qquad$ Sector i net $\qquad\qquad$ Sector i net
$\qquad\qquad$ enlargment effect $\qquad$ enrichment effect

$$+ \sum_{i=1}^{n} [(W_2^i - W_1^i)[f_2^i - f_1^i (1 + p)]].$$

$\qquad\qquad$ Interaction of sector i net enlargement
$\qquad\qquad$ and enrichment effects.

6.7   Conclusions and Implications

This chapter has examined the welfare implications of different types of dualistic economic development. Several alternative approaches for assessing the welfare implications of growth were set forth (Sections 6.2 and 6.3). In Section 6.4 dualistic development was analyzed from the various perspectives. Section 6.5 set out three stylized development typologies. For each the changes in relative inequality and absolute incomes and poverty and the welfare effects of these changes were derived according to the various welfare criteria and contrasts among them were noted. Then, some extensions of the methodology were set forth (Section 6.6).

A number of conclusions and implications may be drawn:

1. *The extent to which different groups participate in economic growth may be readily conceptualized and quantified using the formulas developed in this chapter.* The procedure is easily implementable, subject to availability of straightforward cross tabulations of employment distributions and wage and income structures.

2. *The time paths of relative inequality and absolute poverty depend on the type of economic development as well as its level.* In terms of the three stylized development typologies formulated above, absolute poverty is diminished in traditional sector enrichment growth and modern sector enlargement growth, but is not alleviated in modern sector enrichment growth. Relative inequality declines in traditional sector enrichment growth and rises in modern sector enrichment growth. The usual relative inequality measures show an inverted-U pattern in modern sector enlargement growth. In short, contrary to the beliefs of some, income distribution need not get worse before it gets better, provided a suitable development strategy is followed.

3. *The absolute income and poverty and relative inequality approaches often do not give the same welfare judgments about the desirability of different patterns of growth.* Only for traditional sector enrichment growth and for the later stages of modern sector enlargement growth do these approaches concur in indicating an unambiguous welfare improvement. In the case of modern sector enrichment growth, there is a real substantive disagreement about whether or not growth of that sort is a good thing. However, in the early stages of modern sector enlargement growth, there arises a discrepancy between the various approaches, but it has no apparent welfare economic basis. This is because

4. *Conventional relative inequality measures show an inverted-U pattern in modern sector enlargement growth despite a constant intersectoral wage structure.* This implies that the "worsening" inequality (as ordinarily measured) should *not* be interpreted as a bad thing, nor should the subsequent "improvement" be regarded as an economically meaningful reduction in relative inequality either. Thus, social welfare functions, whether explicitly stated or implicitly assumed, of the form $W = W(Y,I)$, $f_1 > 0$, $f_2 < 0$, where I is any of the Lorenz curve-based relative inequality measures in common use, are *invalid* for this type of growth. In cases of modern sector enlargement growth, it is far better to look only at the rate at which the growth is taking place.

As a corollary of the above:

5. Before we can legitimately interpret a rising relative inequality coefficient in a country as an economically meaningful worsening of the income distribution rather than a statistical artifact, we must know which of the three types of economic development patterns that country has been following. We have shown that a falling share of income received by the poorest 40 percent and rising Gini coefficient can be the result of

> a) Traditional Sector Impoverishment, which is clearly bad in social welfare terms; or

> b) Modern Sector Enrichment, which is good in absolute income terms, indifferent in absolute poverty terms, and ambiguous in relative income terms; or

> c) Modern Sector Enlargment in the early phases, which is good according to widely accepted axiomatic judgments. Simple calculations of relative inequality patterns cannot distinguish among these causes. This implies the following:

6. *Regardless of whether one favors an absolute or relative approach or some combination of them, social welfare judgments about the desirability of a given course of economic development should be made on the basis of the enlargement and enrichment components of that growth.* Equation (12) makes clear that the way we feel about a country's growth pattern depends on changes in its wage structure and occupational structure over the development period. Data on rates of growth of total incomes in various sectors of an economy are insufficient for coming to a welfare judgment. We must also know how many are sharing in each sector's income at each point in time.

7. *To evaluate the participation of the poor in economic development, poverty indices have a number of desirable properties.* They avoid the problems associated with possible ambiguities that arise in interpreting relative inequality measures. They are sensitive to changes in the number of poor (the enlargement effect) and in the severity of their poverty (the enrichment effect). They are easily calculable from the macroeconomic data or sufficiently disaggregated tabulations. The Sen index shares these advantages, plus it reflects the degree of income inequality among the poor and its axiomatic justification is clearly delineated so that users and nonusers alike will know what welfare judgments underlie the measure. Absolute poverty measures in general and the Sen index in particular warrant further use, especially in the study of less developed countries where this type of approach has not received much attention.

6.8   Empirical Significance

The preceding analysis has shown that under certain circumstances the absolute poverty and relative inequality approaches may give very different results concerning the distributional effects of growth in the dual economy. In light of these differences, the choice between the two types of measures should be based on the type of welfare judgments we wish to make. The empirical significance of the choice may be illustrated with reference to two actual cases of particular interest, India and Brazil.

The Brazilian economy achieved a growth in per capita income of 32 percent over the decade of the 1960s, a substantial accomplishment by the standards of less developed countries. Fishlow (1972), Langoni ('1972), and others have examined the distributional question of who received the benefits of this growth, found greater relative income inequality, and concluded that the poor benefited very little, if at all. Yet when the distributional question is reexamined from an absolute poverty perspective by looking at the number of very poor and the levels of income they receive, it is found that the average real incomes among persons defined as poor by Brazilian standards increased by as much as 60 percent, while the comparable figure for nonpoor persons was around 25 percent (Fields, 1977). At the same time, the percentage of persons below the poverty line fell somewhat. It would thus appear that by assigning heavy weight to changes in the usual indices of relative income inequality and interpreting these increases as offsets to the well-being brought about by growth, previous investigators may have inadvertently overlooked important tendencies toward the alleviation of poverty.

In the India case, the problem is just the opposite. Bardhan (1974) reports that relative inequality in India (as measured by the Gini coefficient) exhibited a small but perceptible decline, which some might see as an improvement in income distribution. Yet, due to the lack of growth of the Indian economy, the percentage of people living in absolute poverty increased in both the urban and rural sectors of the economy.

These examples indicate that the choice of an evaluative criterion *does* make a very real qualitative difference. It comes down to a choice between welfare judgments which emphasize the alleviation of absolute poverty or those focusing on the narrowing of relative income inequality. Personally, I am most concerned about the alleviation of economic misery among the very poorest, especially in low-income countries, and therefore give greatest weight to absolute poverty changes. Others with different value judgments who may be more concerned than I with relative income comparisons or with the middle or upper end of the income distribution may wish to rely more on one of the other approaches. The inconsistency between the professed concern of many researchers for the alleviation of absolute poverty and their use of relative inequality measures in empirical research is striking. I hope this will be less prevalent in the future.

7

Labor Market Modeling and the Urban Informal Sector: Theory and Evidence

7.1   Introduction

The goal of economic development is to raise standards of living throughout an economy. Most persons' standards of living are determined by their labor earnings. Consequently, rising real wages at full employment are rightly viewed as a primary means of improving standards of living. For many workers, the best available job is a poor one in the city. This job is not "formal" or "modern" in the sense that those terms are used in the development literature to refer to activities in factories and offices similar to those of the industrialized world. Nor is the worker "unemployed" in the standard ILO sense of not working for pay but actively looking for work. The worker who is employed in a non-modern activity needs to be counted somewhere. Such workers, the jobs they hold, and the incomes they earn have come to be termed the "urban informal sector." In what way does it make sense to talk about an informal sector, as distinct from a formal sector? Mazumdar (1976, p. 656) gives a good answer: It is sometimes maintained that the characteristics which constitute the basis of the formal-informal sector distinction represent a pattern of continuous variation in a typical LDC labor market and, therefore, the dichotomy is unwarranted. There are two reasons for rejecting this contention: (a) whether the relevant characteristics represent a continuum or not is itself a subject of research, and, if we are to go by casual empiricism; then certainly the view that the "formal" sector is separated

The original version of this chapter was published as: Fields, Gary S. (1990). Labour Market Modeling and the Urban Informal Sector: Theory and Evidence, in: D. Turnham, B. Salomé, A. Schwarz, eds., The Informal Sector Revisited, 49–69. © 1990 by OECD Publishing.

sharply in some ways from the rest of the urban market is more valid than the contrary one for many LDC urban markets; (b) even if the difference between two types of employment is one of degree rather than of kind, so long as it is of marked degree the methodology of economics can be applied successfully by operating with models which assume that the labor market is split into two different sectors.

The purpose of this paper is to assess the compatibility between theoretical models of the urban informal sector (UIS) and empirical evidence on the workings of that sector in the context of developing countries' labor markets. My major point is that although the UIS is an excellent idea which has served us well in the 1970s and 1980s, we have need in the next round of research to refine our terminology and our models in light of empirical findings which have come to the fore in the interim. I would contend that what empirical researchers label "the informal sector" is best represented not as one sector nor as a continuum but as two qualitatively distinct sectors. Wage employment or self-employment in small-scale units may be better than or worse than employment in the formal sector. This is not a new point: diversity of earning opportunities and other job characteristics within the informal sector has long been noted – among other places, in the pathbreaking work of Hart (1973) and in the critiques of the informal sector concept by Bienefeld and Godfrey (1975), the ILO Sudan Report (1976), Standing (1977) and Sinclair (1978). But only recently has this view come to the fore: "A third point in which agreement has been reached concerns the degree of heterogeneity within the informal sector. Contrary to the prevailing image of a decade and a half ago to the effect that the informal sector was of a homogeneous nature, it is clear today that there are different segments within this sector" (Tokman, 1986, p. 13).

My view on heterogeneity of the informal sector is somewhat different from that expressed by many others. I am not simply saying that earnings and other aspects of jobs vary within sectors as well as between them. As I see it, the differences within the informal sector are systematic vis-à-vis the formal sector. Let me elaborate.

Consider the situation of a new entrant to the labor market or a new (or potential) migrant to the city. For such a person, a low-paying job in agriculture may be an option, although for those who live in land-scarce economies, even that may not be possible. In the city, the best initial alternative, if available, may be employment in the formal sector. Unemployment in the city is a distinct possibility. In between formal sector employment and open unemployment is employment (or under-employment) in the urban informal sector.

But persons who have been working in the formal sector for a long period of time do not necessarily wish to remain there. As they acquire experience, skills, and money, some of them may endeavor to leave wage employment in the formal sector and set up their own small businesses. Although these businesses are usually small and unregulated and may well lack a fixed work place, these businesses differ from the kinds of jobs described in the previous paragraph in one key dimension: they are not free-entry. At least some human and financial capital, often a considerable amount, is required before one can get into this kind of work.

Consider now the range of activities in which firms are small, workers are unprotected by labor legislation, work hours are variable, and the work place is not fixed. Usually, such employment is called informal. However, based on the distinction drawn in the previous two paragraphs, I would suggest that two very different things are going on within that "sector." Part of it consists of employment which is free-entry, low-wage, and undesirable relative to formal sector employment. However, another part of it consists of employment which is limited-entry, high-wage, and preferred to formal sector employment. From the point of view of the worker, as well as that of the outside evaluator, these two groups are very different in their position relative to the formal sector the first is worse, the second better. In most empirical research, however, these two segments are lumped together and treated as one. As a result of combining two very different groups, the typical empirical study, which purports to offer data on the "informal sector," conceived of as a free-entry sector within the urban economy and broadside by firm size or some other equally indistinct categorizing variable, is rendered dubious, if not downright invalid.

This implies the need for a clear distinction between the two sectors. The terminology I would suggest would be "easy entry informal sector" and "upper-tier informal sector."

Section 7.2 reviews some of the major labor market models of the 1960s for developing countries. This section serves to show both what was present in the thinking of the researchers of the day and what was missing. What was present was labor market dualism, purposeful job search, and unemployment. What was missing was an informal sector.

Section 7.3 presents characterizations of the urban informal sector. This section points up the features that led to the perceived need for an additional sector and presents the definitions of the UIS that were suggested as a result.

Section 7.4 reviews ways that the UIS has been integrated into theoretical labor market models. After presenting each of the major theoretical efforts, the strengths and weaknesses of these various formulations are evaluated.

Section 7.5 and 7.6 set forth some of the empirical evidence on the UIS, from existing studies and from economic anthropology respectively. These findings pose challenges not only to those labor market models which incorporate an urban informal sector but to the very concept of the UIS itself.

Section 7.7 summarizes the main conclusions.

7.2 Some Early Labor Market Analyses

7.2.1 *Stylized Facts of LDC's Labor Markets*

Any realistic analysis of labor markets in developing countries must capture two empirical features of their labor markets: open unemployment and wage dualism.

Open unemployment rates, as tabulated by Turnham (1971), Squire (1981), and others are sizable, often in double-digits. And this excludes underemployment, the rates of which are also found to be substantial (Yotopoulos and Nugent, 1976; Sabot, 1977; Squire, 1981).

Wage dualism arises when apparently homogeneous workers are paid different wages depending on the sector of the economy in which they are employed. Both tabular presentations and multivariate analysis demonstrate wage differentials for observationally equivalent labor; see Berry and Sabot (1978), Fields (1980), Squire (1981) and the references cited therein. From my reading of this evidence, it appears that after standardizing for relevant differences in workers and firms, there remain wage differences between comparable workers in different sectors.

The reasons offered for these apparent differentials fall into two categories – institutional and market – of which the institutional dominate thinking and discussion. Five institutional forces, singly or in combination, have potent influences on wages in most of the developing world. Minimum wage laws are commonplace and when enforced cause wages to be higher than they otherwise would be. Labor unions often are very strong. At times, this is because of the close association between organized labor and the political party in power. Other times, it is because labor unions are encouraged as a means of achieving higher wages for workers. Pay policy for government workers often sets the pattern of wages for the rest of the economy, and those in charge have a propensity to pay high wages to all government workers (including themselves). Also, multinationals often pay high wages, partly to maintain parity between expatriate and local employees and partly (in some instances) to appear to be good corporate citizens and thereby to avoid expropriation or expulsion. Finally, labor codes may require higher wages, fringe benefits, and severance pay, resulting at times in bloated work forces and inflated labor costs. Market reasons for higher-than-market-clearing wages have been offered by other analysts. For example, Stiglitz (1974, 1976, 1982) suggests that firms may find it profitable to raise wages by x percent if this leads to a greater-than-x percent increase in worker productivity due to better nutrition, improved morale, or lower labor turnover.

Not all wages are affected identically by wage floors, either for market reasons (e.g., a more experienced labor force is more valuable in some industries than in others) or for institutional reasons (e.g., trade unions exert differential influence in different industries, certain industries or occupations are exempted from minimum wage laws). The result is a structure of wage differentials. As a stylized version of the differential applicability of wage floors, economists from such disparate fields as development economics, labor economics, and international trade have formulated two-sector models with a wage floor in one sector but not the other. Wage floors would be expected to affect directly the sectors involved and to affect indirectly via migration and other general equilibrium phenomena the other parts of the economy.

7.2.2 Some Early Models

Some models in international trade have two economic sectors with the same wage floor in each. Models from other fields of economics have wage dualism but lack unemployment: the dualistic models of economic development, the trade models with fixed wage differentials, some general equilibrium models of sector-specific wage floors, and some but not all minimum wage models of labor economics. These classes of models differ from I one another in important ways, but have one central feature in common: they do not have both wage dualism and unemployment. It would be desirable to have a model with both.

7.2.3 Models with Wage Dualism and Unemployment

Wage dualism arises due to incomplete coverage by minimum wage laws, strong trade unions in some sectors but not others, and the like. Open unemployment arises form the purposeful movement of labor between sectors on the basis of the expected wages in each, labor may move on the basis of the strict mathematical expectation (i.e., wage multiplied by probability of employment), or the employment probability may be included in some other way. But the equilibrium tendency is toward equalization of wages adjusted for probability of employment. This contrasts with flexible wage models; it is an increase in unemployment in the high wage sectors rather than a fall in the wage that ultimately equilibrates the supply side of the market.

Models with the preceding features have been developed by Todaro (1969), Harris and Todaro (1970), Harberger (1971), Tidrick (1975), Mincer (1976), and others. The core features of this framework are:

(i) A dualistic economy, consisting of a modern urban sector and a traditional agricultural sector, or a covered sector and a non-covered sector;

(ii) Wage dualism, resulting from:

    a) A rigid wage above market-clearing levels in the modern sector, along with

    b) Market-clearing wages in agriculture;

(iii) Migration on the basis of differences in expected wages (the wage if employed adjusted for the probability of employment);

(iv) Persistent urban unemployment;

(v) Tendency toward expected wage equalization.

7.2.4   Evaluation

The Harris-Todaro model (and others in that class) improved enormously on previous models. Harris and Todaro tried to capture the features of the Kenyan labor market (and, we learned later, the features of many other countries' labor markets as well). This they did much better than labor market models which preceded it. However, despite the many attractions of the Harris-Todaro model, and the subsequent extensions and refinements of it, a certain disquiet arose: the urban labor force did not fit neatly into Harris and Todaro's two categories: employed in the modern sector or unemployed. It became increasingly evident that within the urban areas of developing economies, there existed a significant group of people who were neither employed in modern sector jobs nor unemployed. They occupied an intermediate position, sometimes called "underemployment," whereby they were working (hence not unemployed) but the work was by no means modern (nor, for that matter, was the pay). A number of authors studied this sector and made its characteristics known. The result is the widespread recognition of what has come to be called the "urban informal sector."

7.3   Characterizations of the Urban Informal Sector

Around 1970, researchers became aware that people in developing countries were working in an urban sector that was not modern. Included in this sector were small traders, street vendors, shoeshine boys, self-appointed parking attendants, beggars, and others in somewhat shadowy activities, as well as carpenters, masons, tailors and other tradesmen, cooks, taxi-drivers, etc.

The criteria for the informal sector identified in the ILO report on

Kenya (1972, p. 6) were:

  (i) ease of entry;
 (ii) reliance on indigenous resources;
(iii) family ownership of enterprises;
(iv) small scale of operation;
 (v) labor-intensive and adapted technology;
(vi) skills acquired outside the formal school system; and
(vii) unregulated and competitive markets. Informal-sector activities are largely ignored, rarely supported, often regulated and sometimes actively discouraged by the Government. The characteristics of formal-sector activities are the obverse of these…

Of these many possible distinguishing characteristics, which are most crucial? My concern in this paper is with labor market choices. From that point of view, what matters about the informal sector is not its economic efficiency or inefficiency, nor its possible contribution to a country's future wealth, but rather its role as a source of earnings for those who wish to work there. Thus, for my purposes, the critical distinguishing feature of the informal sector is ease of entry or lack thereof.

Mazumdar (1976, p. 656) shares this view of the distinction between the formal and informal sectors. In his words:

> The basic distinction between the two sectors turns on the idea that employment in the formal sector is in some sense or senses protected so that the wage-level and working conditions in the sector are not available, in general, to the job-seekers in the market unless they manage to cross the barrier of entry somehow.

If by definition, the informal sector exhibits free entry, which means that all who are willing to take up employment in that sector can receive a cash income, the mechanism whereby incomes are determined within that sector must be specified. Harberger (1971, p. 574) characterized it thus:

> The second variant associates disguised unemployment not just with low wages but with situations in which the marginal productivity of labor lies below the actual wages earned. This is clearly a quite different concept, which could among other things apply to high-wage as well as to low-wage workers. There are a variety of activities to which this argument applies. A classic example is that of fishermen on a lake. The addition of more fishermen increases the total catch, but not proportionately, yet the last fisherman has an equal chance of making a given catch as the first. The expected catch is the same for all, and is equal to their average productivity. But, owing to the fact that the total catch does not increase in proportion to the number

of fishermen, the marginal productivity of a fisherman is less than what he earns. Other cases, more frequently cited in the economic development literature, are the shoeshine boys in a given square, where the presence of the last boy does not proportionately increase the number of shines, or the hawkers and vendors found in the streets of less developed countries, where the addition of another man selling a given product does not proportionately increase the amount sold but has the effect of somewhat reducing the average amount received by each.

Implicit in Harberger's examples are certain assumptions about institutional arrangements, resulting in average product determining individual incomes. In his fishing example, the assumption is that existing fishermen cannot restrict the marginal fisherman from fishing in their waters and reducing their catch – which is, of course, what free entry means. In his shoeshine example, it is assumed the customers who enter the square in search of shoeshines choose a particular shoeshine boy one n'th of the time – and thus, there is no particular advantage to one location within the square compared with another. These are reasonable assumptions, but the need to make them should be pointed out.

By definition, the formal sector jobs pay better than the informal sector jobs. Because of this, workers naturally aspire to formal sector jobs. But formal sector jobs are not available to all who seek them. Unemployment or underemployment will result.

Which will it be: unemployment or underemployment? The answer depends upon earning opportunities and ease of on-the-job search in the different sectors. In the Harris-Todaro world, a worker has only two options: he can migrate to (or remain in) the city and search for a formal sector job while unemployed, or he can locate in the rural sector and relinquish any chance of getting a formal sector job.

Moving beyond the strict Harris-Todaro specification, we might want to allow for on-the-job search from the rural sector, in which case the two search strategies are search while unemployed in the urban area or search while employed in agriculture. In this case, everyone in the labor force aspires to a modern sector job, because that is the best earning opportunity in the economy. Some search while openly unemployed; others search (albeit with a reduced probability of success) while employed in agriculture. The only persons in the economy who do not search are those who are already in modern sector jobs.

The existence of earning opportunities in the informal sector gives each member of the labor force yet another search option: he might take up a job in the urban informal sector and search from there in the evenings, on weekends, or during the day when working hours are variable. In the typical developing country, most of the formal sector jobs are located in the cities. Urban informal sector workers would therefore be expected to have a better chance of obtaining an urban formal sector job than would an agricultural worker, if for no other reason than simple proximity to places of hiring. Writing in the early 1970s, based upon observation of the Kenyan situation, I characterized the search process as follows:

New arrivals in the cities ordinarily stay with friends or relatives who help house and feed them while they look for work. A dozen or more people crowded into one room is not uncommon. They need not live in housing which is rented or provided as part of job compensation. Squatter setdements and shanty towns house a substantial portion of urban populations, particularly in Africa.

Open unemployment is not very common. Additional household members are expected to contribute to their support. Frequently, they assist with the household chores by preparing meals, washing clothes, or caring for children. Simultaneously, they search for work (albeit on an irregular basis) and are classified as unemployed.

The most fortunate new migrants obtain a permanent modern-sector job as a clerk, messenger, or whatever. However, these are the best jobs and the typical migrant is forced to find some lesser means of earning a cash income. He may secure one or more typically a succession of wage jobs (e.g., house-servant, cook in a small lunch kiosk, assistant in a family shop) or engage in self-employment (e.g., selling produce, newspapers, curios, or shoe shines on the street corner).

The defining characteristics of the (informal) sector are ease of entry and the lack of a stable employer–employee relationship. The urban areas of less developed countries typically have a wide variety of such open entry, casual employment types of jobs. For instance, a person can get started by buying some peas in the market, removing the pods at the side of the road, and selling podded peas to passers-by at a higher price. Prostitution is another occupation which has notoriously easy entry.

Workers in the (informal) sector are ordinarily classified as employed although they themselves and the statisticians who measure those things would be inclined to consider them underemployed. (Fields, 1975, pp. 171–172)

I would maintain that this characterization is equally valid today as a characterization of a broad range of economic activity, not only in Kenya but in a wide variety of developing countries.

Others agree. For example, Oberai and Singh (1984) conducted a study in Ludhiana in the Indian Punjab. They found (p. 509) "that more than 90 percent of migrants seeking work found a job within two months of their arrival, which means that migrants are being absorbed fairly quickly into the urban labor market." But much of this is free-entry self-employment. In Oberai and Singh's words (pp. 516-517): "... a fair proportion of migrants who take up self-employment on arrival start in the informal sector where they work as street vendors, porters, shoeshine boys and the like. Perhaps some of them also work in small family enterprises. All such employment requires little capital or skill. The proportion of migrants who are engaged in the formal sector as own-account workers or employers rises in most cases with length of stay; the increase is particularly sharp during the first few years." And in a study of Jamaica, Doeringer (1988) has written: "In particular, a distinction is drawn between those jobs (generally in what is often called the informal sector) where easy entry and work sharing are the principal determinants of income-earning opportunities, and those which are protected by formal sector internal labor markets. This distinction is critical for understanding how employment and productivity are affected by economic change, and by institutional forces in the workplace."

Thus, the main features of the urban informal sector, as I characterized it in my 1975 paper and as it remains characterized in many people's minds today are:

- *Free entry*, in the sense that all who wish to enter this sector can find some sort of work which will provide them with cash earnings;
- *Income-sharing*, because of the institutional circumstances of that sector's production and sales patterns;
- *Positive on-the-job search opportunities*, in that those who are engaged in the urban informal sector have a non-zero chance of finding a formal sector job;
- *An intermediate search probability*, in that those in the urban informal sector have better chance of finding a formal sector job than do those in agriculture but a worse chance than those who are openly unemployed and searching full-time; and
- *A lower wage in the urban informal sector than in agriculture*, arising endogenously result of the higher on-the-job search opportunity here.

Free entry is the defining feature of the informal sector, and the other characteristics just listed are attributed of that sector in a typical developing economy.

Not everyone shares this view. Tokman (1986), for instance, explicitly rejects it. He writes (p. 3): "As it happens, migrants and newcomers to the labor market are characterized by their lack of capital, both physical and human. This determines the type of activities they can perform, their main requirement being easy entry into the sector." However, he continues (p. 5): "The ease of entry has not been dropped from the analysis and is still kept as an important factor to examine the rules of income determination. However, the organization of production is the main variable, while the characteristics of entry are only used to qualify the differences between the units which use labor, either paid or unpaid, and the individual units of production."

The utility of any concept depends on the use to which it is put. If we regard work in the informal sector as a labor market option for workers, and if we wish to analyze the functioning of that sector's labor market and its linkages with other sectors' labor markets, then the ease or difficulty of entry into the sector is the critical distinguishing feature. For other purposes, such as for designing industrial policy or urban development policy, conceptualizations based on form of organization might be better. But for the purpose of labor market analysis, free entry must take precedence.

7.4 The Urban Informal Sector in Theoretical Labor Market Models

An urban informal sector has been included in some of the better-developed formal theoretical labor market models. The models fall into three broad classes, depending on the extent of freedom of entry into the informal sector and on the nature of the job-search behavior posited.

One class of models posits the behavior: Take an informal sector job if you can't get a formal sector job. The earliest model of which I am aware that contains an urban informal sector, Lopez (1970), has this feature. His starting point was the rural-urban migration model of Todaro (1969). He generalized the Todaro model to include the possibility that those who were not employed in the urban modern sector might possibly be employed in the urban informal sector.

In the first of Lopez's formulations, an urban resident who seeks a formal sector job and is unsuccessful automatically takes up informal sector employment. The problem with this formulation is that by assumption, it excludes the possibility of urban unemployment. Since urban unemployment exists, that possibility must be allowed for.

Another class of models posits different behavior for those who do not succeed in getting formal sector jobs: Take an informal sector job if you can get one. A second variant of Lopez's model allowed for this. A potential migrant from the rural area or a new entrant to the labor force in the urban area would face three possibilities: employment in the modern sector with probability @(t); unemployment in the city with probability [1 - @(t)] k'; and employment in the urban informal sector with probability [1 - @(t)] [1 - k']. In later years, essentially the same model was carried forward independently by Mazumdar (1976).

Note how unemployment arises in this class of models. In any given time period, informal sector jobs are not available to all who might wish them. Rather, Mazumdar felt that new hiring takes place frequently, so that those who are unemployed today have a good chance of being hired tomorrow. He wrote (1976, p. 676): "The labor market in the (informal) sector is assumed to represent, in its broad outline, a casual labor market. Workers are hired on short contract, say for the day. No worker is certain of obtaining a day's work in any particular day, but everybody gets some work over a period of time." Thus, entry into the informal sector is essentially free, in the sense that anyone wishing to enter that sector can do so and share in the available work over time; yet unemployment exists, because not all of the labor hours supplied are actually demanded.

The introduction of unemployment alongside employment in the urban informal sector (or, as it sometimes called, "under-employment") is a clear improvement on models which lacked an informal sector. However, the specific way in which unemployment is introduced is not necessarily the best. From the point of view of job search and job-getting behavior, the formulations of Lopez and Mazumdar are controversial, if not downright problematical: they assume implicitly that those urban workers who are employed in the urban informal sector have the same chance of getting a modem sector job as those who are completely unemployed. This is probably unrealistic, empirically. One observes that urban informal sector workers appear to have a lesser chance of getting a modem sector job than those who are unemployed. One reason for this is that informal sector workers have less time to spend on job search. Put differently, whenever a modem sector job vacancy occurs, the unemployed worker engaged in full-time job search has a better chance of being in the right place at the right time to be hired as compared with the worker who is employed in the informal sector. The presumed greater efficiency of search while unemployed relative to on-the-job search should be brought into the analysis.

This leads to a third class of models with the decision rule: Take an informal sector job only if it pays you to take one. Search while unemployed should be more effective than on-the-job search. This may be included in a three-way choice among the following options:

(i) Remain in the rural area without hope of getting a modem sector job. Earn the agricultural wage.
(ii) Search while unemployed in the urban area. Take a modern sector job if one is offered. Otherwise, be unemployed.
(iii) Search while employed in the urban informal sector, with a lower probability of success than if searching while unemployed. Take a modern sector job if one is offered. Otherwise, earn the informal sector wage.

The first two of these strategies correspond to the Harris-Todaro options. The third is an additional option, first introduced in Chapter 7.5 of my 1975 paper (Fields (1975)).

The considerations entering into the choice between options (*i*) and (*ii*) are familiar from the Harris-Todaro problem, and so require no elaboration here. Regarding option (*iii*), however, questions may arise. Why would anyone search from the informal sector if it means a reduced probability of getting a modern sector job? The answer is that those who search from the informal sector receive a wage while employed in that sector, as opposed to the unemployed who do not (although they might receive transfers from family members).

The opposite question might also be asked: why doesn't everyone search from the informal sector if they can receive a wage while working there? The answer is that they I would all do exactly that if the earnings they could receive were sufficiently high to compensate for the reduced chance of finding a modem sector job. But if not all of them do that, there must be some reason for it. The reason, I suggest, is that if all were to enter the informal sector and search for formal sector employment from there, they would drive the informal sector wage down so low that it would be in some of their interests to alter their behavior. Some would therefore pursue modem sector jobs more intensively and search while unemployed.

Finally, it might also be asked: Why does anyone remain in agriculture? If it is possible to earn a wage in the urban informal sector and have a non-zero chance of obtaining a modem sector job, why stay in agriculture, where the chance of getting a modem sector job is small if not zero? The answer is that workers who stay in agriculture must be compensated for their lack of access to the formal sector by being paid a higher wage than they could earn in the urban informal sector. Put differently, in equilibrium, the wage in the urban informal sector must turn out to be sufficiently below the wage in agriculture for it to be advantageous for some workers to choose to remain in agriculture, as indeed they do.

We are now in a position to understand what must be the case for all three labor market strategies [(*i*)–(*iii*) above] to be chosen: if the chance of getting a modem sector job is highest while unemployed, next highest while employed in the urban informal sector, and lowest (or zero) while employed in agriculture, the wage must be higher in agriculture than in the urban informal sector (which is in turn higher than the transfer income while unemployed). This reasoning therefore predicts that an economy with these features will reach an equilibrium in which urban poverty will be widespread and more serious than rural poverty – a quite plausible explanation for the existence of miserable Third World urban slums.

In Fields (1975), I extended the model just presented in other ways: by allowing for on-the-job search for modem sector employment while in agriculture, by introducing differential educational qualifications and allowing for the possibility that modem sector employers might hire the better educated preferentially, and by embedding all of these extensions of the Harris-Todaro model in a multi-period framework. Because these extensions do not have a bearing on the characterization of the informal sector per se, I shall not elaborate upon them here.

Since the appearance of my 1975 paper (which received favorable attention from, among others, Todaro, 1976 and Krueger, 1983), other models have appeared. Stark (1982) published a model of the informal sector similar in a great many respects (even notation). I do not find any additional insights in that paper which were not already in the models cited above.

Harris and Sabot (1982) reiterated one of the major conclusions of my model: that the urban informal sector wage is predicted to end up below the rural wage. They then adopted a standard job search formulation from labor economics and discussed how this class of models might be generalized to allow for searching from among a wide range of urban wage offers; but because their model is so general, it does not produce any specific results.

The models discussed thus far have not treated skill differences among workers. Yet, it is a well-established empirical fact that workers with more education or training have a higher chance of working in the better sectors of an economy. My 1975 model allows for this (Fields, 1975, Section 8). The possibility is raised that education might be necessary to qualify for better-paying jobs in the formal sector. The model also allows for the possibility that, if there are surplus educated workers relative to the demand for them in the better jobs, some might take their education to the informal sector, where they might be more productive or be hired preferentially for wage jobs.

Cole and Sanders (1985) have formulated a model which also has formal and informal sectors in the urban economy as well as rural sector and workers who differ in educational qualifications. Their model has a number of desirable features, including intersectoral linkages, expected wage equalization among alternative search strategies, and specification of the demand and supply sides of informal sector output. It has a number of defects, though. One is that according to their specification, workers migrate either in search of formal sector jobs or in search of informal sector jobs but that these are mutually exclusive strategies. They thereby exclude on-the-job search from the informal sector – a not very realistic assumption.

Another very recent line of work bears mention. We now know that on-the-job search raises an additional complication not recognized by myself in my 1975 paper or by subsequent authors working in a similar tradition, including McDonald and Solow (1985). This is that workers' choices among search strategies ex ante are not the same as the ex post outcomes. Ex ante, workers begin by allocating themselves between the three postulated search strategies such that the three expected wages are equalized. But when there is on-the-job search, some of those who started in agriculture or in the urban informal sector get modern sector jobs, hence leave the sectors they began in. Consequently, the rural labor force and the urban informal sector labor force will be smaller *ex post* than *ex ante*, and likewise, the urban labor force will be larger than the number of urban searchers *ex ante*. One implication of this is that even in a rational expectations equilibrium, the average urban and rural wages will not equalize. Another is that urban unemployment will be smaller the more efficient is on-the-job search from the informal sector. For details, see Fields (1987).

A final line of work deserves mention. A model with diversity within non-formal urban activities has been constructed by Steel and Takagi (1983). They distinguish "small scale enterprises" from the "residual sector" within nonformal activities. However, a number of specific features of the model make it less than fully satisfactory for analyzing the informal sector:

(i) Some of the key variables are approximated rather than solved directly.

(ii) An earlier error made by Todaro (1969) is repeated: the failure to distinguish the probability that a worker will get a modem sector job (which is a transition probability) from the probability that a worker will have become and will continue to be employed in a modern sector job (which is a state probability).

(iii) All who are engaged in "small scale enterprises" or in the "residual sector" are assumed to be searching for formal sector jobs. However, the small scale sector does not receive workers who have accumulated capital in formal sector jobs. This is inconsistent with empirical evidence on the small scale sector, to which we now turn.

7.5   Challenges and Responses

The empirical observations cited in Section 7.2 and the resultant theoretical formulations contained in Section 7.3 led to a well-defined view of what the informal sector is and how it interrelates with the rest of the labor market. But almost immediately after these views were put forth, and continuing up to the present, empirical researchers have challenged the earlier views. The purpose of this section is to review and critique the available evidence.

7.5.1 *Challenges to the Earlier Views*

The following challenges have appeared in the literature:

Claim 1: What appears to be free-entry isn't. According to Sinclair (1978, pp. 96-97), "the belief that entry into informal occupations is easy is widespread." He cites studies of Indonesia (Sethuraman, 1975) and Brazil (Merrick, 1976), as well as more general analyses (Reynolds, 1969) in support of this view, but then offers contradictory evidence of his own from Nigeria and elsewhere. It has also been argued that past researchers have been fooled by their own observations. In this view, outside observers who look in at the informal sector and see people begging, selling things on the streets, or working in illegal or quasi-legal activities are mistaken in inferring that anyone who wishes to engage in such activities can freely do so. The argument is this: Anyone who tries begging in front of the Hilton Hotel will quickly find that someone very strong and powerful will come along and either shoo that person away, by force if necessary, or demand a sizable amount of protection money to permit the beggar to remain.

The response is that although many activities which might appear to be free-entry in fact are not, it is nonetheless true that there exist opportunities for those who wish to to enter some sorts of urban activities and earn at least some cash, even if earnings are low, the work unsteady, and protection minimal at best. This is all that the established view requires. House's study of Nairobi finds exactly this (0984, pp. 282–284):

> The popular image of the informal sector is that it is easy to enter because skill levels are low and the amount of money required to set up in business is insignificant ... [My findings show that] entry to the sector is clearly not as easy as the popular image would have us believe ... Clearly, business proprietors in the informal sector are urban residents of long standing and not young, recent migrants ...

However, the survey findings reported below reveal that employees in the sector are much younger and more recent immigrants to Nairobi than their employers. For them the informal sector offers the promise of a way into an urban existence, albeit at a bare subsistence level.

Claim 2: The earnings of informal sector workers are lower on average than earnings in the formal sector. However, informal sector earnings are not uniformly lower. Rather, the two distributions exhibit substantial overlap. The theory supposes that workers in the informal sector earn less than formal sector workers, and mat for this reason, they seek to leave the informal sector if they can. The evidence is in part consistent with this, in that the average wages among urban informal sector workers are generally reported to be lower than those among formal sector workers. Among those reporting such findings are Merrick (1975) for workers in Belo Horizonte, Brazil, Webb (1975) for Peru, Kugler et al. (1979) and Bourguignon (1979) for Colombia, and Pang and Liu (1975) for Singapore.

Despite these average differences, the evidence also appears to show that the earnings distributions in the two sectors have substantial overlap. Here, for example, are Webb's findings for Peru:

Table 7.1. Urban labor force by monthly income, in US$, Peru

Income	Informal (%)	Formal Blue-Collar (%)
0–23	32	9
24–26	27	20
47–115	29	60
116–230	8	11
231+	4	1
Average	50	68

Source: Webb (1975)

Taking the self-employed as "an important category of the informal sector," Mazumdar (1976, p. 662) cites the following examples of overlapping distributions: the work of Webb for Peru, showing that 37 percent of the self-employed earned as much or more as the modal earnings of formal sector workers; Sabot's (1975) work on Tanzania, in which the income of the self-employed is shown to be less equally distributed than the income of wage earners; and Mazumdar's own work on Malaysia, in which the male self-employed were found to earn only slightly less at any given age than male employees. And reflecting the view that "the tertiary sector is tacitly accepted to be the substantial part of both the informal sector and the self-employed in the urban labor market," Mazumdar (1976, p. 666) examined the available evidence for Malaysia, Brazil, and Korea and found a "lack of factual basis behind the popular myth about the tertiary sector" (p. 670).

Claim 3: The earnings of informal sector workers are not lower than the earnings of agricultural workers. The theory of Section 7.4 led to the conclusion that the earnings of urban informal sector workers should be less than the earnings of comparable agricultural workers. If earnings are quoted in nominal pesos, rupees, or whatever, one reason that informal sector workers might be observed to have higher earnings than agricultural workers is that the urban cost-of-living is higher than the rural cost-of-living. Of course, such differences should be standardized for.

An example of evidence which at first glance appears to contradict the predictions of the theory is the work of Webb (1975). He classified

Peruvian workers on the basis of their relative importance in the four quartiles of the country-wide income distribution in 1970. He found:

Table 7.2. Percentage of labor force in each category in quartiles, Peru, 1961

	Poorest	Second	Third	Richest
Urban formal	0	4.0	26.0	70.0
Urban Informal	9.5	29.8	39.4	20.0
Rural traditional	45.8	24.9	16.0	13.4

Source: Webb (1975)

From this, he concluded:

> Though urban cost of living differences inflate the apparent real incomes of urban residents, most urban incomes surpass the limiting income for the bottom quartile by a longer than any plausible correction (sic). The common assertion that urban workers (except for a lucky few placed in modern establishments) are no better off than the rural poor, is an erroneous generalization derived from the case of the urban fringe: the poorest (and most visible) 5-10 per cent.

> Webb, 1975, p. 29, cited in Mazumdar, 1976, p. 671.

Claim 4: Because informal sector workers have been in that sector a long time, the "staging area hypothesis" is wrong. The extended Harris-Todaro theory suggests that some number of job aspirants for the formal sector begin their search in the urban informal sector. This is sometimes called the "staging area hypothesis," in that the urban informal sector is regarded as a temporary stopping-off ground through which workers pass as they move into formal employment. It is thought to relate to migration, insofar as people migrate from rural to urban areas in the hopes of improving their chances of being hired for formal sector jobs, most of which are typically located in urban areas.

Some of the evidence purporting to contradict this hypothesis is the following. In Belo Horizonte, Merrick (1975, p. 21) found that the proportions of native-born and migrants in the informal sector were more or less the same. Webb (1975) found that 63 percent of workers in the urban informal sector were migrants and that an identical 63 percent of formal sector workers were migrants. Formal sector workers had resided in the city for an average of 16.9 years, as compared with an average of 15.3 years among informal sector workers. Sabot (1975) found that of migrants in urban Tanzania, 60 percent had been self-employed for 5½ years or more. Mazumdar (1983, p. 257) reports that graduation from the informal sector factory workers at the time of the survey whose first jobs were in other urban wage sectors was about 25 percent. In urban Malaysia, the proportion was a little higher, because the survey included movement out of self-employment. Steel and

Takagi (1983, p. 427) cite a number of other studies showing that workers commonly find "permanent employment" in small firms rather than as temporary positions while in transition to modern sector employment.

What does this mean? It does not tell us anything about workers' intentions about leaving the informal sector, which is my understanding about what the "staging area hypothesis" is all about. At best, we learn from such evidence about workers' opportunities to leave. If we wish to know about workers' intentions to leave, we must get more direct information.

Claim 5: The urban informal sector is not the major source of recruitment for the urban formal sector. Formal sector jobs are often filled by rural residents. The Indian case is well-documented. Banerjee (1983) found that a worker newly-hired into the formal sector of New Delhi was six times as likely to have come from the rural area as from the urban informal sector. Mazumdar (1978) and Poppola (1977) reached the same qualitative finding for Bombay and Ahmedabad respectively.

Although this evidence poses a problem for the Harris-Todaro model, it is not a problem for the extended Harris-Todaro model. The Harris-Todaro model rules out recruitment of rural workers for formal sector jobs by assumption, so evidence that most of those hired in the formal sector come from rural areas is clearly at odds with the assumptions of the model. However, the extended Harris-Todaro model (e.g., Fields, 1975) allows rural workers to have a non-zero probability of finding a modern sector job. If rural workers have a good chance of securing a modern sector job relative to informal sector workers or the unemployed, the extended Harris-Todaro model implies that in societies like India where most of the people are in rural areas, most of the jobs will be filled by rural residents. There is no contradiction here.

Claim 6: Many people are in the urban informal sector by choice, not because they are forced into it. The theory of Section 7.3 suggests that people are in the urban informal sector partly by choice and partly not. They are hypothesized to be in the informal sector by choice in the sense that they could have remained in rural areas, yet they left those areas in the pursuit of something better. They are hypothesized to be in the informal sector not by choice in the sense that once in that sector, they would willingly leave it and move into formal sector employment if such employment were offered, but because no such employment is offered, they remain where they are.

The evidence is at odds with this viewpoint on two counts. 1) Many of those in the informal sector say they are not looking for formal sector jobs. Many say that they migrated to the urban area specifically to take up informal sector employment. For instance, Banerjee (1983, p. 414) found in a study of migrant heads of households in Delhi: "Forty-one per cent of those who entered the informal wage sector continued job

163

search ... Thus, it can be claimed with some confidence that a sizable proportion, possibly one-half or more, of migrants who entered the informal wage sector and the non-wage sector had been attracted to the city by opportunities in these sectors, and did not consider employment there as a means of survival while waiting in the queue for formal sector jobs." A similar conclusion has been reached in unpublished work on Korea by Rhee (1986). 2) A significant number of workers now in the informal sector previously had worked in the formal sector. The net flow of labor was actually found to be from the formal sector to the informal sector in studies by Mazumdar (1981) of Malaysia and Balan et al. (1973) of Mexico.

Of all of the challenges to the empirical relevance of the theoretical model, this is the most serious. I shall return to it later. But first, before accepting the proffered evidence, let us look carefully at the definitions used, and hence what the evidence in fact is.

7.5.2   How the UIS Is Defined in Empirical Studies

Critical to any attempt to judge the preceding evidence is the practical matter of how the urban informal sector concept has been operationalized in these studies. The ILO has taken the lead on this. In the words of Sethuraman (1981, p. 17): informal sector "... consists of small-scale units engaged in the production and distribution of goods and services with the primary objective of generating employment and incomes to their participants notwithstanding the constraints on capital, both physical and human, and knowhow." In practice, the working definition used in many studies is based on firm size; firms employing five workers or fewer are classified as informal. Sometimes, workers in certain occupational categories are also classified as informal; typically, self-employed workers (excluding professionals or those with higher levels of education) and unpaid family workers are so included. PREALC (the ILO's regional program for employment in Latin America) has adopted the following definition: "The informal labor market consists of those persons who develop activities for self-employment, those who work in small firms and those who provide low-productivity personal services" (PREALC, 1974, cited in Tokman, 1979, p. 75. Translation mine.)

Other researchers have defined the urban informal sector in similar ways in their empirical research. Webb defined the informal sector to be small firms, plus all of the self-employed except for those in the liberal professions. Merrick defined the informal sector to be those employers who did not make payments to Brazil's social security system. Banerjee classified workers as belonging to the formal sector if they were employed in government or public sector establishments or in privately owned establishments employing twenty or more workers; all others were classified as informal. Mazumdar regarded workers in the factory sector as formal and those in small-scale enterprises and casual employment as informal.

One is hard-pressed to see how these working definitions of the informal sector conform to the earlier notions based on free-entry. Only Mazumdar's even comes close.

7.5.3 A Restatement of Results

Given the preceding definitions and empirical operationalizations, the actual findings of the studies cited in Section 7.5.1 can be restated. We may say that for some countries, the evidence shows:

(i) Some of the activities which appear to be free-entry are not.

(ii) The earnings of workers in small firms are lower on average than the earnings in large firms. However, the earnings in small firms are not uniformly lower. Rather, the two distributions overlap.

(iii) The earnings of workers in small urban firms are not lower than the earnings of rural traditional workers.

(iv) Those presently working in small firms, in firms not covered by social security, and in self-employment have been in those jobs for long periods of time.

(v) Formal sector jobs are mostly filled by rural residents, not by informal sector workers.

(vi) Many of those who are in small firms and in self-employment are there by choice.

When the studies are viewed this way – in terms of what the evidence actually shows rather than in terms of the labels and terminology of the authors – the early theoretical models are found for the most part not to be seriously challenged or contradicted by the empirical evidence.

There is one exception, though: contrary to the earlier theoretical models, empirical studies show that workers do indeed move into the informal sector by choice. Because this point leads to a major conclusion of this paper, I elaborate on it at some length below.

7.6 Some Economic Anthropology – Type Findings

To get a better handle on the workings of the informal sector labor market, I led a research team in conducting a series of interviews with informal sector workers in the two cities: Kuala Lumpur, Malaysia and San José, Costa Rica. Three major findings emerged.

7.6.1 *Diversity within the Informal Sector*

Informal activities prove to be quite diverse. Some are activities with easy entry and no fixed hours of operation. They may be characterized by self-employment or employment of unpaid family labor or of unskilled labor with non-specific work relations. By contrast, other informal activities exhibit limited entry due to higher set-up costs and/or complicated licensing requirements, irregular hours of operation, and employment of family labor and unskilled labor with semi-specified work relations. These contrast with formal sector enterprises, which are characterized by restricted entry, regular place and hours of operation, and employment of non-family labor with specific work relations. These belong in the category of formal sector, even if they are very small in scale. One example would be professional services companies which, although small in scale, cannot be viewed in any meaningful way as part of the informal sector.

Some examples may help clarify the distinction between the three types of activities. In transportation, trishaws in Malaysia (pedi-cabs) are examples of easy entry activities. They require very little capital investment. They are usually operated and owned by one person. Their owners operate them at irregular hours and at negotiable prices. No particular skill is required to be a pedi-cab driver. Typical of the upper-tier informal activities are the individually owned and operated taxi-cabs. Taxis are much more expensive to purchase than trishaws and the operating costs of taxis are much higher. Hours of operation can be regular or irregular, and the owner may hire a second driver to operate at different times of day (such as the night shift). Finally, there are the large established taxi companies which own a fleet of vehicles and hire a number of drivers to operate them. The taxi-drivers are expected to report to work at regular, agreed-upon hours. Sometimes they are paid fixed wages, sometimes a percentage of the fares. These taxi companies are examples of formal sector activities.

In commerce, street-vending is an obvious representative of free-entry activities. Street-vending (e.g., a sugar cane juice stand or a fruit stand) requires relatively low set-up costs. There is no skill requirement to this work. Street-vending licenses are easily procured. Location rental fees are nominal. Hours of operation are irregular. Paid employees are rare; even unpaid family workers are not very numerous. For the upper-tier informal sector in the commerce industry, examples are small retail stores such as sundry shops. They face higher set-up costs than do street-vendors because of higher rental fees and also because more licenses are involved.

Although these shops are opened and closed at the same hours on most days, they may without notice close up earlier or not open at all at the wish of their owners. These shops are usually family-run with some hired help. The hired workers can be non-relatives, although relatives are sometimes employed with semi-specified responsibilities. Supermarkets owned by a large company exemplify the formal sector in commerce.

In manufacturing, backyard industries belong to the easy entry informal sector. Entry is easy because capital costs are small and rental fees are minimal, since the owners live and work in the same house. These backyard industries use manual labor, sometimes with very few tools. Workers may have to put in long hours to fill an order, or when there is no order, the shop may have to close up. These workers are usually family members or paid relatives and are generally unskilled. The small manufacturing industries in the upper-tier informal sector have higher capital and property costs. Because of the kinds of machinery used and the larger number of workers hired in these activities, licensing requirements may be more complicated and time-consuming. Workers in the upper-tier informal sector are both family members and hired laborers who are either unskilled or semi-skilled. Work relations are semi-formal.

Thus, within the informal sector, we find considerable diversity. The UIS does not consist uniformly of free-entry, low-wage, unorganized enterprises and workers, although, some activities do indeed fit this characterization; I would refer to these as the easy entry informal sector. Others do not. These others have significant barriers to entry, higher capital or skill requirements, and fairly regular labor relations arrangements; yet, they too may also be small, employ family labor, and operate at irregular hours and places. I shall refer to these as the upper-tier informal sector. In Malaysia and Costa Rica, there are really two urban informal sectors.

7.6.2 *Voluntary Participation in Upper-Tier Informal Activities but Not Easy Entry Ones*

Another major conclusion from the interviews is that many people are in informal activities by choice. When asked their reasons for doing what they were doing, many informal workers in Costa Rica gave the following answers most frequently: *i)* They felt they could make more money at the informal sector job they were doing than they could earn in the formal sector, or *ii)* Even though they made a little less money, they enjoyed their work more, because it allowed them to choose their own hours, to work in the open air, to talk to friends, etc.

Here are some examples of such people. One man, 46 years old, sells a peanut-sugar-butter candy called "melcochas" in downtown San José. He has been selling melcochas on the streets for 37 years, and before that his father made and sold them. He was very insistent that he was there voluntarily, doing what he likes to do, and that it pays better than formal sector work. His brother had, at one time, started up a small factory making melcochas, which he then sold to the public. The brother eventually gave up this factory because he realized that he could make more money selling in the streets himself. That is, the informal sector work paid better than formal sector work.

Another interview was with a 50-year-old man selling fruit on a corner. This man had worked in the United States in several paid positions, and could easily have become a formal sector job in Costa Rica. Yet he sold fruits, because he earned more money (US $36 a day) than in any other type of work he could get in San José.

These examples illustrate what I call the constrained voluntary nature of much upper-tier informal activity. That is, given the constrained choices open to them, a great many of informal sector workers are in that sector voluntarily. These people know that job opportunities are available in the urban formal sectors for people like themselves and mat they could get such jobs. Yet, they choose not to seek such jobs, the foremost reason being that they prefer the combination of monetary rewards and psychic aspects of their informal sector jobs.

Of course, not all informal sector activities are of such a type. Many people face such severely constrained options that the informal sector involvement can only be seen as their making the best of a bad situation. Representative of this kind of informal sector activity is a woman sitting on a market street in Kuala Lumpur, garlics set out on a piece of newspaper in front of her for sale. She calls out the price of her products to shoppers who pass by. Whenever she sells off her garlics, she is ready to go home. If the market turns out to be slow for the day, she sometimes stays for longer hours; other times, she sells her products at a substantial discount. If it happens to be raining, she takes the day off. This kind of activity is clearly small in scale. It also has free entry; all anyone has to do to enter similar economic activity is buy a supply of garlics from a rack jobber. The owner is self-employed and manages her business in a very casual (though not necessarily inefficient) way. She is very poor.

7.6.3 Linkages between the Formal Sector and Informal Sector Labor Markets

A third important conclusion is that the upper-tier informal sector and the easy entry informal sector are linked to the formal sector in very different ways. Whereas most participants in the easy entry sector reported themselves dissatisfied with their positions and sought better jobs in the formal sector, those in the upper-tier informal sector had typically come from the formal sector and were glad to leave the formal sector behind.

There are barriers to entry to many upper-tier informal sector activities. One needs skills and tools to repair shoes or watches. Even to sell fruit, one needs capital for the initial stock, contacts with fruit wholesalers in the market, and money to buy a license for a good street location. However, these barriers can be overcome by working in the formal sector.

The formal sector was found to provide training for workers to move into upper-tier small-scale employment. Examples are food industry workers who leave jobs in the formal sector to set up their own small food processing activities, office-workers who leave to work in small family stores, and repairmen who learn their trades in large work places and then leave to set up their own shops. In Costa Rica, a study by the Ministry of Planning found that more than 70 percent of those self-employed in the informal sector had previously held wage or salary jobs in the formal sector. This finding was reaffirmed in our interviews of such workers in San José.

The formal sector also provides the opportunity for workers to accumulate savings to start up their own businesses. Examples are repairmen and small manufacturers who save part of their wages to buy their own machinery, tools, and raw materials for use in their own businesses. In Costa Rica, these savings from formal sector jobs are a much more important source of finance for new businesses than are loans from banks or other financial institutions.

At the other end of the spectrum, the formal sector was found to employ preferentially those workers who have acquired training in the easy entry segment of the informal sector. Examples are managers of appliance stores who had previously worked in small family businesses. These people tend to be young and well-educated. The growth of the formal sector enables workers to move out of the easy entry informal sector into newly-created formal sectors jobs. This is especially true in Malaysia, where the economy has been on a sustained positive economic growth path. It is much less the case in Costa Rica, where the severe economic crisis of the early 1980s led to a loss of formal sector employment. Examples in Malaysia are young people who start out in family stores but end up as clerks in fast-food restaurants or as mechanics in car-repair shops – jobs that have opened up due to the growth of the formal sector.

Although on balance the linkages between the informal sector and the formal sector were found to be positive, there is one identifiable group of losers among informal sector firms: those who fail to respond to the dynamic changes in the economy. Yet, a repeated finding from the interviews in Malaysia and Costa Rica, as surprising as it was consistent, is that those who do not respond often have deliberately decided not to. Many do not want to change. For example, proprietors of small family shops (often older people) prefer to go on operating them in much the same way as before despite growing competition from shopping centers Another reason for losing out due to economic growth, much less common than the first, is technical change. An example is the reluctance of watch repairmen to enter new lines of work despite the fact that demand for their services has plummeted due to the advent of cheap digital watches which cost less to replace than to repair. It was rare for informal sector workers to report that they themselves or others in similar lines of work lost out because they were squeezed by formal sector firms.

7.7 Conclusions

7.7.1 *Major Findings*

The analysis of urban labor markets has gone beyond the simple dichotomy between formal sector and unemployment. The existence of non-formal employment is well-recognized in what has now come to be called the "urban informal sector".

It is clear that urban labor markets in developing countries possess a sector with all the characteristics postulated many years ago: virtually unrestricted entry, low wages or self-employment incomes, irregular work hours and work place, lack of protection and regulation. What distinguishes this sector is that it is not a "target of employment" for job-aspirants. Persons working in that sector are at the bottom of the job structure and hope to get out. Existing theoretical models have done a good job of capturing the essential features of this type of activity.

More recent empirical studies raise some new issues/findings which do not fit neatly into classification of the urban labor market into just the categories of formal employment, informal employment, and unemployment.

When one tries to define the urban informal sector in a manner consistent with the empirical evidence, one finds that there exists yet another category of urban employment: restricted-entry self-employment. The workers in this sector have willingly left formal sector employment, because the wages and/or working conditions are better if they work on their own. This sector is not a free-entry sector: sizable accumulations of financial and/or human capital are required to enter it.

The upper-tier informal sector has not yet been worked into theoretical models. In order to integrate it, researchers will need to specify how this sector works, what determines incomes in it, how workers gain entry into it, etc.

Empirically-implementable ways need to be devised to identify the easy entry self-employment sector in a household survey program.

Because the term "urban informal sector" refers to widely disparate activities, some of which are preferable to formal sector employment and some of which are not, the use of one all-inclusive term invites the neglect of that sector's fundamental duality. To distinguish between the different parts of the informal sector, I suggest the terms "easy entry informal sector" and "upper-tier informal sector."

7.7.2 Implications for Further Study

I have concluded that the urban informal sector consists of two distinct groups which need to be conceptualized and analysed separately. Some activities are easy entry and low-wage, and the workers and enterprises in those activities are unorganized and unprotected. People in those activities seek to get out of them. Other activities have significant barriers to entry, higher capital or skill requirements, and fairly regular labor relations arrangements. People aspire to those activities. It is a mistake to talk of these two segments as if they were one.

The conclusion about the desirability of breaking urban nonformal employment into two groups has important implications, one empirical and one theoretical.

The empirical implication is that the two sectors must be considered as different entities in subsequent empirical studies. It is not obvious how to do this, so it will take much careful thought. As regards existing data sets, researchers will have to investigate their potentiality for yielding up information on questions of interest. As for surveys yet to be administered, they should be designed so that the necessary distinctions can be drawn.

The theoretical implication is that although the models we now have possess quite a number of valuable features which should form the basis for subsequent theoretical efforts, they need to build in another sector: the restricted-entry self-employment sector, into which workers may enter only upon completing a work spell of sufficient length in the formal sector. One way of doing this would be to formulate a three-period model with work in a free-entry job followed by promotion to the urban formal sector and then by work in the restricted-entry self-employment sector as a possible work trajectory. Another would be to build an n-period model with Markov chains linking up the various sectors.

In addition, the model should be generalized in other directions. One desirable development is to refine the analysis of education as a determinant of earnings and intersectoral mobility. Another is to deal with sources of differences among individuals such as their personal characteristics, rural opportunities, and family and social contacts.

Both the empirical and the theoretical tasks are formidable.

8

Changes over Time in Individual Countries

8.1 The experiences of major developing economies[1]

8.1.1 *China*[2]

Economic growth has brought about a sharp reduction in poverty. China combines the most rapid economic growth of any country in the world – 10% a year in real terms – with the largest reduction in poverty ever recorded: a reduction of 500 million persons in the quarter-century ending in 2005 living on less than $2.00 per person per day. *China's urban unemployment rate is now moderate, having fallen in the 2000s*. Rural unemployment data are not available, so the unemployment figures for China are limited to urban areas. The official unemployment rate among local residents in urban areas ("registered unemployment") is 4.2%. In addition, however, the urban unemployment has been estimated approximating the ILO definition – that is, including migrants as well as persons with urban household registration and workers in unregistered employment in addition to workers in registered employment in both numerator and denominator. This so-called "surveyed unemployment rate" (so called because it is based on household survey data) is found to be 5.2% (Yang and Gu, 2010). And when international methods are applied – that is, calculating unemployment as the difference between total employment and labor force and then calculating the unemployment rate as the ratio of unemployment to labor force – China's urban unemployment rate is

The original version of this chapter was published as: Fields, Gary S. (2012). Challenges and policy lessons for the growth-employment-poverty nexus in developing countries, in: IZA Journal of Labor Policy, 1(6). © 2012 by Springer Berlin Heidelberg.

estimated to have peaked at nearly 10% in 2000 before falling to around 6% by 2008 (Arnal and Förster, 2010).

For the most part, the mix of jobs has improved. Urban employment, which pays four times what rural employment does, engages a larger percentage of the labor force than previously. This is because of rural-to-urban migration, not because of birth rate differences; China continues to adhere rigidly to its one-child policy. Workers have been moving out of agriculture (a low-paying activity) and into manufacturing (especially in township and village enterprises) and services. Workers have also been moving out of self-employment and into wage employment. In all of these respects, then, the mix of jobs has improved. In one other respect, though, the job mix has worsened, at least from the point of view of workers: as a consequence of economic and labor market reforms, there was a sharp cut in public sector employment; these were the jobs with the highest pay, most generous benefits, and iron-clad job security.

Real labor earnings have increased sharply. Compared to 1995, real urban earnings are five times higher now and rural labor earnings nearly three times higher. Among formal sector workers, real wages rose rapidly overall, in each ownership type (state-owned enterprises, collectively-owned enterprises, and other ownership types), and in every region of China.

Household income inequality and labor income inequality have both increased. Urban labor incomes were twice rural labor incomes in 1995; they are now four times as high. Urban–rural earnings differentials persist after controlling for human capital variables. Migrants to urban areas earn only about half of what urban residents do.[3] Overall, income inequality in China has been rising.

In summary: The Chinese labor market has played a central role in transmitting economic growth to workers, thereby reducing poverty. There have been huge improvements in many aspects of labor market conditions in the course of Chinese economic growth: reductions in unemployment, improved employment composition, rapidly rising real labor earnings. However, despite an enormous reduction in absolute poverty, income inequality in China is increasing; this issue is receiving a great deal of attention in Chinese policy circles at present.

8.1.2 *India*[4]

Indian economic growth is high and accelerating; the Indian economy was, until very recently, the second-fastest growing economy in the world (after China). The changes in labor market conditions in the course of Indian economic growth are as follows:

Low and falling unemployment. Using the definition of unemployment closest to the ILO's, the data show that India's unemployment rate stayed right around 3% from 1983 to 2004/05, then fell to 2.6% in 2009/10.

Composition of employment. Indian workers remain employed overwhelmingly in informal employment. As stated earlier, 86% of Indian workers are in the informal sector and another 7% are informal workers in the formal sector; just 7% of Indian workers are formal workers. Essentially all of the increase in employment in India has been in informal employment; but because the rate of informal employment is so high and the rate of formal employment so low to begin with, the shares of formal and informal employment in the total have barely changed.

As for other aspects of employment composition, over time, the composition of employment improved so that a larger percentage of the employed were in regular wage employment and casual wage employment and a smaller percentage in self-employment. Still, though, 57% of Indian workers are self-employed and 28% are casual wage employees. As for the composition of employment by economic sector, it too has changed, so that agriculture's share of the total fell and industry's share rose, consistent with a shift to higher-paying activities. (Services' share increased as well, but this change is not easy to interpret owing to the heterogeneity of the services sector.) However, because these changes have been rather slow, the structure of employment is not much different from what it was earlier. Agriculture's share fell from 64.9% of total employment to 54.6% over a twenty-year period; thus, agriculture remains the majority employer in India even now. The education level in India is improving, but it still remains very low: 50% of the female labor force and more than 20% of the male labor force have no education at all, and the education that is received remains highly variable in quality.

Real wages. Where the main improvement in Indian labor market conditions has been recorded is in real wages. Positive wage growth was recorded between 1993/94 and 2004/05 for all sixteen employment groups analyzed. (The sixteen groups are rural male/rural female/urban male/urban female cross-classified by regular/casual and agriculture/non-agriculture.) Between 1993/94 and 2004/05, real wages grew at only about half the rate of growth of the economy as a whole; but between 2004/05 and 2009/10, real wages grew at about the same rate as the economy as a whole. Moreover, these wage increases were at about the same rate in regular wage employment, casual wage employment, and the informal sector; the only important group whose wages rose at a slower rate is formal sector workers.

Inequality. Income inequality in India has been rising. See, for instance, Asian Development Bank (2007) and ILO (2008).

Poverty. In India, the percentage of workers in households below a constant real absolute poverty line fell continuously, overall and for each employment status (regular wage and salaried workers, the self-employed, and casual labor). *In Summary.* Indian economic growth was rapid, labor market conditions improved, but the improvements in types of employment were slow compared to the rapid economic growth. In recent years, though, real wages in most employment categories have been rising apace of economic growth.

8.1.3 *Brazil*[5]

In the period from 1996 to 2004, the Brazilian economy experienced real per capita economic growth of less than 1 percent a year, during which poverty increased. Given the importance of labor income in total income in Brazil as elsewhere, it would be expected that very slow economic growth and an increase in poverty would be accompanied by a mixed pattern of changes in the labor market, with some indicators registering an improvement and some a deterioration. Indeed, the data show exactly that.

There were signs of progress. They include an improved sectoral mix of employment, higher educational levels of the employed, a higher proportion of employed in wage and salaried employment, shorter weekly work hours, a reduced child work rate, higher participation in social security, and a reduction in unpaid work. Many of these changes were very modest in magnitude.

On the other hand, there were also signs of regress. Unemployment rose, median earnings fell, and earnings inequality rose for several groups. The percentage of workers holding signed labor cards and receiving the consequent employment protections fell further from an already low level.

In summary, important labor market problems remain in Brazil. They include high unemployment, low earnings, lack of participation in social security, lack of employment protection, and significant unpaid family work.

8.1.4 *Mexico*[6]

Between 2000 and 2006, the Mexican economy grew at an average annual rate of 2.9% in real terms. During this growth period overall unemployment increased in Mexico by one percentage point from 2000 to 2006. However, the unemployment rate in 2006 was still very low: just 3.6%. Mexico's chief labor market problem is not unemployment; it is low earnings.

The composition of employment improved. Compared to 2000, a smaller percentage of Mexicans were working in the low-paying primary sector (agriculture and related activities) in 2006 and more in the higher-paying trade and services sectors. A larger percentage of workers had completed high school or above and a smaller percentage were illiterate. However, there was hardly any change in the sources of workers' earnings (wage and salaried employment, business, and other).

Real labor market earnings increased, overall and for most groups. Average real monthly earnings grew by 1.2%, which was less than the growth rate of GDP. Wage and salaried workers' average monthly earnings rose, the average earnings of workers deriving their incomes from business declined, and the average earnings of workers with incomes from other sources rose. Earnings rose for both males and females. And they rose for workers in every economic sector (primary, trade, manufacturing, services, public sector, and other).

The poverty rates in Mexico fell using three different poverty lines, in both urban and rural areas.

Income inequality in Mexico fell. A Lorenz-improvement took place, and therefore all Lorenz-consistent inequality measures such as the Gini coefficient register falling inequality.

In summary: Mexican economic growth was accompanied by rising unemployment, improved employment composition, rising real labor earnings, and falling poverty and inequality.

8.1.5   South Africa[7]

Following the fall of apartheid in 1993, the South African economy grew at an average annual rate of nearly 3% in real terms in the next fifteen years. After adjusting for population growth, real per capita GDP averaged 1.4% growth over that same period.

In terms of the labor market indicators identified in this report, we find: *Unemployment in South Africa rose dramatically in the first half of the period and started to fall only in the early 2000s.* Using the standard international definition of unemployment (the ILO definition), the unemployment rate rose from 13.6% in 1993 to 28.9% in 2001 before falling to 23.4% by 2008. Another, broader definition of unemployment is commonly used in South Africa, including in addition persons who were not working, were not searching for work, but report that they are willing to take a job. The broad unemployment rate too rose in the earlier period (from 31.2% to 40.8% between 1993 and 2001) before falling to 28.9% by 2008. Words like "frightful" and "catastrophic" are used to describe unemployment rates of such magnitudes. The exceptionally high unemployment rate in South Africa is accompanied by an exceptionally low rate of informal wage-employment and self-employment. Workers in South Africa have not responded to the lack of wage-employment opportunities by creating their own self-employment positions to the same extent as have workers in most other countries. In most developing countries, informal employment comprises about three-quarters of non-agricultural employment. In South Africa, the rate is one-half. Among the barriers to creation of informal employment in South Africa are geographic separation of would-be self-employed from markets, crime, lack of access to infrastructure, lack of access to services, insufficient skills, hassles from the local authorities, harsh licensing requirements, and insufficient informal credit. Instead, the unemployed in South Africa have attached themselves to households with income from the labor market and/or social grants.

Various indicators of employment composition show a worsening job mix. Among those who are employed in South Africa, we find an increased rate of part-time and casual employment, a higher share of informal employment (defined as those working in a business that is not registered with the government, plus domestic workers), and a shrinking rate of wage and salaried employment as a percentage of total employment over time.

Real monthly wages grew, but in a very unequal way. Average wages increased overall and for most races (African, Indian, and white) but not for coloreds. ("Coloreds" is the South African term for persons of mixed race.) But real wages rose only in the top two labor income deciles; in the other eight, real wages fell. For the poorest decile, the decline was a stunning 43%.

Household poverty rates fell, using the $1.25 PPP dollar and $2.00 PPP dollar poverty lines described above. The fall in poverty is due to South Africa's system of social grants and not to changes in the labor market. Despite the falling poverty rates, the percentages of South Africans recorded as poor using these poverty lines were respectively 17.7% and 30.0% in 2008. The poor in South Africa are overwhelmingly non-white, reflecting the nation's legacy of apartheid.

Income inequality, already at a high level, increased even more. By 2008, the aggregate Gini coefficient of per capita income reached 0.70, which is one of the very highest rates of inequality the world. This was caused in large part by the rising inequality of monthly wages, which was noted above.

In summary: Unlike in most other countries, in the case of South Africa, economic growth did not generally result in improved labor market conditions. Household poverty rates did fall, but not because of changes in the labor market.

Table 8.1. Economic growth and changing labor market conditions in five developing countries

	China, approx. last 25 years	India, approx. last 25 years	Brazil, 1996–2004	Mexico, 2000–2006	South Africa, approx. last 20 years
Economic growth	Highest in the world	Second highest in the world until recently	Slow growth	Moderate growth	Moderate growth
Unemployment rate	Decreased (urban)	Low and falling	Rose	Rose but still very low	Sharp rise, then slow fall
Mix of jobs	Fast improvements	Slow improvements	Mixed pattern of changes	Improved	Worsened
Real labor earnings	Sharp increase	Positive for all labor force groups	Median fell	Slow rise	Rose, unequally
Income inequality	Large increase	Rose	Rose for several groups	Fell	Rose
Absolute poverty	Sharp decrease	Continuous fall	Increased	Fell	Fell because of social grants, not changes
Overall change in labor market conditions	Generally, much better	Improved slowly	Mixed changes	Generally positive	Mixed changes

8.1.6 *The Five Countries Compared*

Table 8.1 presents a qualitative summary of the changes taking place in the five preceding countries. Rapid economic growth resulted in improved labor market conditions in China and India, while moderate and slow growth produced a mixed pattern of changes in South Africa, Mexico, and Brazil.

8.2 Other Countries

A number of earlier studies had been carried out on the question of how labor market conditions changed with economic growth in other developing countries. Their main results are:

The World Bank's 'Working Out of Poverty' series: This project resulted in three country studies: Bangladesh (Paci and Sasin, 2008), Madagascar (Hoftijzer and Paci, 2008), and Nicaragua (Gutierrez, Paci, and Ranzani, 2008). Bangladesh achieved good economic growth, improved labor market conditions, and falling poverty. In Nicaragua, modest economic growth took place, but labor market indicators were mixed: employment grew primarily in the agricultural, manufacturing, and commerce sectors; real wages grew in some sectors but not others; and the poverty headcount did not change. In Madagascar, during a period when economic growth did not take place, the labor market record was mixed: unemployment rose, real earnings increased at the bottom and middle of the earnings distribution but not the top, and poverty fell.

Sub-Saharan Africa (Fox and Gaal, 2008): The study focuses on six countries: Burkina Faso, Cameroon, Ghana, Mozambique, Senegal, and Uganda. GDP growth rates per capita ranged from 2.0% to 6.5% per annum over periods ranging from five to ten years. Wage and salaried employment increased in all six countries, albeit from very low levels. Agriculture continued to be the major sector of employment despite a declining share in all six countries. Labor earnings grew by the largest amount in Mozambique (which achieved the fastest economic growth of the six), by the next largest amount in Uganda (which achieved the second-fastest economic growth), and by lesser amounts in the slower-growing economies.

Turkey (Güder, 2006): Turkey experienced slow average economic growth during the 1988–2004 period. Some of these were positive economic growth years, some negative ones. Employment, real wages, poverty, and employment composition improved during the growth years and reversed when growth was negative.

Taiwan, Indonesia, Costa Rica, and Brazil (Fields and Bagg, 2003): This study reached the following principal findings:

- Economic growth has been the driving force leading to improved labor market conditions and therefore reductions in poverty.
- The faster the economic growth, the faster the fall in poverty.
- Economic growth brought about higher real wages, a movement to more productive and higher paying jobs, and a more educated labor force in each country.
- The role played by the private sector as opposed to the public sector in the upgrading of labor market conditions varied from country to country.
- Economic growth is a critical means for improving employment and earning opportunities and thereby lowering poverty.

Hong Kong, Singapore, Korea, and Taiwan (Fields, 1994): During the rapid economic growth of these economies, full employment was generally maintained, job mixes were improved, real earnings were raised, and poverty rates were lowered. Labor market conditions improved in these economies at rates comparable to their rates of aggregate economic growth.

Barbados, Jamaica, and Trinidad and Tobago (Fields, 1984): Barbados and Trinidad and Tobago grew at just 1-2% per annum in per capita terms over the study period. In both these economies, unemployment remained in double digits, agriculture's share of total employment fell, and real wages rose. Meanwhile, Jamaica suffered a cumulative 26% fall in real per capita GNP over the study period. As a consequence, the unemployment rate more than doubled, real wages fell by 30%, and poverty rates rose; the only positive change was an increase in the share of employment in the best occupations, apparently because of loss of employment in the poorer ones.

8.3   A Comment on "Jobless Growth"

One hears much about the notion of jobless growth – specifically, the claim that in many cases economic growth takes place, yet employment does not increase. This hypothesis is *not* borne out by the data. Actually, the truth is quite the opposite.

In the case of *India*, data from the Indian Planning Commission, the National Sample Survey Organization, the National Commission for Enterprises in the Unorganised Sector, and other sources all show a continuous increase in employment. What has not increased is the *rate of unemployment* in India. There has been little improvement in the *categories* of jobs people are working in, so informal employment remains the norm, but real wages have risen in all job categories. Though the pace of improvement in the types of work performed has been disappointing, economic growth in India has *not* been jobless.

In the case of *South Africa*, government data show an *increase* in employment, followed by an equally sharp *decrease*. But upon further examination, what we see increased and then decreased in South Africa is *formal* employment. Not so for *total* employment in South Africa; it has increased throughout.

A new World Bank research study by Cho et al. (2012) examines data for *133 low and middle income countries* and groups them into four clusters: middle income, rapid growth, and structural change; upper middle income, aging, and declining informality; very low income, young, balanced employment growth; and low income, young, slow productivity growth. In all four clusters, employment as per the ILO definition increased *apace* of labor force growth in every country but one, and in that one, labor force grew at the rate of 1% and employment at the rate of 0%.[8]

In short, there are cases where economic growth has taken place and *formal* employment has increased slowly or even decreased. Yet, as the labor force has grown, so too has employment in other areas. "Jobless" is not only hyperbole; it reflects a limited understanding of what counts as employment and what doesn't.

8.4 In Summary

What the evidence presented in this chapter has shown is that labor market conditions generally improve as economic growth takes place within countries. This is true in low-income and in middle-income countries, in Asia, Latin America, and Africa, and in fast-growing and not-so-fast growing economies. Developing country labor markets have transmitted economic growth to workers in the lower parts of the income distribution and in the poorer employment categories, thereby reducing poverty. The mechanisms responsible include increasing paid employment so that workers engaged in low-paying self-employment can move into positions that pay better, raising the returns to self-employment for those who remain self-employed, upgrading education and skills, and improving labor market programs. The policies underlying these changes are detailed below.

It is worth highlighting what the data do *not* show. It is *not* the case in general that countries' economic growth comes at the expense of labor, either in the sense of workers as a whole being made poorer or in the sense of workers as a whole being left out.

Among the developing countries, the one important documented exception to the generalizations noted in this summary is South Africa. There, it was not the *labor market* that transmitted economic growth to the poor; rather, it was an expanded and more generous system of *social grants* that was responsible. In that case, it was the legacy of apartheid that brought non-labor-market mechanisms to the fore.

Part V

Assessing Changes in Income Distributions

The title of Simon Kuznets's Presidential Address to the American Economic Association was "Economic Growth and Income Inequality" (Kuznets, 1955), as a consequence of which researchers interested in the distributional effects of economic growth at first concentrated on changes in income inequality, including Kuznets himself (e.g., Kuznets, 1963). The early 1970s marked a pivotal point in economics thinking when income inequality came to the fore through the work of Atkinson (1970), Sen (1973), and Chenery et al. (1974), among others. We knew then that we could make inequality comparisons using Lorenz curves and/or inequality indices such as the income share of the richest x%, poorest y%, Gini coefficient, and other measures. But a nagging question remained: exactly what judgments does one make when using Lorenz curves to make inequality comparisons?

Economists did not know the answer, and so I set out with John Fei to work it out. The resultant paper (Fields and Fei, 1978) – Chapter 9 below – formalized the axiomatic foundations of inequality comparisons using Lorenz curves, proving that ranking income inequalities according to the three Lorenz criteria is equivalent to adopting four axioms for making inequality comparisons.[1] Further work on inequality measurement added depth to the profession's understanding; see, for example, Lambert (1989), Foster and Sen (1997), Foster et al. (2013) and the works cited therein.

Income inequality is what mathematicians and logicians call a primitive concept – that is, one that cannot be derived from other concepts. Yet, most of us have some notion, albeit vague, of what inequality is, in contrast to the much more precise notion we have of what an elephant is. Even now, the inequality literature pays scant attention to whether the standard inequality measures measure this underlying notion of inequality. From the time I started thinking about whether inequality measures measure inequality until I worked out an answer I found satisfactory, many years passed, and it was not for lack of trying.

You can try it yourself. Suppose we have an n-person economy and just two income levels, which we can call high and low; for concreteness, suppose y_{high} = $2 and y_{low} = $1. Start with everybody having low incomes and let economic growth increase the percentage with high incomes, keeping y_{high} = $2 and y_{low} = $1, until everybody has an income of $2. Now draw a graph with the percentage of people with high incomes on the horizontal axis and income inequality on the vertical axis. Your graph probably has zero inequality when 0% of the people have high incomes and also has zero inequality when 100% of the people have high incomes. Now comes the controversial part: what is the shape of your graph in the middle? Are you sure that that is the right shape? The relationship between the concept of inequality and measures of it is explored in "Do Inequality Measures Measure Inequality?" (Chapter 10).

Besides considering inequality, many analysts are also interested in poverty – in particular, absolute poverty.[2] I published two books in which absolute poverty featured prominently: Fields (1980) and Fields (2001). In the two decades between them, the literature advanced enormously. On the conceptual side, huge advances were made in developing the concept of poverty and measures of it; see Foster and Sen, 1997, Chapter A.6, for a summary, which includes the then-new $P\alpha$ measure of Foster, Greer, and Thorbecke (1984). I had nothing to do with these conceptual developments other than to learn these new ideas and exposit them. Where I did add to the poverty literature was on the empirical side, doing some country studies myself as well as collecting up the knowledge contributed by others. The results for the developing countries can be summed up in two sentences: Usually but not always, economic growth reduces absolute poverty. And when poverty has not fallen, it is generally because economic growth has not taken place. Further empirical studies in the 2000s support these two empirical conclusions, albeit with more recent evidence (e.g., Chen and Ravallion, 2013; Alvaredo and Gasparini, 2015). What we knew at the turn of the millennium is reproduced in Chapter 11.

To determine whether income distributions were getting better in welfare economic terms, changes in income inequality and absolute poverty have been combined with information on economic growth into what has come to be called "abbreviated social welfare functions".[3] A later strand of income distribution analysis was carried out using first- and second-order dominance. What do the two approaches tell us about changes in economic well-being over time? Do they give the same answers or different ones? The methods and empirical findings as of 2001 are reproduced in Chapter 12. Here too, studies in the 2000s add more country observations and newer data but leave the overall conclusions unchanged (e.g., Asian Development Bank, 2007; Chotikapanich et al., 2014).

The preceding analyses are all based on comparisons of cross-sectional data. By contrast, the question of who benefits from economic growth (and who is hurt by economic decline) can be analyzed by using a different kind of data – panel data – which follow the same individuals or households over time and assessing the changes experienced by these individuals. How should income mobility be conceptualized and measured? My chapter "Income Mobility" in *The New Palgrave Dictionary of Economics* remains fresh, and it is reproduced here (Chapter 13).

As for empirical studies of income mobility, a succession of graduate students and I have looked at macro-mobility (i.e., how much income mobility there is in an economy over a given time interval) and micro-mobility (i.e., which income groups benefit or are hurt how much and why). The empirical evidence established by us and others is summarized in a still-unpublished working paper of mine (Fields, 2010). Moreover, in some countries, analyses of income distribution changes have been conducted using both cross-sectional comparisons and panel data analysis and the results compared. The qualitative conclusions from the two approaches look quite different. One paper demonstrating this difference is "Earnings Mobility, Inequality, and Economic Growth in Argentina, Mexico, and Venezuela" (with Robert Duval Hernández, Samuel Freije, and María Laura Sánchez Puerta). See Chapter 14.

9

On Inequality Comparisons

Is one distribution (of income, consumption, or some other economic variable) among families or individuals more or less equal in relative terms than another?[1] Despite the seeming straightforwardness of this question, there has been and continues to be considerable debate over how to go about finding the answer.

There are two points of contention. One is the issue of cardinality vs. ordinality. Practitioners of the cardinal approach compare distributions by means of summary measures such as a Gini coefficient, variance of logarithms, and the like. For purposes of ranking the relative inequality of two distributions, the cardinality of the usual measures is not only a source of controversy, but it is also redundant.[2] Accordingly, some researchers prefer an ordinal approach, adopting Lorenz domination as their criterion. The difficulty with the Lorenz criterion is its incompleteness, affording rankings of only some pairs of distributions but not others. Current practice in choosing between a cardinal or an ordinal approach is now roughly as follows: Check for Lorenz domination in the hope of making an unambiguous comparison; if Lorenz domination fails, calculate one or more cardinal measures.

This raises the second contentious issue: which of the many cardinal measures in existence should one adopt? The properties of existing measures have been discussed extensively in several recent papers.[3] Typically, these studies have started with the measures and then examined their properties.

The original version of this chapter was published as: Fields, Gary S. and Fei, John C. H. (1978). On Inequality Comparisons, in: Econometrica, 46(2):303–316. © 1978 by The Econometric Society.

In this chapter, we reverse the direction of inquiry. Our approach is to start by specifying as axioms a relatively small number of properties which we believe a "good" index of inequality should have and then examining whether the Lorenz criterion and the various cardinal measures now in use satisfy those properties. The key issue is the reasonableness of the postulated properties. Work to date has shown the barrenness of the Pareto criterion.[4] Only recently have researchers begun to develop an alternative axiomatic structure.[5] The purpose of this paper is to contribute to such a development.

In Section 9.1, we shall postulate three axioms: scale irrelevance, symmetry, and desirability of rank-preserving equalization. Then, in Section 9.2, we will use these axioms to investigate and strengthen previous results by Rothschild and Stiglitz [9] and others regarding the consistency of alternative orderings in terms of Lorenz domination. The principal result of this paper is that the three axioms are sufficient to justify the Lorenz criterion for comparing the relative inequality of two distributions. Like the Lorenz criterion, the axiomatic system so constructed is incomplete. This incompleteness is intentional, for it allows us to ascertain which of the indices in current use do or do not satisfy our axioms (Section 9.3).[6] Those that do are the Gini coefficient, coefficient of variation, Atkinson index, and Theil index. This lends support to their reasonableness. However, they differ in ways which lie outside the scope of our axioms. Hopefully, future researchers will add to our axioms so as to narrow down this incompleteness.

9.1 Three Axioms for Inequality Comparisons

Suppose there are n families in an economy whose incomes may be represented by the non-negative row vector

$$(1.1) \qquad X = (X_1 \quad X_2 \quad ... \quad X_n) \geq 0$$

in the non-negative orthant of the n-dimension income distribution space Ω^+. A point in Ω^+ is a pattern of income distribution. In this paper, we shall exclude the origin $(0 \quad 0 .... 0)$ (i.e., when no family receives any income) from Ω^+. The object of inequality comparisons between two such patterns is to be able to say that one is more or less equal than the other. More specifically, we wish to introduce a *complete pre-ordering*[7] of all points in Ω^+, i.e., a binary relation "R" defined on ordered pairs in Ω^+ satisfying the conditions of comparability and transitivity:

(1.2a)   Comparability. For any X and Y in Ω^+, exactly one of the following is true: (i) XRY ... in which case we write $X > Y$ and read "X is more equal than Y;" (ii) *YRX* ... in which case we write $Y > X$ and read "Y is more equal than X;" (iii) *XRY* and *YRX* ... in which case we write $X \simeq Y$ and read "X and Y are equally unequal."

(1.2b)   *Transitivity.* XRY and YRZ implies XRZ.

We now introduce three properties which we shall propose as axioms for inequality comparisons. Not only do these seem reasonable to us but in addition they have been used by previous writers on inequality.

First, suppose two distributions X and Y are scalar multiples of one another:

$$(1.3) \qquad X = aY, \quad \text{i.e.,} \quad (X_1 \ X_2 \ldots X_n) = (aY_1 \ aY_2 \ldots aY_n), \quad a > 0.$$

Because inequality in the distribution of income and the *level* of income enter as separate arguments into judgments of social well-being, it would seem reasonable and desirable for the *measure* of inequality to be independent of the level of income.[8] For this reason, we require that the two distributions X and Y in (1.3) be ranked as equally unequal.[9] Hence, we postulate:

9.1.1   Axiom of Scale Irrelevance: $X = aY$ $(a > 0)$ implies $X \simeq Y$

This axiom allows us to normalize all distributions X in Ω^+ according to the fraction of income received by each family:

$$(1.4) \qquad [X = (X_1 \ X_2 \ \ldots X_n)] \simeq [\theta = (\theta_1 \ \theta_2 \ldots \theta_n)]$$

where

$$\theta_i = X_i/(X_1 + X_2 + \ldots + X_n) \quad \text{for} \quad i = 1, 2, \ldots, n.$$

The totality of all such normalized patterns, Ω^c, is the subset of points $\theta = (\theta_1 \ \theta_2 \ldots \theta_n)$ of Ω^+ satisfying the conditions

$$(1.5) \qquad \theta_i \geq 0 \quad \text{and} \quad \sum_i \theta_i = 1.$$

Axiom 1 assures us:

Lemma 1.1:   If a preordering R is first defined on Ω^2, then it can be extended uniquely to Ω^+.

Next, suppose the elements in one vector X are a permutation of the elements of Y, i.e., the frequency distributions of income are the same but different individuals receive the income in the two cases. On the principle of treating all individuals or families as the same with regard to income distributions, these two patterns can be characterized by the same degree of inequality. Hence, we state:

9.1.2 *Axiom of Symmetry:*[10] *If $(i_1, i_2, ..., i_n)$ is any permutation of $(1, 2, ..., n)$ then $(X_1 \ X_2 ... X_n) \simeq (X_{i_1} \ X_{i_2} ... X_{i_n})$.*

Let $(i_1^*, i_2^*, ..., i_n^*)$ be a particular permutation of $(1, 2, ..., n)$. Then those $\theta = (\theta_1 \ \theta_2 ..., \theta_n)$ in Ω^c which satisfy the condition

$$(1.6) \qquad \theta_{i_1^*} \leq \theta_{i_2^*} \leq ... \leq \theta_{i_n^*}$$

comprise a rank-preserving subset of Ω^c. There are altogether $n!$ such rank-preserving subsets. Suppose R is defined for any one of them. Then A2 allows us to extend it uniquely to the entire set Ω^c and, by Lemma 1.1, to the full income distribution space Ω^c. For convenience, we shall work with the permutation with the natural order $(1, 2, ..., n)$. Denote the corresponding rank-preserving subset as Ω_0, which includes all points satisfying the conditions

$$(1.7) \qquad \theta_1 \leq \theta_2 \leq ... \leq \theta_n; \qquad \theta_i \geq 0; \qquad \sum_{i=1}^{n} \theta_i = 1.$$

Ω_0 will be referred to as the *monotonic rank-preserving set*. Al and A2 allow us to state the following:

Lemma 1.2: Under AI and A2, if R is first defined on the monotonic rank-preserving set Ω_0, then it can be extended uniquely to Ω^+.

Notice from Lemma 1.2 that after postulating Al and A2, we can restrict our search for "reasonable" properties to the space Ω_0.

Next, let X and Y be two alternative distributions in Ω_0 such that X is obtained from Y by the transfer of a positive amount of income h from a relatively rich family j to a poorer family i, $i < j$. We shall write $X = E(Y)$ and say that X is obtained from Y by a *rank-preserving equalization*. For a particular pair i, j $(i < j)$, there is a maximum amount which can be transferred if the rank is to be preserved. Formally:

Definition: Rank-Preserving Equalization. $X = E(Y)$ if for some i, j $(i < j)$ and $h > 0$,

$$(1.8a) \qquad X_k = Y_k \quad for \quad k \neq i, j,$$
$$X_i = Y_i + h,$$
$$X_j = Y_j - h, \quad where:$$

$$(1.8b) \qquad if \ j = i + 1, \qquad h \leq \tfrac{1}{2}(Y_j - Y_i);$$
$$if \ j > i + 1, \qquad h \leq \min [(Y_{i+1} - Y_i), (Y_j - Y_{j-1})].$$

The next axiom which we shall introduce is:

9.1.3 *Axiom of Rank-Preserving Equalization: In Ω_0, if $X = E(Y)$, then $X > Y$.*[11]

The intuitive justification for this axiom is simply that it is reasonable to regard as more equal a distribution which can be derived from another by a richer person giving a part of his income to a poorer person. Defining the *perfect equality point* as $\Phi = (1/n \ 1/n \ \ldots \ 1/n)$, any income distribution point X in Ω_0 can be transformed into Φ by a finite sequence of rank-preserving equalizations.[12] Thus A3 and the transitivity of the ordering imply:

Lemma 1.3: $\Phi = (1/n \ 1/n \ \ldots \ 1/n) > X$ for all $X \neq \Phi \in \Omega_0$.

The proof is immediate.

Notice that A3 has been introduced only on Ω_0. Suppose now we introduce an R on Ω_0 satisfying all three axioms. By Lemma 1.2, R can be extended uniquely to the entire income distribution space Ω^+. It is clear that A3 is automatically extended. Formally:

Definition: Let X and Y be two patterns of income distribution in Ω^+. We shall say that X is obtained from Y *by a rank preserving equalization*, in notation $X = E(Y)$, if (a) X and Y belong to the same rank preserving subset;[13] (b) X is obtained from Y by the transfer of a positive amount of income h from a relatively rich family (e.g., $Y_q = X_q - h$) to a relatively poor family (e.g., $Y_p = X_p + h$) for $Y_q > Y_p$.

Notice that $X = E(Y)$ is now defined for the entire income distribution space Ω^+. However, this definition coincides with the previous definition (1.8a, b) where both X and Y belong to Ω_0. Thus:

Lemma 1.4: If R is first defined on the monotonic rank-preserving set Ω_0 satisfying A1–A3, the unique extension of R to Ω^+ also possesses the property of desirability of rank preserving equalization, i.e., if $X = E(Y)$, then $X > Y$.

9.2 Ordinal Approach to Inequality Comparisons: Zones of Ambiguity and Lorenz Domination

In the last section, we showed that if we postulate a set of "reasonable" axioms for R on Ω_0, then R can be extended from Ω_0 to the entire income distribution space Ω^+. We have not as yet considered whether the three axioms are sufficient to allow us to compare any two points X, Y in Ω^+ according to the comparability condition (1.2.a). In this section, we examine when inequality comparisons can or cannot be made using A1–A3.

9.2.1 Zones of Ambiguity

We shall now show that there are well-defined ranges in which inequality comparisons can be made using A1–A3 alone and other well-defined zones of ambiguity where comparisons cannot be made without further specification of the rules of ordering. We shall also establish that there is a direct one-to-one correspondence between the zones of ambiguity and the more familiar concept of Lorenz domination, which we examine below.

The first concept we need to introduce is a sequence of equalizations from a given point $Y \in \Omega_0$ according to the following definition:

Definition: X is obtained from Y by a finite *sequence of equalizations*, $X = T(Y)$, when

$$(2.1) \qquad X = E_k (\ldots E_2 \; (E_1 \; (Y)) \; \ldots \;).$$

Starting from a given point Y, we can define three sets Y^*, Y_*, and M as follows:

$$(2.2a) \quad Y^* = \{X | X = T(Y)\},$$

$$(2.2b) \quad Y_* = \{X | T(X) = Y\},$$

$$(2.2c) \quad M = \Omega_0 - Y^* \cup Y^*.$$

Y^* is the set of all points in Ω_0 obtained from Y by a sequence of *equalizing* transfers, while Y^* includes those points in Ω_0 from which a sequence of equalizing transfers will lead to Y. We can also talk about *disequalizing transfers* as the transfer of income from a relatively poor to a relatively rich family, in which case Y^* is the set of all X which can be obtained from Y by a sequence of disequalizing transfers. The set M contains all other points of Ω_0.

It follows from A3 that points in Y^*, obtained from Y by a sequence of equalizations, are more equal than Y, i.e., $X \in Y^*$ implies $X > Y$. Similarly, $X \in Y^*$ implies $X < Y$. From (2.2c), it follows that the set M contains all points which are not unambiguously comparable with Y under A1–A3. A point Z in M can always be transformed into Y by a finite sequence of rank-preserving transfers. However, any such sequence necessarily involves at least one equalization and at least one disequalization

– which is why Z cannot be compared with Y. The theorem we prove below, Theorem 2.1, implies that the Lorenz curves of Z and Y necessarily cross each other. We now consider Lorenz domination.

9.2.2 *Lorenz Domination*

One distribution is said to Lorenz-dominate another if the Lorenz curve of the first distribution never lies below that of the second and lies above it at least one point. For two points X and Y in Ω_0:

Definition: X Lorenz-dominates Y (in notation, $L_X \geq L_Y$) when

(2.3a) $\quad X_1 + X_2 + ... + X_j \geq Y_1 + Y_2 + ... + Y_j \qquad\qquad$ *for* $j = 1, 2, ... n - 1,$

(2.3b) $\quad X_1 + X_2 + ... + X_j > Y_1 + Y_2 + ... + Y_j \qquad\qquad$ *for some* $j < n.$

Notice that

(2.4) $\quad \sum_{i=1}^{n} X_i = \sum_{i=1}^{n} Y_i = 1$ in Ω_0.

Our basic theorem is:

Theorem 2.1: $\quad X \in Y^*$ if and only if $L_X \geq L_Y$.

Thus, the Lorenz Curve of Y is dominated by the Lorenz Curves of all $X \in Y_{,,}$ dominates those of $X \in Y_{,,}$ and crosses those of $X \in M$, i.e., neither dominates the other.

The necessary condition of the theorem (i.e., $X \in Y^*$ implies that the Lorenz curve of X dominates that of Y) is a well-known result.[14] The sufficient condition of the theorem states that whenever the Lorenz curve of X dominates that of Y (i.e., $L_X \geq L_Y$), X can be obtained from Y by a sequence of equalizations which are rank-preserving.[15] This sufficient condition, when proved, along with (2.2.a), will allow us to conclude that Lorenz domination implies greater equality. This may be summarized as:

Corollary 2.2: Under A3, for X, Y in Ω_o, $L_X \geq L_Y$ implies $X > Y$.

9.2.3 *Proof of the Sufficient Condition of Theorem 2.1*

The sufficient condition of Theorem 2.1 holds that whenever X Lorenz-dominates Y, there exists a sequence of rank-preserving equalizations leading from Y to X. In order to prove the validity of this part of the theorem, we must produce a rule for finding the necessary sequence. The derivation of the rule follows.

Consider any two distributions X and Y in Ω_0. Let their difference be denoted by

(2.5a) $d = (d_1\ d_2\ ...\ d_n) = (X_1 - Y_1\ X_2 - Y_2\ ...\ X_n - Y_n),$

(2.5b) $\sum d_i = 0.$

The n elements of d can be partitioned consecutively into r subsets $(D_1\ D_2\ ...\ D_r)$ according to the following rules:

(2.6a)   Every d_i belongs to one D_j.

(2.6b)   Every D_j contains at least one non-zero d_i.

(2.6c)   If $d_i \in D_j$ and $d_p \in D_q$, then $j < q$ implies $i < p$.

(2.6d)   The first element of $D_2, D_3, ..., D_r$ is non-zero.

(2.6e)   All $d_i \in D_j$ are non-positive or non-negative [D_j is called positive (or negative) according to the signs of the d_i in D_j.]

(2.6f)   The D_j alternate in sign.

The partition determined by (2.6.a–f) is unique. Furthermore, if $X \neq Y$, then there is at least one strictly positive d_i and one strictly negative d_i. Thus,

(2.7) $if\ X \neq Y, \qquad r \geq 2.$[16]

We can also define

(2.8) $S_j = \sum_{d_i \in D_j} d_i \qquad for \qquad j = 1, ..., r$

with the properties

(2.9a) $S_j \neq 0, \qquad j = 1, 2, ..., r,$

(2.9b) $S_1, S_2, ..., S_r$ alternate in sign,

(2.9c) $\sum_{j=1}^{r} S_j = \sum_{i=1}^{n} d_i = 0.$

We may now state a *general rule for rank preserving equalizations* from X to Y: (a) Identify the groups according to (2.6). (b) With each transfer, eliminate the gap between X and Y of one family's income by (i) taking from the poorest family (the pth) with non-zero d in the richest group (S_r), (ii) giving to the richest family (the qth) with non-zero d in the next lower group (S_{r-i}), (iii) compute the amount of transfer as the smaller of d_p and $-d_q$. (c) Repeat these steps (a, b) again, each time eliminating the gap for another family's income.

To prove the validity of this rule, we need to draw on the Lorenz domination condition of Theorem 2.1 by the following lemma.

Lemma 2.3:　When $X \neq Y$, $L_X \geq L_Y$ is equivalent to (2.10.a, b)

(2.10a) $\sum\limits_{j=1}^{i} d_j \geq 0$ 　　　　　　　*for* $i = 1, ..., n$,

(2.10b) $\sum\limits_{j=1}^{p} S_j \geq 0$ 　　　　　　　*for* $p = 1, ..., r$.

Proof: (2.3.a, b) imply (2.10.a). Conversely (2.10.a) implies (2.3.a) and, since $X \neq Y$, it also implies (2.3.b). Thus, (2.3.a, b) and (2.10.a) are equivalent when $X \neq Y$. It follows directly from (2.8) that (2.10.a) implies (2.10.b). Thus we need only prove the reverse implication. Suppose $d_i \in D_q = (d_{a+i}\ d_{a+2}\ ...\ d_{a+mq})$. Then define

$$V_i = \sum\limits_{j=1}^{i} d_j = S_1 + S_2 + ... + S_{q-1} + d_{a+1} + ... + d_i.$$

We want to prove $V_i \geq 0$. In this expression,

(2.11a)　$S = S_1 + S_2 + ... + S_{q-1} \geq 0$　　　(by (2.10.b)),

(2.11b)　$S_q = d_{a+1} + ... + d_{a+m_q}$,　　　where all d's have the same sign,

(2.11c)　$V_{a+m_q} = S + S_q \geq 0$　　　(by 2.10.b).

Thus, d_i is one member of a sequence $(V_{a+1}, V_{a+2}, ..., V_{a+m_q})$ which either (i) is monotonically increasing from $S \geq 0$ if D_q is a positive set, or (ii) is monotonically decreasing to $S + S_q \geq 0$ if D_q is a negative set. In either case, $V_i \geq 0$.

　　　　　　　　　　　　　　　　　　　　　Q.E.D.

Notice that (2.9.a, c) and (2.10.b) imply $S_1 > 0$ and $S_r < 0$. Thus (2.9.b) implies r is even. Hence,

Lemma 2.4:　$L_X \geq L_Y$ implies r is even and the S_i can be grouped into $r/2$ pairs with the indicated signs:

(2.12)　$(S_1^+ S_2^-)\ (S_3^+ S_4^-)\ ...\ (S_{r-1}^+ S_r^-)$

Then when $L_x \geq L_Y$, families in the last group S_r^- of X must be relatively poorer than those in Y. The opposite is true for the group S_{r-1}^+.

Before we can prove the validity of the rule, we need one more lemma. In this lemma suppose $Y' = (Y'_1\ Y'_2 \dots Y'_n)$ is obtained from Y by a single rank-preserving equalization. Let

(2.13) $d' = (d'_1 \dots d'_n) = (X_1 - Y'_1\ X_2 - Y'_2 \dots X_n - Y'_n)$.

Then:

Lemma 2.5:   If $L_X \geq L_Y$, there exists $Y' \in \Omega_o$ such that

(2.14a) $Y' = E(Y)$,

(2.14b) $L_X \geq L_{Y'}$,

(2.14c) $d_i = 0$ implies $d'_i = 0$,

(2.14d)   there is at least one integer j such that $d_j \neq 0$ and $d'_j = 0$.

Proof: Suppose the last non-zero d_i in S_{r-1}^+ in (2.12) is d_p and the first non-zero d_i in S_r^- is $d_q\ (q > p)$. Thus, by this choice, we have

(2.15) $d_{p+1} = d_{p+2} = \dots = d_{q-1} = 0$.

Let

(2.16) $h = \min (d_p, -d_q) = \min(X_p - Y_p, Y_q - X_q) > 0$.

When h is transferred from the qth family to the pth family of Y, let the result be denoted by Y'. Then obviously (2.14.a, c, d) are satisfied. To prove (b), we have

(2.17) $d'_1 + d'_2 + \dots + d'_i = \begin{cases} d_1 + d_2 + \dots d_i \text{ for } i < p \text{ or } i \geq q, \\ d_1 + d_2 + \dots + d_i - h = d_1 + d_2 + \dots + d_{p-1} + d_p \\ -h \text{ for } p \leq i < q. \end{cases}$

The first sum $d_1 + d_2 + \dots + d_i \geq 0$ by (2.10.a). In the second sum, $d_1 + d_2 + \dots + d_{p-1}$ is non-negative by Lorenz-domination (2.10.a) and $(d_p - h)$ is non-negative because $h \leq d_p$. Thus $d'_1 + d'_2 + \dots + d'_i \geq 0$ and $L_X - L'_Y$ by (2.10.a).   Q.E.D.

Lemma 2.5 assures us that we can repeat the same operation on Y' by reducing one additional non-zero entry of d'. Since there are only a finite number of non-zero d_i we have:

Lemma 2.6: If $L_X \geq L_Y$, then there exists a sequence of rank-preserving tranfers T such that $X = T(Y)$ and T involves at most m steps, where m is the number of non-zero d_i in d (as given by (2.5)).

The proof of the sufficient condition of Theorem 2.1 follows directly from Lemma 2.6, as does the validity of the rule presented above.

9.2.4   Theorem 2.1 and the Lorenz Criterion

Theorem 2.1 has a ready application to zones of ambiguity and Lorenz-domination. When comparing two distributions X and Y, a simple rule for determining when L_X crosses L_Y (i.e., when $X \in M$) *is to examine the sign of the first and last non-zero d_i and, if they have the same sign, the Lorenz curves must cross.*[17]

From Theorem 2.1, it follows that the axiomatic system A1–A3 constitutes a rigorous justification for the Lorenz criterion for comparing the relative inequality of two income distributions. Of course, the Lorenz criterion is incomplete, and the three axioms are also. Completeness is customarily achieved via cardinality, but the cardinal indices in current use do not necessarily satisfy A1–A3. In what follows, we examine which of the usual indices satisfy our three axioms and which do not.

9.3   Cardinal Index Approach to Inequality Comparisons

The traditional approach for comparing the inequality of two distributions is to compute a cardinal index of inequality I with domain Ω^+:

(3.1) $I = f(X) = f(X_1 \; X_2 \; ... \; X_n), \quad X_i \geq 0.$

Examples are the Gini coefficient, coefficient of variation, range, and others which we shall consider below. Inequality comparisons are made according to the following definition:

Definition: Pre-Ordering induced by an Index: A real-valued index of inequality $I = f(X)$ induces a complete pre-ordering R as follows: for all X, $Y \in \Omega^+$, XRY when $f(X) \leq f(Y)$.[18]

Notice that the *cardinality* of the index (3.1) is unnecessary for the question of determining which is the more equal of two distributions, since the essential information for this purpose is all contained in the pre-ordering R which $f(X)$ induces.

It is the purpose of this section to explore whether R's induced by many familiar inequality indices indeed satisfy the three axioms introduced in Section 1. When a particular index $I = f(X)$ in (3.1) satisfies restrictions (3.2.a-c), the following theorem insures that R satisfies A1–A3:

Theorem 3.1:   The pre-ordering R induced by an index $I = f(X)$ satisfies A1–A3 when:

(3.2a)   homogeneous of degree zero: $f(X) = f(aX)$, $a > 0$;

(3.2b)   symmetry: $f(X_{i_1} X_{i_2} ... X_{i_n}) = f(X_1 X_2 ... X_n)$,
where $(i_1, i_2, ..., i_n)$ is a permutation of $(1, 2, ..., n)$;

(3.2c)   monotonicity of partial derivative:

$$\frac{\partial f}{\partial X_i} = f_i(X) < \frac{\partial f}{\partial X_j} = f_j(X) \quad \text{for } i < j \quad \text{and} \quad X \in \Omega_0.$$

Proof: (3.2a) and (3.2b) respectively insure that the induced ordering satisfies A1 and A2. To show A3 holds on Ω_0, suppose X is obtained from Y by a rank-preserving equalization. It is readily seen that the difference $I(X)-I(Y)$ is negative by (2.2.c) for an equalization of any positive sum. Thus, A3 is satisfied.

Using Theorem 3.1, we may prove:

Theorem 3.2:   The following inequality indices satisfy A1–A3:

(3.3)   Coefficient of Variation: $C = \sigma/\dot{X}$ where $\sigma = \Sigma_i(X_i - X)^2/n$ and $\dot{X} = \Sigma_i X_i/n$.

(3.4)   Gini Coefficient: $G = -1 - \frac{1}{n} + \frac{2}{n^2\dot{X}} [X_1 + 2X_2 + ... + nX_n]$.

(3.5)   Atkinson Index:[19]

$$A = 1 - \left[\left[\left(\frac{X_1}{\dot{X}}\right)^{1-\varepsilon} + \left(\frac{X_2}{\dot{X}}\right)^{1-\varepsilon} + ... + \left(\frac{X_n}{\dot{X}}\right)^{1-\varepsilon} \right] \frac{1}{n} \right]^{1/(1-\varepsilon)}, \qquad \varepsilon > 1.$$

(3.6)   Theil Index:[20] $T = \sum_i X_i \log nX_i$.

At the suggestion of the editor, the proof of Theorem 3.2 is omitted due to space limitations.

   The fulfillment of A1–A3 by these measures strengthens both the axioms and the indices. The axioms are seen to be relevant to a number of measures with which we have considerable experience. In turn, the indices are seen to have several properties whose desirability is a matter of substantial agreement.

Despite the large number of indices which satisfy our three axioms, there are other indices in common use which violate them, particularly A1 and A3. The difficulty with those indices which violate A1 (e.g., *variance*) is that they are not independent of the level of income. Those indices which do not satisfy A3 are in some circumstances insensitive to certain rank-preserving equalizations. One example is the family of *fractile ranges* (e.g., *interquartile range*); any rank-preserving equalizations *within a segment* (e.g., within a quartile) leave the index unchanged, in violation of A3. Another example is the *Kuznets Ratio*:

$$(3.7) \quad K = \sum |\theta_i - 1/n|,$$

which is unchanged by any rank-preserving equalization or disequalization *on the same side of the mean*. To the extent that A1–A3 are reasonable, all indices which violate them are less than satisfactory; their popular use in empirical work cannot be defended by these axioms and must be justified on other grounds.

9.4   Conclusion

In this paper, we have developed an approach to inequality comparisons which differs from the conventional one. Beginning by postulating three axioms, we showed that the axiomatic system so constructed is sufficient to justify the Lorenz criterion for inequality comparisons. However, like the Lorenz criterion, the axiomatic system is incomplete. Past researchers have achieved completeness by the use of cardinal inequality measures. We showed that many but by no means all of the commonly used indices satisfy our three axioms. The ones which do satisfy the axioms agree on the ranking of distributions whose Lorenz curves do not intersect. However, when Lorenz curves do intersect, the various measures partition the income distribution space differently. Since the three axioms are insufficient to determine the specific partition to use, the use of any of the conventional measures implicitly accepts the additional welfare judgments associated with that measure.

The key issue for inequality comparisons is the reasonableness of the ordering criterion, which in the case of cardinal measures is the index itself. An axiomatic approach is probably the ideal method for confronting this issue, because the reasonable properties (i.e., the axioms) are postulated explicitly. At minimum, this approach facilitates communication by enabling (and indeed requiring) one to set forth clearly his own viewpoints and value judgments for scrutiny by others. But in addition, to the extent that one person's judgments (such as those in our three axioms) are acceptable to others, controversies over inequality comparisons may be resolved. We have seen that our three axioms are incomplete insofar as they cannot determine the ordinal ranking uniquely. A feasible and desirable direction for future research is to investigate what further axioms could be introduced to complete the axiomatic system or at least to reduce further the zones of ambiguity.

It is conceivable that beyond some point the search for new axioms may turn out to be unrewarding. In that case, inequality comparisons will always be subject to arbitary specifications of welfare weights. The selection of suitable weights by whatever reasonable criterion one cares to exercise is a less desirable but possibly more practical alternative than a strictly axiomatic approach.

Our research has hopefully made clear that inequality comparisons cannot be made without adopting value judgments, explicit or otherwise, about the desirability of incomes accruing to persons at different positions in the income distribution. Even the Lorenz criterion, which permits us to rank the relative inequality of different distributions in only a fraction of the cases, embodies such judgments. The traditional inequality indices such as those considered in Section 9.3, to the extent they complete the ordering, embody *some* value judgments beyond our three axioms. The axiomatic bases for these judgments are at present vague, and it would be helpful if future researchers could state these implicit value judgments in axiomatic terms so that when a particular inequality index is used we will know exactly what judgments are being made.

10

Do Inequality Measures Measure Inequality?

10.1 Introduction

I first met Aldi Hagenaars at the World Econometric Society Congress in Cambridge, Massachusetts in 1985. At that time, we had a long discussion about the question posed in the title of this chapter. The driving force behind Aldi's research program became clear to me then: a profound concern with people's feelings about their economic well-being accompanied by the quest to devise measures that reflect those underlying feelings.

This chapter follows that tradition. My own research program has dealt with the twin questions of who benefits how much from economic growth and why. Before answering these questions, it is necessary to decide what measure to take to the data to determine if economic growth is welfare-enhancing. For many people, one component of a social welfare judgment is the extent of income inequality.

There is no shortage of inequality measures (Gini coefficient, Theil index, Atkinson index, etc.). The task is to decide what we mean by "inequality" and then to determine which, if any, of the available measures behave as "inequality" does.

The literature offers two principal ways of relating social welfare to the inequality of income.[1] One, due to Kolm (1966) and Atkinson (1970), first constructs a social welfare function defined on the space of incomes

The original version of this chapter was published as: Fields, Gary S. (1998). Do Inequality Measures Measure Inequality?, in: S. Jenkins, A. Kapteyn, B. van Praag, eds., The distribution of welfare and household production, 233–249. © 1998 by Cambridge University Press.

(1) $$W = W(y_1, y_2, ..., y_n)$$

then defines the equally distributed income as the amount of income which, if equally distributed would yield the same social welfare as the actual distribution, and finally measures inequality as the gap between the actual mean income y and the equally distributed income y^*

$$I = I - (y^*/\overline{y})$$

Another way of taking the level of national income and the inequality of its distribution into account in welfare judgments is to rank income distributions in terms of the mean income level $\overline{Y}$, income inequality I and perhaps other things:

$$W = f(\overline{Y}, I, ...), \partial W/\overline{Y} > 0, \partial W/\partial I < 0.$$

Ranking income distributions in terms of income level and income inequality is common practice in a whole host of empirical studies of "growth and equity." This practice receives abundant theoretical support, for instance, in Sen (1973), Blackorby and Donaldson (1977, 1984), Fields (1979), Ebert (1987), and Lambert (1989). Schur-concave social welfare functions provide one justification for this practice; another is diminishing marginal utility of identical interpersonally comparable utility functions.

To be able to rank income distributions in this way, we must determine how the inequality of one distribution compares to that of another, which means that the primitive concept of "inequality" must be made precise. Amartya Sen (1973, pp. 2, 3) has written:

> there are some advantages in . . . try[ing] to catch the extent of inequality in some *objective* sense . . . so that one can distinguish between (a) *"seeing"* more or less inequality, and (b) *"valuing"* it more or less in ethical terms ... There is, obviously, an objective element in this notion: a fifty-fifty division of a cake between two persons is clearly more equal in some straightforward sense than giving all to one and none to the other.

> [First emphasis Sen's, second and third emphases mine.]

It is precisely this objective sense of "seeing" what inequality is which I shall adopt in this chapter in the context of inequality comparisons.

In the literature, much attention has been paid to a number of aspects of inequality including the distinction between relative and absolute inequality, axiomatization of inequality, the Lorenz criterion for inequality comparisons, properties of various inequality measures, and inequality decomposition. In no way do I wish to argue with the main results derived in these areas. Rather, my purpose here is to add to the theory of inequality measurement by dealing with one aspect of inequality which has been largely ignored by economists[2] and by others.[3] This is the question of how inequality changes – in particular, whether it increases, decreases, or remains unchanged – when income grows in specified ways.[4]

The balance of this chapter deals with two distinct conceptual entities, "inequality" and "inequality measures." The next section analyzes how "inequality" might be said to change under various types of economic growth and explores the foundations for alternative views. One approach in terms of "elitism of the rich" and "isolation of the poor" is then described. The following section looks into the behavior of "inequality measures" and the relationship between "inequality measures" and "inequality," and a final section draws some conclusions.

10.2 How Does Inequality Change with Economic Growth?

In this chapter, inequality is analyzed on the space of "incomes" among "persons," ruling out multiple goods and problems of aggregation. The analysis proceeds axiomatically, following a long tradition which dates back at least to Pigou (1912) and Dalton (1920) and has been accepted by many others ever since.[5] It holds that whenever a transfer of income is made from a person[6] who is relatively poor to another who is relatively rich, inequality increases. Notice two things about this way of conceptualizing the primitive concept "inequality." First it is in terms of *conditional* "if ... then" statements. Second, the answer to the question "what is inequality?" is sought by looking at inequality *orderings* on pairs of distributions, addressing the related question "when is one distribution more equal than another?" I shall follow this practice and seek to clarify the meaning of "inequality" by formulating a series of conditional statements on binary comparisons.

Let the economy consist of n "persons," total population being assumed fixed. Let Φ be the share of persons having income y_H and $1-\Phi$ the share having income y_L ($< y_H$). Analyzing this restricted domain is helpful in forming precise views on the meaning of inequality before moving on to analyze inequality on the more general domain of incomes, a task left for the future.

Throughout the rest of this chapter, we shall use the notation $\Phi = nH/n$ and $\Theta = Y_H/Y_L$ whenever $\Phi \in (0,1)$.[7] The term "increase in Θ" shall be understood as signifying an increase in $Y_H/Y_L \forall \Phi \in (0,1)$.

In the two-income world, income growth can take place by increasing Y_H, Y_L, or Φ, or by some combination of these. A simple example shows why inequality rankings are sometimes difficult to make when incomes are growing, even in so simple a world.

Consider an economy consisting of six individuals with an initial distribution of income [1,1,1,1,1,6]. Now suppose the economy experiences income growth of \$5. The change in inequality depends on how that \$5 is distributed.

First let the entire \$5 go to the rich person. We have little difficulty in ranking the new distribution [1,1,1,1,1,11] as *more unequal* than the old.

Suppose instead that the \$5 of income growth is divided equally among all the low income persons, resulting in a new distribution [2,2,2,2,2,6]. Once again, the ranking is likely to be uncontroversial: the new distribution may be said to be *more equal* than the old.

Consider a third possibility: that the \$5 of income growth produces an income gain for *just one* of the low income persons.[8] Compare the two income distributions

$$Y_1 = [1, 1, 1, 1, 1, 6]$$

and

$$Y_2 = [1, 1, 1, 1, 6, 6]$$

Which is more equal, Y_1 or Y_2?[9] The rest of this chapter seeks an answer.

A natural starting point would be Lorenz curve comparisons. One income distribution is said to *Lorenz-dominate* another if the first distribution's Lorenz curve is somewhere above and nowhere below that of the second. The *Lorenz criteria for relating the inequality of two distributions* consist of several parts:

(i) If two distributions X, $Y \in Z$ have the same Lorenz curves L_x and L_y, then they are equally unequal ($=_L$) by the Lorenz criterion, i.e.,

$$L_X = L_Y \Rightarrow X =_L Y$$

(ii) If distribution X Lorenz dominates distribution Y, then X is more equal than Y by the Lorenz criterion *(L)*:

$$L_X \geqslant L_Y \Rightarrow X >_L Y$$

(iii) If the Lorenz curves of X and Y cross, then the inequality of the two distributions cannot be compared using the Lorenz criterion alone.

Together, these are termed ranking $\geqslant_L$.[10]

When economic growth causes the income distribution to change from $Y_1 = [1,1,1,1,1,6]$ to $Y_2 = [1,1,1,1,6,6]$, we may calculate the cumulative income shares Cum $Y_1 = [1/11, 2/11, 3/11, 4/11, 5/11, 1]$ and Cum $Y_2 = [1/16, 2/16, 3/16, 4/16, 8/16, 1]$ and note that their Lorenz curves cross.

Therefore the two distributions' relative inequalities cannot be ranked on the basis of the Lorenz properties alone. Likewise, in a sequence of income distributions whereby an economy progresses from $Y_1 = [1,1,1,1,1,6]$ to $Y_2 = [1,1,1,1,6,6]$ to $Y_3 = [1,1,1,6,6,6]$ to $Y_4 = [1,1,6,6,6,6]$ to $Y_5 = [1,6,6,6,6,6]$, *all* of the associated Lorenz curves cross each other. If we want to say how the inequalities of the different distributions compare, we must go beyond the Lorenz criteria considered thus far and appeal to additional properties.

One way of sharpening our views about what inequality *is* is to look at the sequence of distributions from Y_1 through Y_5 and see what we "see."[11] From simple eyeballing of the sequence Y_1 through Y_5, many different patterns emerge as plausible possibilities. It might be said that inequality decreases monotonically, increases monotonically, follows a U-shaped path, follows an inverted U-shaped path, or even remains unchanged. This does not exhaust the possible patterns.

Experimental evidence confirms the diversity of views for a similar thought experiment. Amiel and Cowell (1992) asked more than 1,000 university students to compare the inequality of two distributions

$$A = [5,5,5,10]$$

and

$$B = [5,5,10,10]$$

40 percent judged A as more unequal, 56 percent judged B as more unequal, and 4 percent judged them equally unequal. When asked to compare

$$B = [5,5,10,10]$$

with

$$C = [5,10,10,10]$$

57 percent judged B as more unequal, 40 percent judged C as more unequal, and 3 percent judged them equally unequal. Furthermore, in three-way comparisons, by far the most common judgment was to deem $[5, 5, 10, 10]$ as less unequal than *both* $[5, 5, 5, 10]$ and $[5,10,10,10]$, a view consistent with the U-shaped pattern.

In addition, Amiel and Cowell's respondents were asked about their views on what I have here called the high income sector-enlargement process. Specifically, the question asked was:

Suppose there is a society consisting of n people. There is one rich person and n-1 identical poor people. One by one, some of those who were poor acquire the same income as the rich person, so that eventually there are n-1 (identical) rich people and just one poor person. Please circle the appropriate response:

Inequality increases continuously.	(7.5%)
Inequality decreases continuously.	(20.5%)
Inequality at first increases and then decreases.	(19.9%)
Inequality at first decreases and then increases.	(36.7%)
Inequality remains the same throughout.	(11.2%)
None of the above.	(4.1%)

(The frequency distribution of valid responses is given in brackets).

Here, as well, the U-shaped pattern is the most common.

At this point, I would invite the reader to consider his or her own rankings of the inequality of Y_1 versus Y_2 versus Y_3 versus Y_4 versus Y_5, of A versus B versus C, and of the high income sector-enlargement process described in the previous paragraph.

10.3 Justifying Alternative Patterns in Terms of "Elitism of the Rich" and "Isolation of the Poor"

If you had trouble making the inequality comparisons asked for above, it may be because you lack a framework for moving beyond Lorenz comparisons. This section may help in that regard.

A philosopher, Temkin (1986), has analyzed essentially the same process, different only in that he has total income falling rather than rising. Temkin's analysis is in terms of individual complaints – how serious the inequality in a situation is from the standpoint of particular individuals in that situation. Alternative principles (additive, weighted additive, and maximin) and referents (relative to the average, relative to the best-off person, and relative to all those better off) lead plausibly, in his view, to most of the various patterns raised above.

In an earlier paper (Fields, 1987), I adopted a different approach, which I also take here. Rather than weighing "individual complaints," I look at the question from a societal point of view. The specific way in which I now prefer to do this is with reference to two concepts – "elitism of the rich" and "isolation of the poor" – which are developed formally in Fields (1993).

Briefly put, *elitism of the rich* (ER) is the following idea. When one person has a high income ($\$y_H$) and everybody else has a low income ($\$y_L$ each), the one rich person may be thought to have a very elite position. In this case the economy may be said to have a high degree of elitism of the rich. Now let a second person acquire a high income, all others' incomes remaining the same (Φ increases). Because each of the rich now has to share his elitist position with someone else, the two rich persons together might be regarded as less elite than one person was when he alone was rich. Thus, elitism of the rich falls. If a third person is enriched, elitism of the rich might be thought to fall further, but not by as much as when the second person was enriched. In general, the larger the fraction rich, the smaller is elitism of the rich and the smaller is the change in elitism of the rich for a given increase in size of the high income group. When everybody is rich, there no longer is any ehtism of the rich.

Elitism of the rich also varies with the ratio of high incomes to low incomes (Θ). Holding the number of persons in the two income groups constant, if the amount received by each high income person increases or if the amount received by each low income person decreases, elitism of the rich should increase.

Figure 10.1. Elitism of the rich.   **Figure 10.2.** Isolation of the poor.

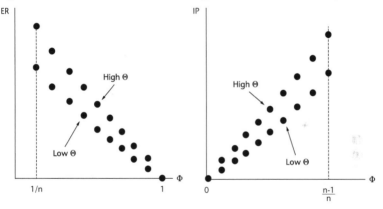

Figure 10.1 summarizes how elitism of the rich varies with Φ and Θ. *Isolation of the poor* (IP) may be defined as a reciprocal notion to elitism of the rich. When everyone in an economy is equally poor, there is no isolation of the poor, because there are no rich from whom to be isolated. When one person escapes poverty, isolation of the poor is created. As the number with high incomes increases, those who are left behind may be regarded, as a group, as increasingly isolated. For this reason, isolation of the poor may be viewed as increasing at an increasing rate as the high income group expands. Finally, when just one person is poor, it can be argued that that one person is very isolated from everyone else, at which point isolation of the poor attains a maximum. Now, holding the numbers in the two groups constant any increase in the ratio between high and low incomes (Θ) should increase isolation of the poor. These properties of isolation of the poor are shown in Figure 10.2.

From these concepts of elitism of the rich and isolation of the poor, we may derive various inequality patterns. Those observers who wish to view inequality solely in terms of elitism of the rich would see inequality as *falling* continuously on the interval $\Phi \in (0,1)$ for any given Θ. The higher is Θ, the higher is inequality. This class, shown in Figure 10.3, will be termed the I class.

Others may wish to view inequality solely in terms of isolation of the poor. These observers would see inequality as *rising* continuously on the interval $\Phi \in (0,1)$ for any given Θ. A higher Θ implies more inequality. Figure 10.4 depicts this class, denoted the I_+ class.

Many observers hold the view that inequality consists of *both* elitism of the rich and isolation of the poor. How might these notions be combined on their common domain, the open interval $(0,1)$?

Elitism of the rich and isolation of the poor need to be expressed in comparable units, which may be done by postulating that for any Φ, $ER(\Phi) = IP(1 - \Phi)$.

Next, elitism of the rich and isolation of the poor need to be combined in some plausible way. Suppose equal weight is given to each. The simplest such mixing function, defined on the open interval $(0,1)$, the common domain of $ER(\cdot)$ and $IP(\cdot)$, is

$$I(\Phi, \Theta) = (ER + IP)/2$$

Alternatively, unequal weights may be posited by using a linear mixing function:

$$I(\cdot) = w\, ER(\cdot) + (1 - w)\, IP(\cdot), \quad w > 0.\, w \neq 1 - w$$

Define the I_{min} class to be those $I(\cdot)$ rankings which are U-shaped as Φ varies on the open interval $(0,1)$ for a given Θ, and which lie on higher contours for higher Θ, as shown in Figure 10.5; denote those which also are symmetric with a unique minimum at $\Theta = 1/2$ as the symmetric I_{min} class. Fields (1993) proves that the preceding properties with *equal* weights generate the symmetric I_{min} class and these properties with *unequal* weights generate a ranking which is a member of the I_{min} class but not the symmetric I_{min} class.

Note two things. First, given $I(\cdot) = w\, ER(\cdot) + (1 + w)IP(\cdot)$, for $w = 1$, we have the I_- pattern shown in Figure 10.3, and for $w = 0$, the I_+ pattern shown in Figure 10.4, which may be attractive to some observers. Second, these are the *only* patterns consistent with the preceding axioms. In particular, the inverted-U pattern *cannot* be generated from the preceding properties.

Figure 10.3. The I_- class of inequality rankings.

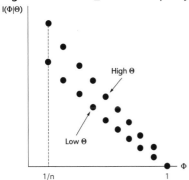

Figure 10.4. The I_+ class of inequality rankings.

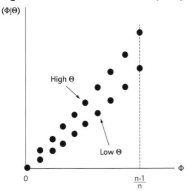

Figure 10.5. The I_{min} class of inequality rankings.

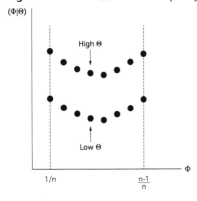

It remains to extend the inequality ordering to the end-points $\Phi = 0$ and $\Phi = 1$. If we adopt the Lorenz axioms, we obtain two additional restrictions on the inequality orderings. One restriction, arising from the transfer principle, is that a situation in which everyone has the same income must be regarded as more equal than any situation in which incomes differ. Accordingly, the Lorenz properties require that a situation of equally distributed incomes be deemed a "most equal point." The other restriction, arising from the income homogeneity principle, is that all equally distributed incomes be deemed "most equal points." If we adopt a natural normalization – that most equal points have *no* inequality – we then have

$$I(Y/n, Y/n, \ldots Y/n) = 0$$

for all total income amounts Y.

The concept of a most equal point accords with the notions introduced earlier of elitism of the rich and isolation of the poor. Suppose that two incomes are possible but that everybody has one of those incomes and nobody has the other. In one case, there is no elitism of the rich, because there are no rich; and in the other case, there is no isolation of the poor, because there are no poor. One would be inclined to say that a situation where all are equally rich or equally poor is more equal than a situation where some are rich and some are poor and that the two situations ("all rich" and "all poor") have the same inequality as one another. Inequality notions in the $I\_^L$, I_+^L and I_{min}^L classes make these judgments.

Combining these judgments with the alternative enlargement patterns as depicted in Figures 10.3 through 10.5, we obtain the three inequality orderings $I\_^L$, I_+^L and I_{min}^L shown in figures 10.6a–6c respectively. All are Lorenz consistent, yet they treat high income sector enlargement in very different ways.

Note, too, that the familiar inverted U-shaped pattern shown in figure 10.6d *cannot* be generated from the preceding axioms. A different justification is needed. I shall not pursue that here.

10.4 Inequality Measures and Inequality

Any relative inequality relation such as those considered in Section 10.2 determines which of two income vectors $X, Y \in Z$ is more equal than the other. An inequality function $I(\cdot)$ which assigns a real number r to X and Y representing the inequality of that vector such that $I(X)$ and $I(Y)$ are ordered by the usual greater than or equal to relation $\geq$ is said to be an *inequality measure* (alternatively, a "numerical inequality measure" or an "inequality index"). A *relative inequality measure* has the additional property that an equiproportionate change in everyone's income leaves inequality unchanged.

Figure 10.6. The I^L classes of inequality rankings.

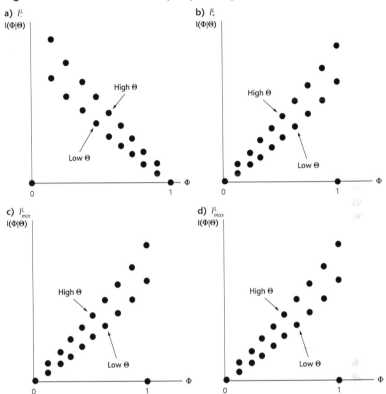

Some relative inequality measures are Lorenz consistent (meaning that they make precisely those judgments specified by the Lorenz properties whenever Lorenz comparisons can be made) and some are not, either because they are only weakly Lorenz consistent (meaning that if one Lorenz curve lies partly above but not below another, the measure may rank the two distributions as equally unequal) or because they are Lorenz inconsistent (meaning that there may be a case in which one distribution Lorenz dominates another and yet the measure deems the first distribution to be more unequal than the second). Among those known to be Lorenz consistent are the Gini coefficient, Theil's two measures, Atkinson's index, and the coefficient of variation. Among those known not to be Lorenz consistent are some which are only weakly Lorenz consistent (income share of the richest $X\%$ or poorest $Y\%$) and others which are Lorenz inconsistent (including the mean absolute deviation and the logarithm of the variance of incomes). Lorenz consistent inequality measures are emphasized hereafter.

It will be said that an inequality measure measures inequality, or equivalently, that the inequality measure is consistent with a specified ranking, when the ordinal ranking assigned by the inequality measure matches the ordinal ranking of inequality assigned by the observer. All that can be hoped for is agreement on conditional statements of the type: "For all those whose inequality notions are of such and such type, such and such inequality measures measure inequality (and such and such other inequality measures do not)."

Consider now the process of high income sector enlargement on the domain of two incomes, as analyzed in Section 10.2. It was shown in Fields (1993), building on the work of Anand and Kanbur (1993), that each of six commonly used inequality measures (Theil's entropy index, Theil's second measure, CV^2, Atkinson index, Gini coefficient, nonoverlapping case, and log variance) starts at zero, increases continuously to an interior maximum at Φ^*, and then decreases to zero.[12]

Thus, Theil's entropy index, Theil's second measure, the CV^2, the Atkinson index, and the Gini coefficient (non-overlapping case) are Lorenz consistent and follow an inverted U-shaped pattern in high income sector-enlargement growth.[13] These commonly used measures therefore go beyond the Lorenz ordering in a way that produces a similar *pattern* of rankings (the inverted U-pattern).[14]

Turning now to the question of symmetry, it is sometimes said that on the two-income domain, inequality should reach a turning point when half the population is in the high income group and half in the low income group, i.e., at $\Phi^* = 1/2$. Do the five Lorenz consistent inequality measures considered above have this property? It can be shown by numerical example that the answer is "no." Those who believe that inequality *should* increase until half the population is in the high income group and decrease thereafter might find this result disturbing.

There is, though, an inequality measure that follows the inverted Ushaped pattern and *does* turn at $\Phi = 1/2$, namely, the log variance. It, however, is not Lorenz consistent.

These five commonly used inequality measures (excluding the log variance, which is not Lorenz consistent) all belong to the *same* subclass, namely, the I^L_{max} subclass depicted in Figure 10.6d. Is it possible to construct Lorenz consistent inequality measures possessing the I^L_{min} pattern depicted in Figure 10.6c? The answer is "yes." An example of such a measure is:

$$I = (\Theta - 1)^{\alpha} (K + 1/4 - \Phi(1 - \Phi))^{1-\alpha}$$

where

$$\Theta = y_H/y_L, \quad \Phi \in (0,1)$$
$$= 1, \Theta = 0,1$$
$$0 < \alpha < 1$$

and

$$K > 0.[15]$$

This index is but one example of a real-valued function with the desired properties. There are many other possible representations, e.g., $I' = (\Theta^2 - 1)^{\alpha} (K + 1/4 - \Phi(1 - \Phi))^{1-\alpha}$. It remains to explore the properties of various alternatives and determine their relative merits.

10.5 Conclusion: Do Inequality Measures Measure Inequality?

This chapter has set out different views which prescribe how inequality rankings "ought" to behave in certain circumstances. The Lorenz axioms have been unchallenged. The contribution of this chapter has been to analyze inequality orderings when Lorenz curves cross.

The findings in this chapter raise two conceptual problems for empirical researchers. One problem confronts those who use these measures in empirical applications but who have not yet decided which enlargement pattern they favor. Use of the standard measures implicitly imposes an ordering. Before using one of these measures, the researcher should ask whether the ordering imposed (the I_{max}^L ordering) is the one he or she wishes to impose.

A different problem arises for those of us who believe that inequality "should" be highest when most people are in one income group and few are in the other. For such observers, the standard measures do not do what they "should" do.

The most important task for future work is to expand the domain to allow for intra-group inequality, and for more than two groups.

11

The Absolute Poverty Approach

In the present time, through the greater part of Europe, a creditable day-labourer would be ashamed to appear in public without a linen shirt.

Adam Smith, Wealth of Nations, 1776

11.1 The Measurement of Poverty

11.1.1 *Introduction*

"Poverty" has been defined as the inability of an individual or a family to command sufficient resources to satisfy basic needs. The workman who, in Adam Smith's day, could not appear in public wearing a proper linen shirt, was ipso facto poor, not only to Smith but to Amartya Sen who, commenting on Smith's observation, wrote: "On the space of the capabilities themselves – the direct constituent of the standard of living – escape from poverty has an absolute requirement, to wit, avoidance of this type of shame. Not so much having equal shame as others, but just not being ashamed, absolutely" (Sen 1984, p. 335).

Nowadays, an income recipient is classified as poor on the basis of more than a single item of clothing. A basket of "basic needs" is defined and costed out. Given this figure in dollars, pesos, or rupees, we classify a recipient unit as poor if its income (or consumption, if that is the chosen

The original version of this chapter was published as: Fields, Gary S. (2001). The Measurement of Poverty (73–94), Does Economic Growth Reduce Absolute Poverty? A Review of the Empirical Evidence (95–104), in: G. Fields: Distribution and Development: A New Look at the Developing World. © 2001 by Russell Sage Foundation and the MIT Press.

measure of economic well-being) is below the cutoff amount. This cutoff amount will be called the "poverty line" and be denoted by z.

Over time, the poverty line needs to be adjusted for changes in the cost of acquiring the basket of basic needs. When the poverty line is adjusted for inflation and only for inflation, the line defines "absolute poverty."[1]

Often it is of interest to concentrate our attention on the poor to the exclusion of the rest of the income distribution – for instance, in gauging how much economic misery there is in an economy or in determining whether economic misery is increasing or decreasing. For such purposes, we may be justified in focusing our attention on the economic condition of poor people while ignoring the incomes of those who are demonstrably non-poor. The idea that the extent of poverty in a population is independent of the incomes of those above the poverty line is sometimes called the "focus axiom," and it justifies gauging poverty solely with reference to the incomes of persons below the poverty line.

The rest of this chapter deals with four topics: setting a poverty line, clarifying the concept of poverty, constructing a poverty measure, and testing for poverty dominance. For detailed results on these topics, see inter alia Foster 1984, Atkinson 1987, Seidl 1988, Ravallion 1994, Zheng 1997, and Foster and Sen 1997.

11.1.2 *Setting a Poverty Line*

In some countries, the poverty line has already been set and the best thing to do is to speak of poverty in the same way that others in the country do. In other countries, though, one may be able to define a single poverty line or an entire range of poverty lines, and will therefore have to make some choices about how to do it. In such instances, a number of decisions will need to be made:

1. *Is the basis income or consumption, and how comprehensively will the chosen concept be measured?* Consumption is regarded as the better indicator of living standards, provided it can be accurately measured. The best measure is a comprehensive one, including imputations for food and other goods produced and consumed at home, basic goods provided free or at subsidized rates by the government, and non-wage benefits such as "free" housing provided by the employer.

2. *What is the recipient unit: individual, family, per capita, or adult equivalent?* Adjustments for family size are needed. One method to adjust for family size is to set different poverty lines for families of different sizes (which enables adjustments for economies of scale). Another

method is to set a poverty line on a per capita or an adult-equivalent basis, then adjust income or consumption accordingly.[2] The number of families in poverty should be used only as a last resort.

3. *Will there be a single poverty line or will there be separate ones for urban and rural areas or different regions of the country?* Typically, the cost of the basic basket of necessities is significantly higher in urban than in rural areas, which is why the South Asian countries have been using separate poverty lines for urban and rural areas for decades.

4. *Is the poverty line income determined scientifically, politically, subjectively, or as a matter of convenience?* Governments of individual countries such as India and the United States as well as international organizations such as the Inter-American Development Bank (IDB) and the Economic Commission for Latin America and the Caribbean (ECLAC) have determined their poverty lines "scientifically" by figuring the cost of purchasing nutritional necessities consistent with local dietary habits and adding to that the cost of housing, clothing, and other nonfood necessities.[3] In other countries, the poverty line is determined politically – for example, in Brazil, "poverty" denotes those persons with incomes less than the national minimum wage.[4] Yet another approach is to define poverty subjectively, in answer to a question such as, "What income level do you personally consider to be absolutely minimal? That is to say that with less you could not make ends meet?" There is a long tradition of analyzing poverty subjectively, especially in the Netherlands but elsewhere in Europe as well (Jenkins et al. 1998). And in some cases, there is no poverty line at all, and "poverty" is defined as a matter of convenience in round numbers: below 100,000 New Taiwan dollars or 100,000 Korean won or one U.S. dollar per person per day.[5] Clearly, the more scientific the basis for setting the poverty line, the better.

5. *What use should be made of indicators other than consumption or income?* The United Nations, through its Human Development Reports, and Nobel Price winner Amartya Sen are among those who have been forceful and consistent voices in favor of broad indices of human development and human capabilities.[6] Although one may quarrel with the specific form of the United Nations's human development index, there is little disagreement about the desirability of moving beyond consumption - and income-based measures when possible. Meanwhile, it is often

the case that data are not available on consumption, income, functionings, or capabilities, so other measures are used instead including social indicators (e.g., school attendance, adult literacy rate, per capita food consumption, percentage of dwelling units with running water, extent of electrification, population per physician) and labor market indicators (e.g., unemployment rates, minimum wages, industrial and occupational composition of employment, extent of wage and salary employment).

Finally, it bears repeating that in setting absolute poverty lines, there are two essentials. First, the poverty line must be adjusted for inflation, so that it remains constant in real currency units; when inflation is running at triple-digit rates, such adjustments may have to be made monthly or even weekly.[7] Second, the only adjustment to be made to the poverty line is for inflation; the poverty line must not be adjusted for economic growth, for then it ceases to be an absolute poverty line.

The answers just given have been very brief. For further discussion of these issues, see Atkinson 1987, Ravallion 1994, Gottschalk and Smeeding 1997, Anand and Sen 1997, and Foster and Sen 1997.

11.1.3 *The Concept of Poverty*

The next steps in measuring poverty in an economy are to gauge the poverty of each recipient unit and then to aggregate them. For concreteness, let us suppose that poverty is to be determined by comparing the "income" of an "individual" (y_i) with the poverty line (z). The individual poverty function $p(y_i, z)$ tells us how much poverty is associated with individual income y; when the poverty line is z. The aggregator function then gives us a measure of poverty in the population as a whole. At issue is what properties the individual poverty function $p(y_i, z)$ and the aggregator function should have in order to produce a "good" poverty measure.

Three commonly used individual poverty functions are the indicator function

$$p(y_i, z) = 1 \quad if \quad y_i < z,$$
$$= 0 \text{ otherwise,}$$

the poverty gap function

$$p_2(y_i, z) = z - y_i, \quad if \quad y_i < z,$$
$$= 0 \text{ otherwise,}$$

and the normalized gap function

$$p_3(y_i, z) = (z - y_i)/z \quad if \quad y_i < z,$$
$$= 0 \text{ otherwise.}$$

It is useful to think of these individual poverty functions as loss functions $L(y_i, z)$, indicating the loss from having income y_i when the poverty line is z. These three particular loss functions – the indicator function, the poverty gap function, and the normalized gap function – are depicted in panels (a)–(c) of Figure 11.2.

To get a poverty measure for the economy as a whole, these individual poverty functions are then aggregated. Denote the number of poor people by q and the total population by n. Aggregation might perhaps be by summing

$$P = \sum_i p(y_i, z),$$

by averaging over the poor population

$$P = \frac{1}{q} \sum_i p(y_i, z),$$

or by averaging over the entire population

$$P = \frac{1}{n} \sum_i p(y_i, z),$$

In view of these possibilities, what would be a "good" poverty measure? We shall proceed by considering a number of examples, to compare the amount of poverty in different situations.

As before, we will suppose that we are given a set Ω of income vectors. Given two vectors X, Y ε Ω, the relation $\geqslant p$ (read "at least as much poverty as") provides a basis for comparing their relative degrees of poverty. When both $X \geqslant p$ Y and Y v p X, we shall say that X and Y "have equal poverty" and write this relation as $\sim p$, for example, $X \sim p Y \Leftrightarrow X \geqslant p Y$ and $Y \geqslant p X$. The binary relations $\geqslant p$ and $\sim p$ are assumed to satisfy reflexivity $\mathbf{R}$ $(X \sim p X$ and $X \sim p X$ for all X ε $\Omega)$ and transitivity $\mathbf{Tr}$ (if $X \geqslant p X'$ and $X' \geqslant p X''$ and likewise for $\sim p$.

In all of the following examples, the poverty line z is taken to be \$2.50 per unit of time.

Consider two income distribution vectors

$$Y_1 = (1, \quad 2, \quad 3, \quad 4)$$
$$\alpha, \quad \beta, \quad \gamma, \quad \delta$$

and

$$Y_2 = (1, \quad 2, \quad 3, \quad 4)$$
$$\alpha, \quad \beta, \quad \gamma, \quad \delta$$

which are identical except that one is a permutation of the other. As with inequality comparisons, unless there is something different about the income recipients in the two cases, it is appealing to say that Y_1 and Y_2 have the same degree of poverty.[8] Accepting this idea as an axiom, anonymity in poverty comparisons is defined as the following property:

Figure 11.1. Four loss-from-poverty functions.

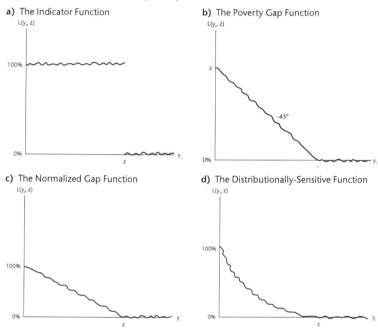

a) The Indicator Function

b) The Poverty Gap Function

c) The Normalized Gap Function

d) The Distributionally-Sensitive Function

ANONYMITY (**A**):   If $X \ \varepsilon \ \Omega$ is obtained from $Y \ \varepsilon \ \Omega$ by a permutation of Y, $X \sim_p Y$.

Our next question is how to compare the degrees of poverty in two economies with different total income amounts. Suppose that everyone's real income doubles, producing the new income distribution vector

$$Y_3 = (2, 4, 6, 8).$$

How does the poverty of Y_3 compare with that of Y_1 and Y_2?

This is where the decision to look at absolute poverty is crucial. For as long as the poverty line z is set as a *constant* real income figure, when everyone's real income rises, poverty must fall (or at least not increase).

Continuing with our example, when the poverty line is $2.50, in Y_1 and Y_2, two people are poor and their average income shortfall is $1, whereas in Y_3, one person is poor and his/her shortfall is $.50. This demonstrates why it is that we do *not* want to have an income-homogeneity axiom for a *poverty* measure, and for this reason, no such axiom is proposed.

Consider now how to compare poverties in populations of different sizes, for example,

$$Y_3 = (2, 4, 6, 8)$$

and

$$Y_4 = (2, 2, 4, 4, 6, 6, 8, 8),$$

again using a poverty line of $2.50. Two answers are reasonable, though they convey different information. On the one hand, it could be said that Y_4 has *twice as much* poverty as Y_3, because Y_4 has two poor people whereas Y_3 only has one, Y_4 has a total poverty gap of $1.00 (=$.50 per poor person x 2 poor persons) whereas Y_3 has a gap of only $.50, and so on. On the other hand, Y_3 and Y_4 both have 25 percent of the population in poverty and the average poverty gap is $.50 in both, so in this sense, Y_3 and Y_4 have *the same* poverty as each other.

When populations of different sizes are being compared, the per capita comparison may convey a better sense of the magnitude of the problem. In most circumstances, we would probably not want to say that India has more poverty than Singapore simply because there are more than three hundred times as many Indians as Singaporeans. So the following axiom may be appealing:

POPULATION HOMOGENEITY.
(ALSO CALLED POPULATION INDEPENDENCE) (P):
If $X \ \varepsilon \ \Omega$ is obtained from $Y \ \varepsilon \ \Omega$ by replicating each income an integral number of times, then $X \sim p \ Y$.

Thus far, we have no basis for making poverty comparisons when income amounts differ. An axiom which has been used by Sen (1976) and others enables such comparisons to be made in some circumstances:

MONOTONICITY AND STRONG MONOTONICITY (M AND SM):
1. Monotonicity: If $X \ \varepsilon \ \Omega$ is obtained from $Y \ \varepsilon \ \Omega$ by adding a positive amount of income to someone who was below the poverty line, holding all other incomes the same, then $Y \geqslant p \ X$.
2. Strong monotonicity: Replace $\geqslant p$ by $> p$.

Finally, we have a transfer principle for poverty measurement, also introduced by Sen (1976). If a transfer of income is made from a poor person to any person who is richer, then poverty must increase. For example, take the income distribution

$$Y_1 = (1, 2, 3, 4),$$

and let the poverty line be $2.50. Now let the person with an initial income of $1 transfer $.25 to the individual with an initial income of $2, producing the new income distribution

$$Y_5 = (.75, 2.25, 3, 4).$$

It might be argued that poverty *increases* when such a transfer is made, because although there are the same number of poor and the same average income shortfall among the poor in the two situations, the transfer of income from a very poor person to a not-so-poor poor person may be said to raise the economic well-being of the recipient by less than it lowers the economic well-being of the donor.[9] By this argument, the loss-from-poverty function is strictly convex on *[0, z]*, as shown in panel (d) of Figure 11.1. In the poverty literature, such functions are said to be "distributionally sensitive." Accordingly, we have the following axiom:

DISTRIBUTIONAL SENSITIVITY (DS):
If, holding all other incomes the same, $X \ \varepsilon \ \Omega$ is obtained from $Y \ \varepsilon \ \Omega$ by transferring a positive amount of income from a poor person α to a richer person β, then $X >_p Y$. (The strict poverty relation $>_p$ is defined as $\geq_p$ but not $\sim_p$.)

We have defined reflexivity (**R**), transitivity (**Tr**), anonymity (**A**), population homogeneity (**P**), monotonicity (**M**) and strong monotonicity (**SM**), and distributional sensitivity (**DS**). Let us now see how a number of commonly used poverty measures stack up against these axioms.

11.1.4 *Four Groups of Poverty Measures*

In this section, we shall consider four groups of poverty measures. These are the poverty headcount and headcount ratio; the Sen index and generalizations; the P_α class; and other miscellaneous poverty measures. Throughout this section, z will be used to denote the poverty line, n the total number of income recipients ("persons"), and q the number who are adjudged to be poor using poverty line z.

The Poverty Headcount and Headcount Ratio

The poverty headcount (H) is defined as the *number* of people in a population who are poor, while the poverty headcount ratio (*H*) is the *fraction* who are poor:

$$H = q$$

and

$$H = q/n.$$

Both of these measures use the individual poverty function

$$p(y_i, z) = 1 \quad \text{if} \quad y_i < z,$$
$$= 0 \text{ otherwise.}$$

Their aggregator functions are, respectively,

$$P = \sum_i p(y_i, z)$$

and

$$P = \frac{1}{n} \sum_i p(y_i, z).$$

Which of the preceding properties are satisfied by H and *H*? As with all the other poverty measures to be considered in this section, H and *H* satisfy reflexivity (**R**), transitivity (**Tr**), and anonymity (**A**). The income distribution (1, 1, 2, 2, 3, 3, 4, 4) has a higher poverty headcount H than does the income distribution (1, 2, 3, 4), therefore H does not satisfy population-homogeneity (**P**). Population-homogeneity is, however, satisfied by the headcount ratio *H*. Because both the poverty headcount H and the headcount ratio *H* are concerned only with the number of people with incomes below the poverty line but not with their incomes, neither satisfies strong monotonicity (**SM**) nor distributional sensitivity (**DS**).[10]

If you find **SM** and **DS** appealing, then the poverty headcount H and the poverty headcount ratio *H* are not good poverty measures for you. Why, then, are these measures used so often? There are three main reasons. One is that poverty headcounts and headcount ratios are straightforward conceptually: when we read that 1.3 billion persons in the world are poor using a poverty line of US\$1 per person per day (World Bank 1999; United Nations 1999), the extent of poverty is easily grasped. Second, some researchers and statistical bureaus have not fully considered the desirability of using measures with the **SM** and **DS** properties or, in some cases, acted on that understanding. And third, even in cases where the analyst is fully aware that other poverty measures are preferable to H and *H*, there may simply be no data enabling poverty comparisons to be made using measures with the **SM** and **DS** properties.[11] For these reasons, the poverty headcount and headcount ratio continue to be used in empirical work.

When micro data are available, as they are increasingly coming to be, one can calculate a variety of other poverty measures even when they are not published by national statistical offices.[12] The two classes of measures that follow are increasingly being calculated by individual researchers.

The Sen Index of Poverty

Let us adopt the following notation:

$\bar{Y}_p$ = the average income of the poor,

$\bar{I}$ = $(z-\bar{Y}_p)/z$ the average (normalized) income shortfall among the poor,

and

G_p = Gini coefficient of income inequality among the poor.

The Sen poverty index, P_{Sen}, is defined as

$$P_{Sen} = H[\bar{I} + (1 - \bar{I})G_p].$$

It is apparent from this formula that the Sen index has the following three characteristics:

(i) Other things equal, the larger is the fraction of income recipients who fall below the poverty line, the larger is P_{Sen};
(ii) Other things equal, the higher is the average income of those below the poverty line, the lower is P_{Sen};[13] and
(iii) Other things equal, the greater is income inequality among the poor, the greater is P_{Sen}.[14]

The Sen index has been generalized by a number of authors; see Foster and Sen 1997 (p. 173) for a summary.

The P_α Class

This class of measures was devised by Foster, Greer, and Thorbecke (1984). It is best understood by considering the ith individual's normalized gap function

$$p_3 (y_i, z) = (z - y_i)/z \quad \text{if} \quad y_i < z,$$
$$= 0 \text{ otherwise.}$$

Consider a poverty measure which weights each individual's normalized gap function by itself – thus, the income of an individual whose income is 10 percent below the poverty line is weighted by 10 percent, the income of an individual whose income is 50 percent below the poverty line is weighted by 50 percent, and so on. Average these squared percentage shortfalls over the entire population.[15] The resultant poverty measure is

$$P_2 \equiv \frac{1}{n} \sum_{i=1}^{q} [(z - y_i)/z]^2.$$

Other members of the P_α class besides the P_2 measure also have intuitive meaning. For $\alpha = 1$, we have

$$P_1 = \frac{1}{n} \sum_{i=1}^{q} [(z - y_i)/z] = \frac{q}{n} \frac{1}{q} \sum_{i=1}^{q} [(z - y_i)/z] = H\bar{I},$$

that is, P_1 is the "per capita income gap" or the "normalized poverty deficit."[16] And for $\alpha = 0$, we have that $P_0 = q/n = H$, the poverty headcount ratio. We see too that as we progress from P_0 to P_1 to P_2, the P_α measure gets more and more sensitive to extremely low incomes.

In the empirical literature, the P_2 measure is being calculated increasingly often.

Other Poverty Measures

Before leaving this presentation of poverty measures, let us briefly note some other measures that one sometimes finds in use. One is *the average (normalized) income shortfall among the poor*, $I = (z - \bar{y}_p)/z$, taken by itself. The problem with this measure is that if an individual just below the poverty line receives a large enough income gain to escape poverty, the average income among the remaining poor $\bar{y}_p$ falls, and therefore I rises. That is, making a poor person richer has *raised* poverty, violating the monotonicity axiom (**M**). This is why, if one finds monotonicity appealing, I is not a good poverty measure to use.[17]

Another poverty measure that has been suggested – actually, the first poverty measure that was sensitive not only to the number of poor but also to the severity of their poverty – is attributable to Watts (1968):

$$P_{Watts} = \sum_{i=1}^{q} \log(z/y_i)/n.$$

Another early poverty measure that is also sensitive to the severity of poverty is the second measure of Clark, Hemming, and Ulph (1981)

$$P_{C\text{-}H\text{-}U} = \frac{1}{c} \sum_{i=1}^{q} [1 - (y_i/z)^c]/n, \quad \text{where } c \leq 1.$$

One finds these measures used only occasionally in empirical work.

11.1.5 *Poverty Dominance*

All of the poverty measures presented in Section 11.1.4 permit complete binary comparisons for any two income distribution vectors X, $Y \in \Omega$. That is, given a particular poverty measure $P(.)$ and a particular poverty line z, the poverty measure $P(.)$ is able to say which distribution has more poverty than the other.

Uncertainty arises in poverty comparisons from two sources: We may not be sure where exactly to draw the poverty line z, and we may not be prepared to commit to a particular poverty measure to the exclusion of others. We could, of course, make numerical calculations for a wide range of poverty lines and poverty measures and see if they all rank X as having more (or less) poverty than Y. But even this would not be conclusive proof; it could be that one of the other poverty measure/poverty line combinations that we didn't try would give the opposite ranking.

Fortunately, dominance methods are now available to test whether one income distribution has more poverty than another for a broad class of poverty measures and a wide range of poverty lines. Unlike inequality measurement, in which dominance theory has a long tradition, dominance analysis in poverty measurement is still a new field. Important contributions have been made by Atkinson (1987), Foster and Shorrocks (1988), Ravallion (1994), and Jenkins and Lambert (1998). Poverty dominance may be nested within the broader concept of "deprivation dominance" (Jenkins and Lambert 1997; Xu and Osberg 1998; Shorrocks 1998).

We begin by noting that most of the poverty measures considered in this chapter – including the headcount ratio, the P_α measure, the Watts index, and the Clark-Hemming-Ulph measure, among others – are members of the general additive class

(1) $P = \sum_{i=1}^{n} p(z, y_i)/n$ such that

1. $p(z, y_i) = 0$ if $y_i \geq z$,   and
2. $p(z, y_i) > 0$ if $y_i \leq z$

The fact that many poverty measures belong to this general class (but not all do – in particular, the Sen index does not) leads us to consider whether there are dominance criteria for these measures. One may pose three related questions:

1. Are there circumstances under which *all* members of the class of poverty measures (1) would rank one income distribution as having more poverty than another for a *given* poverty line z?

2. Given the controversy that usually goes with setting a poverty line, dominance criteria encompassing many poverty lines would be very desirable. In particular, are there circumstances under which a *given* poverty measure belonging to class (1) would rank

Figure 11.2.

a) Poverty Incidence Curves for two Distributions A and B.

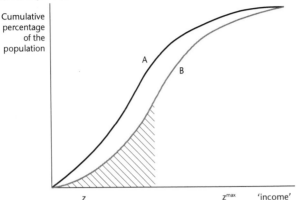

b) Poverty Deficit Curve for Distribution B.

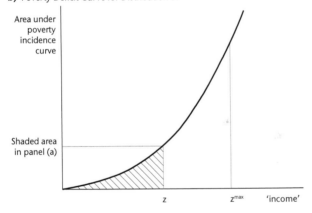

c) Poverty Severity Curve for Distribution B.

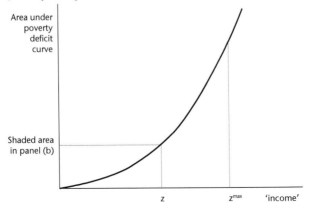

one income distribution as having more poverty than another for a *range* of poverty lines $\underline{z} < z < \dot{z}$?

3. Are there circumstances under which *all* poverty measures belonging to class (1) would rank one income distribution as having more poverty than another for a *range* of poverty lines $\underline{z} < z < \dot{z}$?

This section shows that the answers to all three questions are affirmative. The following notation will be used:

z = poverty line,
y_{min} = lowest income in population,
y_{max} = highest income in population,
z_{max} = highest possible poverty line,
$F_X(z)$ = cumulative density function for distribution X when the poverty line is z, also called the "poverty incidence curve."

For the class of poverty measures given by (1), we now consider three levels of poverty dominance.

First-Order Dominance (FOD)
First-order dominance in poverty measurement is defined as follows: If the cumulative density function for distribution $A(F_A)$ is everywhere at least as high as that for distribution $B(F_B)$ for all z between y_{min} and z_{max}, A *first-order-dominates B*, written A FOD B. (See Figure 11.2.a) An increase in some poor person's income, holding other poor persons' incomes constant, is sufficient but not necessary for first-order dominance.

The relationship between *FOD* and poverty dominance using measures belonging to the class (1) is given by the following theorem:

THEOREM II.I (ATKINSON 1987; FOSTER AND SHORROKS 1988):
A FOD $B \Leftrightarrow pov_A > pov_B$ for all poverty measures belonging to the class (1), or for any monotonic transformation thereof, and for all poverty lines between y_{min} and z_{max}.

As applied to the P_α class, Theorem 11.1 tells us that A FOD $B \Rightarrow pov_A > pov_B$ for all P_α, $\alpha \geq 0$ and for all poverty lines between y_{min} and z_{max}.

Theorem 11.1 gives a condition for ranking two income distributions when their poverty incidence curves do not cross. If they do cross, rankings may be still be possible using the results of:

Second-Order Dominance
Second-order dominance in poverty measurement is defined as follows: Take the areas under the F_A and F_B curves. Call these *poverty deficit curves*,

$D(z)$, as in Figure 11.2.b. If the poverty deficit curve for A is somewhere above and never below the curve for B for all z between y_{min} and z_{max}, A *second-order-dominates* B, written A SOD B.

A subset of the measures belonging to the class (1) will give identical poverty rankings in cases of second-order dominance. Specifically:

THEOREM 11.2 (ATKINSON; FOSTER AND SHORROCKS):
A SOD $B \Leftrightarrow pov_A > pov_B$ for the subset of poverty measures belonging to the class (1) which are strictly decreasing and at least weakly convex in the incomes of the poor, or for any monotonic transformation thereof, and for all poverty lines between y_{min} and z_{max}.

For the P_α class, Theorem 11.2 tells us that A SOD $B \Rightarrow pov_A > pov_B$ for all P_α, $\alpha \geq 1$ and for all poverty lines between y_{min} and z_{max}.

If poverty deficit curves do not cross, Theorem 11.2 provides a criterion for ranking the poverty of different income distributions. However, the poverty deficit curves may cross, in which case poverty rankings may still be possible by turning to:

Third-Order Dominance
Third-order dominance in poverty measurement is defined analogously to second-order dominance. Take the areas under the poverty deficit curves for distributions A and B and call these *poverty severity curves*, $S(z)$. (See Figure 11.2.c.) If the poverty severity curve for A is somewhere above and never below the poverty severity curve for B for all z between y_{min} and z_{max}, A *third-order dominates* B, written A TOD B.

Before stating the next theorem, recall the definition of distributional sensitivity given above. We then have:

THEOREM 11.3 (ATKINSON, FOSTER, AND SHORROCKS):
A TOD $B \Leftrightarrow pov_A > pov_B$ for the subset of poverty measures belonging to the class (1) which are distributionally-sensitive, or for any monotonic transformation thereof, and for all poverty lines between y_{min} and z_{max}.

For the P_α class, Theorem 11.3 tells us that A TOD $B \Leftrightarrow pov_A > pov_B$ for all P_α, $\alpha \geq 2$ and for all poverty lines between y_{min} and z_{max}.

Comparing the Different Levels of Dominance
When we examine the definitions of the various levels of dominance, we see a hierarchical relationship among them: If A FOD B, then the area under the poverty incidence curve for A is necessarily greater than the area under the poverty incidence curve for B, which is the definition of second-order

dominance. Likewise, given second-order dominance, the area under the poverty deficit curve for A is necessarily greater than the area under the poverty deficit curve for B, which is the definition of third-order dominance. Thus:

(2) $$\text{FOD} \Rightarrow \text{SOD} \Rightarrow \text{TOD}.$$

Fact (2) makes precise exactly how far you can go in defining the variety of poverty measures and range of poverty lines for which one income distribution has more poverty than another. For instance, if neither A FOD B nor B FOD A but A SOD B, then you can conclude that A has more poverty than B only for those poverty measures in class (1) which are strictly decreasing and at least weakly convex in the incomes of the poor, or for any monotonic transformation thereof, and for all poverty lines between y_{min} and z_{max}. You would know too that because the poverty headcount ratio is not strictly decreasing in the incomes of the poor, that that measure would not necessarily show greater poverty in A than in B.

Suppose you have decided that you like the P_α class of poverty measures, but you are not sure how far these measures can take you in making ordinal poverty comparisons. Pulling together the preceding results, here is your answer:

1. A FOD $B \Rightarrow pov_A > pov_B$ for all P_α, $\alpha \geq 0$ and for all poverty lines between y_{min} and z_{max}.
2. A SOD $B \Rightarrow pov_A > pov_B$ for all P_α, $\alpha \geq 1$ and for all poverty lines between y_{min} and z_{max}.
3. A TOD $B \Rightarrow pov_A > pov_B$ for all P_α, $\alpha \geq 2$ and for all poverty lines between y_{min} and z_{max}.

Finally, it bears mention that your search for dominance results may be frustrated, because you have chosen a wider than necessary range for possible poverty lines. For example, you may have initially set z_{max} at a very high value (e.g., \$50,000 per capita per year) and then found that the poverty incidence curves cross at a lower income amount z^* (e.g., \$40,000), as shown in Figure 11.3. In such cases, you might want to reset z_{max} to z^*, which would enable you to conclude that A FOD B for all poverty lines in the restricted range $[y_{min}, z^*]$.

11.1.6 *The Concept of Relative Poverty*

Thus far in this chapter, we have dealt only with absolute poverty. Some authors (e.g., Fuchs 1967, 1969; Ruggles 1990; Citro and Michael 1995; Ali 1997; Ali and Thorbecke 1998) take exception to this approach to determining poverty lines, preferring to measure relative poverty instead.[18] For rigorous discussions of absolute versus relative poverty, see Foster and Sen 1997 and Foster 1998.

Figure 11.3. Intersecting Poverty Incidence curves.

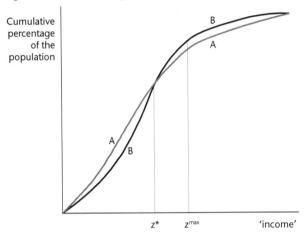

Source: Ravallion 1994 (p. 70)

Actually, "relative poverty" embodies two separate ideas, and the relative poverty measures therefore fall into two categories. In the first type of relative poverty measure, a group that is relatively the poorest (e.g., the poorest 40 percent) is defined, and the poverty measure used is then taken to be the average real income of this poorest group. Consider the following example, in which the income distribution changes from

$$\text{Initial} = \underbrace{(1, 1, 1, 1, 1, 1, 1, 1, 1,}_{9} \underbrace{2)}_{1}$$

to

$$\text{A-C-E-G} = \underbrace{(1, 1, 1, 1, 1, 1, 1, 1,}_{8} \underbrace{2, 2)}_{2}$$

to

$$\text{B-D-F-H} = \underbrace{(1, 1, 1, 1, 1, 1, 1,}_{7} \underbrace{2, 2, 2)}_{3}.$$

The average absolute income of the poorest 40 percent of the population shows no change in this process. If you see no change in poverty in this process, this type of relative poverty measure might be a reasonable one for you. But if you judge that poverty has decreased in this process, then you are assuredly not a relative poverty adherent, at least in this first sense.

There is, however, a second sense in which you might wish to move in the direction of relative poverty, and that is to use a higher poverty line the richer is the country in which poverty is being measured. Ravallion, Datt, and van de Walle (1991) have found empirically that the poverty lines used in countries tend to increase with their per capita consumption levels, and Ali (1997) regards the desirability of raising the poverty line as the mean increases as "obvious to us, Africans living amidst poverty." While there are different ways of adjusting your poverty line z as a function of the mean income or consumption, μ, the easiest such adjustment is to raise z in proportion to increases in μ, producing a thoroughgoing relative poverty measure. This procedure applies either when z has been set "scientifically" to begin with (e.g., as the cost of purchasing the minimal basket of goods and services) or when z has been set relatively from the beginning. Examples of such relative poverty lines are half the median income (Fuchs 1969), two-thirds of the median income, as is done by the Luxembourg Income Study (Atkinson et al. 1995), half the mean income, as is done by the European Union (O'Higgins and Jenkins 1990; Atkinson 1998) or two-thirds of the median income, as is used on occasion by the World Bank.

Now let us examine what happens to relative poverty when the poverty line z increases proportionately with the mean μ. We may start with a given income distribution X and then increase everybody's real income by the same proportion, producing the new income distribution λX, $\lambda > 1$. When z increases proportionately with μ, the number with incomes below such a relative poverty line is unchanged. So too are the average (normalized) income shortfall of the poor $\bar{I}$ and the Gini coefficient of income inequality among the poor. This means that the poverty headcount (H), the poverty headcount ratio (H), the Sen index of poverty (P_{sen}), and the P_α class will all show *no change* in poverty when z changes in proportion to μ.

You now need to ask yourself whether this is what you want. Personally, I would want poverty in a country to *fall* when everyone experiences a given percentage increase in income. If you feel the same, then these relative poverty approaches are not for you.[19]

One alternative is to increase the poverty line when economic growth takes place, but by a smaller percentage than the growth rate. Because this is neither fully absolute nor fully relative, it has been termed a "hybrid" approach by Foster (1998). See Citro and Michael 1995 and Atkinson and Bourguignon 1999 for detailed proposals along these lines.

I prefer a different alternative, which is to choose an absolute poverty line, relatively defined. That is, you can set your z higher in relatively rich countries than in relatively poor ones. This is in fact done: The poverty lines used around the world (in 1985 Purchasing Power Parity [PPP] dollars, per person per day) range from $1 for developing countries as a whole to $2 in Latin America to $4 in Eastern Europe and the Commonwealth of Independence States (CIS) nations to $14.40 in the United States. Once these lines are set, they should be adjusted by the respective countries' rates of inflation and nothing more. The best problem that any country could have would be for its economy to grow so fast for so long that its current poverty line is rendered obsolete!

11.1.7 Summary

"Poverty" has been defined as the inability of an individual or a family to command sufficient resources to satisfy basic needs. A number of technical considerations go into setting a country's poverty line. If we can agree on where to set the poverty line, we can gauge the amount of poverty in a population by measuring the extent of poverty for each constituent individual and then totaling these using a suitable aggregator function. Among the axioms that might be desirable for poverty measures are anonymity, population-homogeneity, monotonicity or strong monotonicity, and distributional sensitivity. The poverty headcount possesses only the first of these properties and the poverty headcount ratio only the first two. However, all four properties are satisfied by the Sen poverty index and the P_α index for $\alpha > 1$. If we are uncertain which poverty measure or which poverty line to use, we may under certain conditions be able to use dominance results to obtain ordinal poverty rankings for a broad class of poverty measures and a broad range of poverty lines; see Section 11.1.5 for details. Finally, and alternatively, if you prefer relative poverty notions to absolute poverty ones, you may prefer one of the types of measures described in Section 11.1.6.

11.2 Does Economic Growth Reduce Absolute Poverty? A Review of the Empirical Evidence

Most economists accept without question that economic growth reduces absolute poverty. Some of the phrases in our profession reflect this: "trickle-down," "a rising tide lifts all boats," "the flying geese," and so on. I shall refer to this view as the "shared growth" position, in that when economic growth takes place, the poor and others share the fruits of it, to a greater or lesser degree.[20]

On the other side is the distinctly less popular view that economic growth might make the poor poorer. To take just one example, Nobel Prize-winning economist Arthur Lewis (1983) gave six reasons why development of enclaves may lower incomes in the traditional sector: The development enclave may be predatory on the traditional sectors; products of the enclaves may compete with and destroy traditional trades; the wage level of the enclave may be so high that it destroys employment in other sectors; the development of the enclave may result in geographical polarization; development of the enclave may lead to generalized improvements in public health and therefore lower death rates; and development of the enclave may stimulate excessive migration from the countryside.

The most respectable present incarnation of this view is in the work of immiserizing growth theorists, who have proven rigorously that it is possible that economic growth *might* make the poor poorer.[21] Whether growth *does* make the poor poorer or not is an empirical question, to which we now turn.

11.2.1 *Inferences from Cross-Section Evidence*

The immiserizing growth hypothesis gained a brief bit of apparent support in the work of Adelman and Morris (1973). They wrote (p. 189): "Development is accompanied by an absolute as well as a relative decline in the average income of the very poor. Indeed, an initial spurt of dualistic growth may cause such a decline for as much as 60 percent of the population." They continued (p. 192): "The frightening implication of the present work is that hundreds of millions of desperately poor people throughout the world have been hurt rather than helped by economic development."

Their results were based on an indirect method that did not survive further scrutiny. One of the most influential subsequent studies was by Ahluwalia (1976b), who compiled data for 62 countries, both developed and developing, for roughly 1970, and regressed the income share of the poorest 20 percent, 40 percent, or 60 percent of the population against log per capita GNP, log per capita GNP squared, and other variables. These shares were then combined with GNP information to produce the average absolute incomes shown in Figure 11.4. We see that as per capita national income increases in the cross-section, the incomes of the poorest *rise* monotonically.

The most direct test of the poverty/national income relationship in the cross-section is to be found in the recent work of Ravallion (1995), based on data from Chen, Datt, and Ravallion (1993). Using an internationally comparable poverty line ($1 of consumption per capita per day in 1985 PPP$), he calculated the poverty headcount index for each of 36 developing countries. The results, shown in Figure 11.5, reveal a pronounced negative relationship between a country's poverty rate and its average level of consumption.

Figure 11.4. Average income levels of low-income groups, international cross-section.

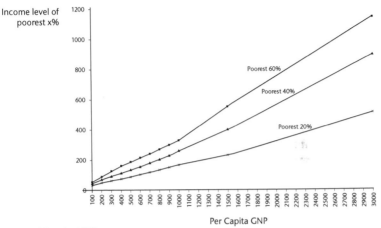

Source: Ahluwalia 1976b.

Figure 11.5. Headcount index against mean consumption.

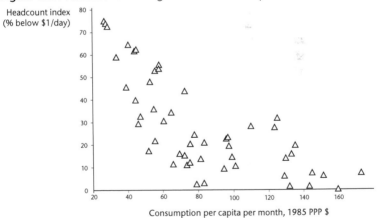

Source: Ravallion 1995 (p. 413).

In follow-up work, Lipton (1998) used data for the same countries as Ravallion, but also including a second year of data where possible. His regressions showed that half the variance in poverty rates (expressed as the percentage of population below the $1 per day consumption line) could be explained by mean consumption. It may be presumed that the countries' individual circumstances and policies help explain the other half.

241

In sum, twenty years of research has shown convincingly that in a cross-section of countries, those with higher per capita income or consumption have less poverty. The cross-sectional version of the absolute impoverishment hypothesis has been thoroughly discredited.

11.2.2 *Intertemporal Evidence*

The results reported in the previous section described the relationship between poverty and national income growth in the cross-section. What about changes in poverty over time within countries? In the Western world, the early studies of changes in income distribution over time in individual developing countries concentrated on inequality rather than on poverty, reflecting the powerful intellectual influence of Simon Kuznets (1955, 1963) and followers.

However, in some countries of the Eastern world such as India, the focus on poverty was there all along (Srinivasan and Bardhan 1974). What was not there for quite some time, however, was statistical information with which to measure how poverty changed with economic growth in individual countries.

Once the data started becoming available in the 1970s, authors around the world performed studies of poverty change in individual countries. Fields (1980) synthesized thirteen of these. Poverty fell in ten of these countries and rose in three. Two of the three countries in which poverty did not fall are ones in which economic growth did not take place. The only country in which poverty rose in the course of economic growth was the Philippines. The apparent political economy explanation ("crony capitalism") is probably the right one.

In a concurrent study, Ahluwalia, Carter, and Chenery (1979) looked at changes in incomes of both the poorest 60 percent and the richest 40 percent for twelve developing countries. Their results show that in *every* case, the real incomes of the poorest 60 percent and the richest 40 percent both increased over time when the economy grew.

In the 1980s and 1990s, additional country studies were carried out, using increasingly comprehensive data sets. These include the work of Fields (1991); Chen, Datt, and Ravallion (1993); Deininger and Squire (1996); Roemer and Gugerty (1997); Timmer (1997); and Bruno, Ravallion, and Squire (1998). All of these studies used so-called "spell analysis."[22] The results were always the same: It is overwhelmingly the case that growth reduces poverty and recession increases it, though in about 10 percent of the cases, poverty did not appear to fall when growth took place.

The finding that economic growth nearly always reduces poverty is sometimes misinterpreted. Of course, not every individual is made richer by economic growth, nor even every population subgroup. Early on, Fishlow (1972) wrote eloquently about the poverty that remained in Brazil despite the so-called economic miracle that had taken place there in the late 1960s and early 1970s, and Griffin and Khan (1978) demonstrated that the percentage of rural people who were poor had increased despite economic growth in a number of South and Southeast Asian economies. The reports on poverty by the World Bank (1990, forthcoming) and the United Nations (1997) remind us that even when the majority of a country's people are found to gain from economic growth, some are left out or even hurt by the growth process.

Economic growth would be expected to alleviate poverty, at least to some extent. How much depends on at least two factors. One is the growth rate itself. A study by Squire (1993) used an internationally comparable poverty line and regressed the rate of poverty reduction in a country against its rate of of economic growth. His results show that a one percent increase in the growth rate reduces the poverty headcount ratio by 0.24 percentage points. Similarly, Ravallion and Chen (1997) found that the larger the rate of change in log mean consumption or income in a country, the larger the decline in a country's log poverty rate. Furthermore, Roemer and Gugerty (1997) found that in the economic growth experiences of twenty-six developing countries, the rate of increase of the incomes of the poorest 20 percent was 92 percent of the rate of GDP growth, while for the poorest 40 percent, the rate of increase was essentially identical to the rate of GDP growth. Thus, in all these studies, faster economic growth has been found to lead to greater poverty reduction.

The rate of poverty reduction would also be expected to depend on the extent of economic inequality. In a very straightforward statistical sense, we would expect to find that economic growth reduces poverty by more if inequality falls than if it does not. This expectation is confirmed in cross-country analysis carried out by Bruno, Ravallion, and Squire (1998). For twenty countries during the period 1984–1993, they regressed the rate of change in the proportion of the population living on less than $1 per person per day against the rate of change in real mean income and obtained a regression coefficient of -2.12 with a t ratio of -4.67. This means that a 10 percent increase in the mean can be expected to produce a roughly 20 percent drop in the proportion of people in poverty. And when the P_2 measure is used instead, the effect is even greater: -3.46 with a t ratio of -2.98. They conclude: "Absolute poverty measures typically respond quite elastically to growth, and the benefits are certainly not confined to those near the poverty line."

To see what role inequality plays in poverty reduction, these authors also ran a multiple regression of the change in poverty (using the proportion of the population living on less than $1 per person per day) as a function of both the change in the mean and the change in inequality as measured by the Gini coefficient and found a coefficient of -2.28 (t = -6.07) on the former and 3.86 (t = 3.20) on the latter. In their words (p. 11): "Measured changes in inequality do have a strong independent explanatory power; indeed, rates of poverty reduction respond even more elastically to rates of change in the Gini index than they do to the mean."

The Bruno-Ravallion-Squire findings show that the change in poverty is related both to economic growth and to changing inequality. First, holding the dispersion of income the same, the faster is the rate of economic growth, the larger is the reduction in poverty. Second, for any given growth rate, the more dispersed the distribution is becoming, the smaller is the reduction in poverty.[23]

The relative importance of these growth and redistributive factors for poverty reduction can be gauged using the following equation devised by Ravallion and Huppi (1991), Datt and Ravallion (1992), and Kakwani (1993). Let poverty in a country at time t be denoted by

$$P_t = P(z/\mu_t, D_t),$$

where z is the poverty line, μ_t is mean expenditure per capita, and D_t is the inequality in the distribution of expenditure per capita. Then the change in poverty between a base year B and a terminal year T can be written as

$$P_T - P_B = \underbrace{P(z/\mu_T, D_B) - P(z/\mu_B, D_B)}_{\text{Growth component}}$$

$$\underbrace{+ \, P(z/\mu_B, D_T) - P(z/\mu_B, D_B)}_{\text{Redistribution component}} + \text{residual}.$$

Applying this methodology to developing countries in Africa, Latin America, and East and Southeast Asia, Demery, Sen, and Vishwanath (1995) came to two conclusions. First, poverty change is largely determined by economic growth. Second, changes in inequality are of secondary importance in the great majority of cases.

An important qualifier needs to be added. In countries' actual experiences, it has proved far easier to generate economic growth than to change the Gini coefficient. In the developing world, GOP per capita grew by 26 percent between 1985 and 1995 (World Bank 1997), while Gini coefficients in the world barely changed over the same period (Deininger and Squire 1998, table 5). In a similar vein, Adelman and Robinson's simulation results showed that even huge changes in policy parameters (such as a doubling of the tax rate, increasing agricultural capital stocks by 30 percent, fixing all agricultural prices at world prices, and subsidizing the consumption of food, housing, and medical services for the poorest 60 percent of households) would change the Gini coefficient in Korea by only one or two Gini points in most cases. The point is that in comparing the elasticities of poverty with respect to growth and with respect to inequality, one should not fall into the trap of thinking that it is as easy to lower inequality by 10 percent as it is to achieve 10 percent growth; the former is far more difficult than the latter.

11.2.3 *Poverty Reduction and Growth: Individual Country Experiences*

The data presented in the previous section showed that the predominant tendency is for poverty to fall when economic growth takes place. This happens in the great majority of cases. Consequently, the shared growth view is clearly a better general description of the growth/poverty relationship than is the immiserizing growth position.

Not only does this conclusion hold in general but it holds for every region of the world. In Asia, the "big five" countries – China, India, Indonesia, Pakistan, and Bangladesh, which together have threefifths of the developing world's people and two-fifths of the poor – have all made "impressive progress" in reducing income poverty (United Nations 1997). Ahuja et al. (1997) report that "poverty has been declining in every East Asian economy for which we have data except Papua New Guinea."[24] Unfortunately, the crisis of the late 1990s in a number of East and Southeast Asian countries has demonstrated that the relationship between growth and poverty holds in times of economic decline as well. Although direct data on poverty are not yet available for the post-crisis period, the dramatic increase in unemployment caused by the crisis is surely leading to an increase in poverty (ILO 1998a; Manuelyan-Atinc and Walton 1998).

In Latin America and the Caribbean (LAC), data compiled by Londoño and Székely (1998) show that poverty rose during the 1980s and fell slightly during the 1990s. The 1980s was a "lost decade" for Latin America, the growth rate in the region being a negative 1.2 percent (Inter-American Development Bank 1991). In the 1990s, the region experienced a modest recovery: a 6 percent increase (total, not per annum) in real GOP per capita and a 4 percent increase in private consumption. Changes in poverty within countries mirror this trend: During the negative growth decade, the poverty headcount ratio rose in ten of the thirteen countries in Latin America and the Caribbean for which we have data, whereas in the recovery, it fell in nine of the thirteen.[25]

In Africa, the experiences that have been documented also show that when growth has taken place, poverty has fallen. This was the case in

Morocco and Tunisia in the latter half of the 1980s (Chen, Datt, and Ravallion 1993), in Ghana from 1987/1988 to 1991/1992 (World Bank 1995; Ghana Statistical Service 1995), in Nigeria from 1985 to 1992 (Canagarajah, Nwafon, and Thomas 1995), and in rural Ethiopia from 1989 to 1994 (Dercon, Krishnan, and Kello 1994; Dercon and Krishnan 1995). However, there were also negative results. In Kenya, lack of economic growth resulted in a constant poverty headcount ratio and continued poverty for an increasing number of people (Mukui 1994; World Bank 1996a). In Tanzania, real per capita income of the poorest 40 percent fell by 28 percent between 1983 and 1991 (Ferreira 1993, cited in Wangwe 1996) – a time during which the economy was contracting at the rate of 1 percent per year. And in Cote d'Ivoire, poverty increased during the 1985–1988 recession, using the poverty headcount ratio, the normalized poverty deficit (P_1) and the squared poverty gap (P_2) for two alternative poverty lines (Grootaert 1994). Note that in each of these cases where poverty did not fall, growth did not take place.

Finally, Eastern Europe and the countries of the former Soviet Union experienced dramatic economic contractions of the early 1990s. While there has been some growth since then in the Eastern European countries, the decline has continued in the countries of the Former Soviet Union. Along with the decline in income, the transition from socialism has also brought increasing inequality. Together, these effects have led to a massive increase in poverty: The poverty headcount ratio for the region as a whole rose from 4 percent in 1987/1988 to 32 percent in 1994 by one estimate (United Nations 1997) and from 4 percent to 45 percent in 1993/1995 by another (Milanovic 1999).

11.2.4 *Conclusion*

The lessons from the available evidence can be summed up simply. Usually but not always, economic growth reduces absolute poverty. On the other hand, when poverty has not fallen, it is generally because economic growth has not taken place.

These findings create a presumption in favor of pursuing economic growth of a type that will reduce poverty. This is hardly a new conclusion, but it is one that is supported by the latest available evidence.

12

Economic Well-Being

12.1 The Meaning and Measurement of Economic Well-Being

Distributional analysis often examines ways of determining whether one income distribution is *more unequal* than another, whether one income distribution has *more poverty* than another, and whether a change from one income distribution to another has more *economic* mobility than another change. This chapter asks a different question: When is one income distribution *better* than another? Here, the "better" society is that into which you would choose to be born, or that which you would choose if you were a social planner.[1] It bears mention that the analytical methods introduced in this chapter apply not only to income distributions but to evaluations of economic states in general.

The chapter begins with an introduction to the types of approaches involved. We then turn our attention to social welfare functions defined first on vectors of utilities or of incomes and then to abbreviated social welfare functions. Some useful theorems on social welfare dominance are then presented. The chapter concludes by demonstrating how the various approaches can lead to different qualitative assessments.

The original version of this chapter was published as: Fields, Gary S. (2001). The Meaning and Measurement of Economic Well-Being (159–172), Empirical Comparisons of Economic Well-being (173–190), in: G. Fields: Distribution and Development: A New Look at the Developing World. © 2001 by Russell Sage Foundation and the MIT Press.

12.1.1 *Types of Approaches*

In this chapter, we shall consider *outcome-based* evaluation criteria – that is, we will base our evaluations on measures calculated for the resultant income distributions, as economists nearly always do. But before proceeding to such measures, it is worth briefly discussing the alternative, which is to assign primacy to the *process* generating the results. Here are some examples. Libertarians argue for a minimalist state, and therefore some would rank income distributions according to which has less government involvement of an undesirable type (Nozick 1974). Trade unionists and their supporters sometimes argue that a wage-employment package is good if and only if it is unionnegotiated. And nearly all of us regard any economic state involving slavery as inferior to one without slavery. It lies outside the scope of this volume to debate such process-based criteria. They are brought up here so that they will not be overlooked.

Turning our attention to an evaluation of *outcomes* (or in Nozick's terminology, *end-states*), one might naturally seek guidance from the fundamental theorems of welfare economics. These may be stated as follows (Atkinson and Stiglitz 1980, p. 343):

FIRST WELFARE THEOREM: *If* (1) households and firms act perfectly competitively, taking prices as parametric, (2) there is a full set of markets, and (3) there is perfect information, *then* a competitive equilibrium, if it exists, is Pareto-efficient.

SECOND WELFARE THEOREM: *If* household indifference maps and firm production sets are convex, if there is a full set of markets, if there is perfect information, and if lump-sum transfers and taxes may be carried out costlessly, *then* any Pareto-efficient allocation can be achieved as a competitive equilibrium with appropriate lumpsum transfers and taxes.

The logical validity of these theorems is unquestioned. The issue is their usefulness.

Figure 12.1 depicts a simple two-person economy in which the participants (indexed by i) have utility levels U_1 and U_2 respectively. Three possible states are depicted: state A, which lies inside the utility possibility frontier, and states B and C which lie on it.[2] Our task is to choose the *best* of the three states.

We know from the first welfare theorem that under the stated conditions, the competitive equilibrium would not be a point like A (which is Pareto-inefficient). Rather, competition would lead to a point like B or C. One criterion for social welfare rankings is to judge income distributions on the basis of *Pareto-improvements*. That is, social welfare is said to have increased if everybody's utility is at least as great and somebody's utility is strictly greater. By this criterion, either B or C is superior to A. But which is better, B or C? The second welfare theorem is of no help. It says that under the stated conditions, B can be achieved as a competitive equilibrium, and so too can C. Even if the "appropriate" lump-sum taxes and transfers could be made (which in the real world does not ever seem to be the case), the standard welfare theorems provide no basis for choosing among Pareto-optima.[3]

Figure 12.1.

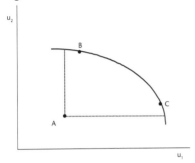

If we are going to make headway on this problem, we need a different way of thinking. In the next two sections, we consider two types of approaches based on social welfare functions.

12.1.2 *Social Welfare Functions Based on Vectors of Utilities or Incomes*

We begin with the class of *welfaristic social welfare functions*. By definition, a social welfare function is *welfaristic* if (i) its arguments are the utilities of the various individuals

(1) $$W = f(U_1, ..., U_n),$$

and (ii) only the utilities of the various individuals enter the social welfare function.[4] Such a welfare function is also called individualistic and, in view of its origins in the work of Bergsan (1938) and Samuelson (1947), a *Bergson-Samuelson social welfare function*. The indifference curves coming from this class of functions are called *Bergson-Samuelson community indifference curves*, about which more will be said later.

The class of Bergson-Samuelson social welfare functions is too general to be of use, so restrictions must be put on it. One is to limit oneself to *Paretian social welfare Junctions*. A social welfare function is Paretian if it approves of any Pareto-improvement:

(2) $\qquad$ $W = f(U_1, ..., U_n),$ $\quad$ $f(.)$ increasing in all U_i.

One special type of Paretian social welfare function is the class of *utilitarian (or Benthamite) social welfare functions*, in which social welfare is taken to be the sum of the individual utilities

(3) $\qquad\qquad\qquad$ $W = U_1 + U_2 + ... + U_n.$

All Paretian social welfare functions regard any state which is Pareta-superior to another as being better in social welfare terms than the other. Notice, however, that the opposite is not true (i.e., if a state is better than another using the Benthamite social welfare function (3), this does not imply that it is also Pareto-superior). For instance, consider two ordered utility distributions such as $X = (1, 2, 3)$ and $Y = (1, 2, 4)$. Y is Pareta-superior to X: One individual is better off and nobody is worse off. Using a social welfare function like (3), social welfare in Y is also higher than in X. On the other hand, if we compare $X = (1, 2, 3)$ to $Z = (4, 2, 1)$ we find no Pareto-improvement, but social welfare function in Z is also higher than in X by (3). This is why Paretian social welfare functions provide a wider scope of comparison among states than the strict Pareto- improvement criterion.

Not all social welfare functions are Paretian. A social welfare function may be non-Paretian, because although it is welfaristic, that is, $W = f(U_1, ..., U_n)$, it is not increasing in all utilities. An example is the *egalitarian social welfare function* which, in a two-person economy, takes the form:

(4) $\qquad\qquad\qquad$ $W = g(|U_1 - U_2|),$ $\quad$ $g' < 0.$

This and other non-Paretian functions are sometimes called an *observer's social welfare function*, because the observer cares about something different from what the participants care about: In this case, the observer cares about $|U_1 - U_2|$ whereas the ith participant cares about U_i alone.

Another reason that a social welfare function may be non-Paretian is that it does not judge all Pareto-improvements to be strictly better. An example is the *Rawlsian social welfare function* in which social welfare depends only on the utility of the worst-off person (denoted by [1], the brackets indicating the individual's position in the utility distribution):

(5) $\qquad\qquad\qquad$ $W = f(U_{[1]}),$ $\quad$ $f(.)$ increasing.

This is not Paretian, because if a Pareto-improvement leaves the worst-off person's utility unchanged, the Rawlsian social welfare function says that welfare is unchanged.[5] What *is* Paretian, however, is the *lexicographic Rawlsian function*, defined as follows: If the poorest person's utility is unchanged, look at the next poorest person's utility, and so on until you find a change. Denote the poorest person whose utility has changed by *[i]*. Social welfare changes as $U_{[i]}$ changes:

(6) $\qquad\qquad W = f(U_{[i]}), \quad f(.)$ increasing.

By this criterion, *any* Pareto-improvement would be judged as welfare-increasing.

Some social welfare functions not only are not Paretian but they are not even welfaristic. A social welfare function is *nonwelfaristic* if it is not a function of the utilities of the individuals involved, that is, it does not accept their preferences. Why might you not want to accept the utility functions of the participants? Suppose the participants exhibit malevolence (sometimes called "envy").[6] Let us represent these malevalent preferences in a two-person economy by the utility functions:

(7a) $\qquad\qquad U_1 = h(Y_1, Y_2), \quad h_1 > 0, h_2 < 0$

and

(7b) $\qquad\qquad U_2 = i(Y_1, Y_2), \quad i_2 > 0, i_1 < 0.$

Malevolence enters in here by writing that the utility of one individual depends negatively on the income of the other. The observer may not want to accept this malevolence; such censoring has been suggested by Harsanyi (1955) and Goodin (1995), among others. An alternative is to use a social welfare function which is monotonic in each person's *income* (but not utility):

(8a) $\qquad\qquad W = j(v(Y_1), \quad v(Y_2), ...),$

(8b) $\qquad\qquad v(.)$ increasing in Y_i

(8c) $\qquad\qquad j(.)$ increasing in all $v(.)$.

This function is nonwelfaristic, because the *v*s are the weights used by the evaluator and not the individuals' own utility functions. Equations (8a–c) also introduce a subtle but vitally important change: Social welfare is now expressed as a function of *incomes* (on which we have data) and not as a function of *utilities* (on which we do not).

To see how this makes a difference, suppose we have a *quasi-Pareto improvement*, defined to be a situation where somebody's income goes up and everybody else's income stays the same. (As always, incomes are assumed here to be expressed in real dollars.) When somebody's income has risen, holding others' incomes the same, (8) would say that social welfare has increased, and accordingly we may say that (8) is a quasi-Paretian social welfare function. However, the welfaristic social welfare function:

(1) $$W = f(U_1, ..., U_n),$$

coupled with malevalent utility functions

(7a) $$U_1 = h(Y_1, Y_2), \quad h_1 > 0, h_2 < 0$$

and

(7b) $$U_2 = i(Y_1, Y_2), \quad i_2 > 0, i_1 < 0$$

is incapable of rendering a social welfare judgment about an increase in one individual's income, holding constant the income of the other.[7]

Figure 12.2.a   **Figure 12.2.b**

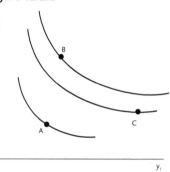

Figure 12.2.c

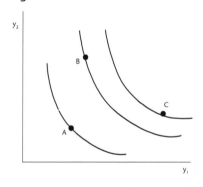

Figure 12.2.a depicts a situation similar to that in Figure 12.1 except that the comparison is now between different points on the space of *incomes* rather than on the space of *utilities*. Moving from A to B or from A to C constitutes a quasi-Pareto improvement, and as such raises welfare for the class of functions given by (8).

What about a comparison between B and C? At first, it might appear that a solution could be found by working with those community indifference curves derived from social welfare functions of type (1), but this is not so, because some members of this class of social welfare function rank B as better than C (Figure 12.2.b) while others rank B as worse than C (Figure 12.2.c). An answer needs to be sought elsewhere.

12.1.3 *Abbreviated Social Welfare Functions*

A different way of making welfare judgments is to use what are called *abbreviated social welfare functions* (Lambert 1993). A social welfare function is *abbreviated* if welfare is expressed as a function of statistics calculated from the income distribution vector, for example,

(9a) $W = w(GNP, INEQ, POV),$

where GNP is a measure of gross national product (in real dollars per capita), INEQ is a measure of inequality, and POV is a measure of poverty. When such functions are applied, it is usually with the stipulation (typically implicit) that social welfare increases if GNP rises, INEQ falls, or POV falls, and thus, assuming differentiability of the *w(.)* function:

(9b) $w_1 > 0, \quad w_2 < 0, \quad \text{and } w_3 < 0.$[8]

Empirically, GNP often increases while INEQ and POV decrease, permitting a welfare statement to be made using the class of functions (9). But about as often, a different pattern of changes is found – about half the time, INEQ increases in the course of GNP growth, which means that the welfare judgment about the distributional effects of economic growth is ambiguous in such cases. The analyst can either accept the ambiguity rendered by (9) or seek another criterion for making comparisons of economic well-being. The next section presents the welfare dominance alternative.

12.1.4 *Welfare Dominance Results*

In certain situations, it may be possible to rank the welfare of one income distribution relative to another for a broad dass of social welfare functions. Three theorems are particularly useful for this purpose.[9]

First, consider ranking two income distributions that have the same mean. The following theorem pertains to such situations:

THEOREM 12.1 WELFARE COMPARISONS WHEN MEANS ARE EQUAL (ATKINSON 1970; DASGUPTA, SEN, AND STARRETT 1973): Let X and Y be two income distributions such that $\mu(X) = \mu(Y)$. Let $L_X(p) > L_Y(p)$ indicate that X Lorenz-dominates Y. Let W_E denote the class of anonymous, increasing, and S-concave social welfare functions. Then,

$L(X) > L(Y)$ if and only if $w(X) > w(Y)$ for all $w \ \varepsilon \ W_E$.

Note carefully what this says: When the means are equal, an income distribution that Lorenz-dominates another is not only more equal but *better* in welfare terms – provided, that is, that we accept the properties of class W_E.[10] What if the means are *not* equal? Two theorems apply in such cases.

THEOREM 12.2 FIRST-ORDER WELFARE DOMINANCE (SAPOSNIK 1981):

Let X and Y be any two income distributions. Define $X(p) \equiv inf\{x \ : \ F(x) \geq p\}$ (i.e., the smallest value of x such that $F(x) \geq p$) and define $Y(p)$ similarly. Let $X >_{FOD} Y$ indicate that X first-order-dominates Y, that is, $X(p) \geq Y(p)$ for all $p \ \varepsilon \ [0, \ 1]$ with strict inequality for some p. Let W_P denote the class of anonymous, increasing social welfare functions. Then, $X >_{FOD} Y$ if and only if $w(X) > w(Y)$ for all $w \ \varepsilon \ W_P$.

First-order dominance is also called "rank dominance," because in the case of populations of equal size, the income of the person in each rank in X is at least as great as the income of the person with the corresponding rank in Y and strictly greater someplace. In other words, the person who ranks poorest in each distribution has a higher income in X than in Y, and likewise for the second person, the third person, and so on. In the case of aggregate data divided, say, into centiles, for one income distribution to first-order-dominate another, the income in the first centile of X must be higher than in Y, the income in the second centile of X must be higher than in Y, and so on up to the ninety-ninth centile. First-order dominance implies first-order poverty dominance, that is, when one income distribution is better than another in the sense of Theorem 12.2, the better one necessarily has less poverty than the other.

Note what makes first-order dominance different from Pareto dominance: In first-order dominance, we are comparing anonymous people in particular positions, whereas for Pareto dominance, we need to compare the before and after incomes for named persons.[11]

First-order dominance is an easy-to-use criterion in aggregate data. To implement it, check whether the real income is higher at the first quantile (decile or centile) in X than in Y, likewise for the second quantile, the third quantile, and so on.

It may turn out that the $X(p)$ and $Y(p)$ curves cross, as in Figure 12.3. In this case, welfare rankings may still be possible, based on the following result:

THEOREM 12.3 SECOND-ORDER WELFARE DOMINANCE (SHORROCKS 1983, BASED ON KOLM 1976):
Let X and Y be any two income distributions. Define the Generalized Lorenz curve $GL_X(p) \equiv \mu_X L_X(p)$, that is, the ordinary Lorenz curve multiplied by the mean, and define $GL_Y(p)$ similarly. One distribution X is said to second-order dominate another Y (which we write as $X >_{SOD} Y$) if and only if $GL_X(p) \geq GL_Y(p)$ for all $p \; \varepsilon \; [0, 1]$ with strict inequality for some p. Then for the class of anonymous, increasing, and S-concave social welfare functions W_E, $X >_{SOD} Y$ if and only if $w(X) > w(Y)$ for all $w \; \varepsilon \; W_E$.

Theorem 12.3 gives another easy-to-use criterion for making welfare comparisons of two income distributions X and Y. Draw the two generalized Lorenz curves, that is, the ordinary Lorenz curves multiplied by their respective means. One income distribution is judged to be *better* than another (i.e., it gives higher welfare) if its generalized Lorenz curve lies somewhere above and nowhere below the other's, and for this reason, second order welfare dominance is also called "Generalized Lorenz curve dominance."[12] By the Shorrocks-Kolm theorem, ranking by generalized Lorenz curves is equivalent to using social welfare functions which:

1. are anonymous,

2. are increasing in all incomes,

3. are S-concave.

Figure 12.3. Crossing of quantile functions.

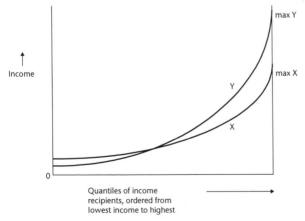

This tells us what is required to justify welfare comparisons using generalized Lorenz curves. But before using this criterion, you will have to think whether *your* social welfare function satisfies these three properties.[13]

Before concluding this section, it is important to remark on the relationship between first- and second-order welfare dominance. Observe that the class of social welfare functions in Theorem 12.3 is a subclass of the class in Theorem 12.2. It follows that first-order welfare dominance implies second-order welfare dominance, or in different terminology, that rank dominance implies Generalized Lorenz dominance. It is an empirical question how often first-order dominance fails but second order dominance holds.

12.1.5 *Similarities and Differences among the Various Approaches*

Section 12.2 considered several types of social welfare functions defined on participants' utilities. The absence of utility information in data renders such functions unusable in practice.

The abbreviated social welfare function approach of Section 12.3 and the welfare dominance approaches of Section 12.4 both provide income-based criteria for helping determine if one income distribution is better or worse than another. (Again, please remember that "income" is being used in this chapter as shorthand for whichever indicator of economic well-being one chooses to use.)

The usefulness of the two approaches, as well as the differences between them, will be illustrated theoretically in this section. A useful heuristic device for doing this is to consider the three stylized economic growth types first introduced in Fields (1979a).[14]

Keeping within the dualistic development tradition of Lewis (1954), Fei and Ranis (1964), and Kuznets (1966), let us suppose that there are two economic sectors, which we shall call "modern" and "traditional." The workers in these sectors each earn incomes y_M and y_T respectively, $y_M > y_T$. The two sectors respectively comprise population shares f_M and $f_T = 1 - f_M$.

Now let us define three stylized growth types. *Traditional sector enrichment* entails an increase in y_T, holding y_M and f_M constant. *Modern sector enrichment* involves an increase in y_M, holding y_T and f_M constant. Finally, *modern sector enlargement* occurs when f_M increases, holding y_M and y_T constant.

Traditional sector enrichment results in an increase in GNP, a reduction in inequality (by virtue of a Lorenz-improvement), and reduced poverty (for any standard poverty measure provided that the poverty line, z, is set at least as great as y_T and less than y_M). The class of abbreviated social welfare functions given by (9) deems such growth to be welfare-improving.

Modern sector enrichment produces an increase in GNP, an increase in inequality (by virtue of Lorenz-worsening), and no change in poverty (again, provided that the poverty line z falls in the range $y_T \leq z < y_M$). The class of social welfare functions given by (9) evaluates the increase in GNP positively and the increase in inequality negatively, and therefore cannot generate a verdict as to whether this type of growth is welfare-improving or not.

Modern sector enlargement also raises GNP. The Lorenz curves for the initial and final distributions can be shown to cross each other (Fields 1979a). When Lorenz curves cross, an inequality measure can always be found which registers an increase in inequality and another can be found which registers a decrease in inequality. Furthermore, as f_M varies from zero to one, a number of commonly used inequality measures first increase up to a critical value f_{M^*} and then decrease.[15] If you choose one of those measures, as f_M increases, you will then have an increase in GNP, a fall in poverty, and an increase in inequality for modern sector enlargement growth in the range $f_M < f_{M^*}$. Modern sector enlargement growth is therefore evaluated ambiguously in this range. It is only once $f_M > f_{M^*}$ that GNP grows, INEQ falls, and POV falls, so that this type of growth can be judged by the abbreviated social welfare function approach to be welfare-enhancing.

What if we instead use the welfare dominance approaches of Section 12.4? Theorem 12.2 applies to each of the three stylized growth typologies, and in each, it registers an unambiguous verdict: *in traditional sector enrichment, in modern sector enrichment, and in modern sector enlargement, economic growth is welfare-enhancing according to the welfare dominance approaches.* This is because some real incomes have increased and none have decreased, producing first-order dominance.

The abbreviated social welfare function approach and the welfare dominance approaches diverge in the following way. The abbreviated social welfare function approach allows for the possibility that increased inequality might possibly overpower GNP growth, in the sense that an observer who is sufficiently inequality-averse might prefer a no-growth situation to an inequality-increasing pattern of growth. On the other hand, the welfare dominance approaches do not allow this – for those who adhere to such methods, any time some real incomes increase holding other real incomes the same, social welfare must be deemed to have increased, regardless of whether inequality has increased or not. It is this different treatment of inequality that is the critical factor distinguishing the abbreviated social welfare function approach from the first- and second-order welfare dominance methods.

12.1.6 Conclusions

This chapter has considered several methods for judging whether one income distribution is *better* than another – better in the sense that if you could choose, you would choose to belong to or bring about the first income distribution rather than the second. Your first decision is whether to choose which is preferred on the basis of the income distributions themselves or on the basis of the processes by which these distributions were generated. Assuming that your basis will be a comparison of the income distributions, your next decision is what kind of social evaluation function to use. Utility-based social welfare functions, while fine in theory, cannot be used empirically. You need to use something that can be calculated from available data on incomes or expenditures.

Two approaches for dealing with census or survey data were distinguished: abbreviated social welfare functions and welfare dominance methods. These were shown to make a difference in certain stylized growth types. The crucial distinguishing feature is the different ways in which these two approaches treat inequality. Does the choice make a difference empirically? It turns out that it does.

12.2 Empirical Comparisons of Economic Well-Being

There are at least two empirically implementable ways of deciding whether one income distribution is better or worse than another. The first uses an abbreviated social welfare function in which economic well-being depends positively on gross national product (in real dollars per capita) and negatively on changes in inequality and poverty. The second approach involves dominance methods. This chapter applies these methods to a number of country cases from the developing world, comparing and contrasting the findings empirically.

12.2.1 *Comparisons of Economic Well-Being: The Methods Reviewed*

The "abbreviated social welfare functions" were of the form

(9) $\qquad W = w(GNP, INEQ, POV), \quad w_1 > 0, \ w_2 < 0, \ \text{and} \ w_3 < 0.$

such that social welfare is a positive function of GNP (in real dollars per capita) and a negative function of inequality and poverty in the country. Empirical analysis has shown that income inequality increases about half the time when economic growth takes place and decreases about half the time. It follows that for about half the growth experiences in the world, the class of social welfare functions given by (9) would record *ambiguous* changes in economic well-being as these countries grow.

The welfare dominance approach was reflected in Theorems 12.1–12.3. Theorem 12.1 dealt with the case where mean income is unchanged. Since empirically, the mean nearly always changes, this theorem is of little practical interest.

Theorems 12.2 and 12.3 apply to cases where the mean changes. One distribution first-order-dominates another if, for each population group, the per capita income in the first distribution is higher than in the second. For instance, if the population groups are deciles, first-order dominance holds if the per capita income is higher in one distribution than another for the first decile, for the second decile, and so on. Theorem 12.2 states that if one distribution first-order-dominates another, the first distribution is *better* than the second for all social welfare functions which are anonymous and increasing in all incomes.

If neither distribution first-order-dominates the other, we may still have second-order dominance. One distribution second-order dominates another if, for each population group, the *cumulative* per capita income is higher in the first distribution than in the second for each cumulative population group. Again, illustrating for the case of deciles, second-order dominance holds if one distribution has higher per capita income than another for the first decile, for the first two deciles taken together, and so on. Theorem 12.3 states that if one distribution second-order dominates another, the first distribution is *better* than the second for all social welfare functions which are anonymous, increasing in all incomes, and S-concave.

Comparisons of economic well-being using dominance methods have been carried out for five developing countries: Taiwan, Thailand, Indonesia, Brazil, and Chile. These results are presented below, where they are compared and contrasted with the results using abbreviated social welfare functions.

12.2.2 *The Case of Taiwan*

Taiwan's economy has had one of the world's highest economic growth rates since the 1960s. A welfare dominance analysis for the period 1980–1992 has been conducted by Chiou (1996).

Between 1980 and 1992, per capita income in Taiwan grew at a 6.1 percent annual rate. However, Taiwan's income distribution became more unequal (Figures 12.4 and 12.5). Because GNP increased and inequality did also, the class of abbreviated social welfare functions of the form

$$W = w(GNP, INEQ, POV), \ w_1 > 0, \ w_2 < 0, \ w_3 < 0$$

would be unable to say whether social welfare in Taiwan had improved or not.

First-order dominance testing gives an unambiguous answer. Table 12.1 and Figure 12.6 show that the real incomes of each quintile of households in Taiwan were about double in 1992 what they had been in 1980. Thus, all evaluators who accept a social welfare function which is anonymous and increasing in all incomes would say that the 1992 income distribution in Taiwan was better (in a social welfare sense) than the 1980 distribution, notwithstanding the ambiguity recorded by the abbreviated social welfare function.

Figure 12.4. Taiwan: Lorenz curves of family income, 1980 and 1992.

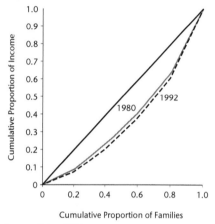

Cumulative Proportion of Families

Source: Chiou 1996.

Figure 12.5. Taiwan: The rising Gini coefficient of household income.

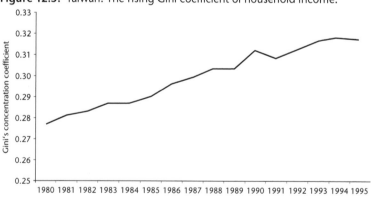

Year

Source: Republic of China 1995 (table 4).

Table 12.1. Taiwan's mean income by quintile, 1980 and 1992 (mean family income per month in 1991 NT dollars)

	Quintile				
	1	2	3	4	5
1980	144,799	226,620	288,680	371,467	599,992
1992	225,600	405,159	536,331	710,493	1,183,164

Source: Chiou 1996.

Figure 12.6. First-order dominance and Taiwan's income distribution, 1980 and 1992.

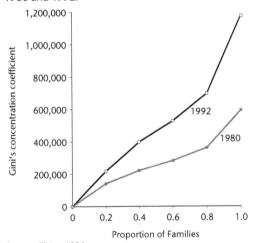

Source: Chiou 1996.

Table 12.2. Thailand: Economic growth and changing inequality

	1975	1981	1986	1992
Mean expenditures	947.5	1250.0	1261.3	1911.4
	Economy grew		*Economy grew*	
Inequality measure				
Gini coefficient	35.74	39.71	42.62	45.39
	Inequality rose		*Inequality rose*	
Mean log deviation	0.209	0.259	0.301	0.342
	Inequality rose		*Inequality rose*	
Theil index	0.245	0.305	0.335	0.406
	Inequality rose		*Inequality rose*	
One-half of the square of the coefficient of variation	0.497	0.653	0.550	0.801
	Inequality rose		*Inequality rose*	

Source: Calculations by Ahuja et al. 1997 (table 4.2) based on Thai Socioeconomic Survey data.

12.2.3 *The Case of Thailand*

A welfare dominance analysis for Thailand has been presented in Ahuja et al. 1997 comparing four years: 1975, 1981, 1986, and 1992. GDP per capita in Thailand grew at an annual rate of 4.6 percent per capita between 1965 and 1980 and at 6.4 percent between 1980 and 1995; the corresponding per capita GDP growth rates in purchasing power parity (PPP) dollars were 4.4 percent for 1965–1980 and 5.5 percent for 1980–1995. However, this growth was quite uneven: Mean expenditure grew rapidly from 1975 to 1981, essentially stagnated from 1981 to 1986, and again grew rapidly between 1986 and 1992 (Figure 12.7). Our question, therefore, is what distributional changes took place in Thailand during the 1975–1981 and 1986–1992 growth episodes?

Figure 12.7. Thailand: Growth of mean expenditures, 1975–1992.

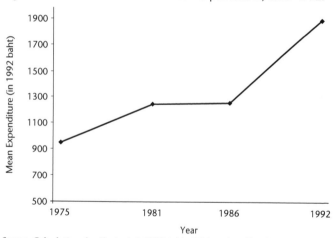

Source: Calculations by Ahuja et al. (1997, table 4.2) based on Thai Socioeconomic Survey data.

Let us begin with the abbreviated social welfare approach. Inequality data appear in Figure 12.8 and Table 12.2. The Lorenz curves essentially coincide at the very lowest end of the expenditure distribution and then show Lorenz-worsenings during the 1975–1981 growth episode and again during the 1986–1992 growth episode. The increases in inequality during these growth episodes are confirmed by the four inequality measures presented in Table 12.2, all of which increased when the economy grew from 1975 to 1981 and again when the economy grew from 1986 to 1992.

Figure 12.8. Real expenditure Lorenz curves, 1975–1992.

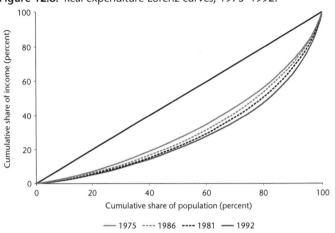

Source: Calculations by Ahuja et al. (1997, figure 4.5) based on Thai Socioeconomic Survey data.

Table 12.3. Thailand: Economic growth and changing poverty

Poverty line/ measure	1975	1981	1986	1992
Poverty line: $2 a day (1985 prices)				
P(0) Headcount	41.80	30.36	33.80	15.69
	Poverty fell		*Poverty fell*	
P(1) Poverty gap	12.09	7.87	10.05	3.45
	Poverty fell		*Poverty fell*	
P(2) Poverty severity	4.79	2.87	4.15	1.14
	Poverty fell		*Poverty fell*	
Poverty line: $1 a day (1985 prices)				
P(0) Headcount	5.92	2.84	5.49	0.97
	Poverty fell		*Poverty fell*	
P(1) Poverty gap	0.94	0.39	1.08	0.16
	Poverty fell		*Poverty fell*	
P(2) Poverty severity	0.25	0.09	0.34	0.04
	Poverty fell		*Poverty fell*	

Source: Calculations by Ahuja et al. (1997, table 4.2) based on Thai Socioeconomic Survey data.

Poverty changes in a country reflect the combined effect of economic growth and inequality change. Table 12.3 shows that despite the increase in inequality that took place in Thailand, economic growth nonetheless reduced poverty as measured by three different poverty indices for two alternative poverty lines. Figure 12.9 goes a step further: The graph shows that for all expenditure levels up to 360 baht per capita, the 1981 cumulative distribution function lies below the 1975 curve, and the 1992 curve lies below the 1986 one. Applying the poverty dominance methods presented in Section 12.5, this means that poverty fell from 1975 to 1981 and again from 1986 to 1992 for *all* poverty measures in the class

(10) $P = \sum_{i=1}^{n} p(z, y_i)/n$ such that

1. $p(z, y_i) = 0$ if $y_i \geq z$, and

2. $p(z, y_i) > 0$ if $y_i \leq z$

and for *all* poverty lines between 200 and 360 baht.

Figure 12.9. Thailand: Cumulative distribution functions, detail of low-income range, 1975–1992.

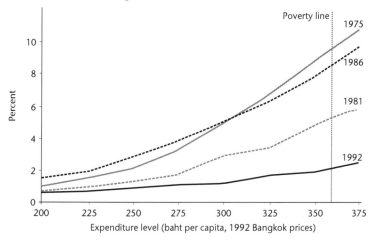

Source: Ahuja et al. (1997, figure 4.7), based on Thai Socioeconomic Survey data

Summing up what happened to the components of the abbreviated social welfare function approach, between 1975 and 1981 and again between 1986 and 1992, economic growth took place, inequality rose, and poverty fell. The abbreviated social welfare function

(9) $W = w(GNP, INEQ, POV)$, $w_1 > 0$, $w_2 < 0$, and $w_3 < 0$.

is therefore not able to say whether social welfare has improved or not.

Were we to instead use the welfare dominance method of Theorem 12.2, we would get an unambiguous answer. As Figure 12.10 shows, the 1981 curve dominates the 1975 curve and the 1992 curve dominates the 1986 one. Thus, by the first-order dominance criterion, the 1975–1981 economic growth led to a better distribution of economic well-being, as did economic growth during the 1986–1992 period.

Figure 12.10. Thailand: Cumulative distribution functions, 1975–1992.

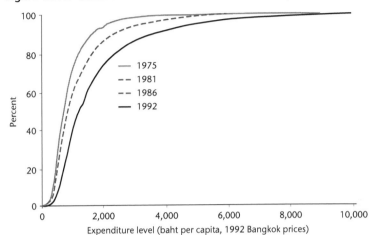

Source: Ahuja et al. (1997, figure 4.6), based on Thai Socioeconomic Survey data

12.2.4 *The Case of Indonesia*

Essentially the same result arises for Indonesia as arose for Thailand. Data from the Susenas surveys for Java have been analyzed by Cameron (forthcoming) covering the years 1984 and 1990. Between 1984 and 1990, mean per capita income on Java grew by 23.5 percent. The three basic distributional facts she finds (Figure 12.11) are:

1. The 1990 distribution first-order-dominates the 1984 distribution.

2. The 1984 distribution Lorenz-dominates the 1990 distribution.

3. The 1990 distribution Generalized-Lorenz-dominates the 1984 distribution.

As we have learned, i implies iii. Thus, the dominance approach to economic well-being judges 1990 to be better than 1984. On the other hand, the abbreviated social welfare function approach records growth in mean income and rising inequality, and therefore evaluates the 1984–1990 experience ambiguously.

12.2.5 *The Case of Brazil*

Our next case is that of Brazil. Income inequality has been getting progressively more unequal, as gauged by successive Lorenz-worsenings from 1960 to 1970 to 1980 to 1990 (Figure 12.12). Yet, economic growth took place from 1960 to 1970 and again from 1970 to 1980 (Figure 12.13). During these intervals, we see for Brazil, as we did for other countries, that the rising GNP and rising inequality are evaluated ambiguously by the abbreviated social welfare function

$$W = w(\text{GNP, INEQ, POV}), \quad w_1 > 0, \ w_2 < 0, \ \text{and} \ w_3 < 0.$$

Nonetheless, real incomes were higher in each decile of the Brazilian income distribution in 1980 than in 1960 (Figure 12.14), so by the first order dominance criterion, the 1980 distribution was better than the 1960 one.[16]

Figure 12.11. Indonesia: Dominance comparisons, 1984 and 1990.

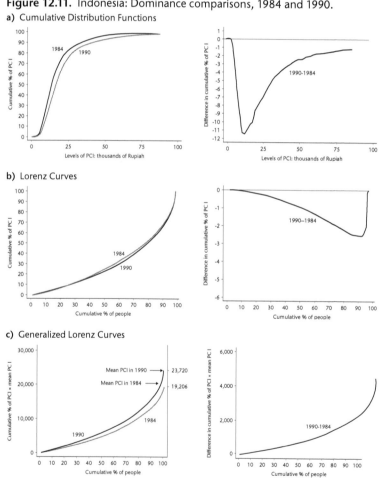

a) Cumulative Distribution Functions

b) Lorenz Curves

c) Generalized Lorenz Curves

Source: Cameron, Lisa, 2000, Poverty and inequality in Java: examining the impact of the changing age, educational and industrial structure, Journal of Development Economics 62(1), 149–180.

Figure 12.12. Thailand: Cumulative distribution functions, 1975–1992.

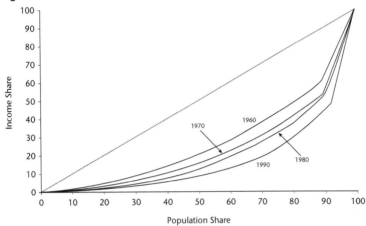

Source: Ahuja et al. (1997, figure 4.6), based on Thai Socioeconomic Survey data

Let us now consider the 1980–1990 period in Brazil. In those years, GNP fell and inequality and poverty rose. The abbreviated social welfare function would therefore say that social welfare worsened in Brazil during this period of time. In addition, Figure 12.14 shows that real incomes fell from 1980 to 1990 in every income decile, which means that by the first-order dominance criterion, the 1990 distribution of income was worse than the 1980 one. So in this case, the abbreviated social welfare function approach and the first-order dominance approach are in agreement – unhappily, showing a *worsening* of economic well-being over the decade of the 1980s.

Figure 12.13. Brazil: Average income level of the economically active population (1960–1990).

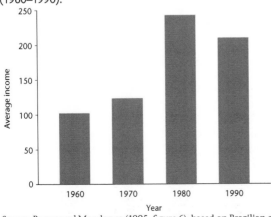

Source: Barros and Mendonça (1995, figure 6), based on Brazilian census data.

269

12.2.6 *The Case of Chile*

The final case to consider is Chile. Income distribution data at the national level are available for the period 1987–1994.[17]

Real per capita income grew at a 5.8 percent annual rate over these seven years. Between 1987 and 1994, the distributions of household income per capita and household income per adult-equivalent both showed Lorenz-improvements, and therefore falling inequality (Table 12.4). Rapid economic growth accompanied by falling inequality would be expected to produce falling poverty. Table 12.5 shows that poverty did indeed fall for a variety of poverty lines and poverty measures. Because growth has taken place and inequality and poverty have fallen, all functions in the class of abbreviated social welfare functions:

$$W = w(\text{GNP}, \text{INEQ}, \text{POV}), \quad w_1 > 0, \ w_2 < 0, \ \text{and} \ w_3 < 0.$$

register improved economic well-being.

Figure 12.14. Brazil: Average income of each tenth of the distribution of economically active population with positive income.

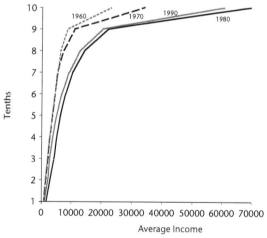

Source: Barros and Mendonça (1995, figure A.8.c), based on Brazilian census data.

In view of these changes, it would not be surprising to find that the 1994 distribution dominates the 1987 distribution. Indeed, first-order dominance does arise (Figure 12.15).

We may conclude that economic well-being in Chile improved by both the abbreviated social welfare function and the first-order-dominance criteria.

Table 12.4. Chile: Lorenz curves, 1987–1994

a) Decile income shares: Household incomes per capita

	1987		1994	
	Decile	Cumulative	Decile	Cumulative
Decile 1	1.21	1.21	1.28	1.28
Decile 2	2.19	3.40	2.33	3.61
Decile 3	2.95	6.35	3.11	6.72
Decile 4	3.77	10.12	3.96	10.68
Decile 5	4.72	14.84	4.96	15.64
Decile 6	5.94	20.78	6.22	21.86
Decile 7	7.66	28.44	7.91	29.77
Decile 8	10.37	38.81	10.60	40.37
Decile 9	15.89	54.70	15.95	56.32
Decile 10	45.30	100.00	43.66	99.98

b) Decile income shares: Household incomes per adult equivalent

	1987		1994	
	Decile	Cumulative	Decile	Cumulative
Decile 1	1.34	1.34	1.43	1.43
Decile 2	2.41	3.75	2.57	4.00
Decile 3	3.17	6.92	3.36	6.36
Decile 4	3.97	10.89	4.18	11.54
Decile 5	4.88	14.77	5.14	16.68
Decile 6	6.04	21.81	6.33	23.01
Decile 7	7.66	29.47	7.93	30.94
Decile 8	10.24	39.71	10.55	41.49
Decile 9	15.71	55.42	15.76	57.25
Decile 10	44.58	100.00	42.73	100.00

Source: World Bank 1997, pp. 11 and 13.

12.2.7 Conclusions

Empirical analysis has shown that income inequality increases about half the time when economic growth takes place and decreases about half the time. It follows that for about half the growth experiences in the world, the class of social welfare functions given by

(9) $W = w(GNP, INEQ, POV), \quad w_1 > 0, \ w_2 < 0, \ \text{and} \ w_3 < 0$

would report ambiguous changes in economic well-being in these countries' growth experiences. What was not clear a priori is what dominance methods might reveal. What we have found is that dominance methods in fact give rankings for the five developing countries in which they have been applied, and what they show is that by the first-order-dominance criterion, economic growth improved economic well-being in Taiwan from 1980 to 1992, in Thailand from 1975 to 1981 and again from 1986

271

to 1992, in Indonesia from 1984 to 1990, in Brazil from 1960 to 1980, and in Chile from 1987 to 1994.

Table 12.5. Poverty measures in Chile

a) Chile: Poverty measures: Household incomes per capita

		1987	1994
Indigence line	P$15,050		
Headcount		0.2209	0.0996
Poverty deficit		0.0756	0.0336
FGT (2)		0.0382	0.0184
Poverty line L	P$30,100		
Headcount		0.5137	0.3386
Poverty deficit		0.2274	0.1269
FGT (2)		0.1299	0.0663
Poverty line H	P$34,164		
Headcount		0.5679	0.3940
Poverty deficit		0.2647	0.1554
FGT (2)		0.1560	0.0831

b) Chile: Poverty measures: Household incomes per adult equivalent

	1987	1994
Indigence line P$15,050		
Headcount	0.1268	0.0511
Poverty deficit	0.0412	0.0192
FGT (2)	0.0213	0.0118
Poverty line L P$30,100		
Headcount	0.4069	0.2308
Poverty deficit	0.1568	0.0762
FGT (2)	0.0822	0.0382
Poverty line H P$34,164		
Headcount	0.4726	0.2852
Poverty deficit	0.1905	0.0978
FGT (2)	0.1028	0.0492

Source: World Bank 1997, p. 18.

It is sometimes thought that first-order dominance is such a stringent criterion that it is not likely to be fulfilled empirically very often. It may therefore come as a surprise to you, as indeed it did to me, that first-order dominance gives rankings in *all* of the cases we have reviewed.

The theoretical possibility that the abbreviated social welfare function method and dominance methods might disagree has long been known. We now know that in a number of cases—Taiwan, Thailand, Indonesia, and Brazil—the choice of method also makes an important *empirical* difference in evaluating the welfare effects of economic growth.

Figure 12.15. Chile: First-order dominance, 1987–1994.

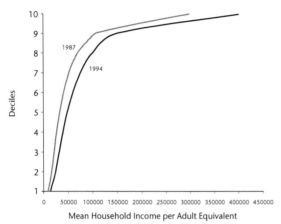

Source: World Bank 1997b (pp. 11–13).

On the other hand, when it comes to evaluating the welfare effects of economic decline, the two methods may turn out to be in closer accord. We have looked at the case of Brazil for the 1980–1990 period. There, the two approaches were indeed in agreement: (1) All components of the abbreviated social welfare function changed in the direction of worsening welfare, so all functions of this class consequently show declines in economic well-being, and (2) The first-order dominance criterion produced falling real incomes for each decile of the population, which implies a decline in economic well-being for all social welfare functions which are anonymous and increasing in all incomes.

What distinguishes the conclusions reached by the two approaches is the way they treat inequality. In the abbreviated social welfare function approach, any increase in inequality will cause the welfare effects of economic growth to be evaluated ambiguously. By contrast, in the welfare dominance approach, as long as real incomes have increased for each quantile group, such as a decile or a quintile, it doesn't matter what has happened to their income shares. This is yet one more reason for you to consider carefully how important inequality is to you as compared with other aspects of income distribution.

13

Income Mobility

What is income mobility? Extensive surveys of the income and earnings mobility literatures may be found in Atkinson, Bourguignon, and Morrisson (1992), Maasoumi (1998), Solon (1999), and Fields and Ok (1999a). ('Income' refers to income from all sources while 'earnings' refers to income earned in the labor market.) Mobility analysts agree on one defining feature: 'income mobility' is about how much income each recipient receives at two or more points in time. In this way, income mobility studies are distinguished from studies of the inequality and poverty aspects of income distribution, both of which are based (typically) on anonymous cross-sections or (less frequently) marginal distributions of the joint distributions.

The following notation is used throughout this article. Let $x = (x^1, ..., x^n)$ denote a vector of 'incomes' in an initial year. This vector is 'personalized' in the sense that the same recipient units are followed over time. It is conventional to array the recipients in the base year from lowest income to highest. Whether this convention is followed or not, it is essential to keep the same order for subsequent years (or generations). Denote the ordered vector in a subsequent year by $y = (y^1, ..., y^n)$. The micro-mobility data, also termed in the literature the pattern of 'distributional change', is summarized by the transformation $x \rightarrow y$ in the two-period case or more generally the transformation $x \rightarrow y \rightarrow z \rightarrow ...$ in the T-period case. The extent of mobility associated with the transformation $x \rightarrow y$ will be denoted by $m(x, y)$.

The original version of this chapter was published as: Fields, Gary S. (2008). Income Mobility, in: The New Palgrave Dictionary of Economics, 2nd ed. © 2008 by Palgrave Macmillan.

Beyond agreeing that income mobility studies are about transformations of the type $x \rightarrow y \rightarrow z \rightarrow ...$, the literature is marked by considerable disagreement. This is because the term 'income mobility' connotes precise but *different* ideas to different researchers. It is for this reason that mobility analysts often have trouble communicating with each other, with other social scientists, or with the general public. Furthermore, these differences in notions of what income mobility is remain even after agreement is reached on a number of other aspects of the mobility under consideration. These other aspects, discussed in the following paragraphs, are whether the context is intergenerational or intragenerational, what the indicator of social or economic status is, and whether the analysis is at the macromobility or micro-mobility level.

One issue is whether the aspect of mobility of interest is intergenerational or intragenerational. In the *intergenerational* context, the recipient unit is the family, specifically a parent and a child. In the *intragenerational* context, the recipient unit is the individual or family at two different dates. The issues discussed in this article apply equally to both.

Second, agreement must be reached on an indicator of social or economic status and the choice of recipient unit. For brevity, I shall talk about mobility of 'income' among 'individuals'.

Third, the mobility questions asked and our knowledge about mobility phenomena may be grouped into two categories, macro and micro. *Macro*-mobility studies start with the question, 'How much economic mobility is there?' Answers are of the type '*a* percent of the people stay in the same income quintile', '*b* percent of the people moved up at least $1,000 while *c* percent of the people moved down at least $1,000', 'the mean absolute value of income change was $*d*,' and 'in a panel of length T, the mean number of years in poverty is t^*.' The macro-mobility studies often go beyond this question to ask, 'Is economic mobility higher here than there and what accounts for the difference?' Answers would be of the type, 'economic mobility has been rising over time', '*A* has more upward mobility than *B* because economic growth was higher in *A* than in *B*', and 'incomes are more stable in *C* than in *D* because *C* has a better social safety net'. Micro-mobility studies, on the other hand, start with the question, 'What are the correlates and determinants of the income or positional changes of individual income recipients?' The answers to these questions would be of the type, 'unconditionally, income changes are higher for the better educated' and 'other things equal, higher initial income is associated with lower subsequent income growth'.

These three issues – intergenerational versus intragenerational, changes in the distribution of what among whom, and macro-mobility versus micro-mobility – help determine which kind of mobility analysis is being undertaken. Yet major differences remain. It is to these that we now turn.

13.1 Mobility Concepts and Measures

At least 20 mobility measures have been used in the literature. Many empirical mobility studies divide base- and final-year incomes into quantiles (for example, quintiles or deciles) and calculate immobility ratios, mean upward movements, and the like (Fields, 2001). Other studies estimate correlation coefficients between base-year and final-year incomes (Atkinson, Bourguignon and Morrisson, 1992). In the intergenerational mobility literature, it is common to calculate intergenerational elasticities, that is, the coefficient obtained when the logarithm of the child's income is regressed on the logarithm of the parent's (Solon, 1999).

In each case, we may ask, what are the various measures measuring? The essential answer is this: *different indices measure different underlying entities*. Whenever one of these underlying entities is measured, other information contained in the joint distribution of initial and final incomes is lost.

What are the different underlying entities that the various income mobility measures measure? The first distinction to be drawn is between measures of time independence and measures of movement. The question asked by *time-independence* studies is, how dependent is current income on past income? One commonly used measure of time-independence is the beta coefficient commonly calculated in the intergenerational mobility literature by regressing the log-income of the child on the log-income of the parent.

Movement studies ask a different question, namely: in comparisons of incomes of the same individuals between one year and another, or of parents and children between one generation and another, how much income movement has taken place? The various movement indices in the literature may usefully be classified into five categories or concepts ('concepts' because they are different underlying entities, not alternative measures of the same underlying entity).

Positional movement (or 'quantile movement') is about the movement of individuals among various positions (quintiles, deciles, centiles, or ranks) in the income distribution. An individual experiences positional movement if and only if he or she changes quintiles, deciles, centiles, or ranks. Positional movement in a population is greater the more such positional changes there are and/or the larger these positional changes are. King (1983) derived a broad class of positional movement indices axiomatically, one member of which is

(1) $$M_K(x, y) = 1 - \exp{-\frac{\gamma}{n} \sum_{i=1}^{n} \frac{|z_i - y_i|}{\mu(y)}},$$

where γ is the observer's degree of immobility aversion, z_i is the income level agent i would have obtained if his or her rank order did not change during the process $x \rightarrow y$, and $\mu(y)$ is the mean income in distribution y.

Like positional movement, *share movement* is relative but it is relative in a different way. Share movement takes place if and only if an individual's income rises or falls relative to the mean. Thus, an individual can experience upward or downward share movement even if his or her income in dollars is unchanged and/or if he or she does not change position within the income distribution. Share movement in the population reflects the frequency and magnitude of these individual share changes. One attractive index of share movement in a population is the mean absolute value of share changes

(2) $$M_S(x, y) = \frac{1}{n} \sum_{i=1}^{n} \left| \frac{y_i}{\mu_y} - \frac{x_i}{\mu_x} \right|,$$

where $\mu(x)$ and $\mu(y)$ are the means of distributions x and y respectively.

Another concept is *non-directional income movement* (also called 'flux'), which gauges the extent of fluctuation in individuals' incomes. To illustrate, suppose that in a two-person economy one person's income goes up by $10,000 while another's goes down by $10,000. Those who see an average income change of $10,000 are non-directional income movement adherents. Two indices of non-directional income movement have been suggested by Fields and Ok (1996; 1999b):

(3) $$M_{F-O_1}(x, y) = \frac{1}{n} \sum_{i=1}^{n} |y_i - x_i|$$

and

(4) $$M_{F-O_2}(x, y) = \frac{1}{n} \sum_{i=1}^{n} |\log y_i - \log x_i|.$$

Suppose, however, that, when one person's income goes up by $10,000 and another's goes down by $10,000, the observer cares not only about the amounts of the income changes but also about their direction. Directional income movement may be judged using a linear or a concave valuation function. One valuation function which embodies concavity is the mean change in log-incomes (Fields and Ok, 1999):

(5) $$M_{F-O_3}(x, y) = \frac{1}{n} \sum_{i=1}^{n} (\log y_i - \log x_i).$$

As a fifth and final notion of income movement, consider how the income changes experienced by individuals cause the inequality of longer-term incomes to differ from the inequality of base-year incomes. *Mobility as an equalizer of longer-term incomes* would judge that a pattern of income change $(1, 3) \rightarrow (1, 5)$ would *disequalize* longer-term income relative to the base, while a pattern of income change $(1, 3) \rightarrow (5, 1)$ would *equalize* longer-term income relative to the base. This concept is well-established in the literature (Schumpeter, 1955; Shorrocks, 1978b; Atkinson, Bourguignon, and Morrisson, 1992; Slemrod, 1992; Krugman, 1992; Jarvis and Jenkins, 1998), but only recently has a class of measures of this concept been proposed (Fields, 2005). One family within this class is

(6) $$\delta \equiv 1 - (I(a)/I(x)),$$

where x is the vector of base-year incomes, y is the vector of final-year incomes, a is the vector of average incomes, the i'th element of which is $a^i \equiv \frac{x^i + y^i}{2}$, and $I(.)$ is a cross-sectional inequality measure such as the Gini coefficient or the Theil index.

We thus have six mobility concepts and a large number of measures. Because these concepts are fundamentally different from one another, it is important for analysts to choose the concepts that are of greatest interest to them and then measure those concepts. Let us now turn to a brief empirical review of studies that have used two or more of these concepts.

13.2 Different Mobility Concepts in Practice

The previous section distinguished between time independence, positional movement, share movement, non-directional income movement, directional income movement, and mobility as an equalizer of longer-term incomes. How do these six concepts and the measures of them compare in empirical work? Specifically, which country has more mobility than another? Has mobility been rising or falling over time within a country? Are some groups in the population more or less mobile than others?

The answers to these questions have been shown empirically to depend on which mobility concept is used. In comparing *OECD countries*, some countries were found to be more mobile than others with the use of measures of some concepts and less mobile than others with the use of measures of other concepts (OECD, 1996; 1997). When we looked over time, in the United States measures of four concepts (time independence, positional movement, share movement, and income flux) all peaked in 1980–5 but measures of two other concepts did not: directional income movement exhibits a saw-tooth pattern, while mobility as an equalizer of longer-term incomes exhibits a peak followed by a valley (Fields, Leary and Ok, 2002; Fields, 2005). In *France*, mobility differences among demographic groups have been explored (Buchinsky et al., 2004). The answers to the questions 'Who has more mobility: women or men? Better-educated or less-educated workers?' were shown to differ depending on which mobility concept was used. By gender, women in France have *more* time independence and positional movement than men, *less* share movement than men, *about the same* non-directional and directional movement in logs, and *about the same* amount of mobility as an equalizer of longer-term incomes. By education, those with the highest educational attainments have less time independence and positional movement, and if anything *more* share movement, flux, and directional income movement in logs. In *Argentina*, too, measures of the six different concepts produced qualitatively different results (Sánchez Puerta, 2005). Looking at changes over time, some mobility indices increased, some decreased, and some showed no clear trend. Comparing population subgroups (genders, educational levels, age ranges, regions, initial quintiles, and initial sector), some groups were found to have higher earnings mobility for some concepts and lower earnings mobility for others; no group was found to have higher mobility than others for every mobility concept. Finally, in both *Venezuela* and *Mexico*, the time trend of mobility was found to vary according to the notion of mobility measured (Freije, 2001; Duval Hernández, 2005).

The conclusion is that at both levels, macro and micro, it makes an important qualitative difference which mobility concept is being gauged. When a layperson asks an economist which of two situations is the more mobile, the answer 'It depends' is not very satisfying. An answer of the type 'Current incomes are more dependent on past incomes in the United Kingdom than in the United States (that is, the UK is *less* mobile in this respect than the USA), but the United Kingdom has more quintile movement than the United States (and therefore is *more* mobile than the USA in this sense)' is more informative, even if less clear-cut than the questioner may have been hoping for.

13.3 The Axiomatic Approach to Income Mobility

We have seen that there are different income mobility concepts and that the indices measuring these concepts behave differently from one another. How is the analyst to decide which notion(s) best capture(s) the essence of 'income mobility' for him or her? One approach is to proceed axiomatically, that is, to say that 'for me, mobility is such and such' and then to see which concepts, if any, embody these axioms.

Two broad approaches to axiomatization may be found in the literature. In one approach, mobility is conceptualized in social welfare terms (Atkinson, 1980; King, 1983; Chakravarty, Dutta and Weymark, 1985; Dardanoni, 1993; Gottschalk and Spolaore, 2002; Ruiz-Castillo, 2004).

In the other, a descriptive approach is used, wherein analysts specify the properties they wish income mobility concepts and measures to possess, and then proceed to deduce which indices, if any, have these properties (Cowell, 1985; Fields and Ok, 1996; 1999b; D'Agostino and Dardanoni, 2005). The work of Shorrocks (1978a; 1978b) makes use of both of these approaches. This difference between the ethical and the descriptive axiomatizations in the mobility literature parallels the two strands of the inequality literature (Foster and Sen, 1997): for Atkinson (1970), inequality is the amount of social welfare lost because incomes are distributed the way they are rather than being distributed perfectly equally, whereas for Sen (1973, p. 2), inequality is objective in the sense that 'one can distinguish between (*a*) "seeing" more or less inequality, and (*b*) "valuing" it more or less in ethical terms'. Note that under both the ethical and the descriptive approaches the amount of mobility recorded has or may have welfare significance. For example, many observers would say that an economy with more directional income movement has performed better than an economy with less directional income movement.

The literature offers a wide variety of axioms, some of which were designed with particular mobility concepts in mind, others of which have been explored to help sharpen what is meant by 'mobility'. Shorrocks (1993) presents 12 axioms for mobility and shows that they are mutually incompatible. In view of their incompatibility, there is a need for judgments as to which ones an analyst wants a measure to embody.

Fields and Ok (1999a) and Fields (2001) have suggested that analysts choose among the axioms by considering their views on simple examples. For example, consider the following three situations:

(i) $(1, 3) \rightarrow (1, 3)$
(ii) $(1, 3) \rightarrow (2, 6)$
(iii) $(2, 6) \rightarrow (4, 12)$

and the corresponding degree of mobility $m(x, y)$. (As above, $\rightarrow$ denotes a change in the ordered (personalized) vector of incomes.) The axiom of strong relativity, if accepted, would maintain that $m(\lambda x, \alpha y) = m(x, y)$ for all $\lambda, \alpha > 0$ and all $x, y \in \Re_+^n$. If strong relativity is accepted, it requires that Situations I, II, and III all have the same mobility. In Situation I, the only sensible amount of mobility for there to be is zero, and therefore strong relativity requires that Situations II and III also have zero mobility. An analyst who sees non-zero income mobility in Situations II and III is therefore not a strong relativity adherent.

Similarly, (weak) relativity specifies that $m(\lambda x, \alpha y) = m(x, y)$ for all $\lambda > 0$ and all $x, y \in \Re_+^n$. This axiom requires that Situations II and III have the same mobility, though not necessarily the same mobility as Situation

I. Therefore, an analyst who sees more mobility in Situation III than in Situation II is not a (weak) relativity adherent either.

The literature offers characterizations of some of the mobility measures that have been used – for example, Fields and Ok's (1996; 1999b) measures of nondirectional and directional income movement and Chakravarty, Dutta and Weymark's (1985) index of mobility as welfare change. More commonly, though, the axioms are used to state a number of desirable properties and then display a measure or a family of measures consistent with these properties.

In summary, a fruitful way for the analyst to choose which mobility concept(s) is (are) most salient for oneself is to consider the axiomatic judgments underlying each of the concepts. To date, some but not all of the income mobility concepts have been so characterized.

13.4 Other Issues

The income mobility literature has a number of other issues that remain more or less contentious, not because the different views have not been worked out but because different analysts hold genuinely different positions on a number of important matters.

13.4.1 *Is All Distributional Change 'Mobility' or Only Some of It?*

Lurking in the background of some writings on income mobility is a fundamental difference of opinion about what income mobility is. For the majority of analysts, the notion of 'income mobility' has both absolute and relative components. For example, if all incomes double, most would judge there to be more mobility than if all incomes remain unchanged. For some analysts, though, the notion of 'income mobility' is relative only; therefore, the change in the mean needs to be taken out, and 'mobility' applies only to what is left.

Thinking of 'mobility' in this way can lead to some controversial judgments. For example, Chakravarty, Dutta and Weymark (hereafter CDW) (1985) propose the following mobility index:

(7) $$M_{CDW} = (E(y_{agg})/E(b)) - 1,$$

where $E(.)$ is an equality measure, y_{agg} is a vector of aggregate incomes over the observation period, and b is the benchmark vector of incomes under the assumption of complete relative immobility following the first period. In the case in which $E(.)$ is a relative equality measure, the term $E(b)$ is replaced by $E(x)$, where x is the vector of first-period incomes. In the view of these authors (CDW, 1985, p. 8): 'Socially desirable mobility is associated with income structures having positive index values while socially undesirable mobility is associated with income structures having negative index values.' Thus, given their index, CDW judge that mobility contributes positively to social welfare if and only if y_{agg} is distributed more equally than x. Thus, if all incomes rise but the percentage gains are larger at the top end of the income distribution than they are at the bottom, mobility would be judged by CDW to have been socially *undesirable*, in direct contradiction to the quasi-Paretian welfare judgment that an increase in some incomes with no decline in others raises social welfare. This difference of views – whether 'income mobility' includes the growth aspect of distributional change or whether 'mobility' is what remains after growth has been taken out – underlies much of the mobility literature, but rarely is it made explicit.

13.4.2 *What Is 'Relative Mobility'?*

As already noted, the term 'relative mobility' is used ambiguously, sometimes to refer to mobility notions characterized by strong relativity $m(\lambda x, \alpha y) = m(x, y)$ for all $\lambda, \alpha > 0$ and all $x, y \in \mathfrak{R}^n_+$ and sometimes to refer to those characterized by weak relativity $m(\lambda x, \lambda y) = m(x, y)$ for all $\lambda > 0$ and all $x, y \in \mathfrak{R}^n_+$. Note that for both of these relativity notions the basis for determining whether a given individual is experiencing upward or downward relative mobility is that individual's change in *income* relative to the *income* changes of others.

However, the term 'relative mobility' is used in yet another sense, namely, to refer to *positional* movements. On this view, an individual experiences relative mobility if and only if he or she changes position (quintile, decile, centile, or rank) from base year to final year. For example, Jenkins and Van Kerm (2003) break down trends in income inequality into a 'pro-poor income growth' component and an 'income mobility' component. The 'income mobility' component involves rerankings and only re-rankings. Thus, for them as for some others, mobility is positional movement and nothing more.

Finally, D'Agostino and Dardanoni (2005) have yet a different definition of relative mobility. For them, relative mobility involves a change in an individual's relative standing with respect to all others, whereas absolute status is something that can be derived by looking at data regarding the individual taken in isolation.

This last point raises the issue of what is meant by 'absolute mobility', to which we now turn.

13.4.3 *What Is 'Absolute Mobility'?*

The term 'absolute mobility' is used in at least three different ways in the income mobility literature. One way is to express a concern with gains and losses of *income* rather than *income shares* or *positions*. In this sense, the concept of directional income movement and the various measures of that concept are about absolute mobility. Second, 'absolute mobility' is sometimes used to mean that the analyst is concerned with the *absolute value* of income changes, as would be the case in studies of non-directional income movement, or flux. Third, the term is used in the sense of *translation invariance*, in the sense that, if all initial and final incomes are increased by the same amount, the new situation has the same absolute mobility as the original one, that is, $m(x + \alpha, y + \alpha) = m(x, y)$.

As is the case elsewhere in economics, when a term has more than one meaning within the same literature, it is probably best to drop the term altogether. Henceforth, researchers would do better to speak of dollar-based, absolute-value-based, or translation-invariant income mobility measures in preference to 'absolute mobility'.

13.4.4 *Is 'Income Mobility' Decomposable, and if so, how?*

Consider the total income mobility recorded in a population. Under what circumstances can the total be broken down into component parts?

Of the six income mobility concepts considered above, one involves the timeindependence aspect of mobility and the other five involve the movement aspect of mobility. The time-independence aspect of mobility is not decomposable. However, there have been decompositions of various movement measures.

One type of decomposition is subgroup decomposability, that is, if the population is divided into J subgroups, the total income mobility in the population as a whole equals a (possibly) weighted average of the mobility in each of the subgroups:

(8)
$$m(x, y) = \sum_{j=1}^{J} w_j m_j(x, y).$$

A number of income mobility measures are subgroup decomposable; examples are Fields and Ok's (1996; 1999b) non-directional income movement measures

$$m_1(x, y) \equiv \frac{1}{n} \sum_{i=1}^{n} |y_i - x_i| \qquad \text{and}$$

$$m_2(x, y) \equiv \frac{1}{n} \sum_{i=1}^{n} |\log y_i - \log x_i|$$

and their directional income movement measure

$$m_3(x, y) \equiv \frac{1}{n} \sum_{i=1}^{n} (\log y_i - \log x_i).$$

A second kind of decomposition is into substantively meaningful components. There is a long tradition in the sociology literature (for example, Bartholomew, 1982) of breaking down the movement of individuals among occupations or social classes into two component parts: (*a*) changes that can be attributed to the increased availability of positions in the better occupations and social classes ('structural mobility') and (*b*) changes that can be attributed to increased movement of individuals among occupations and social classes for a given distribution of positions among these classes ('exchange mobility'). Bridging the economics and sociology literatures, Markandya (1982; 1984) proposes two alternative decompositions of income mobility along these lines. The first defines exchange mobility as the proportion of the change in welfare that could have been obtained if the income distribution had stayed constant through time, in which case structural mobility is defined as the residual welfare change. The second defines structural mobility as the change in welfare that would have taken place if the two-period or two-generation transition matrix had exhibited complete immobility, in which case exchange mobility is defined as the residual. Along similar lines, Ruiz-Castillo (2004) shows how the CDW (1985) index of welfare due to mobility could be decomposed into either (*a*) a precisely defined structural component and a residual representing exchange mobility or (*b*) a precisely defined exchange component and a residual representing structural mobility. In all these cases, the residual component makes the decomposition exact but in a rather unexciting way.

The results just cited do not mean that an exact additive decomposition of income mobility is impossible. Fields and Ok (1996) show that their mobility index $m_1\ (x,\ y) \equiv \frac{1}{n}\sum_{i=1}^{n} |y_i - x_i|$ decomposable into the sum of appropriately defined structural and exchange components. In the case of a growing economy, the decomposition equation is $m_1\ (x,\ y) = (\sum_{i=1}^{n} y_i - \sum_{i=1}^{n} x_i) + 2\sum_{\{i:y_i < x_i\}}(x_i - y_i)$. An analogous decomposition holds for a contracting economy. Along similar lines, Fields and Ok (1999b) show that their directional movement measure $m_3\ (x,\ y) \equiv \frac{1}{n}\sum_{i=1}^{n} (\log y_i - \log x_i)$ is decomposable into social utility growth and social utility transfer components. In all of these cases, the weakness of Markandya's and Ruíz-Castillo's residual approaches is averted.

13.5 What Other Empirical Issues Arise?

Empirical researchers should bear in mind two additional issues. One is that, as an empirical matter, the longer the observation period, the greater is the amount of mobility registered (Atkinson, Bourguignon and Morrisson, 1992). Therefore, care should be taken not to compare, for example, two-year mobility in one context with, for example, five-year mobility in another.

Second, measurement error is a serious issue. There is an ample literature on mismeasurement of earnings *levels* but, as yet, only a very limited literature on mismeasurement of earnings *changes* (Deaton, 1997; Bound, Brown and Mathiowetz, 2001). A task for the future is to estimate empirically the effect of measurement error on estimates of both macromobility and micro-mobility.

13.6 Conclusions

The income mobility literature is fundamentally unsettled. This is because the very term 'income mobility' connotes different things to different people. This article has reviewed a number of dimensions in which differences arise: which of six notions most accurately captures the fundamental idea of 'income mobility', which indices best measure each of the concepts, which axioms best characterize the essence of 'income mobility', how income mobility has been evolving over time in different countries, which demographic groups have more mobility than others in different settings, and which theoretical refinements to the notion of 'income mobility' hold the greatest promise.

Given the unsettled state of the field, before researchers 'do a mobility study', it is important that we specify which concept or concepts of mobility we are considering, which measures of these concepts we are using, and which questions we are answering. More than once, when I have given seminars, a member of the audience has raised his or her hand and said, 'But that's not what mobility *is*'. Let us do all that we can to clarify what we are talking about so that we do not talk past one another any more than we have to.

14

Earnings Mobility, Inequality, and Economic Growth in Argentina, Mexico, and Venezuela

14.1 Motivation and Questions

Who gains the most income when economies grow? Who loses the most income when economies contract? Are those groups that gain the most income in good times the ones that lose the most income in bad times? In this paper, we answer these questions for the changes in labor market earnings for three Latin American countries: Argentina, Mexico, and Venezuela.

The literature offers two distinct but complementary ways of answering questions like these. The more traditional way is to compare data from anonymous cross-sections. Exemplary of this tradition are Kuznets's (1955) seminal work relating inequality and growth and the literature on pro-poor growth and the development of growth incidence curves (e.g., Ravallion, 2004). These literatures are surveyed in Atkinson (2015). More recently, a growing strand of work uses panel data to follow the same individuals or households over time and gauge changes in their economic circumstances; Jäntti and Jenkins (2015) provide a comprehensive overview.

The two types of analysis – anonymous cross-sections and panel data – might produce the same qualitative results – for example, the anonymous rich gaining more than the anonymous poor and the panel rich gaining more than the panel poor – but this is not necessarily to be expected. To see why, consider a benchmark case and deviations from it.

Henry Aaron (1978) famously said that watching the distribution of

The original version of this chapter was published as: Fields, Gary S., Duval-Hernández, Robert, Freije, Samuel and Sánchez Puerta, María Laura (2015). Earnings mobility, inequality, and economic growth in Argentina, Mexico, and Venezuela, in: The Journal of Economic Inequality, 13(1):103–128. © 2015 by Springer Science+Business Media New York.

income change is "like watching the grass grow." Picture, then, a process of economic growth which leaves the Lorenz curve unchanged or approximately so. Suppose that within an unchanged Lorenz curve, each income recipient were to keep the same position within the income distribution. In this case, the panel data would show the same percentage change in income for each panel person. And, of course, in a time of economic growth, the same percentage change for everyone would mean a larger gain in currency units (here, pesos in Argentina and Mexico, bolivares in Venezuela) for the people who started higher up in the income distribution than for those who started further down. Such a pattern would be what we call "divergent mobility" in real local currency units.

Researchers have many reasons to expect that most panel income changes would be fairly small: among them, most people deriving their incomes from the same sources over time, most people working in the same jobs from one year to the next, and most income sources yielding more or less the same incomes over time. Accordingly, nearly all quantile transition matrices have shown the majority of entries lying along the principal diagonal, with (in a quintile transition matrix) the (5,5) cell exhibiting the highest frequency and the (1,1) cell the second highest frequency.

As for the pattern of deviations from proportionality, numerous forces are at work, some going in one direction and some the other. Consider first those that lead to divergence. The theory of cumulative advantage posits that individuals with higher incomes and earnings in the base year experience the largest earnings gains (Merton, 1968). Wealthier individuals' ownership of physical and human capital, access to social and political connections, and greater ability to borrow and save, could all contribute to cumulative advantage. Complementing cumulative advantage in contributing to divergent mobility is the notion of poverty traps (Azariadis and Stachurski, 2005). According to this theory, those individuals who lack a minimum level of human, physical, and social assets are consigned to a life in poverty from which they cannot escape. Yet another factor that may contribute to larger gains for the initially well-to-do compared with others is labor market twist. This idea holds that in an increasingly globalized and technology-dependent world, the demand for skills is outpacing the available supply, bidding up the earnings of skilled workers while lowering the relative earnings of the unskilled, with skill-biased technical change propelling individuals with the highest human and physical capital endowments ahead the most (Acemoglu and Autor, 2011). Together, the preceding factors reinforce one another, exemplifying positive feedback in changes in economic well-being, defined by Nobel laureate James Meade (1976, p. 155) as "self-reinforcing influences which help to sustain the good fortune of the fortunate and the bad fortune of the unfortunate."

On the other hand, there are also reasons to expect convergent income changes. For life cycle reasons, young people will disproportionately experience income gains and older people income losses. Some people are casual employees, working some days and weeks and not others; whether one has work is one source of instability. Other working people are regularly engaged in work in which unstable earnings are the norm, and these people do well some of the time and badly some of the time. And in a segmented labor market, some people have the good fortune of being able to move up out of the poorer jobs and into better ones while others have the exact opposite experience.

In sum, the benchmark case (approximately unchanged Lorenz curves, little movement within the income distribution) could hold but it need not. Divergent and convergent forces are pulling in opposite directions.

So far, we have discussed the case of positive economic growth. Economic growth is positive in most countries most of the time, but what if economic growth is negative? Again, suppose that the Lorenz curve remains unchanged and that each income recipient keeps the same position in the income distribution as before. In times of economic decline, the income losses would be largest in pesos or bolivares for those who started highest in the income distribution compared to those who started further down – the exact opposite of what would be encountered in times of economic growth. We term the opposing patterns in times of positive and negative economic growth *symmetry* of mobility. But some of the factors mentioned above – in particular, cumulative advantage, poverty traps, and labor market twist – work in the other direction; in other words, Meade's positive feedback influences operate so that those who started ahead remain ahead even in times of economic decline, leading to *asymmetry* of mobility.

We thus have two major questions. First, do panel income changes favor the income recipients who started at the top of the income distribution (*divergent* mobility) or those who started at the bottom (*convergent* mobility)? And second, are the groups that are found to gain the most when the economy is growing those that are found to lose the most when the economy is contracting (*symmetry* of mobility) or is the pattern asymmetric in the sense that the same groups do best both in times of economic growth and in times of economic decline?

14.2 Contributions to the Empirical Literature on Latin America

This paper uses panel data to answer the divergent/convergent mobility question and the symmetry/asymmetry of mobility question for three

Latin American economies: Argentina, Mexico, and Venezuela. We study the variations in patterns of individual earnings changes over a large number of one-year panels in each of the three countries. In most but not all years covered by this study, economic growth was positive; and in several years, the relative inequality of earnings rose, in our three countries and in Latin America as a whole (Gasparini and Lustig, 2011). Given these macroeconomic changes and given our sense that most people remain approximately where they were within the income distribution, we expect to find two patterns in panel data: first, that panel earnings changes would be divergent in percentages on several occasions, and second that panel earnings changes would be divergent in the country's currency units almost all the time – that is, on average, the higher is one's initial earnings, the higher is one's earnings gain in pesos or bolivares.

Throughout this paper, earnings mobility is measured as changes in real labor market earnings in local currency. We use both changes in earnings as well as changes in logearnings (the latter to approximate proportional changes). We adopt two measures of initial advantage: one based on the reported initial level of earnings, and another one based on the component of earnings predicted by socio-demographic characteristics permanently attached to the worker. This last measure is a proxy of longer-term advantage, and permits a mobility analysis that is less sensitive to transitory changes in earnings and to measurement error.

For the most part, to the extent that earnings gains and losses of different income groups in positive growth and negative growth periods have been studied in Argentina,Mexico, and Venezuela, the answers have mainly relied on comparable cross-sections (Gasparini and Lustig, 2011). In this way, researchers have looked at anonymous individuals and households: e.g., those in the poorest 20% of the income distribution versus others, thus comparing the evolution of income distribution through the use of growth incidence curves. This type of analysis does not link changes in inequality with the evolution of individual incomes over time.

In contrast, in this paper, we look at panel data and calculate earnings changes for each panel person, thus removing anonymity. The study of mobility patterns in labor markets in developing economies is still a fresh area of research where much remains to be learned; see Baulch (2011) for a review of the literature on developing countries in general and our paper (Fields and Duval-Hernández, 2007) for Latin American countries in particular.[1] More recent studies for these economies include Fields and Sánchez Puerta (2010), Cuesta et al. (2011), and Krebs et al. (2012).

14.3 Data and Economic Context

Argentina, Mexico, and Venezuela are chosen for our mobility study both for reasons of data availability and for inherent interest. The available data sets permit the same questions to be answered in a consistent manner in each of the three countries. We are able to measure the changes in real earnings from a given month in one year to the corresponding month a year later. These one-year-long panels begin in 1996 for all urban Argentina, in 1987 for all urban Mexico, and in 1994 for all Venezuela. Moreover, each country has a large number of comparable panels – seven in the case of Argentina, eighty-five in the case of Mexico, and fourteen in the case of Venezuela – ranging over widely different macroeconomic conditions.

The data sources for the three countries are similar in a number of respects. In each, the sample under investigation consists of men and women who were in the labor force both in a given survey and in a follow-up survey one year later. The dependent variables in each case are changes in labor earnings and changes in log-earnings from one year to the next. In each case, earnings are measured in real local currency units (i.e., 1999 pesos for Argentina, 2002 pesos for Mexico, and 1996 bolivares for Venezuela). The surveys also contain information on a set of demographic characteristics like gender, age, education, and geographic region indicators that will be used to predict longer-term earnings (see Section 14.4). To capture earnings changes among workers and to exclude new labor force entrants and retirees, we limit the analysis to individuals aged 25 to 60 in the base year.

For Argentina, the data used come from the Encuesta Permanente de Hogares (EPH or Permanent Household Survey), a rotating panel following urban households for a maximum of a year and a half. For the years used in this paper, the survey was conducted in May and October each year in provincial capitals and areas with more than 100,000 inhabitants for a total of 28 urban areas. Argentina is predominantly urban (86%); just the May-to-May changes are used here. The urban areas surveyed represent 61 percent of the country and 71 percent of urban areas. The survey contains detailed questions on employment and incomes, together with information on household demographics, housing questions, and questions on education. The survey methodology changed after May 2003; therefore, the years used in this paper are 1996–97 to 2002–03 for all urban Argentina.

For Mexico, the data used come from the Encuesta Nacional de Empleo Urbano (ENEU or National Urban Employment Survey), a survey conducted on urban households to trace labor market characteristics in urban areas. This survey is a rotating panel with quarterly data for five periods. In order to maintain consistent geographical coverage over time, the present analysis is based only on the cities that remain in the panel throughout the 1987–2010 period. The urban centers surveyed cover 35 percent of the total population and about 57 percent of the population living in areas with more than 15 thousand inhabitants. Although the coverage of the ENEU has expanded to now survey rural areas as well, we only use data on urban households since the rural panels didn't exist for the first fifteen years of our data.[2] In 2005 the ENEU was replaced by the Encuesta Nacional de Ocupación y Empleo (ENOE or National Survey on Occupation and Employment), which updated the questionnaire and the sampling scheme of the ENEU. However, for the most part the trends observed in the key variables used in this study remain comparable with the ones previous to 2005.

For Venezuela, the data source is the Encuesta de Hogares por Muestreo (EHM or Household Sample Survey). This survey has been conducted twice a year since 1969. For this study, the data run from 1994–95 to 2003–04. It is a nationwide survey, initially intended for measuring unemployment and other characteristics of the labor market.[3] Currently, the EHM is a multipurpose survey that includes questions not only about labor market variables such as labor force participation, earnings and unionization but also about family composition and characteristics of dwellings. Every six months, one sixth of the sample is replaced by a new set of households from the same sampling cluster. This feature enables researchers to produce panel data for those dwellings that remain in the sample up to a maximum of six observation data points. Since the household identification code was not consistent during 1997–98 and 2000–02, these data points needed to be dropped.

14.3.1 *Growth and Inequality Context*

Before presenting the empirical methods followed in this paper, we briefly discuss the evolution of GDP growth and earnings inequality for our three countries. More details can be found in the supporting Online Appendix of the paper.

Unfortunately, during our periods of study our three economies experienced not only positive economic growth but severe economic downturns. Between the years 1996 and 2003, the Argentinean economy experienced extraordinary macroeconomic variability. During the mid-nineties it experienced moderate growth followed by a recession at the end of the decade and a severe collapse of the economy at the end of 2001. In the case of Mexico, the economy experienced an upward trend in real GDP from 1987 to 1994 thanks to the liberalization reforms implemented in those years. In December 1994, the Peso crisis hit the economy and output suffered a sharp downturn, from which it started recovering rapidly. From 1997 onwards, the Mexican economy continued its slow growth, with temporary downturns around the years 2001–02 and 2009. Finally, the Venezuelan economy experienced years of moderate economic growth from 1995 to 1997 and from 2000 to 2001. Each of these growth episodes was followed by a moderate to severe contraction. By the fourth quarter of 2002 the economy rebounded and in 2003 it experienced one of the highest growth rates of the decade.

During the years of this study, absolute and relative earnings inequality changed substantially in the three countries. Absolute inequality was fluctuating in Argentina and Venezuela, while in Mexico it had an inverted-V pattern. As for relative inequality, it rose steadily in Argentina with the exception of the last year, in Mexico it presented an inverted-V pattern, and in Venezuela different relative inequality measures display crossing patterns.

14.4 Empirical Methods

The dependent variable in this study is one-year mobility for each country, i.e., change in earnings and log-earnings for the same individuals from a given month in one year to that same month a year later. Changes in log-earnings are used to approximate proportional changes. The analysis of these proportional changes is important because a given change in income will have a very different impact on well-being depending on whether the individual is poor or rich, e.g., during periods of economic decline a reduction in 100 pesos might represent a drastic change for a poor person, but not for a rich one. For unemployed individuals and individuals with zero earnings we impute them an earnings level of 1 peso/bolívar in order to avoid excluding them from the sample when conducting the analysis of log-earnings.

The data for one-year mobility are analyzed in a number of ways, depending on the hypothesis being tested. The tests for divergence or convergence are based on a) a pooled sample, which uses all of the one-year-long panels, as well as b) each individual panel. The tests for symmetry/asymmetry involve a comparison of all of the positive-growth years with all of the negative-growth years.

14.4.1 *Earnings Dynamics and the Divergence of Earnings Hypothesis*

We start by displaying quintilemobility profiles. These tables show the relationship between earnings and log-earnings change and initial reported earnings quintile groups, over the whole sample and for periods of growth and decline separately. They are the mobility equivalent of poverty profiles and give us a first quick look at whether the rich or the poor have larger earnings (or log-earnings) changes and whether these patterns are consistent over periods of growth and recession.

Next we perform a regression analysis over each of our yearly panels to test in more detail the divergence of earnings hypothesis. To motivate this analysis consider the following simple earnings dynamics model.

Let y_t denote the earnings of an individual in the population at time t.[4] As previously mentioned, our goal is to estimate how an initial advantage in earnings relates to earnings changes. With our data containing individual observations for two periods one year apart, it is natural to formulate a population regression model like

$$(1) \qquad \Delta y_t = y_t - y_{t-1} = \beta_0 + \beta_1 y_{t-1} + u_t.$$

The parameters of this model provide an answer to the question of whether initially advantaged individuals (in terms of earnings) are getting ahead faster than the rest, or alternatively whether the earnings of poorer and richer workers are converging. In particular, the population parameter β_1 measures the expected difference in Δy_t for two individuals who differ by one peso or bolívar in their initial earnings. If $\beta_1 < 0$, it means that earnings changes are negatively related to initial earnings, in which case from one year to the next we would observe convergence in the incomes of initially advantaged and disadvantaged workers. If, on the other hand, $\beta_1 > 0$, this would signify greater earnings gains the greater is initial advantage and hence to a divergent process of earnings dynamics. Finally, if $\beta_1 = 0$, earnings changes would on average be unaffected by the initial advantage of the worker.

While this model is simple and intuitive, we should be careful when interpreting it. In particular, it is possible to observe negative values of β_1 if for instance workers are subject to individual transitory earnings shocks that wear out over time. In other words, in the short run we might observe that earnings are converging just because workers who received an initial positive (negative) earnings shock are now adjusting back to their lower (higher) permanent level of earnings, even if the longer-term earnings do not converge in general. Although strictly speaking this does not create any problem to the model in Eq. 1, we usually do not want to confound transitory adjustments in earnings with a more meaningful convergent process in earnings trajectories over a longer period of time.

To investigate whether convergence between rich and poor is taking place in a more permanent sense, we need to somehow eliminate the impact of earnings reverting to the conditional mean. Thus we need to come up with an operational definition of transitory earnings. To do so, we propose a simple model of earnings determination that can be estimated with short-lived panel datasets like ours.

In particular, we decompose yt as the sum of a component related to characteristics permanently attached to the worker and another component that will be considered transitory earnings. In other words, we propose the model

$$(2) \qquad\qquad y_t = z\gamma_t + \delta\tau_t + \epsilon_t,$$

where z is a *(1 x k)* vector of observable socioeconomic characteristics permanently attached to an individual (like gender, age, education level, etc.), δ is a scalar capturing unobserved characteristics permanently attached to the individual, γ_t and τ_t are time-varying coefficients capturing the influence of these characteristics on earnings, and ϵ_t is the transitory shock component previously mentioned. Thus, $y_t^p = z\gamma_t + \delta\tau_t$ forms the component of earnings associated with permanent characteristics of the worker, and the remaining ϵ_t will be dubbed transitory earnings. Note that we allow y_t^p to be time-varying, since the coefficients associated to these permanent characteristics can change across periods.

To give empirical content to this model, we need to be explicit about the relation between each of these components. In particular, we assume that in the population these three components are uncorrelated among themselves, i.e.,

$$\text{cov} (z_j, \delta) = \text{cov} (z_j, \epsilon_t) = \text{cov} (\delta, \epsilon_t) = 0 \ \forall t, \forall j = 1, ..., k.$$

Furthermore, we will assume that t follows an AR(1) process, i.e.,[5]

$$\epsilon_t = \rho\epsilon_{t-1} + v_t \qquad v_t \sim \text{iid} (0, \sigma_v^2) \qquad |\rho| < 1.$$

The assumptions of uncorrelatedness between the different components of earnings imply that we cannot give a structural interpretation to the coefficient vector γ_t. These assumptions are not too restrictive for the purpose at hand, insofar as we are not trying to estimate the returns to socioeconomic characteristics of the worker, but rather implement a decomposition of the embodied permanent advantage of workers.

The transitory earnings term will contain earnings shocks uncorrelated with the vector z and the scalar δ, which are the characteristics permanently attached to the worker. We implement this definition of transitory shocks because we lack a long series of yearly observations for each individual in the panel. If we had such a dataset we could in principle define as transitory those shocks whose effects die out over time or that are uncorrelated with some long-run trend in earnings.[6]

The AR(1) assumption made on this transitory shock is a common specification in the income mobility literature. Although many papers include more general ARMA(p,q) structures, such structures cannot be identified with our short-lived panels.

With this framework, we can now proceed in two stages, first estimating Eq. 2 in period $t-1$ to get the component of initial earnings associated with permanent characteristics of the worker and then using the predicted values of this regression in a second stage where we estimate the relationship between Δy_t and y_{t-1}^p:

$$(3) \qquad \Delta y_t = \alpha_0 + \alpha_1 y_{t-1}^p + e_t.$$

In Eq. 3, the parameter α_1 captures how earnings changes are related to the component of initial earnings associated with permanent characteristics of the worker. Since this parameter is not affected by transitory shocks reverting to the mean, it will be a better measure of how earnings changes are related to a more permanent measure of initial advantage.

In practice, we do not observe the unobserved individual-specific shocks contained in δ in Eq. 2, which implies that we can only estimate in a first stage the component of earnings associated with *observed* permanent characteristics, namely $y_{t-1}^z = z\gamma_{t-1}$. However, given the orthogonality between δ and z, it will suffice to know y_{t-1}^z in order to be able to consistently estimate α_1 in a regression

$$(4) \qquad \Delta y_t = \alpha_0 + \alpha_1 y_{t-1}^z + v_t.$$

This claim, as well as a full exposition of the econometric model is presented in detail in the Online Appendix of the paper.

In summary, we can use a Two-Stages Least Squares (2SLS) procedure to consistently estimate our parameter of interest α_1, namely the impact of a more permanent measure of earnings on earnings changes.

In our empirical specification the vector z of observable permanent characteristics of the worker includes age, gender, education, and region.[7]

14.4.2 *Testing the Symmetry of Gains and Losses Hypothesis*

As previously mentioned, we formulate the symmetry of gains and losses hypothesis, which is the idea that those earnings groups which experience larger positive earnings gains when the economy grows are the same as those that experience larger earnings losses when the economy contracts.

In the context of a regression equation like Eq. 1, which relates earnings changes to initial earnings we can test whether there is symmetry of gains and losses for each of our countries by pooling the data from several panels for years of growth and recession for a given economy. In particular, we can estimate a model

(5) $$\Delta y = \beta_0 + \beta_1 y_{t-1} + \beta_2 NG + \beta_3 y_{t-1} * NG + u,$$

where NG is a dummy indicating whether in the year in which earnings changes are being considered, GDP growth was negative.[8] In other words, this model assumes that earnings changes during periods with positive growth are given by the equation

$$\Delta y = \beta_0 + \beta_1 y_{t-1} + u,$$

while during periods with negative growth the equation is

$$\Delta y = (\beta_0 + \beta_2) + (\beta_1 + \beta_3) y_{t-1} + u.$$

With an equation like Eq. 5, we can test the aforementioned symmetry of gains and losses hypothesis. In particular, if during a period of positive growth richer individuals experience the largest earnings gains, i.e., if $\beta_1 > 0$, then symmetry would imply that it is also the rich that lose the most during periods of negative growth. In terms of our Eq. 5, this would mean that $\beta_1 + \beta_3 < 0$, or simply $\beta_3 < -\beta_1 < 0$.

Similarly, if during a period of positive growth the richer individuals experience the smallest earnings gains, i.e., if $\beta_1 < 0$, then symmetry of mobility would imply that it is also the richer individuals who lose the least during periods of negative growth. In terms of our Eq. 5, this would mean that $\beta_1 + \beta_3 > 0$, or $\beta_3 > -\beta_1 > 0$.

These two conditions can be tested with a one-tailed t-test over the parameters estimated from Eq. 5. In particular we can test the symmetry of gains and losses hypothesis by testing the following one-sided hypotheses:

Parameter	H_0	H_1
$\beta_1 > 0$	$\beta_1 + \beta_3 \leq 0$	$\beta_1 + \beta_3 > 0$
$\beta_1 < 0$	$\beta_1 + \beta_3 \geq 0$	$\beta_1 + \beta_3 < 0$

Since these are tests for a linear combination of the parameters β_1 and β_3 they can be performed with a one-sided t-test with $n-k-1$ degrees of freedom. The specific form of the t-statistic is the following

(6) $$t = sgn(\hat{\beta}_1) \frac{\beta_1 + \beta_3}{se(\beta_1 + \beta_3)}$$

where $sgn(x)$ is a function that takes value 1 if x is positive, 0 if $x = 0$, and -1 if $x < 0$. By pre-multiplying the ratio by the sign of $\hat{\beta}_1$ we ensure this statistic will be positive if the estimated patterns are asymmetric.

A rejection of the null will be taken as evidence of asymmetric mobility patterns over the business cycle.[9]

14.4.3 Robustness Checks

Measurement Error

So far we have assumed that earnings were measured without error. However, based on validation data in developed countries, we know that this assumption is seldom true. Furthermore, measurement error in earnings is rarely just random noise as the traditional Classical Measurement Error model used to assume (see Bound et al., 2001).

The analysis of the impact of a general form of measurement error on the regression estimates of Eq. 1 has been presented in detail in Gottschalk and Huynh (2010). Using data for the U.S.A., the authors find that measurement error leads to a substantial understatement of inequality (due to mean reversion in the measurement error), but estimates of our parameter β_1 in Eq. 1 are largely unaffected by such error when dealing with a model of log-earnings.

The reason for such a lack of impact on the OLS estimates of Eq. 1 with log-earnings is that with nonclassical measurement error, the attenuation effect on the parameter estimates is offset by the strong correlation between measurement errors across periods.

The consequences of nonclassical measurement error on the estimates arising from the model in Eq. 4 are derived analytically in the Online Appendix of the paper. From that derivation we can conclude that measurement error will have no impact on the estimates of α_1 as long as this error is uncorrelated with the observed permanent characteristics included in the vector z.

To the extent that a substantial part of the measurement error occurs due to reactions to transitory fluctuations in earnings (see Bound et al., 1994; Gottschalk and Huynh, 2010), it is plausible that the inconsistency in our 2SLS estimates when earnings are measured with error is small.

Nevertheless, lacking any validation data for our countries (and for any developing country to the best of our knowledge), we cannot judge whether the conclusions found by Gottschalk and Huynh for Eq. 1 or the conditions mentioned in the previous paragraph hold in our data. At best, we can report on the analytical implications of a general form of measurement error on our estimates and refer to the available empirical evidence for developed nations.

Other methods for dealing with measurement error in the context of earnings changes regressions include instrumenting using either second measurements of earnings or variables that are caused by earnings

(Glewwe, 2010) and constructing pseudo-panels and tracking the mobility of average cohort earnings (Antman and McKenzie, 2007).[10] While these papers correctly point out that 2SLS does not necessarily leads to consistent estimates of β_1 in the presence of measurement error, we contend that the parameter β_1 is an interesting economic object on its own, one that on many occasions can be even more interesting than the original β_1 itself.[11]

In particular, α_1 provides an estimate of how earnings changes are related to a more permanent measure of initial advantage, and hence it gives a measure of mobility cleaner from the mean-reverting impact of transitory shocks and cleaner from measurement error too.

Additional Specifications
In addition to the methods previously discussed, we estimated four additional models.

One robustness check we performed was to estimate the model in Eq. 4 adding sector of economic activity (formal/informal) as a regressor among the set of characteristics of the worker included in the vector z. Although for many individuals, the sector of economic activity will be a transitory state, for some others it will be more permanent as they will tend to stay in one sector for most of their active life.

An alternative method that we explored involved approximating the individual's longer-term earnings by averaging their earnings over several periods observed in the panel. This method captures the impact of both observable factors and unobservable time-invariant characteristics and it will work best if the panel has many observations per individual (i.e., if T is large) and if these observations are spaced widely over time. Under these conditions the effects of transitory income fluctuations and measurement error would be averaged out and their impact would be minimal. We performed these estimations but do not regard them as our preferred specification because in our case T is not very large and the time observations are close to one another.[12]

We also estimated our key models dropping from the sample the individuals who had earnings equal to zero in either the initial or the final period.

Finally, we estimated an alternative version of our predicted model where we "purged" earnings of life-cycle effects before estimating Eq. 4.

14.5 Results

14.5.1 *Mobility Profiles*

Tables 14.1, 14.2, and 14.3 provide a first exploration of the mobility data and give preliminary answers to the questions posed in Section 14.1. In these tables we display mobility profiles for the population classified according to their quintile group in the initial earnings distribution. This exercise is presented for earnings in levels for all years pooled together.[13]

In these mobility profiles, we observe that for all the countries larger positive gains (smaller negative losses) are observed for individuals at the bottom of the initial period earnings distribution. This evidence goes against the divergence hypothesis.[14]

As a first test of the symmetry hypothesis, these same tables also separate out periods of positive and negative GDP growth. We find convergent earnings changes in both the positive growth and the negative growth periods. This is evidence against the symmetry of gains and losses hypothesis, since the same income groups that gain the most when positive growth takes place are the ones who gain the most (lose the least) when there is negative growth.

14.5.2 Regression-Based Tests: Divergence of Earnings

A more precise test of the divergence of earnings hypothesis is obtained by estimating Eq. 1, namely regressing earnings change on initial reported earnings for each country for each one-year panel under the assumption of linearity. These point estimates, along with their 95% confidence intervals, are reported in the left column of Figure 14.1. The right column of that same figure presents the estimates for the regression for changes in log-earnings on initial log-earnings. In all years and for all countries, the regression coefficients are significantly negative. Thus, when initial reported earnings and log-earnings are used as a measure of initial advantage, in all three countries, it is those with the lowest initial reported earnings who exhibit the largest average earnings gains. The divergence of earnings hypothesis for initial reported earnings is decisively rejected by this test.

As noted above, this negative relationship between earnings change and initial earnings could be the result of earnings in any given year adjusting back to their longer-term levels after a transitory shock. This negative relationship could also be the result of measurement error. Accordingly, we approximate longer-term earnings using the prediction method described in Section 14.4 and use these as regressors in the earnings change Eq. 4. The regression coefficients for this exercise are plotted in Figure 14.2, on the left side for earnings change in currency units on initial predicted earnings in currency units, and on the right side for change in log-earnings on initial predicted log-earnings.

Table 14.1. Average earnings changes by initial reported earnings quintile group

	Mean	Std. Dev.	Obs.	H_{01}
Positive and negative growth years combined				
Total population	-30.5	527.4	53,349	***
Breakdown by initial reported earnings quintile group	H_{02}: ***			
Lowest quintile group	226.6	488.7	11,211	***
Quintile group 2	4.5	192.5	10,954	***
Quintile group 3	-28.5	240.5	11,237	***
Quintile group 4	-67.7	332.6	9,895	***
Highest quintile group	-321.2	913.7	10,052	***
Periods of positive growth				
Total population	4.4	504.8	22,422	***
Breakdown by initial reported earnings quintile group	H_{02}: ***			
Lowest quintile group	243.2	478.2	4,537	***
Quintile group 2	25.1	218.2	4,678	***
Quintile group 3	-2.9	232.7	4,255	***
Quintile group 4	-37.2	348.8	4,682	***
Highest quintile group	-219.1	861.8	4,270	***
Periods of negative growth				
Total population	-55.83	541.7	30,927	***
Breakdown by initial reported earnings quintile group	H_{02}: ***			
Lowest quintile group	223.2	499.7	6,294	***
Quintile group 2	-11.6	181.5	6,135	***
Quintile group 3	-37.8	218.9	6,530	***
Quintile group 4	-81.9	318.2	5,974	***
Highest quintile group	-387.8	932.9	5,994	***

Pooled data for Argentina

***, **, * H_{0j} rejected at 1, 5, 10 % of significance

H_{01}: mean equal to zero, H_{02}: equality of means by groups

Earnings are measured in 1999 pesos. Source: Authors' calculations based on Encuesta Permanente de Hogares (1996–03)

The results using predicted earnings differ qualitatively from the ones using initial reported earnings and also differ across the three countries. In the case of Argentina, earnings change is usually related significantly to predicted earnings, and all of the significant coefficients are negative. Thus, in Argentina, the results using predicted earnings confirm the results using initial reported earnings: divergence is rejected in favor of convergence or neutrality of earnings changes. A similar conclusion is obtained when looking at proportional earnings changes as approximated by changes in log-earnings. However, in the case of Mexico,

Table 14.2. Average earnings changes by initial reported earnings quintile group

	Mean	Std. Dev.	Obs.	H_{01}
Positive and negative growth years combined				
Total population	-87	4,889.1	286,062	***
Breakdown by initial reported earnings quintile group	H_{02}: ***			
Lowest quintile group	992	2,202.6	57,216	***
Quintile group 2	513	2,052.4	57,209	***
Quintile group 3	351	2,515.7	57,243	***
Quintile group 4	51	3,276.7	57,188	***
Highest quintile group	-2,342	9,305.0	57,206	***
Periods of positive growth				
Total population	-38	4,890.2	245,404	***
Breakdown by initial reported earnings quintile group	H_{02}: ***			
Lowest quintile group	1,004	2,208.5	49,086	***
Quintile group 2	534	2,095.1	49,080	***
Quintile group 3	378	2,517.2	49,084	***
Quintile group 4	103	3,327.8	49,102	***
Highest quintile group	-2,210	9,306.9	49,052	***
Periods of negative growth				
Total population	-384	4,872.4	40,658	***
Breakdown by initial reported earnings quintile group	H_{02}: ***			
Lowest quintile group	913	2,161.7	8,133	***
Quintile group 2	401	1,809.0	8,135	***
Quintile group 3	146	2,237.9	8,127	***
Quintile group 4	-290	3,239.7	8,153	***
Highest quintile group	-3,096	9,248.7	8,110	***

Pooled data for Mexico

***, **, * H_{0j} rejected at 1, 5, 10% of significance

H_{01}: mean equal to zero, H_{02}: equality of means by groups

Earnings are measured in 2002 pesos for Mexico. Source: Authors' calculations based on Encuesta Nacional de Empleo Urbano (1987–2004) and Encuesta Nacional de Ocupación y Empleo (2005–10)

earnings change is related significantly to predicted earnings only occasionally, and the coefficients change sign. Thus, in Mexico, convergence always appears for initial reported earnings; but for predicted earnings, the earnings changes are significantly convergent in a small number of cases, especially after the 1994 Peso crisis, significantly divergent in a small number of cases, and insignificant in the great majority of cases. In the log-earnings specification, most of the coefficients for Mexico are statistically insignificant. Finally, in the case of Venezuela, the results for predicted earnings are also mixed: earnings change is significantly and

Table 14.3. Average earnings changes by initial reported earnings quintile group

	Mean	Std. Dev.	Obs.	H_{01}
Positive and negative growth years combined				
Total population	-9,518	250	152,747	***
Breakdown by initial reported earnings quintile group	H_{02}: ***			
Lowest quintile group	32,552	58,437	32,129	***
Quintile group 2	5,672	49,228	33,661	***
Quintile group 3	-4,422	50,900	32,650	***
Quintile group 4	-15,284	70,258	25,446	***
Highest quintile group	-74,754	172,970	28,861	***
Periods of positive growth				
Total population	-3,998	87,679	72,617	***
Breakdown by initial reported earnings quintile group	H_{02}: ***			
Lowest quintile group	34,806	58,207	14,923	***
Quintile group 2	8,653	50,777	17,338	***
Quintile group 3	-1,456	43,940	13,989	***
Quintile group 4	-7,585	67,932	12,185	***
Highest quintile group	-59,721	147,905	14,182	***
Periods of negative growth				
Total population	-14,522	105,486	80,130	***
Breakdown by initial reported earnings quintile group	H_{02}: ***			
Lowest quintile group	30,597	58,567	17,206	***
Quintile group 2	2,505	47,324	16,323	***
Quintile group 3	-6,645	55,447	18,661	***
Quintile group 4	-22,357	71,605	13,261	***
Highest quintile group	-89,278	193,033	14,679	***

Pooled data for Venezuela

***, **, * H_{0i} rejected at 1, 5, 10% of significance

H_{01}: mean equal to zero, H_{02}: equality of means by groups

Earnings are measured in 1996 bolivares for Venezuela. Source: Authors' calculations based on Encuesta de Hogares por Muestreo (1995–2004) for Venezuela

negatively related to predicted earnings in seven panels, significantly and positively related to predicted earnings in one panel, and insignificant in six panels. In contrast, most of the coefficients in the model with predicted proportional changes are statistically insignificant. When using predicted earnings as explanatory variable, coefficients become much smaller, within the [–0.3, 0.3] range, and non-significant in many cases; rather than the [–0.8, –0.3] range observed when using reported initial earnings. In other words, the strong convergence patterns become much weaker or even neutral.

Figure 14.1. Regression coefficients of earnings change in levels and logs on initial reported earnings in levels and logs, with 95% confidence intervals.

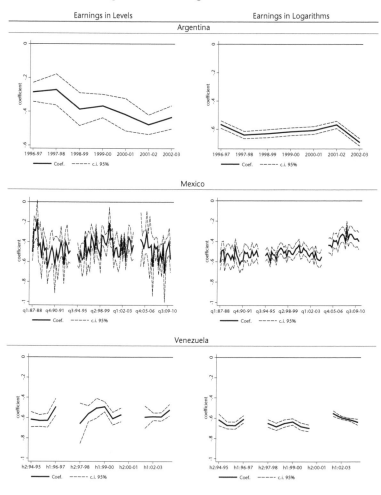

The fact that for Mexico and Venezuela, several coefficients of the predicted earnings variable are negative and statistically significant when working with earnings in levels but insignificant when working with the logarithmic specification indicates that in those periods earnings changes were negatively related to our constructed measure of longer-term earnings advantage, yet the losses were proportional to predicted longer-term advantage.[15]

In sum, in our three countries, the divergence hypothesis for earnings receives no support at all when using initial reported earnings and only

Figure 14.2. Regression coefficients of earnings change in levels and logs on initial predicted earnings in levels and logs, with 95% confidence intervals. Predictions based on time-invariant characteristics.

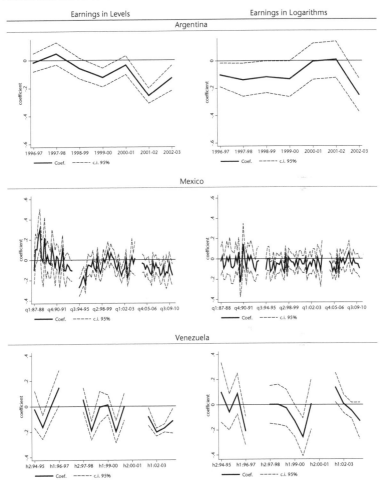

infrequent support when using predicted earnings in pesos or bolivares. In particular, when using initial reported earnings in each country, we find significant convergence both in logs and in levels. When using predicted permanent earnings, the coefficient is not significantly different from zero in most cases, and only in very few cases do we find statistically significant divergence in earnings.

Table 14.4. Earnings change regressions by periods of positive and negative GDP growth

	Reported earnings OLS		Predicted earnings 2SLS	
	ΔEarn	Δln(Earn)	ΔEarn	Δln(Earn)
Initial y	-0.29*** (0.02)		-0.006 (0.02)	
Initial ln(y)		-0.62*** (0.01)		-0.14 (0.038)
Initial y *NG	-0.12*** (0.03)		-0.12*** (0.03)	
Initial ln(y) *NG		0.019* (0.01)		0.075 (0.05)
NG	14.67 (15.66)	-0.40*** (0.06)	7.19 (13.13)	-0.75*** (0.26)
Constant	157.7*** (11.36)	3.32*** (0.044)	7.82 (10.03)	0.87*** (0.20)
N	53,349	53,349	53,349	53,349
R-squared	0.22	0.31	0.006	0.005

Pooled data for Argentina

***, **, * H_0: $\beta = 0$ rejected at 1, 5, 10% level of significance. Robust std. err. in parentheses

y: Earnings measured in 1999 pesos

NG is a dummy variable for periods with negative GDP growth

Initial y and Initial $\ln(y)$ represent the coefficient of initial earnings and log-earnings respectively during periods of positive economic growth. To obtain the corresponding coefficients for periods of negative economic growth sum that coefficient to the one of Initial $y*NG$ (or Initial $\ln(y)*NG$)

Predicted initial earnings are based on a First-Stage regression of earnings on age and its square, education and its square, gender, and regional dummies. A similar model applies to log earnings

Authors' calculations based on Encuesta Permanente de Hogares (1996–2003)

14.5.3 *Regression-Based Tests*: *Symmetry of Gains and Losses*

As already discussed, our three countries all experienced periods of economic growth as well as periods of economic decline. The second question is whether when positive growth and negative growth years are compared, those income groups for whom earnings changes are the most positive when the economy is growing are those for whom earnings changes are the least positive or the most negative when the economy is contracting. When the pattern of gains and losses is not symmetric, we adopt the following terminology: if the same individuals gain significantly more regardless of whether the economy is growing

Table 14.5. Earnings change regressions by periods of positive and negative GDP growth

	Reported earnings OLS		Predicted earnings 2SLS	
	ΔEarn	Δln(Earn)	ΔEarn	Δln(Earn)
Initial y	-0.47***		-0.05***	
	(0.012)		(0.006)	
Initial ln(y)		-0.50***		-0.04
		(0.004)		(0.006)
Initial y *NG	-0.04*		-0.06***	
	(0.024)		(0.016)	
Initial ln(y) *NG		0.04***		0.028*
		(0.011)		(0.017)
NG	-12.46	-0.41***	-42.75	-0.34***
	(104.4)	(0.091)	(60.42)	(0.134)
Constant	2071.5***	3.9***	179.9***	0.31***
	(50.27)	(0.033)	(22.95)	(0.05)
N	286,062	286,062	286,062	286,062
R-squared	0.27	0.26	0.06	0.03

Pooled data for Mexico

***, **, * H_0: $\beta = 0$ rejected at 1, 5, 10% level of significance. Robust std. err. in parentheses

y: Earnings measured in 2002 pesos

NG is a dummy variable for periods with negative GDP growth

Initial y and Initial $\ln(y)$ represent the coefficient of initial earnings and log-earnings respectively during periods of positive economic growth. To obtain the corresponding coefficients for periods of negative economic growth sum that coefficient to the one of Initial $y*NG$ (or Initial $\ln(y)*NG$)

Predicted initial earnings are based on a First-Stage regression of earnings on age and its square, education and its square, gender, and regional dummies. A similar model applies to log earnings

Authors' calculations based on Encuesta Nacional de Empleo Urbano (1987–2004) and Encuesta Nacional de Ocupación y Empleo (2005–10)

or contracting, the pattern of gains and losses is said to be "structural." Alternatively if the gains for different groups are not significantly different from one another in positive growth and/or in negative growth periods; such a pattern is said to be "insignificant."

Tables 14.4, 14.5, and 14.6 present the estimations of Eq. 5

$$\Delta y = \beta_0 + \beta_1 y_0 + \beta_2 NG + \beta_3 y_0 * NG + u,$$

for earnings in levels and in logarithms using initial reported earnings and predicted earnings as alternative measures of initial advantage. To reiterate, these regressions are estimated using pooled data across all years for each economy. Empirically, we observe that the parameter β_1 measures

Table 14.6. Earnings change regressions by periods of positive and negative GDP growth

	Reported earnings OLS		Predicted earnings 2SLS	
	ΔEarn	Δln(Earn)	ΔEarn	Δln(Earn)
Initial y	-0.558***		-0.090***	
	(0.013)		(0.014)	
Initial ln(y)		-0.627***		-0.089***
		(0.005)		(0.025)
Initial y *NG	-0.03109		-0.028***	
	(0.025)		(0.02)	
Initial ln(y) *NG		0.016***		0.124***
		(0.007)		(0.036)
NG	967.4	-0.249***	-6,497.3***	-1.533***
	(2,212.8)	(0.079)	(1,585.5)	(0.360)
Constant	41050***	6.103***	3,261.1***	0.865***
	(980.9)	(0.055)	(1,035.4)	(0.248)
N	152,747	152,747	152,747	152,747
R-squared	0.36	0.30	0.12	0.03

Pooled data for Venezuela

***, **, * H_0: $\beta = 0$ rejected at 1, 5, 10% level of significance. Robust std. err. in parentheses

y: Earnings measured in 2002 bolivares

NG is a dummy variable for periods with negative GDP growth

Initial y and Initial $\ln(y)$ represent the coefficient of initial earnings and log-earnings respectively during periods of positive economic growth. To obtain the corresponding coefficients for periods of negative economic growth sum that coefficient to the one of Initial $y*NG$ (or Initial $\ln(y)*NG$)

Predicted initial earnings are based on a First-Stage regression of earnings on age and its square, education and its square, gender, and regional dummies. A similar model applies to log earnings

Authors' calculations based on Encuesta de Hogares por Muestreo (1995–2004)

the relation between earnings changes and initial earnings during periods of positive economic growth. A quick look across our results tables shows that for virtually all years and all of our econometric specifications, there is *convergence* (i.e., $\beta_1 < 0$) during periods of economic growth.[16]

Given the finding of convergence during periods of economic growth, if symmetry of gains and losses is to hold, then we must have divergence in periods with negative growth, i.e., $\beta_1 + \beta_3 \geq 0$, or equivalently $\beta_3 \geq -\beta_1 > 0$. In Tables 14.4, 14.5, and 14.6 the coefficient β_3 appears either under the label "Initial $y*NG$" or "Initial $\ln(y)*NG$".

Looking first at the results in levels (i.e., pesos or bolivares), the coefficient is always negative. We can thus infer that earnings changes are not symmetric if we look at the specifications using earnings (either reported or predicted) in levels.

Table 14.7. Test of symmetry hypothesis

	Reported earnings		Predicted earnings	
	Levels	Logs	Levels	Logs
Argentina	19.23***	87.00***	6.82***	1.97**
Mexico	24.43***	44.88***	7.47***	0.67
Venezuela	27.26***	118.09***	8.4***	-1.34

One-sided t-statistics

H_0: Individuals that experience larger earnings when the economy is growing are the same as those that experience larger earnings losses when the economy is contracting

Turning to the logarithmic specifications, we see that only in the case of predicted log-earnings in Venezuela does the condition $\beta_3 \geq -\beta_1 > 0$ hold. To formally test the symmetry hypothesis we perform the t-test proposed in Eq. 6. The results for this test are presented in Table 14.7. There we see that in nearly all the specifications, earnings changes are asymmetric, namely the income groups that gain the most (lose the least) during periods of economic growth are the same ones that gain the most (lose the least) during periods of economic downturn. There are two exceptions, which correspond to the specification for predicted log-earnings in Venezuela and Mexico. As previously mentioned in the case of Venezuela there is divergence in predicted log-earnings during periods with negative growth and convergence during periodswith positive growth. In the case ofMexico (under this same specification) there is convergence throughout but the convergence coefficient for periods with negative growth is not statistically significant, so we cannot reject the hypothesis of symmetry.

We have obtained three main findings. First, using pooled data, both for levels and logs, and reported earnings we observe strong convergence (i.e., a coefficient around –0.50) but no evidence of symmetry in any country. Second, using pooled data and our preferred specification with predicted permanent earnings, we find evidence of weak convergence (i.e., a coefficient in the range [–0.1, 0.0]), but no evidence of symmetry when using changes in levels. Third, when using changes in logs we still find weak convergence in all countries, but we fail to reject the symmetry hypotheses in Mexico and Venezuela. Divergence and symmetry of mobility are overwhelmingly rejected.

14.5.4 *Reconciling the Panel and Cross-Section Results*

The reader may have noticed a seeming contradiction. We have mentioned that cross-sectional absolute and relative inequality had ups and downs in each of our three countries. However, we have also found in the panel data analysis that the mobility patterns are nearly always convergent or neutral, rarely divergent. The cross-sectional inequality findingsmean that during several periods those anonymous individuals at the upper end of the earnings distribution gained at least as much in pesos or bolívares, as those at the lower end of the earnings distribution. On the other hand, the mobility evidence compiled from analysis of panel data means that among those particular individuals who are followed over time, those who started at the lower end of the earnings distribution gained at least as much in pesos or bolivares as those who started higher in the earnings distribution. How can these two findings be reconciled?

It is important to note, contrary to what many observers may believe, that convergent mobility does not imply falling inequality. For instance, Furceri (2005) and Wodon and Yitzhaki (2006) both show that "beta-convergence" (a negative relationship between change in log-income and initial log-income) is mathematically compatible with "sigmadivergence" (i.e., rising inequality as measured by the variance of logs). A detailed reconciliation between different measures of panel income change and relative inequality change is presented in Duval-Hernández et al. (2014). In that work it is shown that rising inequality can be compatible with convergent earnings changes if earnings changes are large enough so that some individuals switch positions in a widening income distribution.[17]

To examine this mechanism, we explore more closely what happens with the distributions of earnings and earnings changes. In particular, for each country we select a period with rising absolute and relative inequality and positive economic growth, and we examine the distribution of earnings looking at the individuals anonymously and in a panel setting. For these periods in the three countries, we perform two sets of calculations.

The first set of calculations, presented in Figure 14.3, displays the initial and final period log-earnings of 27 illustrative individuals. To select these individuals, we split the population according to the quintiles of the initial period earnings distribution, and then for each quintile group we randomly select an individual located at the 5th, 25th, 50th, 75th, and 95th percentile of a given quintile group.[18] We also select two individuals non-randomly, namely, the one individual with the highest initial earnings and the one with the highest final earnings. We plot the location of initial period log-earnings (top line) and final period log-earnings (bottom line), looking at the distributions anonymously (left column) and tracking individuals over time (right panel).[19]

As previously mentioned, relative and absolute inequality rose in these periods. Yet behind the rise in inequality, the figure tracking individuals over time reveals two important facts, namely: a) earnings change substantially for a minority of earners, and b) most of these large earnings

Figure 14.3. Earnings distributions for 27 illustrative individuals in a period of rising inequality.

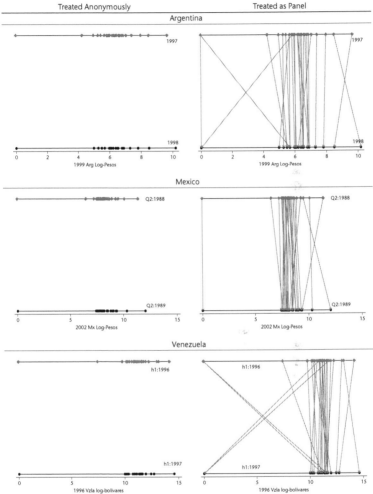

changes occur in a crossing pattern, resulting in convergent mobility.

In other words, part of the reason why we find non-divergent earnings in spite of studying periods with rising inequality is that in the panel distribution of earnings there are a few individuals experiencing large reversals of fortunes. Whether such large reversals of fortunes are due to transitory shocks, measurement error, or some other more lasting force is something that deserves further research in countries with more observations on individuals' incomes over time and, ideally, with both survey and administrative data.

The second set of calculations includes the full samples for the selected panels. For each country, we have classified workers in two ways, a cross-sectional approach and a panel data approach. The cross-sectional approach classifies workers into those belonging to the top quintile of real earnings in each year according to their earnings in that year and everyone else; it then calculates the mean earnings gain for these two cross-sectional (or anonymous) groups. The results, presented in column 2 of Table 14.8, show that in each country the cross-sectional top quintile group always gained the most. By contrast, the panel data approach classifies workers according to their initial earnings, and average earnings changes over time are then calculated for those individuals who started in the top quintile group and the bottom 80% regardless of where they ended up. The pattern from this second approach, presented in the last column of that table, is the exact opposite to the previous one, namely in each country the panel people who gained the most were those who started in the lowest earnings quintiles. Remember: these calculations are for the exact same people. What differs is the method for calculating earnings changes, not the sample of earners.

In summary, not only can cross-sectional methods and panel data methods produce qualitatively opposite pictures of who gains the most when economic growth takes place but they do produce qualitatively opposite pictures for our three countries.

14.6 Conclusions

In this paper, we have used panel data for Argentina, Mexico, and Venezuela to ask who has larger earnings changes in local currency units: those who started at the top of the distribution or those who started at the bottom? Given that economic growth was positive in most years and that relative earnings inequality rose often, and given our sense that most people remain approximately where they began within the income distribution, we expected to find two patterns in panel data: first, that earnings changes would be divergent in percentages on several occasions, and second that earnings changes would be divergent in pesos or bolivares all or nearly all the time – that is, on average, the higher is initial earnings, the higher is mean earnings gain in national currency units. But we found the opposite: convergent earnings changes in pesos or bolívares nearly all the time. Try though we might to get a predominantly divergent pattern of earnings changes in the three countries using a number of different specifications, we could not. Divergence is not the norm; convergence is. Specifically, we found that the divergence of earnings hypothesis receives no support at all when looking at a measure of initial reported earnings (or log-earnings). When we used a measure of predicted earnings that approximates longer-term earnings (and hence is less sensitive to mean-reverting transitory shocks) we obtained only scant support for the divergence hypothesis in the case of Mexico and Venezuela and no support at all in the case of Argentina. Most of the changes in earnings were either unrelated or negatively related to this measure of longer-term advantage.

We also tested whether the income groups that gain the most when the economy is growing are the ones that gain the most or gain the least when the economy is contracting. Support for the hypothesis of symmetric mobility was found only in Venezuela and for only one of the econometric specifications, namely the model of log-predicted earnings. In Mexico, for that same specification, we found no statistically significant pattern. In all other specifications, rather than symmetry, we found that earnings changes were "structural" in the sense that poorer individuals gained more than others regardless of whether the economy was growing or contracting. Therefore, in our three countries, the symmetry of mobility hypothesis was overwhelmingly rejected.

Finally, contrary to common perception, our research shows that periods of rising inequality are not necessarily associated with divergence in earnings among a panel of people, either unconditionally or after controlling for the potential confounding effects of transitory shocks adjusting back to the mean and of measurement error.

Overall, the analysis performed in this paper shows that much can be learned by analyzing panel data, knowledge that would not have been obtained by analyzing comparable cross-sections. In the future, researchers would do well to perform both panel data analysis and cross-section analysis. Both types of analysis are meaningful. They are, however, different from one another.

Part VI
Bringing the Components Together

The papers in the previous three chapters set the developing country context, explored labor market models, and addressed changes in various aspects of income distributions. In this part, I demonstrate possible ways of bringing empirical knowledge, theoretical modeling, and policy evaluation criteria together to reach welfare economic judgments about which policies should or not be pursued.

The first paper in this section ("Private and Social Returns to Education in Labor Surplus Economies" – Chapter 15) is a very early attempt of mine to apply the five-part policy framework laid out in Chapter 1. The policy analyzed is educational expansion and the policy evaluation criterion used is social cost-benefit analysis. The model is a multisector labor market model with educational differences among workers. The key innovation of this paper was a model in which educating more people who then get hired preferentially has serious negative externalities for those persons who do *not* get educated. Standard analyses based on Mincer equations (Mincer, 1974) and rate of return calculations (e.g., Montenegro and Patrinos, 2014) do not take account of these external effects. At the conclusion of his Nobel speech, James Heckman challenged the profession to develop microeconomic-data-based general equilibrium theory for evaluating the impacts of large scale programs (Heckman, 2001, p. 734), and new research is now moving in this direction (for a summary, see Edsall, 2014). The conclusion I reach is rather nihilistic: that we know less about the social costs and benefits of education than we think we do, with the consequence that we also know less about which educational policies to pursue.

The second paper in this section (Chapter 16) reverts to the basic Harris-Todaro model (1970) without extensions. Harris and Todaro's own policy analysis, and decades of additional policy analyses that followed, were conducted in terms of the effects of policy changes on unemployment. Unemployment is arguably *one* meaningful component to include in social welfare analysis, but it would be hard to find anyone today who would contend that unemployment should be the *only* consideration. Later analysis broadened the welfare economic criteria to include total labor earnings, inequality, poverty, and income distribution dominance in assessing policies of urban employment creation, urban wage restraint, and rural development. This analysis is to be found in "A Welfare Economic Analysis of Labor Market Policies in the Harris-Todaro Model."

Finally, a challenge for future work is to develop more realistic multi-sector labor market models of developing economies and subject them to richer welfare economic analysis. Three working papers which I am co-authoring are abstracted in Chapter 19 below. One is a model including two self-employment sectors rather than one. The second is a

China-specific model in which that country's unique household registration system is a central feature. And the third is a model of India featuring agricultural peak and slack seasons and migration from farm to city and back again in accordance with seasonal peaks and troughs.

Good labor market policy requires good labor market models. Although much has been learned, much important work remains to be done.

15

Private and Social Returns to Education in Labor Surplus Economies

The conceptual framework for the human capital approach to investment in education was developed mainly with reference to full employment economies. When we turn to the assessment of educational
problems in less developed countries, we often encounter a situation
of surplus labor.

In the sense used by Fei and Ranis,[1] there is surplus labor when removal
of a worker leads to no reduction in output; the marginal product of the
last worker is zero, and workers are paid their average products. However,
a situation of surplus labor also exists when there is general unemployment throughout an economy, as in India, or in large segments of an
economy, as in most other less developed countries. Such a situation
is the result of institutionally rigid wages set, for any number of reasons, above the market-clearing rate. Marginal products are positive but
unemployment persists. Throughout this discussion, I will use the term
'surplus labor' in the rigid wage sense.

The purpose of this paper is to consider the cost-benefit criterion for
resource allocation in labor surplus economies calling particular attention to the contrasts with full employment economies. The specific plan
is as follows. Section 15.1 reviews the debate over the applicability of
cost-benefit analysis to problems of investment in education. Section
15.2 draws two important distinctions which are not always clear to educational planners and enumerates the likely benefits, both private and

The original version of this chapter was published as: Fields, Gary S. (1972). Private and Social
Returns to Education in Labour Surplus Economies, in: Eastern Africa Economic Review,
4(1):41–61. © 1972 by Oxford University Press.

social, from education. Section 15.3 considers the case of full employment economies. Section 15.4 looks at the private returns to education in labor surplus economies in relation to the demand for education. Section 15.5 considers the social costs and benefits in labor surplus economies. Section 15.6 raises the problems of measuring marginal social rates of return and demonstrates the inadequacy of wage differentials as a measure of marginal social benefit. Section 15.7 summarizes the main points.

15.1 In Defense of a Cost-Benefit Approach to the Economics of Education

In order to assess the returns from social projects, economists and other social scientists have relied on cost-benefit analysis as the major technique for evaluation and decision-making. The *cost-benefit criterion* may be stated as follows:

> A project is profitable if the marginal social benefits (broadly defined) exceed the marginal social costs. The higher the ratio (or difference) between discounted benefits and costs, the more worthwhile the project.

The merits and deficiencies of cost-benefit analysis as a criterion for social decision-making have been discussed at length in the literature. Perhaps the most comprehensive look at the subject is the 1965 survey article by Prest and Turvey.[2] As they describe cost-benefit analysis:

> Cost-benefit analysis is a practical way of assessing the desirability of projects, where it is important to take a long view (in the sense of looking at repercussions in the further, as well as the nearer, future) and a wide view (in the sense of allowing for side-effects of many kinds on many persons, industries, regions, etc.), i.e., it implies the enumeration and evaluation of all the relevant costs and benefits.

The authors then go on to give an exhaustive list of the main questions which must be answered in practical applications of the technique. These questions involve the specification and valuation of costs and benefits, choice of interest rate, and relevant constraints. Specific sub-issues under these headings are discussed in detail. While the problems are many and complex, Prest and Turvey conclude that cost-benefit analysis is a very useful technique, although they caution the reader that applications to the public-utility areas of government are apt to be more fruitful than in the social service areas.

Cost-benefit analysis has been applied in many studies evaluating educational and training projects.[3] In addition to the many practitioners in the area, such leading economists as Arrow,[4] Becker,[5] Blaug,[6] Bowen,[7] Bowman,[8] Hansen,[9] and Weisbrod,[10] are among the firm believers in the social rate of return to education as a criterion for social investment. However, such a view is not unanimously held. Perhaps the strongest objection to the rate of return to education concept was raised by Merrett,[11] who, after considering the problems of enumerating costs and benefits and estimating rates of return by econometric techniques, concluded quite simply that 'research into the rate of return on education should be discontinued'. Balogh and Streeten[12] scorn the social rate of return to education as the 'coefficient of ignorance'. Others submit that a manpower planning approach is much more fruitful than cost-benefit.[13] In general, there is little disagreement with the notion of cost-benefit analysis in principle. The contention is that the practical problems of the technique are so serious as to render it useless in educational research.

My own view is that the economist's main contribution to social decision-making in the field of education is to raise explicitly the right questions pertaining to the marginal social costs and benefits of an educational endeavor.[14]

The manpower planner who plans supply to match demand asks the wrong questions. He asks. 'What is the absorptive capacity of the economy for persons with different skills and educational attainments?', and does not consider the costs of schooling at all. If employers say (or his calculations lead him to believe) that an extra graduate would be hired, the manpower planner directs the education system to produce an extra graduate. He does not ask. 'What is the nature of the work the graduate will perform and what benefits will he confer on society?' Nor does he ask, 'How much will it cost society to educate another graduate? Do the benefits justify the costs?' If educational expansion follows the path recommended by the manpower planner, an overproduction of education (in terms of costs and benefits) would be expected. This is because the demand for educated persons does not reflect the costs of education. When private firms (and government ministries for that matter) report shortages of educated manpower, they are saying in effect that it is worthwhile to them to pay a salary and other fringe benefits in exchange for an educated man's services. If they were also required to pay the costs of education. the demand for educated labor would surely decrease. Thus, the manpower planner's goal of equating supply to demand would result in an overproduction of education.

The problems of evaluating the marginal social costs and benefits of education in labor surplus economies are challenging (if not downright discouraging) to advocates of a cost-benefit approach. However. economic research has exhibited an encouraging tendency to improve over time. As researchers are made more aware of the limitations of the initial efforts of their colleagues, as they seek new ways of dealing with conceptual and measurement problems, and as new and better data sets become available. more thorough and precise analysis will, hopefully, emerge.

15.2 Two Important Distinctions

Traditionally, economists have calculated average rates of return to education while generally neglecting to point out that they are in fact averages and not marginals. Further, the distinction between private and social rates of return seems to be little more than a difference of a few percentage points after adjusting for mortality, taxes, and public subsidization of schooling costs. Policy recommendations are often proposed on the basis of average returns. To help clarify these concepts and to be sure our terminology is consistent, let us review two main distinctions which have troubled educational planners.

Marginal versus Average
The average measures the mean outcome of an activity. The marginal measures the increment resulting from a change from the existing level. We note that the cost-benefit criterion is expressed in terms of marginals, not averages. In some circumstances, the average is a very good approximation to the marginal. As we shall see, however, the existence of unemployment due to institutional wage rigidities gives us good reason to believe that the marginal and average social returns to investment in education in labor surplus economies may diverge sharply.

Private Returns versus Social Returns
The costs incurred and benefits received by society are not identically equal to the costs and benefits to the individual, although they may be of the same general magnitude. The social costs of education include the value of the resources used to construct and maintain school facilities and to train teachers, the output foregone by employing highly-educated persons in teaching rather than in some other occupation, the output foregone by having potentially productive workers in school rather than on the job, and, if the government's budget is more or less fixed, the other government projects which must be foregone in order to provide students with financial aid. In contrast, the private costs to the student (and/or his family) include foregone earnings and out-of-pocket schooling costs. Social costs and private costs differ to the extent that (a) the general taxpayer subsidizes direct schooling costs, and (b) private foregone earnings differ from foregone aggregate production.

A stream of benefits may be considered at one level from the viewpoint of additional income, either national income or personal disposable income. More generally, benefits may be viewed as increments to social welfare or personal utility, one component of which is income. The welfare-utility approach is conceptually more appealing, although it may be of little value operationally.

Social welfare is presumed to depend positively on the present value of aggregate output (net of education costs), the fraction of the labor force employed, the fraction of the labor force educated beyond a certain level, and equality of opportunity and income distribution. Of course, there is no consensus social welfare function; the weights assigned to different components vary from individual to individual and policy maker to policy maker. Personal utility is presumed to depend positively on the present value of net lifetime disposable income and the quality, status, and other nonpecuniary aspects of the job a person holds.[15] Neglecting the problems of trying to specify the form of social welfare and personal utility functions, the social and private benefits of education differ to the extent that additions to private incomes diverge from the marginal productivity to society. The marginal social return to education is the difference (or ratio) between the marginal social benefits and the marginal social costs if one more person is educated. Similarly, the marginal private return to an individual from additional education is the net increment to personal utility if he becomes educated. We note that the cost-benefit criterion is expressed in terms of marginal social returns, not private.

The composition and total magnitude of the returns to investment in education depend critically on the nature of the labor markets for educated persons. The cases of excess demand for and excess supply of educated persons will be considered in turn.

15.3 Returns to Education in Full Employment Economies

By way of contrast with labor surplus economies, let us briefly consider situations of full employment, which apply not only to full employment economies but also to occupations requiring either very high-level or very specific training in economies which otherwise have surplus labor. In cases where wages are flexible and adjust so as to achieve full employment or where wages are rigid but set below the market-clearing level so that demand for educated labor exceeds the supply, graduates can easily find a job utilizing their skills and can expect only brief periods of frictional unemployment.

When a person is educated for a full employment or excess demand occupation, at a minimum, society gains the value of his marginal product on his new job, which may be very large if the presence of an additional educated person helps to relieve a skilled labor bottleneck which had been retarding production. There may be shortages of less educated persons to fill the job he would have had, but a replacement is often available. Even if a replacement is not available, there will be higher output to the extent that the educated worker's marginal product is higher on his new job than it would have been if he were not educated and worked in some lower-level job, and the output gains from relief of bottlenecks are still realized. Society benefits from higher output, additional employment, and a greater fraction of its labor force educated. Society incurs the costs enumerated in the previous section.

The educated person himself benefits from a higher-level job which generally offers higher pay, more stable employment, and superior working conditions and other non-pecuniary benefits.[16] He may experience gains in utility from higher status or from a richer or more fulfilling life. Turning to the private costs, due to the abundance of job opportunities at most educational levels in full employment economies, foregone earnings may be substantial. In addition, out-of-pocket costs may be very large, since students in full employment economies are often charged a large fraction of the costs of their education. While the benefits may be considerable, so also may be the costs, so that private rates of return, while positive, are not found to be particularly great.

Since there is virtually full employment of graduates, if wages reflect marginal productivity, the economic benefits to society and to the individual are similar.[17] Furthermore, private costs and social costs are of the same order of magnitude. Thus, one would expect, as is indeed the case, the average social and private returns in full employment economies to be quite similar.

Since the newly-educated person in full employment economies becomes employed in a high-level job which utilizes his schooling and is paid about[18] the same wage as those educated earlier, the marginal benefits are approximated by the averages. There is little reason to expect the marginal social cost to differ appreciably from the average. Thus, the conventional 'social rate of return' is a useful guide to educational decision-making in full employment economies.

We turn now to the case of labor surplus economies.

15.4   Private Returns and the Demand for Education in Labor Surplus Economies

Private Costs
The private costs of education in labor surplus economies are in many cases quite small. The earnings foregone by an individual depend not

only upon the wage rate but also upon the probabilities of employment, underemployment, and unemployment. The younger the individual and the lower his educational attainment, the lower the wage and the likelihood of employment. In labor surplus economies, in which there are large numbers of unemployed and underemployed in search of work, the probability of employment for a school-aged person may be very low indeed. Hence, foregone earnings may be a small item to the individual. Furthermore, under existing institutional arrangements in many less developed countries, either the entire amount or a large fraction of the out-of-pocket costs of education are paid by the central government.[19] The higher the education level, the more likely this is to be the case. The out-of-pocket costs of schooling may therefore be very small or, to the extent that students receive cash allowances, even negative. In sum, the private costs of education in labor surplus economies may amount to very little.

Private Benefits
The private benefits from education in labor surplus economies may be very large. Percentage wage differentials between different skill levels in labor surplus economies, particularly those in Africa, are much greater than in full employment economies.[20] Furthermore, those with the most education, and those trained in specific excess-demand skills, experience much more stable employment than persons with less education. Expected lifetime income for university graduates may be several times as high as for secondary school leavers, who in turn may expect to earn several times as much as primary school leavers. These high private benefits, compared with the low private costs, lead to a very high rate of return for most educational investments.[21]

The Demand for Education
Education is demanded by families who would like their children educated at a particular level. The demand for a given level of education may be presumed to depend on the *average private*[22] rate of return to that level of education, which is greater

(a) the higher the salaries and non-pecuniary benefits realized by persons with that level of education,
(b) the lower the unemployment of persons with that level,
(c) the lower the school fees at that level,
(d) the lower the salaries and non-pecuniary benefits realized by persons with only the previous level of education,
(e) the greater the unemployment of persons with only the previous level,

(f) the greater the probability of admission to the next level of schooling,
(g) the lower the school fees at the next level,
(h) the higher the salaries and non-pecuniary benefits realized by persons with the next level of education,
(i) the lower the unemployment of persons with the next level.

This demand for education is not expressed in textbook fashion whereby citizens demand different quantities in a marketplace at different prices. Rather, demand for education is manifested through the political process as citizens bring pressure to bear on government officials to increase the number of school spaces, not only at the given level but at prerequisite levels as well.

The demand for a given level of education also depends on capital market conditions. The policy of paying the full costs of higher levels of education for virtually everyone who can find spaces in the schools exchanges one imperfection for another, resulting in a very high private demand for education. The original imperfection was that capital markets did not operate sufficiently well to allow students from low-income families to borrow long-term funds to pay the short-term costs of their schooling in cases where the marginal private benefits exceeded the marginal private costs. This capital market imperfection seriously retarded private demand amongst the local population. Particukrly in the newly independent countries of Africa, this situation was judged socially undesirable in view of the goal of equality of educational opportunity for citizens. The full-subsidy scheme introduced a new imperfection. Not only does it exclude the very real capital costs from the price of investing in human capital but it also excludes all out-of-pocket costs as well, which leads to a very high private rate of return. Without any constraints imposed by the necessity of financing educational investment by recourse to a capital market, the very high private rate of return is readily translated into a very high private demand for education which is much greater than it would have been under the original scheme. Enrolments are limited not by a private rate of return which bears any relation to the true social costs and benefits, or by unavailability of capital, but rather by the capacities of the educational institutions. The likely consequences—dissatisfaction and political pressure to expand the educational system beyond a socially optimal size—may be more serious than the original state of affairs.

The Effect of Increasing the Supply of Educational Spaces on the Demand for Education[23]

If the government bows to political pressure and decides to educate another person, what will happen to the demand for education? The result depends critically on the labor market behavior of the educated and employers. Let us consider three alternative cases.[24]

Case I: Labor market stratification.
Suppose a person seeks to avoid a low-level job which he regards as 'menial' or 'dirty'. He therefore desires to be educated in order to qualify for a high-level job for which there is already a surplus of qualified workers, even though he (and they) expect to be unemployed at least part of the time. From the point of view of an employer, education may make a person less desirable for a job. For instance, the morale of a secondary school graduate employed as a sweeper may be so low that an illiterate would be more productive. In such a situation, (1) highly-educated workers enter the market for skilled jobs only, (2) employers do not wish to hire highly educated workers for low-level jobs, (3) workers with little education are unqualified for high-level jobs, and (4) employers prefer to hire persons with low education for low-level jobs. The net effect of this situation is to entirely separate the high-skill and low-skill labor markets, except that the acquisition of an education (or at least the certificate) is the means by which a person moves from one to the other.

Rigid wages were presumed initially to be the cause of unemployment. If workers at each level are employed until the marginal product of the last worker hired equals the wage rate, employment is determined, which then determines output. If another person is educated, he enters the skilled labor force, thereby reducing the expected probability of finding a job and reducing expected life-time income for skilled workers. Simultaneously, the expected probability of finding an unskilled job is increased, since there is one fewer job-seeker, which raises the expected lifetime income of unskilled workers. The difference (or ratio) between expected lifetime income for skilled and unskilled workers is reduced. Since demand for education depends positively on the expected lifetime income differential, which is now smaller, an increase in the supply of education would cause there to be less demand for education.

Case 2: 'Pure bumping'.
In contrast to the labor market stratification case, let us suppose that young people demand education on the margin specifically in order to stand a better chance of being hired for low-level jobs and that employers prefer to hire persons with more education at the prevailing wage rate, either because they are (or are believed to be) more productive or simply because employers prefer to associate with the better educated. For whatever reason it occurs, preferential hiring by educational level will lead to the general upgrading of hiring standards, and of the labor force

in general, so long as the educational system produces more graduates than are needed to fill skilled positions and some of them are willing to seek employment at a lower level.

As in the labor market stratification case, since wages are rigid, if productivity effects are neglected, employment and output are determined. Ordinarily there will be fewer educated persons seeking unskilled jobs than the number of unskilled jobs available. If the government now decides to educate another person, due to preferential hiring, the educated person moves to the front of the queue for unskilled jobs and is hired first at the unskilled wage rate, 'bumping' a less-educated person from a job. This lowers the probability of getting an unskilled job and also lowers the present value of expected lifetime income for the unskilled. Since there are still the same number of educated workers looking for the same number of high-level jobs in the skilled labor market, the expected lifetime income for persons in the skilled labor market is unchanged. The difference (or ratio) between expected lifetime income for educated and uneducated workers is increased, resulting in a greater demand for education and even more political pressure.

Case 3: 'Modified bumping'[25]
As an alternative to the 'pure bumping' case, it is noted that school leavers probably do not automatically disqualify themselves from the market for high-level jobs. Rather, they first look for high-level jobs, the unsuccessful get discouraged, and then 'bump' the less educated out of lower-level jobs.[26] In this case, an increase in the supply of education does not lead to an unambiguous prediction concerning the effect on demand.[27]

As before, employment and output are determined. If another person is educated, there are now more seekers for high-level jobs. This lowers the probability of finding high-level employment, thereby lowering the present value of expected lifetime income for the educated. However, since the unsuccessful will, after a time, accept lower-level employment, the probability of a less educated person finding a job is reduced, which lowers the present value of expected lifetime income for the uneducated. Since both expected income streams fall, one cannot determine a priori whether the private rate of return to education, and hence demand, goes up or down. The direction of change depends on such factors as the number and skill distribution of job openings, the number of educated jobseekers relative to the total number of new jobs, the wage structure, and schooling costs. In any event. we would expect this 'modified bumping' process to lead to the same kind of gradual upgrading of hiring standards as in the 'pure bumping' case.

The two bumping cases suggest the possibility that the private demand for education at all levels can constantly increase at the same time as employment prospects for those with a given educational attainment continually worsen. This process could continue indefinitely as people seek to be relatively the best educated.

In my judgment,[28] this chain of events is the major historical explanation of the growth of primary and secondary, and even to some extent, university education, in developed economies. It would explain such seemingly unnecessarily high educational requirements as a secondary school diploma to work on the automobile assembly line in Detroit, a university degree to work as a bank teller, and a post-graduate degree to teach primary school in New York City. Furthermore, if central governments only partially satisfy the demand, the disequilibrium will be resolved as citizens get together and construct their own community schools. This process, I believe, explains Kenya's post-independence growth of Harambee (self-help) community secondary schools, the simultaneous worsening of job prospects for secondary school leavers, and the persistence of high demand for education.

15.5 Social Returns to Education in Labor Surplus Economies

In labor surplus economies, the marginal social rate of return to education for labor surplus occupations might be very small or even negative. This is because the marginal social costs (in real terms) ate positive and very possibly large and the marginal social benefits are positive and often quite small. Let us consider the social costs and benefits in some detail.

Social Costs
In labor surplus economies, the social costs of education may be very much higher than the private costs. Typically, labor surplus economies have a large and perhaps redundant supply of unskilled and uneducated labor, with severe shortages of both physical and human capital. The educational system is a large user of both human and non-human capital. A glance at the capital budgets, wage bills of teachers, and number of teacher training spaces relative to educa tion for other occupations, confirms this view.[29] Thus, the resources devoted to education in labor surplus economies are extremely valuable in the light of the important alternative uses to which they could be put.

There is an important counter-argument to the view that the educational system is a large user of capital with valuable alternative uses.

With respect to human capital, in some countries many teachers are themselves only generally educated secondary school graduates of whom there is a surplus.[30] If these persons were to enter the non-education labor market, they might find that they would fare no better than other secondary school leavers. Perhaps the low salary level of teachers as compared with those of other white-collar professionals is primarily a reflection of low opportunity productivity. With respect to physical capital, the resources used to construct schools might simply not be supplied otherwise. To the extent that labor is specially volunteered and physical materials are gathered or made, the real resource cost of educational expansion may be quite small.

Another substantial component of the social costs of education is the financial aid granted to students. In many less developed countries, students in secondary and post-secondary education pay none or only a small fraction of the costs of their education, receive housing and other payments in kind, and in addition may receive a small cash living allowance. If the government's budget is relatively flexible, this is merely a transfer from taxpayers to students to enable them to pay the costs of their schooling. But if the government's budget is more or less fixed, the value of the financial aid is represented in real terms by the social welfare which would be realized if the money were used on the next best projects.

In contrast to full employment economies, the output foregone by having potentially productive workers in school in labor surplus economies is minimal. By the definition of a labor surplus economy, there are large numbers of unskilled workers. To the extent that uneducated persons are temporarily withdrawn from the labor force while in school, there are plenty of others to fill the jobs they would have held. There would be a loss of output only to the extent that the persons selected for further education are niore productive on the job than those who replace them.

Social Benefits

Suppose that in a labor surplus economy, society educates another person and the educated person uses his newly-acquired skills to fill a high-level job which would otherwise have been vacant. This is equivalent analytically to the labor shortage case described in Section 15.3, and society gains all the benefits enumerated therein.

Suppose instead that an additional person is educated at a level which only qualifies him for jobs for which other persons are already queueing. To give a concrete example, suppose there are two kinds of jobs, clerks and gardeners. Secondary education is required to be a clerk. No education is required for gardeners. Let us assume for the moment that the provision of education is costless in both real and budgetary terms to the country in question.[31] (We will relax this assumption shortly.) What are the benefits to society of having one more educated person?

Labor Market Stratification

If the graduate enters the labor force for clerks (the labor market stratification case of Section 15.4) and the wage rate for clerks is fixed at level W_C^*; above the market-clearing wage, employment of clerks is unchanged at equilibrium level E*, since demand curve D (the marginal product of labor curve) does not shift. (See Figure 15.1.) Whether this particular worker is hired, or some other secondary leaver is hired, society gains no additional output. The marginal social rate of return to investment in education in output terms is therefore negative in this case.

Figure 15.1. Labor market for clerks in case of labor market stratification.

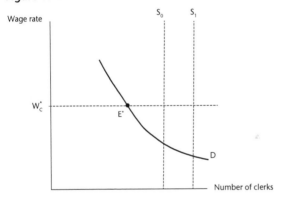

Figure 15.2. Labor market for clerks in case of bumping.

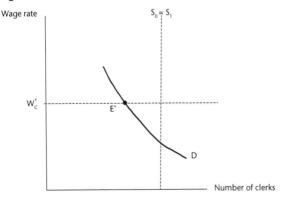

Bumping

Suppose instead that the marginal graduate enters the labor force for a less skilled occupation, in this case gardening; or equivalently, his presence in the labor force for clerks induces some other person in that labor force to seek a job as a gardener instead. Then the situation is as in Figures 15.2 through 15.4. Unemployment among clerks is the same as it was previously, since supply and demand in that labor market are unchanged (Figure 15.2). Figures 15.3 and 15.4 illustrate the labor market for gardeners. The original supplies of educated and uneducated gardeners are represented by S_0 in Figures 15.3 and 15.4 respectively. The D_0's are the demand curves, E_0^*'s the initial equilibria, and W_g^* the common rigid wage rates. Since by assumption educated gardeners are hired first and demand exceeds supply, all educated gardeners are employed. The presence of an addional supply of educated gardeners (shift of supply curve to S1 in Figure 15.3) will increase employment of educated gardeners by the same amount. The greater availability and employment of educated gardeners will lead to the displacement of uneducated gardeners, either immediately by firing, or over time by replacement of retirees. If the level of employment of educated gardeners has no effect on the productivity of uneducated gardeners, the demand curve for uneducated gardeners will shift from D_0 to D_1, the leftward shift of the demand curve for uneducated gardeners equalling the rightward shift in the supply of educated gardeners. Hence, total employment of gardeners would be unchanged. To the extent that educated gardeners are more productive than uneducated ones, output is increased.

Figure 15.3. Labor market for educated gardeners in case of bumping.

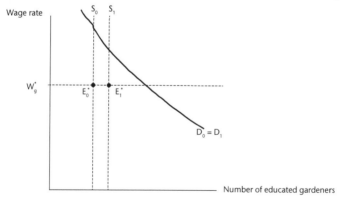

If the presence of additional, highly productive educated gardeners raises the productivity of the uneducated gardeners, the shift of the demand curve for uneducated gardeners will be to some intermediate position such as D_1' in Figure 15.4. In this case there will be an increase in total employment of gardeners with subsequently greater output. The greater the productivity of educated workers relative to uneducated and the stronger the positive effects of employment of educated workers on the productivity of uneducated workers, the greater the output effects of educating more persons.

Figure 15.4. Labor market for uneducated gardeners in case of bumping.

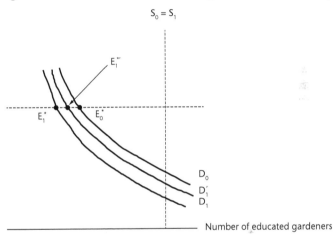

The productivity gains realized from a better-educated work force may be very small in many areas of the modern sector. Literacy may do little to raise the productivity of domestics. gardeners, and the like. General secondary education may do little for such persons as bus drivers, repairmen, and craftsmen. Society gains little additional output by educating the labor force at such levels. However, this is not always the case. In the crucial agricultural sector, there is some evidence to suggest that secondary, or even primary, education raises the output of farmers by improving organizational ability, facilitating optimal choices of crops and inputs, and making the farmer more receptive to innovations, information, and expert assistance.[32] To the extent that this is the case, the output effects may be considerable.

Another possible source of productivity gains relates to the educational system as a rrieans of discovering outstanding young people to become future national leaders. This argument has long been recognized by economists. As Marshall wrote:

We may then conclude that the wisdom of expending public and private funds is not to be measured by its direct fruits alone. It will be profitable as a mere investment to give the masses of the people much greater opportunities and to get the start needed for bringing out their latent abilities. And the economic value of one industrial genius is sufficient to cover the expenses of a whole town.[33]

I believe this argument has some merit. However, the number of budding young industrial geniuses is probably not very large. It is doubtful that poor countries can afford the large outlays required for the probably small and definitely uncertain benefits.

When costs of supplying education are introduced, it is questionable whether the positive output effects resulting from productivity gains exceed the negative output effects of using scarce physical and human capital to produce education. Although more teachers will be employed, employment in the output-producing sector would fall. This is because each unit of labor has less capital to work with and would be illustrated by leftward shifts of the demand for labor curves in Figures 15.2 through 15.4. Aggregate employment might well fall. There is presumably some social benefit from the fact that a larger fraction of the labor force is educated. However, there would be an adverse effect on income distribution (and thus a presumed negative social benefit) if the educated person comes from a well-to-do family and educational expansion is financed by a regressive tax structure. So all in all, there might be little if any social benefit from educating another person. The marginal social rate of return to investment in education might be negative in many labor surplus economies.

15.6 An Example of the Measurement of Rates of Return to Education in Labor Surplus Economies

The difficulty of computing a marginal social rate of return in labor surplus economies results from stringent data requirements. An aggregate production function and demand for labor functions *by educational category* are required in order to estimate additional and foregone output. These need to be expressed in the context of expected growth of the economy, which necessitates estimates of technical change and demographic trends. Few labor surplus economies have the required data. However, a static approximation, which only requires point estimates of marginal rates of substitution between one type of labor and another and between labor and capital, might prove feasible.

Traditionally, observed earnings differentials have been used to measure the output effects on society of additional education. However, a crucial and generally neglected point is: *in labor surplus economies, wage differentials are an inadequate measure of social productivity gains, even if employed workers are paid the value of their marginal products by their employers.* As a result, the average social rate of return as conventionally calculated may be a completely misleading guide to social decision-making on educational investments.

For illustrative purposes, let us consider the following hypothetical data under the assumptions of the 'modified bumping' case of Section 15.4. Suppose the state of the economy is:

Wage of clerks (shs / day)	20
Employment of clerks	50
Supply of clerks	100
Wage of gardeners (shs/day)	10
Total employment of gardeners	40
Supply of educated gardeners	25
Employment of uneducated gardeners	15
Supply of uneducated gardeners	75

Let us now use these data to illustrate some important points.

Allocation of Educated Workers to Different Labor Markets
It may be hypothesized that educated workers allocate themselves among labor markets so that the mathematical expectations of the wages in the respective labor markets (wage times number of jobs divided by labor force) are equal. In our example, an educated person would expect to earn 10 shs/day either as a clerk or as an educated gardener ($20 \times \frac{50}{100} = 10 \times \frac{25}{25}$). In the absence of systematic non-pecuniary preferences for one occupation or the other, or for certainty in preference to uncertainty (or vice versa), equality of expected wages is an equilibrium condition. For instance, suppose ten more persons are educated. If any of these persons enters the labor market for clerks, the expected wage for clerks ($20 \times \frac{50}{100+n}$ where n=the number who enter the labor market for clerks) would be less than for educated gardeners. The labor market for educated persons would be in disequilibrium, which would be resolved only if ten educated persons enter the labor market for gardeners.[34]

The Appropriate Wage Ratio for the Private Rate of Return
The expected wage for uneducated persons is the uneducated wage times the probability of an uneducated person being employed: $10 \times \frac{15}{75} = 2$. The educated-uneducated expected wage ratio is therefore $\frac{10}{2} = 5$. This expected wage ratio, along with private costs, determines the private rate of return and the private demand for education. When there is unemployment, the relevant wage ratio is not the wage ratio for employed clerks compared

to employed gardeners (20/10). Neither is the correct ratio the wage of the average employed educated person ($20 \times \frac{50}{75} + 10 \times \frac{25}{75} = 16\frac{2}{3}$) compared to the average employed uneducated person (10).[35]

The average private rate of return is that internal rate of return which equates the stream of discounted expected educated-uneducated wage differentials to the private costs of schooling. To calculate the average private rate of return in our hypothetical economy, let us assume:

(i) the current expected income differential (8 shs/day=2,000 shs/ year) is expected to prevail for ever,
(ii) education takes one period, and
(iii) the private costs of being educated (out-of-pocket cost plus foregone earnings) is shs 1,000.

Then the average private rate of return is given implicitly by $2000(\frac{1}{1+r} + \frac{1}{(1+r)^2} + ... + \frac{1}{(1+r)^T}) = 1000$, where T is the relevant time horizon, presumably retirement. For sufficiently large T, the left hand side is approximately $\frac{2000}{r}$.

Substituting and solving for r, we find an average private rate of return of 200 percent. From the individual's point of view, it would be an understatement to say that education would be a very lucrative personal investment.

Measurement of Social Productivity
If we take the stream of expected educated-uneducated wage differentials projected over time compared to the current average cost of educating one more person, the average internal rate of return which equates the two streams is what is commonly called 'the social rate of return'. Under assumptions (i), (ii), and

(iv) the social cost of educating one person is shs 10,000, the average social rate of return is given implicitly by $2,000(\frac{1}{1+r} + \frac{1}{(1+r)^2} + ... + \frac{1}{(1+r)^T})$ = 10,000 and is found to be 20 percent. By the conventional calculations, educational investment would appear desirable.

The internal rate of return which equates the marginal social benefits to the marginal social costs is 'the marginal social rate of return'. This rate may be large, small, zero, or negative, depending on the size of the productivity gains resulting from education. Nothing in the data we have so far tells us which is the case. We simply cannot infer whether investment in education is a good investment or not.

If educated gardeners are only slightly more productive than uneducated ones, the marginal social rate of return is small or even negative and the investment would be undesirable. Suppose in our example,

(v) an educated gardener is 2 percent more productive than an uneducated one.

The marginal social rate of return is given implicitly by $50(\frac{1}{1+r} + \frac{1}{(1+r)^2} + \ldots + \frac{1}{(1+r)^7}) = 10,000$, the solution of which gives a marginal social rate of return of one-half of one percent.[36] Although the average private and social rates of return (200 percent and 20 percent respectively) are very high, we would all agree that educational investment would be undesirable.

Care must be exercised in using average private and social rates of return. The private rate of return is an important index of the strength of the private demand and political pressure for educational expansion. The average social rate of return gives us an upper limit on the marginal rate. An average social rate of return which is below the rates which could be earned on other social projects is a clear indication that the educational investment is *not* desirable on economic grounds, but a higher rate is of little help. As a guide to decision-making for educational planners, the average private and social rates of return neither ask the right questions nor measure the right phenomena.

To the best of my knowledge, only one empirical cost-benefit study calculates a *marginal* social rate of return. Using shadow wage rates obtained by solving the dual of a linear programming model for Greece, Psacharopoulos[37] estimated marginal social rates of return to investment in education. For our purposes, the most interesting conclusion is: 'In the case of Greece, investment priorities with respect to investment in skills estimated on the basis of observed labor earnings would have suggested a change *in the wrong direction* of the educational output.' (Emphasis added.)

15.7 Conclusion

Let us conclude by summarizing some of the main points raised in the paper. The intention of this paper was to consider a specific criterion for decision on educational investments, the benefit-cost criterion, which evaluates *marginal social* costs and benefits. Some educational planners and advisors unfortunately fail to distinguish marginal from average returns or private returns from social ones.

The composition and magnitude of the private and social returns to education depend largely on the nature of the labor markets for educated persons. More specifically, if a person is educated for an excess demand occupation, the marginal social rate of return is approximated by the average social rate of return as conventionally measured. In contrast, education in labor surplus economies may confer a very high private rate of return on the educated person while at the same time the average social rate is high and the marginal social rate is small or negative. This would be the case unless bumping is accompanied by large productivity gains attributable to increased education. Furthermore, if bumping is prevalent, the private rate of return to education may actually rise if more education is supplied. Disequilibrium in the political marketplace for education might never be resolved unless edl)cation is offered to almost everyone.

Observed earnings differentials are a very poor approximation to the output gains to society from additional education in labor surplus economies. For such countries, the average social rate of return may convey a grossly distorted impression about the desirability of an educational investment. While few labor surplus economies at present have the data needed to accurately compute a marginal social rate of return, the data might be sufficient to permit point estimates of the relevant parameters in order to construct a first approximation.

16

A Welfare Economic Analysis of Labor Market Policies in the Harris-Todaro Model

16.1 Introduction

Since its introduction in 1970, the Harris-Todaro (HT) model has become the workhorse for analyzing labor market policies in dualistic labor markets. In the intervening years, many aspects of the model have been studied including unemployment, development policies, tax and transfer policies, and many others; see Todaro and Smith (2003) for a review. However, one aspect of the model has not yet received thorough attention, and that is the welfare economics of labor market policies in an HT economy. The purpose of this study is to help fill that gap.

The chapter proceeds as follows. In Section 16.2, I present the original Harris-Todaro model and review prior analyses of the effects of various labor market policies in that model. Three labor market policies were considered by Harris and Todaro themselves. The first was a policy of modern sector job creation, which I call modern sector enlargement (MSENL). MSENL could come about by a tripartite agreement, as in Harris and Todaro; by a government-sponsored employment creation scheme, as many countries have done; or by technical change and/or capital accumulation in the modern sector, which can (but need not) shift the demand curve for modern sector labor outward. The second policy considered by Harris and Todaro was rural development; focusing on the labor market effects of such a policy, I label it traditional sector enrichment (TSENR).

The original version of this chapter was published as: Fields, Gary S. (2005). A welfare economic analysis of labor market policies in the Harris-Todaro model, in: Journal of Development Economics, 76(1):127–146. © 2005 by Elsevier B.V.

A third policy considered by Harris and Todaro was a policy of wage limitation in the urban economy; I call this modern sector wage restraint (MSWR).[1] The review of past literature in Section 16.2 demonstrates that prior work has provided valuable lessons but is not yet complete in analyzing the benefits of the various policies.

The rest of the chapter develops new results. Section 16.3 completes the inequality analysis. Section 16.4 then performs a welfare economic analysis of labor market conditions based on an "abbreviated social welfare function" ("abbreviated," because they are functions of variables which themselves are summary statistics of different aspects of the labor market).[2] The labor market indicators used in the abbreviated social welfare function here are total labor earnings, unemployment, inequality of labor incomes, and poverty rates. Section 16.5 turns to dominance analysis in the labor market (Hadarand Russell, 1969; Saposnik, 1981; Foster and Sen, 1997). Section 16.6 compares the welfare economic results for labor market changes using the different approaches. The main conclusions are highlighted in Section 16.7.

Before proceeding, let me add a word about what the results of this chapter imply and do not imply about policy. If a government is choosing between MSENL, TSENR, and MSWR policies, it needs to consider not only the consequences of putting the policy into effect, which is what is analyzed here, but also the costs of putting the policy into effect. MSENL and TSENR both require expenditures of resources to create more modern sector jobs or to achieve rural development, respectively (unless, that is, an outside donor provides the money as an outright grant to the country). On the other hand, MSWR is costless (economically if not politically); actually, it saves the government money if the government is itself a modern sector employer. The social costs of these policies need to be taken account of along with the social benefits before a policy recommendation can be offered.

16.2 Analysis of Labor Market Policies in the Simplified HT Model

16.2.1 *The Model*

The Harris-Todaro model was formulated to represent a labor market in a dualistic economy. The two sectors of the economy are a modern sector, denoted here by M, and an agricultural sector (A). The two sectors are geographically distinct, with the modern sector being located in the urban area and the agricultural sector in the rural area. For institutional reasons such as trade unions, sector-specific minimum wages, and the like, the real wage in the modern sector WM in the HT model is set rigidly above the real wage in agriculture W_A.[3]

In the model, L workers (all assumed identical and fixed in number) allocate themselves between job search strategies in order to maximize expected earnings. In the original Harris-Todaro model, the two search strategies are an urban search strategy and a rural search strategy. Once workers have chosen their strategies, employers hire workers randomly from among the available pool. Those workers employed receive wages W_M and W_A in the modern and in the agricultural sector, respectively, and the unemployed receive nothing. At this point, the game ends.

The urban search strategy produces a modern sector job paying WM with probability p. With complementary probability $1-p$, an urban job searcher is unemployed; in the absence of unemployment insurance, unemployment results in an income of zero. The expected wage for a prospective worker who adopts an urban search strategy is therefore:

$$(1) \qquad E(W_U) = W_M\,p.$$

Employment in the modern sector EM depends negatively on the modern sector wage through an ordinary downward-sloping labor demand curve:

$$(2) \qquad E_M = e(W_M),\ e' < 0.$$

In the original HT model, the available jobs were assumed to be filled in a random way with each of the LM members of the urban labor force having the same chance of being hired for a given job as any other:

$$(3) \qquad p = E_M/L_M.$$

L_M is determined endogenously from the HT equilibrium condition, defined below.

Rather than pursuing an urban job, a prospective worker might adopt a rural job search strategy. Harris and Todaro assumed that doing this precluded the possibility of obtaining an urban job. On the other hand, the agricultural labor market was assumed to clear so that a job at wage W_A is available to anyone who wants one. A rural job-seeker would therefore earn W_A with probability one:

$$(4) \qquad E(W_R) = W_A.$$

The Harris-Todaro model is both a disequilibrium model and an equilibrium one. The model explained why workers would continue to migrate into urban areas despite the existence of urban unemployment: this would happen as long as $E\ (W_U)$ was still above $E\ (W_R)$. The model also explained why unemployment would exist in equilibrium. In a

Harris-Todaro equilibrium, the expected wage from an urban search strategy $E\ (W_U)$ and that from a rural search strategy $E(W_R)$ would equal one another:

(5) $$E(W_U) = E(W_R)$$

This arises, because $W_M > W_A$ implies $p < 1$: that is unemployment exists in equilibrium. Combining eqs. (1)–(5), we have that in an (interior) HT equilibrium,

(6) $$W_M \frac{E_M}{L_M} = W_A$$

In the original HT formulation, the wage in the agricultural sector, W_A, depended inversely on the agricultural sector labor force L_A. However, many authors (Fields, 1975; Anand and Vijay, 1979; Heady, 1981; Stiglitz, 1982; Sah and Stiglitz, 1985; Bell, 1991) have found it convenient to work with a simplified Harris-Todaro model in which the agricultural wage remains constant over the relevant range. In the simplified model, the causal structure is then: W_M and L are exogenous. W_A is invariant. W_M determines E_M. W_M, W_A, and E_M together determine L_M. L and L_M determine L_A. That simplified model is used here as well. The limitation is deliberate: as I shall show below, many ambiguous results are found. If ambiguities arise in the original model, they also arise in the general model that nests the original model as a special case.

The HT model has been generalized to allow for an urban informal sector, on-the-job search from agriculture, duality within the rural sector, educational differences among workers, job fixity, mobile capital, endogenous urban wage setting, risk-aversion, a system of demand for goods, and many other factors (Fields, 1975; Corden and Findlay, 1975; Calvo, 1978; Moene, 1988, 1992; Khan, 1989; Chakravarty and Dutta, 1990; Bourguignon, 1990; Basu, 1997). My reason for working with the original model is to show that many policy ambiguities are found even there.

16.2.2 *Effects of Labor Market Policies on Labor Market Conditions in Prior Work Using the HT Model*

In the original HT model and in other papers that followed, labor market policies were evaluated in terms of their effect on unemployment. The focus on unemployment was justified by the atemporal nature of the model. In an HT equilibrium, the amount of unemployment (all urban) is given by:

(7) $$\text{UNEM} = L_M - E_M = \frac{W_M}{W_A} E_M - E_M \left(\frac{W_M}{W_A} - 1 \right) E_M$$

From Eq. (7), the two famed policy conclusions of the HT analysis can be seen immediately: that as long as W_M and W_A remain constant, any attempt to eliminate urban unemployment through urban job creation (raising E_M) would raise unemployment, not lower it; and that the solution to urban unemployment is rural development (raise W_A).

The original HT paper considered a third policy: that of urban wage restraint. The authors stated that for plausible parameter values, lower urban wages would be expected to raise employment in both the modern and the traditional sectors of the economy. Subsequently, Fields (1997) determined that a policy of urban wage restraint would lower unemployment if the demand for labor in the modern sector is sufficiently inelastic (specifically, if $\eta > -(\frac{1}{2})y$, where $y = (\frac{W_M}{W_A} - 1)$ and η is the arc wage elasticity of demand for labor in the modern sector evaluated between W_A and W_M and raise unemployment if the demand for labor is sufficiently elastic $(\eta > -(\frac{1}{2})y)$.

Work by Gupta (1988), Rauch (1993), and Temple (1999, 2003) shifted the HT policy analysis from unemployment to labor market inequality. Gupta showed that MSENL could increase or decrease the Gini coefficient. Working with a multiple period version of the HT model, Rauch deduced that as formal sector employment expands with economic growth, the inequality of lifetime income measured by the log-variance follows an inverted-U path. Temple presented three sufficient conditions for inequality to rise and three similar sufficient conditions for inequality to fall. Unfortunately, these were in terms of endogenous variables (the unemployment ratio, the number of unemployed, and the number employed in each of the two sectors), so the comparative static analysis is not yet complete.

16.2.3 *Contributions of this Chapter*

As compared with earlier policy analyses in the basic HT model, this chapter makes the following contributions. First, I complete the analysis of inequality changes for Harris and Todaro's three main policy options: MSENL, TSENR, and MSWR.[4] Inequality is gauged here is in terms of Lorenz curves, which Bourguignon and Temple also used, as well as by intersectoral wage differentials.[5] Second, I present a full labor market analysis using an abbreviated social welfare function in which the goodness of labor market conditions depends positively on total labor earnings and negatively on unemployment, inequality, and poverty, all in the current period. In previous work, only unemployment and inequality were analyzed, and never together in the same social welfare function.[6] Third, I conduct an alternative labor market analysis using more recent methods of welfare dominance, which have not been applied before in the HT literature.

Before proceeding, I would note that the analysis that follows is concerned with evaluating only the labor market conditions that result from various labor market policies in the HT model. This chapter does not attempt to consider broader welfare judgments in terms of the economy's utility possibility frontier, as analyzed by Harris and Todaro (1970) and followers.[7]

16.3 Inequality Analysis

16.3.1 Inequality Analysis in Terms of Lorenz Curve Comparisons

A robust way of judging which of two income distributions is more or less equal than the other is to compare their Lorenz curves; see Figures 16.1–16.4. Income recipients are ordered from lowest income to highest, and the cumulative shares of income received by each cumulative share of population are plotted. In the case of a perfectly equal distribution of income, the Lorenz curve lies along the 458 line, while in the case of a perfectly unequal distribution of income, it lies along the bottom and right axes. When comparing the inequalities of two distributions, if the Lorenz curve of distribution A lies strictly closer to the 458 line at some point than the curve for distribution B and never further away, then we can conclude that A is more equally distributed than B, and all Lorenz-consistent inequality measures would judge A to be more equal than B.[8]

Constructing Lorenz curves in the Harris-Todaro model is aided by the following observations (Bourguignon, 1990; Temple, 1999). In the model, there are just three incomes – W_M for those employed in the modern sector, W_A for those employed in agriculture, and 0 for the unemployed. Any Lorenz curve will therefore consist of three piecewise linear segments and will bend twice, at "kink points" labeled K_1 and K_2. Because the lowest income is zero, the first segment OK_1 is entirely flat. The middle segment K_1K_2 has slope W_A, which also is the average income in the population, and therefore K_1K_2 also has a slope of $45°$.[9] The third segment of the Lorenz curve K_2P is constructed simply by connecting the end of the second segment with the upper corner.

We are now ready to construct Lorenz curves for each labor market policy in the HT model and see how inequality changes. In each case, the original Lorenz curve is depicted by dashed lines and the new Lorenz curve by solid lines.

The first policy, MSENL, is drawn in Figure 16.1. This policy increases both the amount of employment at wage W_M and the amount of unemployment at wage zero. The increase in E_M moves K_2 leftward while the increase in UNEM moves K_1 rightward. (Superscripts 0 and MSENL respectively denote the original point and the new one under MSENL.) Because W_A remains the same and average income equals W_A, the total income in the economy remains the same ($W_A L$). Therefore, the third segment $K_2 P$ has the same slope $W_M/W_A L$ after MSENL has taken place as it did before. The resultant Lorenz curve following MSENL is therefore $OK_1^{MSENL} K_2^{MSENL} P$ which lies partly below the original Lorenz curve $OK_1^0 K_2^0 P$ and never above it. Hence, we have a Lorenz-worsening. We may thus conclude that *a policy of modem sector enlargement increases income inequality*.

Figure 16.1. Lorenz-worsening for MSENL.

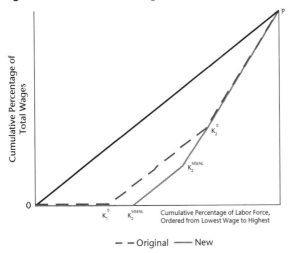

Figure 16.2. Lorenz-improvement for TSENR.

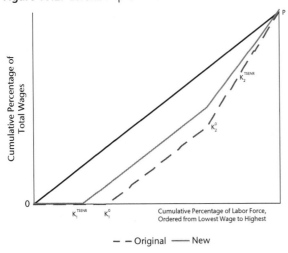

The second policy is TSENR, analyzed in Figure 16.2. Because W_A rises, L_U falls, so the first kink point moves leftward. W_M and E_M are unchanged. The constancy of E_M implies that K_2^{TSENR} and K_2^0 have the same horizontal coordinate. As for the vertical coordinate, the increase in W_A of TSENR means that the slope of the third segment, $W_M/W_A L$, has decreased, and therefore K_2 TSENR must lie above K_2^0. The slope of the middle segment $K_1 K_2$ remains equal to one. We therefore have a new Lorenz curve $OK_1^{TSENR} K_2^{TSENR} P$ that lies partly above the original Lorenz curve and never below it. Thus, *traditional sector enrichment reduces income inequality.*

Figure 16.3. Lorenz-improvement for MSWR, Case i.

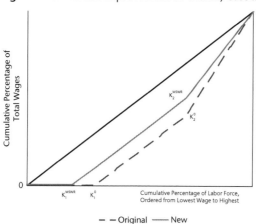

Figure 16.4. Lorenz-crossing for MSWR, Case ii.

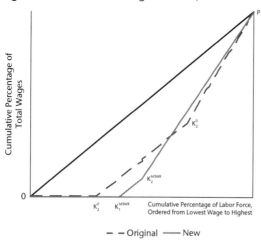

The third policy is MSWR, which lowers W_M, inducing a rise in E_M. Whether this combination of forces (lower W_M, higher E_M induces an increase or a decrease in the number of workers adopting an urban search strategy (L_U) depends on the wage elasticity of demand for labor in the modern sector. As analyzed in Fields (1997), there are two cases.

Case i is when W_M falls and E_M rises a little, causing $W_M E_M$ to fall. If $W_M E_M$ falls, L_U falls. This happens if $\eta > -(\frac{1}{2})y$. The decrease in L_U causes the first kink point K_1 of the Lorenz curve to move to the left. The original E_M^0 people now have lower wages, therefore a smaller wage share than before (this, because with W_A unchanged, total wages are unchanged also). Thus, the new Lorenz curve lies above the original one at K_2^0. The new Lorenz curve $OK_1^{MSWR}K_2^{MSWR}P$ therefore lies above the original Lorenz curve $OK_1^0K_2^0P$. Thus, *when the demand for labor in the modern sector is sufficiently inelastic, modern sector wage restraint reduces income inequality.*

Case ii is when the fall in W_M induces a sufficiently large rise in E_M so that $W_M E_M$ rises and so too does L_U. This happens if $\eta > -(\frac{1}{2})y$. A higher L_U moves K_1 to the right, so the new Lorenz curve is below the original one at K_1^0. For the same reason as in the preceding paragraph, the new Lorenz curve is above the original one at K_2^0. By continuity, the two must cross in between. When Lorenz curves cross, some Lorenzconsistent indices (for example, in this case, the income share of the poorest) show an increase in income inequality while others (e.g., the income share of the richest) show a decrease. Thus, *when the demand for labor in the modern sector is sufficiently elastic, modern sector wage restraint produces an ambiguous effect on income inequality.*

16.3.2 *Inequality Analysis in Terms of Changes in W_M/W_A*

There is another way of judging wage inequality, which is simply to look at the ratio of wages among workers in the different sectors. Gauging inequality in this way, we find:

- For MSENL, inequality is unchanged.
- For TSENR, inequality falls.
- For MSWR, inequality falls, regardless of the elasticity of demand for labor in the modern sector.

16.3.3 *Summary of the Inequality Analysis*

The results on inequality are summed up in Table 16.1. In two cases, the inequality judgments based on wage ratios conflict with the inequality judgments based on Lorenz comparisons.

Table 16.1. Inequality changes resulting from various labor market policies in the Harris-Todaro model

Labor market policy	Inequality change using Lorenz comparisons	Inequality change using wage ratios
MSENL	+	unchanged
TSENR	-	-
MSWR, sufficiently inelastic demand for labor	-	+
MSWR, sufficiently elastic demand for labor	ambiguous	+

MSENL = modern sector enlargement; TSENR = traditional sector enrichment; MSWR = modern sector wage restraint.

Let us now use these inequality changes in a welfare analysis of changes in the labor market.

16.4 Welfare Economic Analysis of Labor Market Conditions Using an Abbreviated Social Welfare Function

16.4.1 *The Abbreviated Social Welfare Function Approach*

To perform comparative static analysis comparing labor market outcomes under different policies, I work with a class of social welfare functions in which an increase in labor earnings is regarded as good and an increase in unemployment, inequality, or poverty is regarded as bad.[10] These social welfare judgments are represented by a class of abbreviated social welfare functions of the form

$$SW = f(\text{Total labor earnings; unemployment; inequality; poverty}),$$
$$f_1 > 0, f_2 < 0, f_3 < 0, f_4 < 0.$$

Previous policy analyses in the Harris-Todaro framework have considered unemployment and inequality (partially). It remains to complete the analysis of inequality using the results of Section 16.3 and to bring in total labor earnings and poverty.[11]

16.4.2 *Results for Total Labor Earnings*

In the simplified HT model with a fixed W_A, total labor earnings equals W_A times the number of workers. Thus, for a fixed number of workers, as long as W_A is constant, which is the case in MSENL and MSWR, total earnings are unchanged. But in the case of TSENR, W_A rises, and average earnings rise accordingly.

16.4.3 *Results for Poverty*

A reasonable place to set a poverty line in an HT economy is in the range $W_A < z < W_M$. Setting the poverty line in this range allows some but not all of the working people to be classified as "working poor." The precise location of z is deliberately left imprecise, as is the precise measure of poverty given z.

One criterion for assessing poverty is the poverty headcount ratio, viz., the fraction of people with incomes below z. For all z in the range $W_A < z < W_M$, the poverty headcount ratio is $\frac{L-E_M}{L}$. By this criterion, MSENL and MSWR raise E_M and therefore lower the poverty headcount ratio, while TSENR keeps E_M constant and therefore leaves the poverty headcount ratio *unchanged*.

Below, I shall show that when combined with the results for unemployment, inequality, and total labor earnings, we now have enough information to know whether each of these policies (MSENL, TSENR, or MSWR) is welfare-improving, welfare-reducing, or welfare-ambiguous.[12] It would therefore be superfluous to get into poverty dominance methods in this context.[13]

16.4.4 *Abbreviated Social Welfare Function Results When Inequality Is Gauged Using Lorenz Curves*

The results for each of the components of the abbreviated social welfare function are brought together in the four middle columns of Table 16.2. The welfare evaluation using the abbreviated social welfare function

$$SW = f \text{ (Total labor earnings; unemployment; inequality; poverty)},$$
$$f_1 > 0, f_2 < 0, f_3 < 0, f_4 < 0.$$

is given in the final column. We see:

- MSENL: Although unemployment and inequality rise, which decreases welfare, the poverty headcount ratio also falls, rendering the social welfare consequences *ambiguous*.
- TSENR: The one desirable element (total labor earnings) rises and the three undesirable elements (unemployment, inequality and poverty) all fall. TSENR is therefore *welfare-improving*.

Table 16.2. Changes in labor market welfare resulting from various labor market policies in the Harris-Todaro model when inequality change is measured using Lorenz comparisons

Labor market policy	Change in total labor earnings	Change in unemployment	Change in inequality using Lorenz comparisons	Change in poverty using poverty headcount ratio	Change in labor market welfare using social welfare function (Eq. (8))
MSENL	0	+	+	-	ambiguous
TSENR	+	-	-	0	+
MSWR, sufficiently inelastic demand for labor	0	-	-	-	+
MSWR, sufficiently elastic demand for labor	0	+	ambiguous	-	ambiguous

MSENL = modern sector enlargement; TSENR = traditional sector enrichment; MSWR = modern sector wage restraint.

Table 16.3. Changes in labor market welfare resulting from various labor market policies in the Harris–Todaro model when inequality change is measured using wage ratios

Labor market policy	Change in total labor earnings	Change in unemployment	Change in inequality W_M/W_A	Change in poverty using poverty headcount ratio	Change in labor market welfare using social welfare function (Eq. (8))
MSENL	0	+	0	-	ambiguous
TSENR	+	-	-	0	+
MSWR, sufficiently inelastic demand for labor	0	-	-	-	+
MSWR, sufficiently elastic demand for labor	0	+	-	-	ambiguous

MSENL = modern sector enlargement; TSENR = traditional sector enrichment; MSWR = modern sector wage restraint.

- MSWR: MSWR will leave total labor earnings unchanged and will reduce poverty regardmess of the elasticity of demand for labor in the modern sector. However, the effects of MSWR on unemployment and inequality depend on the labor demand elasticitry. If labor demand is sufficiently elastic, unemployment will increase and the inequality effect is ambiguous. Taking these results together, in the case of a sufficiently inelastic demand for labor, MSWR is *welfare-increasing*. On the other hand, in the case of a sufficiently elastic demand for labor, the effect of MSWR on welfare is ambiguous.

16.4.5 *Some Final Comments on Policy Evaluation Using Abbreviated Social Welfare Functions*

Three final remarks are in order.

First, up to now in the welfare analysis, inequality has been measured using Lorenz curves. An alternative way of bringing inequality into the analysis is to use the wage ratio among the employed, W_M/W_A. It is immediately apparent that MSENL leaves this ratio unchanged, while TSENR and MSWR both lower it. Measuring inequality in this way and otherwise using the abbreviated social welfare function (Eq. (8)), we have the welfare results shown in Table 16.3. These results are not very interesting because the overall evaluation (final column) is the same here as it was when inequality was gauged using Lorenz curve comparisons (Table 16.2).

Second, it is worth pointing out that in no way can we say from the preceding analysis that any labor market policy is or is not *Pareto*-improving. This is for two reasons. The first, and obvious one, is that the Pareto criterion requires that we look at welfare changes for each identified person in the economy and the HT model has no way of identifying which people are which. But even if we were to look at income changes of anonymous people, we should be careful not to infer from the + entries in Tables 16.2 and 16.3 that all classes of people would be at least as well off as before. Most notably, modern sector wage restraint reduces the economic well-being of all workers employed in the modern sector. Third, to repeat a point made earlier, the analysis here has considered only the benefits but not the costs of the respective policies. A fuller analysis would have to factor in the costs as well.

16.5 Welfare Economic Analysis of Labor Market Conditions Using First-Order Dominance

In certain situations, the welfare of one income distribution may be ranked relative to another for a broad range of social welfare functions. We have a theorem due to Saposnik (1981), building on earlier work of Hadar and Russell (1969) and others, which says that one distribution X first-order-dominates another distribution Y for the class of anonymous, increasing social welfare functions if and only if the income of the person in each rank in X is at least as great as the income of the person with the corresponding rank in Y and strictly greater someplace.[14] In other words, (weakly) fewer persons are below any income amount in X than in Y with a strict inequality someplace. Dominance methods may be used to make welfare comparisons between an initial HT equilibrium and the new equilibrium that would result following a policy change. What is involved is to figure how many people receive each income amount, look for differences between the two sets of numbers, and then see whether these differences are all in the same direction (i.e., all higher or all lower). Figures 16.5–16.8 present the results for each labor market policy in the HT model.

Figure 16.5 displays the results for the policy of MSENL. The dashed step function OADL denotes the income distribution corresponding to the original HT equilibrium. OA is the number of people unemployed in the original equilibrium and earning zero, AD is the number employed in agriculture and earning W_A, and DL is the number employed in the modern sector and earning W_M. After MSENL has taken place, more workers are employed in the modern sector, more are unemployed, and fewer are employed in agriculture, producing the new step function marked by solid lines, OBCL. Comparing the two distributions, they coincide in ranges OA, BC, and DL and differ in ranges AB and CD. The post-MSENL distribution is worse than the original distribution in range AB (this is the number of workers who had been earning W_A before but now are earning zero) and better than the original distribution in range CD (this is the number of workers who had been earning W_A before and are now earning $W_M > W_A$). In this way, we may conclude that the post-MSENL distribution neither welfare-dominates the original distribution nor is welfare-dominated by it. In other words, the class of anonymous and increasing social welfare functions is ambiguous for MSENL. In similar fashion, we may gauge the welfare effects of the other policies. Figure 16.6 shows the results for TSENR. This policy raises the wage of those working in agriculture and increases their number. Consequently, the number of unemployed is reduced. The size

357

Figure 16.5. No welfare dominance for MSENL.

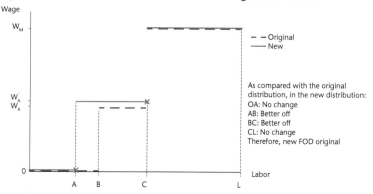

Figure 16.6. The new situation dominates the original for TSENR.

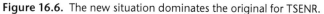

Figure 16.7. No welfare dominance for MSWR, case of a sufficiently inelastic demand for labor.

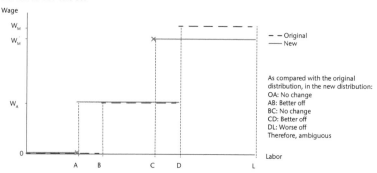

Figure 16.8. No welfare dominance for MSWR, case of a sufficiently elastic demand for labor.

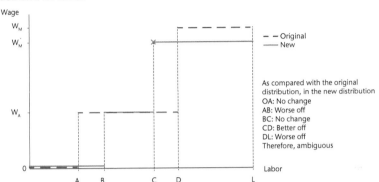

of the modern sector and the earnings level of those employed in the modern sector are unchanged. As a result, the new distribution first-order-dominates the original one. We may thus conclude that TSENR is welfare-improving using the class of anonymous and increasing social welfare functions.

Figures 16.7 and 16.8 analyze MSWR for the two elasticity ranges. As long as the elasticity of demand for labor in the modern sector is non-zero, more people are employed in the modern sector but at a lower wage than before. Those who gain modern sector jobs are better off than they had been before, but those who were employed in the modern sector and who remain so are worse off than before. This is enough to show that MSWR has an ambiguous effect on welfare for the class of anonymous and increasing social welfare functions.

Table 16.4 sums up the welfare analysis using dominance methods. Before concluding this section, it bears mention that similar lines of reasoning may be used to conduct a poverty-dominance analysis. "Poverty-dominance" means that one distribution has unambiguously less poverty than another for a broad class of poverty lines and poverty measures. See Appendix on p. 363 for details.

16.6 Comparing the Approaches and Understanding the Welfare Judgments They Make

The welfare economic results from Sections 16.4 and 16.5 for the abbreviated social welfare function approach and the first-order-dominance approach are summed up in columns 2 and 3, respectively, of Table 16.5. It is interesting to understand why the welfare evaluations are similar in some cases and different in others.

Table 16.4. Changes in welfare in the labor market resulting from various labor market policies in the Harris–Todaro model using first-order-dominance methods

Labor market policy	Unemployed (wage=0)	Agricultural workers (wage=W_A)	Modern sector workers (wage=W_M)	Change in labor market welfare using first-order-dominance
MSENL (Fig. 16.5)	More of them	Fewer of them, unchanged wage	More of them	No dominance, therefore ambiguous
TSENR (Fig. 16.6)	Fewer of them	More of them, higher wages	Same number of them and same wage for each	Dominance, therefore welfare
MSWR, sufficiently inelastic demand for labor (Fig. 16.7)	Fewer of them	More of them, unchanged wage	More of them, but each is now poorer	No dominance, therefore ambiguous
MSWR, sufficiently elastic demand for labor (Fig. 16.8)	More of them	Fewer of them, unchanged wage	More of them, but each is now poorer	No dominance, therefore ambiguous

MSENL = modern sector enlargement; TSENR = traditional sector enrichment; MSWR = modern sector wage restraint.

Table 16.5. Comparing the changes in labor market welfare resulting from various labor market policies in the Harris–Todaro model

Labor market policy	Change in labor market welfare using social welfare function (Eq. (8))	Change in labor market welfare using first-order dominance
MSENL	ambiguous	ambiguous
TSENR	+	+
MSWR, sufficiently inelastic demand for labor	+	ambiguous
MSWR, sufficiently elastic demand for labor	ambiguous	ambiguous

MSENL = modern sector enlargement; TSENR = traditional sector enrichment; MSWR = modern sector wage restraint.

First of all, for TSENR, we see that the two approaches agree that TSENR improves labor market conditions. Why? Because fewer people are unemployed and all in agriculture are earning higher wages than before. (In the modern sector, the same number is employed and they all earn the same amount as before.)

Second, the two approaches disagree about whether MSWR is a good thing when modern sector labor demand is sufficiently inelastic. In this case, under MSWR, total labor earnings are unchanged, unemployment falls, inequality falls, and poverty falls – these are the arguments that enter into the abbreviated social welfare function approach, which is why it renders an unambiguous ranking. But the welfare dominance approach gives negative weight to the fall in W_M, which is why this approach evaluates MSWR ambiguously. Should policy evaluators be worried about the reduction in these rents? This is an ethical question on which reasonable people can and do disagree.

Third, both methods give ambiguous evaluations about MSWR when modern sector labor demand is sufficiently elastic. However, the reasons for the ambiguity are not the same in the two cases. In the abbreviated social welfare function approach, the higher unemployment that the policy generates is valued negatively but the reduction in the number of people below the poverty line is valued positively. However, using the dominance approach, the ambiguity at the top end of the income distribution: more people than before are earning W_M, but W_M, is lower than it was previously.

Finally, both approaches give ambiguous answers for MSENL. For the abbreviated social welfare function approach, the reason is that MSENL raises unemployment, which counts negatively, but it lowers the poverty headcount ratio, which counts positively. For the welfare dominance approach, although more people now get zero wages, which is bad, more people now get W_M, which is good.

16.7 Concluding Remarks

This chapter has analyzed the welfare economics of labor market policies in the Harris-Todaro model. Three policies considered by Harris and Todaro have been evaluated: MSENL, TSENR, and MSWR.

The novelty of this chapter has been to widen the terms of the analysis. Harris and Todaro themselves, and many others who followed them (myself included), analyzed policies in terms of their unemployment effects. More recent analysis been conducted in terms of inequality effects, and this chapter has added to that strand of work. In addition, I have gone beyond these variables to also include poverty and total labor earnings within the abbreviated social welfare function framework. I have also evaluated the various labor market policies using welfare dominance methods applied to the labor market.

When the labor market analysis is broadened beyond unemployment alone, Harris and Todaro's justifiably famous policy recommendations—avoid modern sector employment creation and instead seek rural development—are partially but not fully supported. Rural development would indeed produce better labor market outcomes on all of the dimensions considered (if, as in HT, the costs of rural development can be ignored). Modern sector employment creation is not unambiguously a bad thing, though. The increase in unemployment and inequality of labor earnings (putative "bads") should be balanced against the increased number of high-wage jobs and the consequent reduction in the poverty headcount ratio (putative "goods"). Modern sector wage restraint was also favored by Harris and Todaro. However, the results here show that such a policy does not unambiguously improve labor market outcomes. This is because the lowering of wages itself receives negative welfare weight and because inequality can rise if the demand for labor is sufficiently elastic.

I have shown in this chapter that even when the underlying labor market model is quite straightforward (which is my reason for working with the simplified version of the original HT model), the welfare evaluation of various policy alternatives depends critically on *which* welfare economic approach is adopted. Qualitatively different policy judgments are obtained depending on whether the welfare judgment is a function of unemployment alone, inequality alone, an abbreviated social welfare function, or first-order welfare dominance. These different welfare economic approaches have produced qualitatively different results. Thus, in the HT model, it is not enough just to be concerned about distribution. *How* distributional concerns are brought into the policy analysis can and does make an important difference.

APPENDIX

Poverty Dominance Analysis

Let y_i denote the income of the ith individual, z denote a poverty line, and $p(y_i, z)$ be a function indicating how much is contributed to economy-wide poverty by an individual whose income is y_i when the poverty line is z. Most of the poverty measures in common use, including the headcount ratio and the P_α measure, are members of the general additive class

(A.1) $$p = \Sigma_{i=1}^n p(y_i, z)/n \qquad \text{such that}$$

(i) $$p = (y_i, z) = 0 \text{ if } y_i \geq z, \qquad \text{and}$$

(ii) $$p(y_i, z) > 0 \text{ if } y_i \leq z.$$

The fact that many poverty measures belong to this general class (but not all do – in particular, the poverty index created by Sen (1976) does not) leads us to consider whether there are dominance criteria for the class of measures given by Eq. (A.1). That is, are there circumstances under which all poverty measures belonging to class (A.1) would rank one income distribution as having more poverty than another for a range of poverty lines $\underline{z} < z < \bar{z}$?

The answer is affirmative, provided that first-order poverty dominance can be shown to hold. First-order poverty dominance is defined as follows: If the cumulative distribution function for distribution $X(F_X)$ is everywhere at least as high as that for distribution $Y(F_Y)$ for all z between $\underline{z}$ and $\bar{z}$, X first-order-poverty-dominates Y. Atkinson (1987) and Foster and Shorrocks (1988) proved that X first-order-poverty-dominates Y if and only if $pov_X > pov_Y$ for *all* poverty measures belonging to class (A.1), or for any monotonic transformation thereof, and for *all* poverty lines between $\underline{z}$ and $\bar{z}$.

In the text, poverty lines were considered in the range $W_A < z < W_M$. We see in the relevant ranges of Figures 16.1–16.4 (up to but not including the people earning W_M in each case) that the new distribution poverty-dominates the original one for TSENR and for MSWR – case i, but neither distribution poverty-dominates the other for MSENL or for MSWR – case ii. The reasons for these differences are as follows:

- For TSENR, the number of poor is the same, but more of the poor are earning the agricultural sector wage, which is higher than before.

- For MSWR – case i, fewer people are poor and fewer people are unemployed earning zero. The remaining poor are earning the same agricultural wage as before, so their economic position is unchanged.
- For MSENL, there are fewer poor but more of the poor are unemployed, earning nothing.
- For MSWR – case ii, fewer people are poor, but some people who had been earning the agricultural wage are now unemployed and earning nothing.

To reiterate, these poverty dominance results hold for *all* poverty functions of class (A.1).

One subclass of particular interest is the set of P_α measures, defined as $P_\alpha = \frac{1}{n}\Sigma poor\ \frac{z-\pi}{z}$. For the P_α class, the preceding theorem tells us that if X first-order-poverty-dominates Y, the $pov_X > pov_Y$ for all P_α, $\alpha > 0$ and for all poverty lines between W_A and W_M.

Part VII
Concluding Thoughts

The final paper in this volume (Chapter 17) presents "Directions for Future Research". The chapter is divided into three parts.

First, building on the analysis in Chapter 8, which examined what was known as of 2012 about "Challenges and Policy Lessons for the Growth-Employment-Poverty Nexus in Developing Countries", gaps in knowledge are being filled. Where the field now stands and what new work is being conducted is briefly summarized in the section on "Further Empirical Evidence about the Growth-Employment-Poverty Nexus in Developing Countries".

Second, it was shown in Chapter 14 that the qualitative conclusions from analyzing income distribution changes by comparing cross-sections can be quite different from those using panel data analysis for the same countries. Why the anonymous cross-section and the panel data approaches may produce different answers and under what circumstances has until recently been an open question. In two new working papers, co-authors and I analyze the relationship between rising and falling income inequality on the one hand and convergent or divergent income mobility on the other. This work is summarized in the section "Learning More about Anonymous versus Panel Income Approaches to Analyzing Income Distribution Changes".

Finally, a challenge for future work is to develop more realistic multi-sector labor market models of developing economies and subject them to richer welfare economic analysis. Three working papers which I am co-authoring are abstracted in the section "Toward More Realistic Labor Market Models and Welfare Economic Analysis". One is a model including two self-employment sectors rather than one. The second is a China-specific model in which that country's unique household registration system is a central feature. And the third is a model of India featuring agricultural peak and slack seasons and migration from farm to city and back again in accordance with seasonal peaks and troughs.

Good labor market policy requires good labor market models. Although much has been learned, much important work remains to be done.

17

Directions for Future Research

17.1 Further Empirical Evidence about the Growth-Employment-Poverty Nexus in Developing Countries

First, building on the analysis in Chapter 8, which examined "Challenges and Policy Lessons for the Growth-Employment-Poverty Nexus in Developing Countries", the existing literature is far from complete. With generous financial support of the World Institute for Development Economics Research (UNU-WIDER), Guillermo Cruces, David Jaume, Mariana Viollaz, and I are in the midst of conducting a systematic study of how labor market conditions have changed in the course of economic growth in sixteen Latin American countries in the 2000s. This study is entitled "The Growth-Employment-Poverty Nexus in Latin America".

In brief, the analysis shows that the 2000s were a time of strong improvement in the growth-employment-poverty nexus in Latin America, quite unlike the experience of the OECD countries at the same time. More specifically, in the great majority of Latin American countries in the 2000s, economic growth took place and brought about improvements in almost all labor market indicators and consequent reductions in poverty rates. But not all improvements were equal in size or caused by the same things. To understand why some countries progressed more in some dimensions than did others, we performed a number of additional analyses. Across countries, economic growth was not all that mattered; external factors were particularly important for changes in labor market conditions, while reductions in poverty were strongly related to improvements in earnings and employment indicators.

Of course, like the rest of the world, Latin America suffered from the global economic crisis of 2008. But the downturns in Latin America were milder and more short-lived. Although the 2008 crisis affected different countries differently, nearly all labor market indicators were at least as high or higher by 2012 than immediately before the crisis in all countries but one (Honduras). This contrasts sharply with the effects of previous crises in the region, in which most or all gains in labor markets during the periods of economic growth were wiped out by the subsequent crises. It is too soon to tell if this was a unique experience or if it represents a new resilience for the region.

In conclusion, the growth-employment-poverty nexus in Latin America changed much more favorably than was the case in the OECD countries in general and the United States in particular. It would be interesting to know about developing economies in other regions of the world. Such studies define one of the current research frontiers.

17.2 Learning More about Anonymous versus Panel Income Approaches to Analyzing Income Distribution Changes

Second, Chapter 14 showed that the qualitative conclusions from analyzing income distribution changes by comparing cross-sections can be quite different from those using panel data analysis for the same countries. Why the anonymous cross-section and the panel data approaches may produce different answers and under what circumstances has until recently been an open question. In two new working papers, Robert Duval Hernández, George Jakubson, and I analyze the relationship between rising and falling income inequality on the one hand and convergent or divergent income mobility on the other.

As shown in Part V of this volume, most of the research assessing whether income distributions were getting better in welfare economic terms was based on comparisons of cross-sectional data (Chapters 9 through 12). Additionally, income distribution changes can be analyzed using panel data following the same individuals or households over time (Chapters 13 and 14). The analysis in Chapter 14 of Argentina, Mexico, and Venezuela and other studies have demonstrated that the cross-section and panel data approaches can give qualitatively different empirical results.

Why and under what circumstances the two approaches agree or disagree qualitatively is being analyzed in ongoing work by Robert Duval Hernández, George Jakubson, and myself. One paper ("*Changing Income Inequality and Panel Income Changes*") explores the following combinations: i) rising inequality and divergent mobility, ii) rising inequality and convergent mobility, iii) falling inequality and divergent mobility, and iv) falling inequality and convergent mobility. This paper presents a series of theorems concerning various possibilities and impossibilities. This is done for several income change regressions and various ways of measuring inequality. Some of the results derived in this paper illustrate why a given combination is possible, or they specify under which measures of convergence/inequality a given combination is mathematically impossible.

A second companion paper ("Analyzing Income Distribution Changes: Anonymous versus Panel Income Approaches") illustrates how these theoretical reconciliations look in practice by using panel data on earnings for Mexico. Furthermore, in this second paper, we propose a method to gauge which observable factors account for the equalization in incomes brought by panel income changes. While regression decomposition techniques have been applied to account for changes in the inequality of two "anonymous" distributions, we are the first to show how to apply these techniques to account for the equalization of earnings in panel data. The empirical results of this decomposition exercise show that the equalization that earnings changes bring over a year in Mexico is mainly driven by changes in the employment status and sector of workers.

17.3 Toward More Realistic Labor Market Models and Welfare Economic Analysis

Good labor market policy requires good labor market models. A third challenge for future work is to develop more realistic multisector labor market models of developing economies and subject them to richer welfare economic analysis than is normally the case.

Co-authors and I are in the midst of developing three new theoretical models. One is a model including two self-employment sectors (or as it is sometimes called, "informal sector") rather than one. The second is a China-specific model in which that country's unique household registration system is a central feature. And the third is a model of India featuring agricultural peak and slack seasons and migration from farm to city and back again in accordance with seasonal peaks and troughs in labor demand.

The guiding analytical framework as presented in Chapter 1 highlighted:

Figure 17.1. A Visualization of the Five-Part Policy Evaluation Framework.

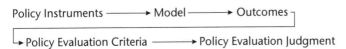

Some past models have been discussed at length. Note that these are multi-market models: how one labor market works, how another labor market works (and perhaps additional others), and how the two (or more) markets are linked. The Lewis and Harris-Todaro models are examples of such multimarket models. However, these models are old and some features pertinent to today's key developing economies have not yet been formalized.

The best labor market models involve the interplay of theory and data. The empirical reality of developing country labor markets is that they have multiple segments and multiple strata. "Multiple segments" means that for workers of any given type, some jobs are better than others. "Multiple strata" means that workers differ in their type along some sort of hierarchy – for example, according to level of human capital or occupation.

A comprehensive labor market model would be one that recognizes multiple segments and multiple strata, formulates how each labor market segment and stratum works, and specifies how the various segments and strata link to one another via the migration of workers and the movement of firms. Specifically:

(i) How do supply and demand for labor and wage determination processes operate in each of the major sectors of the rural economy (which is where the majority of most developing countries' labor markets live and work)?

(ii) How do supply and demand for labor and wage determination processes operate in each of the major sectors of the urban economy (which is where the majority of many nations' economic activity is concentrated)?

(iii) What are most important rural-urban linkages, specifically through migration of both permanent and seasonal types?

Some features of a comprehensive labor market model are generic in nature. Human capital plays an important role in the sense that workers with more skills, often acquired through education and training, have the ability to perform certain jobs which those in the lower strata of the skills distribution lack. As well, a general feature of labor markets around the world is that they are segmented in the sense that 1) some jobs are better than others and 2) there are not enough of the good jobs for all who want them and are capable of performing them.

Looking forward, more multimarket labor market modeling is needed. Abstracts of three models under development follow.

A. Three Heterogeneities in a Labor Market Model for Developing Economies
Arnab K. Basu, Nancy H. Chau, Gary S. Fields, and Ravi Kanbur

The classic Harris-Todaro framework has become the workhorse model of labor markets in developing countries, structuring the analysis and much of the discourse on labor market policy. However, there are at least three features of developing country labor markets that need to be added to this framework: duality in self-employment between what we term "free-entry self-employment" and "high-wage self-employment"; a continuum of abilities among workers; and the presence of both younger and older workers in the labor force. In this paper we show how these "three heterogeneities" can be incorporated into a tractable multisector labor market model for developing countries. Most importantly, we show that these heterogeneities matter. They matter because they allow us to pose analytical and policy questions which cannot be addressed by standard models. And they matter because the propositions of standard models are overturned when they are introduced.

B. A Multisector Labor Market Model for India
Kalyani Raghunathan and Gary S. Fields

The development of an all-India labor market model entails a number of country-specific factors. The modeling effort begins with a rural labor market model, proceeds to an urban labor market model, and then links the two via migration in peak and slack season.

- The central features of the theoretical model of rural labor markets in India include:
- Two agricultural seasons, a peak season and a slack season.
- Wage laborers in agriculture.
- A large number of landlords and workers.
- Uniform daily wages across workers within a particular season, regardless of their skill level.
- Profit-maximization on the part of landlords.
- Income-maximization on the part of workers.
- Full employment of rural labor in the peak season.
- Unemployment of rural labor in the slack season.

Beyond refining the rural labor market model, the next step in the modeling effort will be to develop an urban labor market model for India. The main features of the urban labor market model being developed are:

- A job hierarchy with three occupations, called free-entry, office work, and managers.
- Educational differentials among workers.
- Different employment opportunities for workers with different levels of education.
- Income-maximization on the part of less-educated workers.
- Utility-maximization on the part of better-educated workers, whereby educated workers receive large disutility if they were to work in the free-entry sector, which consequently they do not do.
- Above-market-clearing wages for managers and office workers.
- Choices for workers between risky and safe job search strategies.
- Wages in the free-entry sector which vary (inversely) with the number of people in that sector.

The third step will be to model rural-urban linkages in India, the main features of which will be:

- Seasonality: a peak agricultural season and a slack agricultural season.
- Workers may migrate from rural to urban areas or from urban to rural areas.
- Given what other workers are choosing, workers of each type (rural or urban) and each educational level (better-educated and less-educated) will choose their search strategies in order to maximize their expected incomes.

The net result will be an all-India model combining a rural India model, an urban India model, and a model with rural-urban linkages. This model will generate, both for the baseline case and for a number of possible policy interventions:

- The number of people employed in each location (rural and urban), each season (slack and peak), and each occupation (agriculture, urban free-entry, office worker, manager).
- The number of people unemployed.
- A complete income distribution, including the number of people employed at each possible wage.
- Evaluation of the policy effects including an abbreviated social welfare function and first-order dominance.

C. A Theoretical Model of the Chinese Labor Market
Gary S. Fields and Yang Song

This paper constructs a theoretical labor market model for China, and utilizes the model to examine the effects of various labor market policies on economic well-being. Two key features of the model are a segmented labor market involving three sectors – state-owned enterprises, private enterprises, and agriculture – and China's unique household registration system (hukou). The paper first describes the model's features, then specifies the equations of the model, then obtains a closed form solution given initial conditions, and then deduces welfare consequences of several policy interventions, which include promoting rural development, reducing the cost-of-living in urban areas for rural hukou holders, and offering some rural workers the chance to convert from rural to urban hukou status. Using two alternative welfare criteria including first-order stochastic dominance and an abbreviated social welfare function, it is shown that the rural development policy is unambiguously welfare-improving, while the other two policies have ambiguous effects on social welfare.

Notes

Introduction by the Author

1. "Developing countries" is itself a euphemism, replacing what used to be called "underdeveloped countries" or "less developed countries." Sadly, many developing countries are not developing, but still that is the terminology now used. Developing countries are now categorized into a number of groups: low-income, lower-middle-income, upper-middle-income, and high-income countries. As of 2015, the countries in each group are defined according to the following criteria. Low-income countries are those with a gross national income (GNI) per capita, calculated using the World Bank Atlas method, of $1,045 or less in 2014 (for example, Afghanistan and Mozambique); Lower-middle-income countries are those with a GNI per capita of more than $1,045 but less than $4,125 (Bolivia and India); Upper-middle-income countries are those with a GNI per capita of more than $4,125 but less than $12,736 (Brazil and China); High-income countries are those with a GNI per capita of $12,736 or more (Chile and Singapore). Source: http://data.worldbank.org/about/country-and-lending-groups.
2. Unemployment rates are actually lower in the developing countries than they are in the developed countries (ILO, 2014, Figure 1.2).

Chapter 1

1. Surowiecki (2008).
2. Deaton (1997).
3. Heckman (2001).
4. Ravalion (2008).
5. Banerjee and Duflo (2011).
6. Karlan and Appel (2011).

Chapter 2

1. Margin of Life is the title of an excellent photojournalistic account by Capa and Stycos (1974).
2. The Brazil data are from the World Bank's World Development Report 1994. The United States data are from the U.S. Bureau of the Census.
3. For profiles of who these poor are, see World Bank 1997a, forthcoming, and United Nations 1997, 1998.

4. "Enlargement of choices" features prominently in the work of the United Nations' Human Development Reports (various). "Capabilities and functionings" are central to the work of Nobel Prize winner Amartya Sen (e.g., Sen 1984, 1985, 1992, 1997, 1999).

5. The first three of these were first published in Fields 1980.

6. Gini coefficients measure inequality. They range from zero in the case of perfect equality (everybody having the same income) to one in the case of perfect inequality (one person having everything and everyone else having nothing).

7. For simplicity, this example assumes that there is no unemployment.

8. How the Gini coefficient is calculated is explained in Chapter 2 of Fields 2001.

9. Assume that the person who initially had an income of $2 kept that income in both economies. The income changes in country G are then given by the following table:

Number of People	Initial income share	Final income share	Difference
8	1/11 = 0.091	1/12 = 0.083	-0.008
1	1/11 = 0.091	2/12 = 0.167	0.076
1	2/11 = 0.182	2/12 = 0.167	-0.015

We see that each of the ex post poor had a final year income share of 1/12 = .083, an initial year income share of 1/11 = .091, and thus a decline in income share of .008. In that same country, both of the ex post nonpoor had a final year income share of 2/12; one had a base year income share of 2/11 and the other a base year income share of 1/11. These two individuals' changes in share are +.076 and -.015, producing an average income share change of +.031. The difference between the average share change of the non-poor and of the poor is then +.031- (-.008) = +.039. Similar calculations for country H produce a disparity of +.033- (-.014) = +.047. It is on this basis that one might conclude that there was a more disparate income mobility experience between the poor and the nonpoor in Country H than in Country G.

Chapter 3

1. Excellent older books make many of the points presented in this chapter, but with data that are now obsolete. My favorites are Turnham (1971, 1993) and Squire (1981). A wealth of current information is published by the ILO, which is the source for much of the following data. The ILO publishes an online data source called Key Indicators of the Labor Market, which presents information on twenty indicators including participation in the world of work, employment indicators, unemployment indicators, educational attainment, wages and labor costs, the characteristics of job-seekers, education, wages and compensation costs, labor productivity, and working poverty. This information is presented for the world as a whole, by region of the world, country-by-country, and year-by-year since 1980. The database, a guide to its use, and an executive summary of findings are available at http://kilm.ilo.org/KILMnetBeta/default2.asp, accessed 7/18/10. Another

ILO source presenting an excellent overview of labor market conditions in the world is its annual publication Global Employment Trends.

2. The Universal Declaration of Human Rights is at http://www.un.org/en/documents/udhr/index.shtml, accessed 10/23/09.

3. ILO (2009b, p. 9).

4. The source for these particular quotations is the World Bank's Voices of the Poor volumes; see Narayan et al. (2000, pp. 26 and 34). Other informative sources are World Bank (1995), Inter-American Development Bank (2003), Asian Development Bank (2005), and Chen and Vanek (2005).

5. Unemployment rates for the world and for different regions are taken from ILO, Global Employment Trends , January 2011.

6. Calculated by the author from data in "Economic and Financial Indicators," the Economist, August 14, 2010, p. 77.

7. Bourguignon (2005) and http://www.bls.gov/fls/flsfaqs.htm#developing countries, accessed 1/27/09.

8. See, for example, Ghose et al. (2008, p. 59).

9. Fox and Gaal (2008, p. 3) and Turnham (1971, p. 74).

10. The source is the manager of the ILO Statistical Development and Analysis Group. See Peek (2006) for details.

11. Hamlin (2008).

12. U.S. Bureau of Labor Statistics (2007).

13. See Key Indicators of the Labor Market, Table 17, available at http://kilm.ilo.org/KILMnetBeta/default2.asp, accessed 1/18/10.

14. ILO, Global Employment Trends , January 2011, p. x.

15. ILO (2007c).

16. See http://www.ilo.org/global/Themes/Employment_Promotion/Informal Economy/lang--en/index.htm, retrieved 2/17/

17. Jütting and de Laiglesia (2009).

18. For a good introduction, see Chen, Hussmanns, and Vanek (2007).

19. Collins, Morduch, Rutherford, and Ruthven (2009).

20. Harriss-White (2003, p. 28).

21. These points come from World Bank (2007) and Chen et al. (2005, p. 8). Also see ILO (2009a), www.wiego.org, and Kristof and WuDunn (2009).

22. ILO (2009a) and Foster and Rosenzweig (2008).

23. Asian Development Bank (2005) and Fox and Gaal (2008).

24. The terminology in the text follows international usage as prescribed by the ILO. "Paid employment" includes those persons working for wages or salaries, with or without a formal contract. "Self-employment" includes two groups: "employers," who have at least one paid employee, and "own-account workers," who employ no one.

25. Kucera and Roncolato (2008).

26. Fox and Gaal (2008, pp. 3 and 11).

27. See ILO (2009a) for regional rates and Ghose et al. (2008) for country-specific data.

28. Fox and Gaal (2008).

29. NCEUS (2009, p. 59).

30. For overall data, see, for example, World Bank (2005, p. 32) and Millennium Challenge Corporation (2008, p. 3). Data for specific countries come from Tao (2006, p. 517) and Fox and Gaal (2008, p. 15).
31. For an overview and analysis, see Ahmad et al. (1991).
32. Smith, 2005, p. 91, emphasis in the original.
33. Levy (2008).
34. ILO (2008), p. 122.
35. NCEUS (2009). Following the lead of the International Conference of Labor Statisticians and the International Labor Organization, the following defi-ni-tions are used. "The unorganized sector [also called the informal sector] consists of all unincorporated private enterprises owned by individuals or households engaged in the sale and production of goods and services operated on a propri-etary or partnership basis and with less than ten total workers." "Unorganized workers consist of those working in the unorganized enterprises or households, excluding regular workers with social security benefits, and the workers in the formal sector without any employment/social security benefits provided by the employers." The organization Women in Informal Employment: Globalizing and Organizing (WIEGO) has been influential in broadening attention to in-clude informal employment in the formal sector. See www.wiego.org.
36. The ILO itself has launched a Global Campaign for Social Security and Cov-erage for All; see ILO (2007b). For more on social protection, the website of the World Bank's social protection unit at http://web.worldbank.org/WB-SITE/EXTERNAL/TOPICS/EXTSOCIALPROTECTION/0menuPK:282642~pa gePK:149018~piPK:149093~theSitePK:282637,00.html, accessed 7/23/08, or the Asian Development Bank (2005, Section 5.2).
37. Felipe and Hasan (2006, p. 41).
38. Banerjee and Duflo (2008, pp. 18–19).
39. Sen, Mujeri, and Shahabuddin (2007).
40. Charmes (2009).
41. Luce (2007, pp. 50–52).
42. Abraham (2009).
43. Wittenberg (2002, p. 1194).
44. For a description of such jobs in Africa, see Fox and Gaal (2008, Chapter 4).
45. One news item stated that the government of Kenya was threatening to bring charges against "unscrupulous merchants" who charged higher prices for milk in remote rural areas than the price charged in the cities. That the cost was higher to get the milk to the small rural shops and the sales were slower, and the storage costs therefore higher, was simply irrelevant in the view of the newspaper vendor.
46. And I learned too why families like his sent the men to the city and left the women in the countryside. In much of Africa, men do not do heavy physical work—that is women's work. If the men were to stay on the farm while the women went off to the city, the only task that would get done is supervi-sion. So the men were sent to the city to earn whatever they could while the women tilled the land, fetched the firewood, hauled the water, and did all the other heavy lifting.

47. Banerjee and Duflo (2007, p. 162; 2011, Chapter 9). Others call them petty entrepreneurs, microentrepreneurs, or the self-employed in the informal economy.

48. Banerjee and Duflo (2008, p. 26). These authors then added, "If the middle class matters for growth, it is probably not because of its entrepreneurial spirit." A special report in the Economist ("Bourgeoning Bourgeoisie," 2009, p. 17) reached a very different conclusion: "The middle class's ... distinctive contribution to growth is its gift for entrepreneurship."

49. Examples are Appleton, Song, and Xia (2005) and Bardhan (2010) for China; Glinskaya and Lokshin (2005) and Hasan and Magsombol (2005) for India; and Stroll and Thornton (2002) for several African countries.

50. I have taken the predominant view in a variety of places, among them, Fields (2007a). A prominent dissenter to the segmented labor markets view is Rosenzweig (1988).

51. See Maloney (2004) and World Bank (2007).

52. Günther and Launov (forthcoming). In their study, all individuals who work in the public sector or who have a written contract with a company with formal bookkeeping are classified as formal employees.

53. An Indian reader told me: "I am doubtful if Indian readers would take this example seriously. There is a market for blood here and there are enough 'cheap blood sellers' who sell it at lower prices than the wages mentioned. I personally have never heard of such instances of trapping workers for blood. There are umpteen number of people happily ready to sell blood. In fact there are professional blood sellers in the country that sell blood at fixed prices." Having to sell blood for a living is an outrage too.

54. Alice's story is told in United Nations (2007). See also Gertler, Shah, and Bertozzi (2005) for Mexico.

55. For a graphic account of sex slavery and other outrages against women, see Kristof and WuDunn (2009).

56. ILO (2006) and Edmonds (2008).

57. http://www.ilo.org/ipec/facts/WorstFormsofChildLabour/lang--en/index. htm, accessed 1/25/

58. BBC News (1998).

59. The term "employment problem" appears to have been originated by Turnham (1971) in an OECD study. The ILO picked up on the term in its 1972 Kenya report (ILO, 1972) and subsequent works on other countries (Thorbecke, 1973).

60. ILO (2010).

61. The figures in this paragraph come from unpublished joint work with Paul Cichello and Murray Leibbrandt. One good source on the legacy of apartheid in the South African labor market is Nattrass and Seekings (2005).

Chapter 4

1. In our discussion we shall employ a somewhat different wage determination process from that of Harris and Todaro. The Harris-Todaro model fixes the ur-

ban wage rate in real terms. The rural wage is specified as the marginal product of labor in agriculture, which depends on the number of agricultural workers and the terms of trade between agricultural products and manufactures. Harris and Todaro specified the agricultural wage in this way in order to be able to consider the welfare implications of various government policies with regard to rural-urban migration in a general equilibrium framework. Since our present concern is with employment and underemployment and other labor market conditions, we shall subsequently treat the rural-urban terms of trade as contained in the rural and urban wages and ignore changes in relative price levels. Furthermore, we will treat the agricultural wage rate as fixed. While this is primarily for expositional purposes, it is also likely that given the small size of the modern urban sector compared to the agricultural sector, the wage e potential migrant could earn in agriculture would vary to a relatively small extent over the relevant range and can be treated as constant.

2. Evidence for eight less developed countries (East Pakistan, Egypt, Ivory Coast, Ceylon, Brazil, India, Philippines, and Venezuela) is given in Turnham (1970, p. 77).

3. Turnham (1970, p. 57)

4. In subsequent chapters we will distinguish between the total number of jobs and the jobs for which hiring is taking place and between skilled and unskilled jobs and educated and uneducated workers.

5. Except for those engaged in Illegal activities which they do not report to census enumerators.

6. From the first year the series is available until the last.

7. Turnham (1970, p. 46)

8. Under more general conditions whereby agricultural workers also have some positive chance of obtaining modern sector employment, any value of h (the murky-modern relative job search parameter), greater than n (the rural-urban relative job search parameter) would pive the same result.

9. For evidence on this point, see Blaug, Layard, and Woodhall (1969), Krueger (1971), Skorov (1968), and unpublished data from the 1971 Nairobi Household Survey. The formal analytics of the preferential hiring model have been worked out in my dissertation (Fields (1972)) and in a subsequent paper [(Fields (1974b)), which contrasts the cases of preferential and nonpreferential hiring. After the dissertation was completed, I became aware of a paper by Thurow (1972) which constructs a similar (but nonmathematical) model of 'job competition' in the United States.

10. In his earlier work, Todaro (1969) had formulated the problem as workers migrating in response to differences in present values of expected future income, with the probability of being employed at the end of any given period being the probability of having a job at the beginning of the period plus the probability of acquiring a job during the period. The probability of acquiring a job was expressed as the ratio of job hiring to unemployed job-seekers.

11. This corresponds to a rate of involuntary turnover in urban jobs equal to one in discrete time, infinity in continuous time.

12. I have seen no direct evidence on the rate at which workers employed in

the modern sectors of less developed countries lose their jobs. However, the oft-heard statements by job-seekers to the effect that 'if I secure a modern-sector job, I have it made for life' suggests that involuntay turnover rates are generally very low.

13. The probabilities of *becoming employed* and losing one's job are the so-called 'transition probabilities'. They are used to construct projected 'state probabilities' of being employed and unemployed, which in turn are used to derive the present values of expected income streams given in eqs. (36) and (37). A Markov process is one in which the transition probabilities are assumed constant over time. A brief but clear introduction to Markov processes is found in Kemeny and Snell (1962). For a more detailed treatment, see Kemeny and Snell (1960).

14. $1-\{[(28.5\%+27\%)/(32\%+27\%)]\ (0.985)+1(0.015)) = 6\%$.

15. This predicted increase in the urban unemployment rate as the number of modern-sector jobs increases contrasts with Harris and Todaro's prediction that job creation would lead to more absolute unemployment but a lower unemployment rate. This difference is due to the hypothesis in the present model that potential migrants consider the probability of being hired for an urban job. A small increase in the number of modern-sector jobs leads to a larger increase in the number of jobs for which hiring is taking place and therefore to a large increase in the number of unemployed urban job-seekers.

16. It should be noted that because f_u is unchanged in the new equilibrium, only those who are fortunate enough to be hired in the new jobs enjoy higher expected incomes. The present value of expected future income for the unemployed, those employed in the murky sector, and those in agriculture remain at their previous levels.

17. For an analysis of the ways in which the private demand for education interacts with political and economic forces to determine the allocation of resources to education and the size of the educated labor force, see Fields (1974a, 1974b).

Chapter 5

1. Heterogeneity of labor adds additional complexity that is not warranted at this point. In the case of worker heterogeneity, labor market outcomes have been shown in Fields (1974, 1975) to be very sensitive to the way in which one models the behavior of firms and different groups of workers and the interrelationships among the markets for different labor categories.

2. In cases where unemployment insurance exists, the wages $W_j, j = M, A, T$ may be thought of as the amount by which wage exceeds unemployment benefits.

3. In the minimum wage models of Mincer (1976) and Gramlich (1976), the analogue is 'remain in non-covered employment'.

4. Fields (1975) and McDonald and Solow (1985) do likewise.

5. From this restriction, it follows that the urban traditional sector wage W_T will be less than the agricultural wage W_A – which helps explain the miser-

able slums found in the cities of most developing countries.

6. A concave utility function could easily be introduced but is omitted in order to highlight the result on intersectoral wage differentials derived in Section 6.3. It would also be possible to extend the model to a multi-period context and allow for decisions to be made on the basis of expected present values. In this case, the expected wage in each period would depend on the individual's search strategy, which in turn depends on the transition probabilities between various labor market states and others – all of which are endogenous. While it is indeed possible to do such an extension (see Fields (1975) and McDonald and Solow (1985)), it is not at all clear that it would add anything in the present context. It is best to leave multi-period complexities for another time.

7. If E_M jobs are to be filled, the number filled by those adopting Search Strategy I is πL_I, the number filled by those adopting Search Strategy II is $\pi \theta L_{II}$, and the number filled by those adopting Search Strategy III is $\pi \varphi L_{III}$. Summing these and substituting $\pi = E_M/J_M$, one obtains the total amount of employment as

$$(E_M/J_M)L_I + (E_M/J_M)L_{II}\theta + (E_M/J_M)L_{III}\varphi = (E_M/J_M)(L_I + \theta L_{II} + \varphi L_{III}) = (E_M/J_M)(J_M) = E_M$$

satisfying the adding-up condition.

8. If *all three* wages were invariant with respect to the sizes of their respective labor forces, the three expected values would be equal only by chance. One search strategy would be dominated by the others and would drop out, leaving us with a two-sector model.

Chapter 6

1. In some countries economic growth has been accompanied by declining relative income inequality, and hence alleviation of absolute poverty; see the studies by Fei, Ranis, and Kuo (1978) for Taiwan, and Ayub (1976) for Pakistan. In other countries relative income inequality did not improve, but the overall income growth was large enough to raise the position of the poor as well; this may be inferred from data contained in the studies of Argentina, Mexico, and Puerto Rico by Weisskoff (1970); of Brazil by Fishlow (1972); and of Colombia by Berry and Urrutia (1976). Bardhan's (1974) country study of India is the one case I have seen where absolute poverty has been shown to increase in severity over time; undoubtedly other "fourth world countries" share a similar plight.

2. For instance, Fishlow (1972) demonstrates that given the existing pattern of income distribution in Brazil, the economy would have to grow at a rate of 5 percent per year for twenty years before the poor would attain incomes of $100 per capita.

3. These conclusions are drawn from Berg (1969). He also presents evidence that while skilled-unskilled wage differences widened, skilled-unskilled wage ratios have generally narrowed.

4. This is not to downplay the importance of capital and other sources of income and wealth in determining economic position. Rather, since most

people in less developed countries receive most or all of their income from the work they do, and since variation in labor income is the most important source of overall income inequality, a high-wage-sector-low-wage-sector dichotomy would appear more relevant than any other dualistic classification.

5. The assumption of identical wages for all workers within a given sector is simply for algebraic and diagrammatic convenience and is not necessary for any of the results above. Intrasectoral wage diversity is allowed for in a model in an Appendix that is available from the author upon request.

6. See Rothschild and Stiglitz (1973) and Fields and Fei (1978).

7. See Atkinson (1970).

8. Consider statements of the form "Income of the richest X percent grew by A percent but income of the poorest Y percent grew by only B percent (less than A); therefore, income growth was disproportionately concentrated in the upper income groups." This interpretation is correct if average income among those who were originally the richest X percent of the people rose much faster than among those who were originally the poorest Y percent. However, the interpretation is incorrect if what mainly happened was that the high-income sector expanded to include more people. From cross-sectional data on income growth of the richest X percent and poorest Y percent, we cannot tell which.

9. This statement applies only to studies based on data from comparable cross-sections such as are available for many countries. The statement does not apply to longitudinal data, which as of now are rare.

10. The formula for the Gini coefficient in our dualistic model is
$$G = 1 - \frac{[W^r + (W^m - W^r)(f^m)^2]}{[W^r + (W^m - W^r)f^m]}.$$
This is a quadratic function. By inspection, $G = 0$ when $f^m = 0$ and $f^m = 1$, and $G > 0$ if $0 < f^m < 1$. Thus, the Gini coefficient follows an inverted-U path. To determine the location of the maximum, find
$$\frac{\partial G}{\partial f^m} = \left\{ \frac{[W^m - W^r]}{[W^r + (W^m - W^r)f^m]^2} \right\} \left\{ \frac{-2f^m W^r + W^r}{-(f^m)^2(W^m - W^r)} \right\},$$
and equate the result to zero. Since the first term in brackets is strictly positive, we need work only with the second term. Setting it equal to zero and applying the quadratic formula to solve for f^m, we find that
$$f^m_C = \frac{-W^r \pm \sqrt{W^m W^r}}{W^m - W^r}$$

It is evident that one of the roots,
$$(f^m)_c = (-W^t - \sqrt{W^m W^t}/(W^m - W^t),$$
is negative, so must be rejected. Considering now the other root,
$$(f^m)_c = \sqrt{W^m W^t - W^t}/(W^m - W^t),$$
the fact that $W^m > W^t$ implies both numerator and denominator are positive and therefore $(f^m)_c > 0$. Likewise, $W^m > W^t$ implies that $\sqrt{W^m W^t} < W^m$, and therefore $(f^m)_c < 1$. Thus, G achieves an economically meaningful critical value at
$$f^m = \sqrt{W^m W^t - W^t}/(W^m - W^t),$$
and that root is strictly between zero and one.

11. In his original study (1955) Kuznets produced a number of numerical examples consistent with the inverted-U pattern in modern sector enlargement growth, using as his measure of relative inequality the difference in percentage shares between the first and fifth quintiles. He did not, however, establish its inevitability (under the same maintained assumptions as those employed here). After the first draft of this chapter was completed, I learned that the result in Proposition 3.d had been proved earlier by Swamy (1967) using the coefficient of variation. The result has since been reconfirmed independently by Robinson (1976) using the log variance.

Chapter 8

1. These countries are chosen because of their importance and the availability of data.
2. The following data on China come from Tao (2006), Cai and Du (2006), Cai and Wang (2010), Yang, Chen, and Monarch (2010), and Song (2012).
3. According to China's residential registration system ("hukou"), all persons are classified as either "urban residents" or "rural residents." A "rural resident" who migrates to an urban area remains classified as rural unless that person is able to negotiate the difficult process of transferring his/her registration from rural to urban.
4. The data in this section come from National Commission for Enterprises in the Unorganised Sector (2009), Ghose (2011), and World Bank (2011).
5. The data for Brazil come from Fields and Raju, (2007).
6. The data for Mexico come from Rangel (2009).
7. The data for South Africa come from Kingdon and Knight (2008), Banerjee, Galiani, Levinsohn, McLaren, and Woolard (2008), and Leibbrandt, Woolard, McEwen, and Koep (2010).
8. The paper does not identify that country or any other country by name.

Chapter 9

1. Throughout this paper, we shall talk in terms of income distributions among families. All results apply, however, without modification to comparisons of inequality in the distribution of any quantifiable economic magnitude.

2. Cardinality of inequality is redundant and controversial for purposes of ranking of distributions in the same sense that cardinal utility is redundant and controversial in the analysis of consumer choices. See Hicks (5, p. 17).

3. See Champernowne (2), Kondor (7), Sen (10, Chapter 2), and Szal and Robinson (12).

4. For an axiomatic development of the Pareto criterion, see Sen (10).

5. Noteworthy are the axiomatic approaches in the work by Kondor (7) on relative inequality indices and by Sen (11) on absolute poverty measures.

6. Indices of inequality, including those mentioned above, are cardinal measures which naturally introduce a pre-ordering. Thus, rigorously, it is the pre-ordering R induced by the index which satisfies our axioms.

7. Intuitively, a complete pre-ordering has exactly the same meaning as the ranking of commodity bundles by ordinary(ordinal) indifference curves in consumer analysis.

8. Note that in positing that the measure of relative inequality is independent of the level of income, we do not wish to suggest that our feelings about inequality are invariant with income level. On this, see Hirschman and Rothschild (6).

9. Following Atkinson (1), we would note that this condition is analogous to constant relative inequality aversion. For further applications of this notion to inequality comparisons, see also the papers by Rothschild and Stiglitz (9) and Dasgupta, Sen, and Starrett (4).

10. A2 is sometimes referred to as the axiom of anonymity in the literature (see Sen (10)). Sen also includes an illuminating discussion highlighting the conflicts between A2 and a Benthamite utilitarian approach to social judgments (in which social welfare is taken as the sum of individual utilities).

11. Precedent for this axiom dates back at least half a century to Dalton (3), who called this the "principle of transfers."

12. This assertion is easily proven by constructing a sequence of transfers from families above the mean to those below.

13. For some permutation i_1 i_2 ... i_n, if $Y_{i1} \leq Y_{i2} \leq ... \leq Y_{in}$ then $X_{i1} \leq X_{i2} \leq ... \leq X_{in}$.

14. See Atkinson (1), Rothschild and Stiglitz (9), and Dasgupta, Sen, and Starrett (4).

15. Rothschild and Stiglitz have proven that when the Lorenz Curve of X dominates that of Y, it is possible to construct a sequence of transfers which may or may not be rank-preserving, i.e., they may move out of and back into Ω_0. The sufficient condition which we shall prove in the text is a stronger version requiring that such a sequence be rank-preserving and stay within Ω_0.

16. The number *(r - 1)* may be thought of as a *crossing index* since if we were to plot the two distributions X and Y with two curves they would cross *(r - 1)* times.

17. However, if they have opposite signs, they may or may not cross and it is necessary to compare the full distributions.

18. Notice that (3.1) measures *inequality* and therefore a more equal distribution has a lower index.

19. See Atkinson (1).

20. See Theil (13).

21. See Kuznets (8).

Chapter 10

1. Use of the term "income" is purely for verbal convenience. Inequality of consumption or of anything else could be treated identically.
2. But see Fields (1987, 1993).
3. But see Temkin (1986).
4. Attention here is limited to the ordinal aspects of the problem. To avoid possible misunderstanding of the purpose of this chapter, let me state explicitly that it is not about the question of when one distribution is better than another. Possible criteria for such judgments include comparisons of income level and income inequality, the Pareto criterion on the space of incomes, the Rawlsian maximin criterion, comparisons of generalized Lorenz curves, Kolm's criteria for optimal justice, and various dominance criteria. These criteria from welfare economics, as well as others from ethics and political philosophy, are reviewed and developed by Sen (forthcoming). But all of these criteria are for welfare rankings and this chapter is about inequality rankings, on which Sen's earlier work (Sen, 1973) is a classic.
5. See, for instance, Sen (1973), Atkinson (1983), Foster (1985), and the references cited therein.
6. "Person" stands for whatever recipient unit is relevant, which may be an individual, a family, or per capita.
7. When $\Phi = 0$ or 1, $\Theta = 1$.
8. Analysis of this process is of more than academic interest: Simon Kuznets won a Nobel Prize in part for showing that the gradual shift of economic activity from low income to high income sectors is the essence of modern economic growth and for analyzing inequality change under such a process (Kuznets, 1955, 1966).
9. Again please remember that the question is "which is more equal?", not "which is better?" The great majority of observers rank Y_2 as better than Y_1.
10. Ranking inequalities using $\geqslant_L$ is equivalent to making inequality comparisons using four basic properties: anonymity, income homogeneity, population homogeneity, and the Pigou-Dalton transfer principle. For details, see Dasgupta, Sen and Starrett (1973), Rothschild and Stiglitz (1973), and Fields and Fei (1978). Contrary to these relative approaches, Kolm (1976) and Eichhorn and Gehrig (1982) are among those who have adopted more absolute perspectives on inequality comparisons. For a review of the literature on non-relative views, see Ebert (1987).
11. Aldi Hagenaars liked this approach; we had a long, fruitful talk about it.
12. Such a result was already known for the Gini coefficient from the work of Knight (1976) and Fields (1979) and was implied by work on the coefficient of variation by Swamy (1967), on the log variance by Robinson (1976), and on the generalized entropy class, the Atkinson index, and the income share of the poorest p percent by Kakwani (1988).
13. The log variance, although not Lorenz consistent, also follows an inverted U-shaped pattern.
14. A higher value of Atkinson's inequality aversion parameter ε produces a

smaller value of Φ^*. As $\varepsilon \to \infty$, the Atkinson index produces peak inequality at $\Phi = 1/n$, thus representing the I^L-ordering. I am grateful to Tony Atkinson for pointing this out to me.

15. $L > 0$ guarantees that $I > 0$ for all Φ, in particular, at the interior minimum. The necessity of including such a parameter was first pointed out to me by Aldi Hagenaars and James Foster.

Chapter 11

1. This is in contrast to "relative poverty," which is taken up in Section 11.1.6.

2. The setting of equivalence scales is complex and requires detailed technical analysis. Despite the existence of the topic in the literature for more than a century no consensus has been reached. Two good surveys of the main issues are those by Ravallion (1994, pp. 17–25) and Deaton (1997, pp. 241–270).

3. What is defined as a necessity varies from country to country. Contrast, for instance, Council of Economic Advisers (1964) and Orshansky (1965) for the United States, with Dandekar and Rath (1971), Minhas et al. (1987), and Srinivasan and Bardhan (1988) for India. Because of these variations, we can think of countries having "absolute poverty lines, set relatively." For a recent overview, see Lipton and Ravallion (1995).

4. About which two things should be said: (1) Because the minimum wage is revised regularly by the Brazilian government and therefore is not constant in real terms over time, it is not a good measure of absolute poverty. (2) Sadly, in published income distributions, the category "less than one minimum wage" has more income recipients than any other.

5. The latter is a figure often used by the World Bank.

6. Sen's work is summarized in Foster and Sen (1997, Chapter A.7) and in Sen (1997).

7. It should be noticed that adjusting the poverty line by using a general price index entails a potential problem. The basket of goods of the price index may be different from the basket of goods used to define the poverty line. In this case, the poverty line may be over-/under-adjusted.

8. And, as with income inequality, if there were such differences, we would have wanted to have adjusted the base accordingly, for example, by basing our poverty comparisons on per capita incomes or per-adult-equivalent incomes rather than total incomes.

9. One justification for this would be diminishing marginal utility of income using interpersonally comparable social evaluation functions.

10. Suppose that a poor person transfers enough money to a richer poor person so that the recipient is lifted above the poverty line. The poverty headcount falls – exactly the opposite of what distributional-sensitivity requires.

11. For example, the U.S. government regularly publishes poverty headcount ratios going back to 1959 and updates these annually. But if you want a time series on measures using the SM or DS properties, you will have to make the calculations yourself, because no such table is published by the government.

12. One helpful computer program is POVCAL, available from the World Bank

at http://www.worldbank.org/lsms/tools/povcal/.

13. For instance, using a poverty line of \$2.5, compare the amount of poverty in $Y_1 = (1,2,3,4)$ with that in $Y_6 = (1.2,2.4,3,4)$. These two distributions have the same poverty headcount ratio and the same Gini coefficient among the poor. By (s.2), Y_6 has less poverty by P_{Sen} than does Y_1.

14. Again, using a poverty line of \$2.5, compare the amount of poverty in $Y_1 = (1, 2, 3, 4)$ with that in $Y_7 = (1.5, 1.5, 3, 4)$. These two distributions have the same poverty headcount ratio and the same average income shortfall among the poor, but Y_1 has positive income inequality among the poor whereas Y_7 does not. By (iii), Y_7 has less poverty gauged by P_{Sen}, than does Y_1.

15. For individuals with incomes at or above the poverty line, the shortfall is zero, and the weight is zero.

16. The per capita income gap $H\bar{I}$ arises also for the Sen index when there is no inequality among the poor. In this case, $G_p = 0$ and $P_{Sen} = H\bar{I}$.

17. It would be much better to combine $\bar{I}$ with H and G_p and use the Sen index.

18. Other authors measure both relative and absolute poverty; for instance, Atkinson (1983a) and Blackburn (1994).

19. Be careful not to confuse poverty and inequality here. It is perfectly consistent for you to maintain that a proportionate increase in all incomes leaves relative *inequality* unchanged while reducing absolute *poverty*.

20. Whether it is to greater or to a lesser degree is, of course, what inequality is all about. Chapter 3 reviewed the growth-inequality evidence. The evidence reviewed in this chapter is on "absolute poverty," namely, the extent of poverty when a fixed real poverty line is used.

21. A good summary may be found in Bhagwati and Srinivasan (1983, Chapter 25). Bhagwati himself now dismisses these theoretical p ossibilities as the work of "ingeninous economists (properly) making their mark by proving the improbable" (Bhagwati 1991).

22. A "spell" is a period from one survey to another, for example, Malaysia 1970–1976 is one spell, Malaysia 1976–1979 another, and so on. "Spell analysis" means that individual countries can be included as many times in the growth-poverty analysis as their household censuses and surveys permit.

23. In cases of economic decline, poverty rises by more the more negative is the rate of economic growth and the larger is the rate of increase of dispersion.

24. Papua New Guinea's per capita GDP grew at about a 2 percent annual rate during this period of time. The countries covered in their study are China, Malaysia, Thailand, Indonesia, the Philippines, Papua New Guinea, Lao PDR, Vietnam, and Mongolia.

25. Poverty rose in the 1980s and fell in the 1990s in Brazil, Guatemala, Honduras, Panama, Peru, and Venezuela, in each case reflecting the negative economic growth of the 1980s and the positive economic growth of the 1990s. Another study that also reaches the conclusion that economic growth usually reduced poverty in Latin American countries is that by Ganuza, Morley, and Taylor (1998).

Chapter 12

1. We are excluding purely self-interested choices of the type "I prefer A to B, because my income is higher in A than in B."

2. Points lying on the utility possibility frontier are said to be *Pareto-optimal* or *Pareto-efficient*. This means that one person cannot be made better off (in utility terms) without making another person worse off. A *Pareto-improvement* takes place when somebody is made better off and nobody else is made worse off. Moving from A to B in Figure 12.1 would be a Pareto-improvement, as would a move from A to C.

3. There is, however, another criterion which *does* provide a ranking. This is the rule suggested by Buchanan and Tullock (1962) (see also Sen 1970), which states that if x is neither Pareta-superior nor Pareto-inferior to y, then x and y are socially *indifferent*. As a practical matter, Pareto-superiority is rarely attained, so by the Buchanan-Tullock criterion, nearly every social state would be ranked as indifferent to nearly every other.

4. The U_is in (1) are usually thought of as literal representations of the utility functions of the individuals themselves. However, U_i is also used to denote the individual component of social welfare that is associated with each individual, for example, the weight the evaluator assigns to the ith individual's income or consumption (Atkinson 1970; Sen 1973; Foster and Sen 1997, p. 116). Atkinson himself has expressed regret for not having used a letter other than U in this context (Atkinson 1983b, p. 5).

5. Recall the comrnent on Rawlsians' perceptions of poverty measures in Chapter 2, note 15.

6. "Envy," though, has come to be used in economics in the specific sense that an individual prefers someone else's bundle of goods to his or her own. For a discussion of the concept of envy, see Hammond (1989).

7. This is because although the recipient's utility has increased, the nonrecipient's utility has decreased, rendering the welfaristic social welfare function (8a–c) ambiguous.

8. But for an alternative view on inequality, see Welch (1999).

9. This discussion is based on work by Shorrocks (1983), Kakwani (1984), Pyatt (1989), Lambert ((1989)1993), and Bishop and Formby (1994).

10. Taking the household as the unit of analysis, "anonymous" means that all households are treated identically regardless of which particular ones receive how much income. "Increasing" means that social welfare increases whenever one household's income increases, holding other households' incomes the same. "S-concave" means that the function registers higher economic well-being whenever a transfer of income is made from someone who is relatively high-income to someone who is relatively low-income.

11. The following example illustrates the difference. In distribution X let person α have \$100 and person β have \$200. In distribution Y let person β have \$150 and person a have \$300. Because both the poorest person and the second poorest person have higher incomes in Y than in X, we may say that Y first-order dominates X. But because person β is worse off in Y than in X, Y does

not Pareto-dominate X.

12. However, if generalized Lorenz curves cross, this criterion cannot be used to determine which income distribution is better. Thus, the SOD welfare ordering is partial in the same way that inequality comparisons using ordinary Lorenz curves are partial.

13. If you are not sure about the definitions, look again at note 10.

14. The welfare analysis that follows builds on that contained in Fields (1979a) but moves beyond it to include certain additional features that didn't yet exist at that time.

15. This follows from a result contained in Anand and Kanbur (1993b), applied to the special case of zero within-sector inequality. See also Robinson (1976), Knight (1976), and Fields (1979a).

16. For the price index used by Barros and Mendonça, growth was also positive between 1960 and 1970 for each decile except the seventh. For alternative price indices, income growth is recorded for that decile as well.

17. These are the CASEN (Caracterización Socioeconómica Nacional) data, covering all of Chile. (An earlier, 1985 survey is thought to be poorer in quality than and incomparable to the subsequent ones.) Earlier studies in Chile used data covering Greater Santiago only.

Chapter 14

1. The recent strand of the mobility literature which uses panel income changes also includes papers by Grimm (20) and Palmisano and Peragine (27). Using methods different from ours, these papers find convergent mobility for Indonesia, Peru, and Italy and non-symmetric patterns for Indonesia and Italy. (The symmetry issue was not investigated in Peru.)

2. In 1994 there were small changes to the questionnaire of the survey. These changes generate a break in the series reported here.

3. Since 1997, the Venezuelan sample does not separate urban from rural households. However, according to the Venezuelan National Statistics Institute, the sample is nationally representative.

4. Throughout this section we shall assume that earnings are measured without error. In a later subsection we will discuss how our conclusions are affected by violations of this assumption. For the sake of brevity, we omit writing the model in logarithms. We also omit individual subscripts to avoid clutter.

5. The assumptions on independence and identical distribution of the vt shocks can be relaxed to allow for correlations between the shocks of certain groups of individuals (clusters, families, etc.) and to allow for heteroskedasticity of a general form, since at the end we will eliminate the impact of this transitory component on earnings changes. For expositional simplicity we stick to the more conventional homoskedastic representation.

6. See for instance Gottschalk (18).

7. Although age and education are both time-varying characteristics, in our dataset, age changes by only one year for everyone, and education virtually remains unchanged, due to our focus on a sample of working adults. For this

reason we treat the base period values of these variables as time-invariant for a given individual. It can be argued that region is not time invariant as people often migrate. Yet since we are focusing on a population of stayers in the panel, we will consider it as a fixed characteristic too.

8. For robustness we have also used average earnings growth from the microdata, instead of GDP growth, as an indicator of recession/growth. This responds to the concern of some researchers (see for instance the annex of Ravallion (29)), that macrodata show different trends than microdata. In all our economies, average earnings changes from household surveys follow growth of GDP closely, albeit sometimes the recovery in earnings after a rise in GDP comes with a lag of few periods. Our results are qualitatively similar using both indicators.

9. The p-value for this t statistic can be calculated as the upper-tail of a Student's t-distribution with $n-k-1$ degrees of freedom, or in the case of the 2SLS regressions as the upper tail of a standardized normal.

10. By eliminating any within-cohort mobility, the pseudo-panel approach of Antman and McKenzie (4) provides estimates similar in spirit to ours, by focusing on a measure of convergence less affected by transitory fluctuations in earnings and measurement error. The pseudo-panel method might still lead to biases if there is time-varying cohort-level measurement error. Also the pseudo-panel analysis can entail certain biases in that it might fail to track a consistent group of individuals over time for reasons such as migration, deaths, and household dissolution and creation. For a critique of these methods in mobility studies, see Deaton ((10), p. 120).

11. For the precise mathematical relationship between α_1 and β_1 refer to equation (A.7) in the Online Appendix.

12. For Argentina there are four semi-annual observations per individual, for Mexico there are five quarterly observations, and for Venezuela there are six semi-annual observations.

13. A similar exercise for the logarithm of earnings is included in the Online Appendix of the paper.

14. In all of the cases the null hypothesis of equality of means across the five quintile groups (H02) is rejected at the 1 % level of significance.

15. The different robustness checks mentioned at the end of Section 4 lead to results that are very similar to the ones reported here. For details refer to the Online Appendix Figs. A3–A5 and to Duval-Hernández (11), Sánchez Puerta (30), and Fields and Sánchez Puerta (14).

16. Only in the specification using predicted earnings in levels in Argentina is the β_1 coefficient statistically insignificant.

17. A succinct way to model this is to assume that earnings are the sum of a random walk capturing permanent earnings and an autoregressive process capturing transitory shocks (see for instance Moffitt and Gottschalk 2002). This way cross-sectional inequality can rise because of the random walk, yet the autocorrelation component would generate convergence. We thank an anonymous referee for suggesting this idea.

18. In other words, we have randomly selected individuals located at the following percentile groups of the initial earnings distribution: 1, 5, 10, 15, 19,

21, 25, 30, 35, 39, 41, 45, 50, 55, 59, 61, 65, 70, 75, 79, 81, 85, 90, 95, and 100 percentile groups.

19. If the individuals in the 1st percentile group of the distribution had earnings equal to zero we added 1 peso/bolívar to their earnings, so their log-earnings would be depicted as 0 in the graph.

Chapter 15

1. Fei and Ranis (1964).
2. Prest and Turvey (1965).
3. A summary of the applications to education is contained in Psacharopoulos and Hinchliffe (1970). See also Wood and Campbell (1969).
4. Arrow (1968).
5. Becker (1964).
6. Blaug (1967).
7. Bowen (1968).
8. Bowman (1962).
9. Hansen (1963).
10. Weisbrod (1962).
11. Merrett (1966).
12. Balogh and Streeten (1963).
13. Their views are summarized in Bowen (1968).
14. For similar views, see Cash (1969) and Blaug (1967).
15. The omission of leisure as an argument in the utility function is intended to avoid the unnecessary complication of considering labor-leisure choices. Any gain in personal utility resulting from increased leisure may be subsumed under the private benefit package under lifetime diposable income.
16. I say 'generally' because there are cases in which persons may choose to be educated in order to receive additional non-pecuniary benefits at the expense of lower pay and/or less stable employment. Monetarily speaking, an economics major with a B.A. may earn more selling insurance than he would with a Ph.D. as an Economics professor. Many of us made such a choice, presumably on the basis of non-pecuniary benefits. It may also be that employment is less stable for the graduates in some fields. For instance, aerospace engineers in the United States chose an occupation which offered high salaries and the excitement of a new scientific endeavor. Thoughtful observers foretold the instability of the labor market, but many engineers are today regretfully experiencing the consequences of their lack of foresight.
17. In a forthcoming paper, Joseph E. Stiglitz examines educational systems in developed economies when viewed as a means of providing information on different persons' marginal productivities to employers. Although it is difficult and costly to evaluate the marginal product of any one ~r:;on prior to hiring, Stiglitz sees educational attainment as a means of identifying a group of potential employees who, on average, are more productive than another group with less education. The private benefits of education result from employers paying higher wages to those with more education, because

they are perceived (perhaps correctly) as more productive. Stiglitz concludes that to the extent that education serves a screening function, the social benefits of education are likely to be considerably less than the private benefits.

18. He may be paid less due to inexperience or because the highest paying jobs have already been filled by persons educated earlier.

19. For instance, in Kenya, school fees cover around one-fourth of the gross cost of primary . education and one-fifth of the costs of secondary education. No fees are charged at post-secondary teacher's training colleges or agricultural training institutions. Kenyan university students studying in East Africa are in theory charged £300 per year tuition, but bursaries are so extensive that fees pay only about 6 percent of the costs of the University of Nairobi. For these and other facts on the educational system of Kenya, see Fields (1971).

20. Berg (1966).

21. In Kenya, a university graduate can expect to earn about 3.4 times as much as a secondary school leaver over his lifetime. (fhis is the ratio of undiscounted lifetime earnings according to government salary scales allowing for unemployment of secondary schoolleavers.) The private internal rate of return, unadjusted for background factors of ability, to university education over secondary school is over 30 percent per year. The rates to teacher training are of a similar magnitude. For the details of these calculations, see Fields (1972).

22. The specification of the average private rate of return is consistent with the economist's standard assumption that there are no quality differences between workers with the same education-skill characteristics. The marginal private rate of return would be appropriate if the marginal student's labor market expectations (in the sense af mathematical expected value, not subjective Bayesian prior notions) differ from the average. Ibis would be the case if those already being educated are higher in ability than the marginal student and therefore, (a) are less likely to Bunk, (b) expect to rank higher in their classes and be hired for the choicest positions, or (c) have higher probabilities of continuing onward for further education. For simplicity, these factors are neglected in the remainder of the paper.

23. Besides demand effects of an increase in supply, a number of other questions remain. Will the disequilibrium characterized by excess demand for schooling be resolved if more education is supplied? Does a stable equilibrium exist? In what ways does it depend on the wage structure, employment probabilities, etc? Are there multiple equilibria? These and other questions will be dealt with formally in a forthcoming paper with George E. Johnson.

24. An interesting study beyond the scope of this paper would be to try to classify the labor markets of a number of less developed countries into one or another of these types and to seek cultural explanations for the resultant pattern.

25. I wish to thank the participants in the Institute for Development Studies Economics Seminar for their helpful suggestions on this point.

26. They might continue for a time to look for high-level jobs while employed in low-level jobs. But the combination of reduced job-search time due to being fully employed and depreciation of their human capital tends to confine them to the lower levels.

27. A further source of ambiguity which, for simplicity, I have omitted from the discussion is the fact that the education system employs educated persons and uses scarce capital. If another person (or group of persons) is educated, school facilities must be expanded. This removes scarce resources from the production of output, thereby lowering the marginal product of labor and reducing employment. However, it also increases employment opportunities in the educational sector. One can only speculate on the relative magnitudes of the parameters with respect to specific cases, since they differ from one country to another. Few unambiguous results are attainable.

28. This judgment is shared by Lewis (1968).

29. Out of the approximately 11,000 post-secondary student~ (excluding those at foreign universities) in Kenya, about two-thirds are enrolled in teacher education courses. Education accounts for 15 percent of the Kenya government's budget and 10 percent of its development expenditures. Personal emoluments to teaching and non-teaching staff in schools amounted to £10 million, which is 8 percent of the budget. See Fields (1969).

30. In 1969, about one-fourth of the teachers in Kenya bad less than university education and no teacher training. Source: Republic of Kenya (1969). Moorthy and Thore propose an accelerator model for educational expansion, which they then test using Indian data. Their basic conclusion is that as low-level education is expanded, this requires an additional supply of 'deep' (i.e. high-level) levels of education. They then qualify their position by noting that 'the education acceleration principle may be much more vigorous in a country of full employment than in India which at the moment is characterized by a large unemployed educated labor force especially at the non-technical levels'. See Moorthy and Sten (1959).

31. The world powers, development agencies, and missionary groups, among others, are likely candidates for this to be the case.

32. See Moris (1967).

33. Marshall (1968).

34. These need not be the same ten as the ones just educated.

35. For instance, the well known World Bank study on rates of return to education in Kenya in effect uses such a measure. See Thias and Carnoy (1969).

36. 50 = Wage of employed gardener (10 shs / day)
    × number of work days per year (250)
    × productivity factor (2 percent).

37. Psacharopoulos (1970).

Chapter 16

1. Harris and Todaro also considered a "limited" wage subsidy, which they analyzed at length, and migration restriction, which they rejected on ethical grounds.

2. The terminology is due to Lambert (1993).

3. Stiglitz (1974, 1976) considered instead the possibility of these wages being set above the market-clearing level for efficiency wage reasons, but that variant is not pursued here.

4. The inequality effects of MSENL in the HT model were first studied by Gupta (1988). Temple (1999) considered technical progress in agriculture, which effectively corresponds to TSENR, and in manufacturing, which is essentially MSENR. Temple also analyzed urban wage restraint and a small uniform wage subsidy (which had been introduced into the HT literature by Bhagwati (1974)). The analysis here builds upon and extends these earlier inequality analyses.

5. Gupta measured inequality using the Gini coefficient and Rauch used the log-variance. For a critique of the log-variance, see Foster and Ok (1999).

6. For example, Chakravarty and Dutta (1990) formulated social welfare functions depending on mean income and inequality but not unemployment. Papers are still being written analyzing welfare in the HT model using just mean income; a current example is Marjit and Hamid (2003).

7. Basu (1997) provides a review.

8. However, if the two Lorenz curves cross, then neither can be said to be unambiguously more equal or unequal than the other. In this case, two Lorenz-consistent measures can always be found, one of which shows A to be more equally distributed than B and the other showing A less equally distributed than B.

9. In the generalized HT class of models, WA is the average income in the population if and only if there is no on-the-job search from agriculture (Fields, 1989).

10. I do not use expected wages, because to do so would treat a situation in which all workers receive W_A as equivalent to one in which some are employed and receive $W_M(>W_A)$ while others are unemployed and receive nothing.

11. The social welfare function $f(.)$ should be thought of as including the four labor market components (total labor earnings, unemployment, inequality, and poverty) but not be limited to them.

12. A policy is welfare-ambiguous if it can be shown that for some measures or parameter values, the policy raises welfare, while for others, it lowers welfare.

13. The limitations of the poverty headcount ratio for gauging poverty are well known. One is that the headcount ratio considers only the number of poor but not the average severity of their poverty nor the inequality of incomes among them. The other limitation is that the headcount ratio is sensitive to the precise place where the poverty line z is drawn. One solution to these problems is to create poverty measures which are sensitive to the severity of poverty and the inequality of incomes among the poor and to calculate these measures for a variety of poverty lines. This is what Sen (1976) and Foster et al. (1984) did. Another solution is to apply poverty dominance methods (Atkinson, 1987; Foster and Shorrocks, 1988; Ravallion, 1994; Foster and Sen, 1997). This involves choosing minimum and maximum poverty lines and a broad class of poverty measures. The poverty dominance results follow from the welfare dominance results to be presented in Chapter 19.5 and will be remarked upon there.

14. "Anonymous" means that all workers are treated identically regardless of which particular ones earn how much income. "Increasing" means that social welfare increases whenever one worker's earnings increase, holding other workers' earnings the same.

References

Introduction by the Editor

Assaad, R. (2014): Making sense of Arab labor markets: the enduring legacy of dualism, in: IZA Journal of Labor & Development, vol. 3(6): 1–25.

Bargain, O., Dolls, M., Immervoll, H., Neumann, D., Peichl, A., Pestel, N., Siegloch, S. (2015): Tax Policy and Income Inequality in the United States, 1979–2007, in: Economic Inquiry, vol. 53(2): 1061–1085.

Bosch, M., Maloney, W. F. (2010): Comparative analysis of labor market dynamics using Markov processes: An application to informality, in: Labour Economics, vol. 17(4): 621–631.

Clemens, M. A., Özden, Ç., Rapoport, H. (2014): Migration and Development Research is Moving Far Beyond Remittances, in: World Development, vol. 64(C): 121–124.

Cowell, F. A. (2000): Measurement of inequality, in: Atkinson, A.B., Bourguignon, F. (Eds.), Handbook of Income Distribution, Elsevier, Vol. 1, Chapter 2: 87–166.

Ferreira, F., Robalino, D. (2010): Social Protection in Latin America – Achievements and Limitations, World Bank Policy Research Paper 5305.

Fields, G. S. (2001): Distribution and Development – A New Look at the Developing World. Cambridge, MA: The MIT Press and Russell Sage Foundation.

Fields, G. S. (2004): Dualism in the Labor Market: A Perspective on the Lewis Model after Half of a Century, in: Manchester School, vol. 72 (6), 724–735.

Fields, G. S. (2012): Working Hard, Working Poor: A Global Journey, New York: Oxford University Press.

Fields, G. S. (2014): Self-employment and poverty in developing countries: Helping the self-employed earn more for the work they do, IZA World of Labor.

Gang, I. N. (2015): Laudation on the Presentation of the 13th IZA Prize in Labor Economics to Gary S. Fields, given on January 4, 2015 at the Sheraton Boston Hotel (at Copley Square), Rutgers University, mimeo.

Günther, I., Launov, A. (2012): Informal employment in developing countries, in: Journal of Development Economics, vol. 97(1): 88–98.

Jäntti, M., Jenkins, S. P. (2015): Income Mobility, in: A.B. Atkinson, F. Bourguignon (Eds.), Handbook of Income Distribution, Vol. 2, Chapter 10: 807–935. Elsevier.

Kapsos, S., Bourmpoula, E. (2013): Employment and Economic Class in the Developing World, ILO Research Paper No. 6, International Labour Office.

Krueger, A. O., Hal, L. B., Monson, T., Akrasanee, N. (Eds.) (1981): Trade and employment in developing countries, National Bureau of Economic Research, Chicago: University of Chicago Press.

Rauch, J. E. (1991): Modelling the informal sector formally, in: Journal of Development Economics, vol. 35(1): 33–47.

Scarpetta, S., Pierre, G. (2015): Development and Employment: A Mutual Relationship, International Encyclopedia of the Social & Behavioral Sciences, Second Edition: 269–275.

United Nations (2014): World Urbanization Prospects: The 2014 Revision, New York: United Nations, Department of Economic and Social Affairs, Population Division.

World Bank (2012): World Development Report 2013: Jobs, Washington, DC: World Bank.

Zenou, Y. (2011): Search, migration, and urban land use: The case of transportation policies, in: Journal of Development Economics, vol. 96(2): 174–187.

Zimmermann, K. F., Biavaschi, C., Eichhorst, W., Giulietti, C., Kendzia, M. J., Muravyev, A., Pieters, J., Rodríguez-Planas, N., Schmidl, R. (2013): Youth Unemployment and Vocational Training, Foundations and Trends, in: Microeconomics, 2013, 9 (1–2): 1–157.

Chapter 1

Banerjee, A. V., Duflo, E. (2011): Poor Economics, New York: Public Affairs.

Deaton, A. (1997): The analysis of household surveys: a microeconometric approach to development policy, Baltimore, MD. World Bank by Johns Hopkins University Press.

Heckman, J. J. (2001): Micro Data, Heterogeneity, and the Evaluation of Public Policy: Nobel Lecture, in: Journal of Political Economy 109(4): 673–748.

Karlan, D., Appel, J. (2011): More Than Good Intentions, New York: Dutton.

Ravallion, M. (2008): Evaluating Anti-Poverty Programs, in: Schultz, T. P., Strauss, J. (Eds.), Handbook of Development Economics, Volume 4, Amsterdam: North-Holland.

Surowiecki, J. (2008): What Microloans Miss, in: The New Yorker, March 17.

Chapter 2

Adelman, I., Morris, C. T. (1973): Economic Growth and Social Equity in Developing Countries, Stanford: Stanford University Press.

Ahluwalia, M. S. (1974): Income Inequality: Some Dimensions of the Problem, in: Chenery, H. B, et al. (Eds.), Redistribution with Growth, Oxford: Oxford University Press.

Ahluwalia, M. S. (1976a): Income Distribution and Development: Some Stylized Facts, in: American Economic Review, May, 1976, 128–135.

Ahluwalia, M. S. (1976b): Inequality, Poverty and Development, in: Journal of Development Economics 1976, 3, 307–342.

Ahluwalia, M. S., Carter, N. G., Chenery, H. (1979): Growth and Poverty in Developing Countries, in: Chenery, H., Structural Change and Development Policy, Oxford University Press.

Ahuja, V., Bidani, B., Ferreira, F., Walton, M. (1997): Everyone's Miracle?: Revisiting

Poverty and Inequality in East Asia, World Bank.

Ali, A. A. G. (1997): Dealing with Poverty and Income Distribution Issues in Developing Countres: Cross Regional Experiences, Paper presented at the African Economic Research Consortium Bi-Annual Research Workshop, Nairobi, December, 1996, Revised: January.

Anand, S., Kanbur, S.M.R. (1993a): Inequality and Development: A Critique, in: Journal of Development Economics, 41 (1) 19–43.

Anand, S., Kanbur, S.M.R. (1993b): The Kuznets process and the inequality-development relationship, in: Journal of Development Economics, 40(1), 25–52.

Anand, S., Ravallion, M. (1993): Human Development in Poor Countries: On the Role of Private Incomes and Public Services, in: Journal of Economic Perspectives, Winter.

Anand, S., Sen, A. K. (1997): Concepts of Human Development and Poverty: A Multidimensional Perspective, Background paper for Human Development Report 1997, New York: United Nations.

Atkinson, A. B. (1970): On the Measurement of Inequality, in: Journal of Economic Theory, 1970.

Atkinson, A. B. (1998): Poverty in Europe, Oxford: Blackwell.

Atkinson, A. B., Rainwater, L., Smeeding, T. B. (1995): Income Distribution in OECD Countries: Evidence from the Luxembourg Income Study, Paris: OECD.

Barros, R. P. d., Mendonça, R. S. P. d. (1995): The Evolution of Welfare, Poverty and Inequality in Brazil Over the Last Three Decades: 1960– 1990, IPEA, March.

Bruno, M., Ravallion, M., Squire, L. (1998): Equity and Growth in Developing Countries: Old and New Perspectives on the Policy Issues, in: Tanzi, V., Chu, K. Y. (Eds.), Income Distribution and High-Quality Growth, Cambridge and London: MIT Press.

Cameron, L. (1998): Income Ineqaulity in Java: relating the increases to the changing age, educational and industrial structure, University of Melbourne, unpublished manuscript.

Chen, S., Datt, G., Ravallion, M. (1994): Is Poverty Increasing in the Developing World?, World Bank Working Paper, 1993. Abridged version published in Review of Income and Wealth, December.

Chen, S., Ravallion, M., Data in Transition: Assessing Rural Living Standards in Southern China, in: China Economic Review, Vol. 7, No. 1, 23–56.

Chiou, J. R. (1996): A Dominance Evaluation of Taiwan's Official Income Distribution Statistics, 1976–1992, in: China Economic Review.

Cline, W. (1975): Distribution and Development: A Survey of the Literature, in: Journal of Development Economics, 1, 359–400.

Coondoo, D., Dutta, B. (1990): Measurement of Income Mobility: An Application to India, in: Dutta, B., et al. (Eds.), Economic Theory and Policy: Essays in Honor of Dipak Banerji, Bombay and New York: Oxford University Press.

Danziger, S., Gottschalk, P. (1995): America Unequal, New York: Russell Sage Foundation.

Dasgupta, P., Sen, A. K., Starrett, D. (1973): Notes on the Measurement of Inequality, in: Journal of Economic Theory.

Deininger, K., Squire, L. (1996): A New Data Set Measuring Income Inequality, in:

The World Bank Economic Review 10:3.

Deininger, K. (1998): New Ways of Looking at Old Issues: Inequality and Growth, in: Journal of Development Economics, December, v57, n2, 259-287.

Drèze, J., Lanjouw, P., Stern, N. (1992): Economic Mobility and Agricultural Labour in Rural India: A Case Study, in: Indian Economic Review, Special Number, 25-54.

Fields, G. S. (1980): Poverty, Inequality, and Development, Cambridge University Press.

Fields, G. S. (1989): A compendium of Data on Inequality and Poverty for the Developing World, Cornell University, processed.

Fields, G. S. (1991): Growth and Income Distribution, in: Psacharopoulos, G. (Eds.), Essays on Poverty, Equity, and Growth, Oxford and New York: Pergamon.

Fields, G. S. (1994): Poverty Changes in Developing Countries, in: van der Hoeven, R., Anker, R., (Eds.), Poverty Monitoring: An International Concern, New York: St. Martin's Press.

Fields, G. S. (2001): Distribution and Development: A New Look at the Developing World, Russell Sage Foundation and MIT Press, forthcoming.

Fields, G. S., Jakubson, G. H. (1994): New Evidence on the Kuznets Curve, Cornell University.

Fields, G. S., Newton, A. (1996): Changing Labor Market Conditions and Income Distribution in Brazil, Costa Rica, and Venezuela, Cornell University, processed.

Fishlow, A. (1995): Inequality, Poverty and Growth: Where Do We Stand?, Annual Bank Conference on Development Economics, World Bank, May.

Flemming, J., Micklewright, J. (1999): Income Distribution, Economic Systems and Transition, in: Atkinson, A. B., Bourguignon, F. (Eds.), Handbook of Income Distribution.

Fuchs, V. (1969): Comment on Measuring the Size of the Low-Income Population, in: Soltow, L. (Eds.), Six Papers on the Size Distribution of Wealth and Income, New York: National Bureau of Economic Research, 198-202.

Glewwe, P., Hall, G. (1998): Are Some Groups More Vulnerable to Macroeconomic Shocks than Others? Hypothesis Tests Based on Panel Data from Peru, in: Journal of Development Economics, 56:1, August, pages 181-206.

Gottschalk, P., Smeeding, T. M. (1997): Cross-National Comparisons of Earnings and Income Inequality, in: Journal of Economic Literature 35, 632-87.

Grootaert, C., Kanbur, R. (1996): The Lucky Few Amidst Economic Decline: Distributional Change as Seen Through Panel Data, in: Grootaert, C., Analyzing Poverty and Policy Reform: The Experience of Côte d'Ivoire, Aldershot, UK: Avebury.

Grootaert, C., Kanbur, R., Oh, G. T. (1997): The Dynamics o f Welfare Gains and Losses: An African Case Study, in: The Journal of Development Studies, Vol.33, No.5, June.

Herrera, J. (1999): Ajuste Económico, Desigualdad, y Movilidad, DIAL, July.

Jalan, J., Ravallion, M. (1999): Do Transient and Chronic Poverty in Rural China Share Common Causes?, World Bank, processed, February.

Jalan, J., Ravallion, M. (1998): Transient Poverty in Post Reform China, in: Journal of Comparative Economics 26.

References

Kanbur, R., Lustig, N. (1999): Why is inequality back on the Agenda?, paper presented at the Annual Bank Conference on Development Economics, World Bank, Washington, D.C., April.

Kolm, S. C. (1976): Unequal Inequalities I and II, in: Journal of Economic Theory.

Kuznets, S. (1955): Economic Growth and Income Inequality, in: American Economic Review, March, 1–28.

Kuznets, S. (1963): Quantitative Aspects of the Economic Growth of Nations: VIII, Distribution of Income By Size, Economic Development and Cultural Change, January, Part 2, 1–80.

Lambert, P. J. (1989): The Distribution and Redistribution of Income: A Mathematical Analysis, Oxford: Blackwell.

Lipton, M. (1998): Successes in Anti-Poverty. Geneva: International Labour Office.

Londoño, J. L., Szequely, M. (1998): Sorpresas Distributivas después de una década de reformas: América Latina en los noventa, in: Pensamiento Iberoamericano. Revista de Economía Política, Special Issue, 195–242.

Milanovic, B. (1999): Explaining the Increase in Inequality During the Transition, Paper presented at the IMF Conference "A Decade of Transition: Achievements and Challenges," Washington, DC, February.

Nee, V. (1994): The Emergence of a Market Society: Changing Mechanisms of Stratification in China, Cornell University, Working Papers on Transitions from State Socialism #94.1, April.

Nee, V. (1996): The Emergence of a Market Society: Changing Mechanisms of Stratification in China, in: American Journal of Sociology, January.

Nee, V., Liedka, R. V. (1997): Markets and Inequality in the Transition from State Socialism, in: Midlarsky, M. I. (Eds.), Inequality, Democracy, and Economic Development, New York: Cambridge University Press.

O'Higgins, M., Jenkins, S. (1990): Poverty in the EC: Estimates for 1975, 1980, and 1985, in: Teekens, R., van Praag, B. M. S. (Eds.), Analysing Poverty in the European Community: Policy Issues, Research Options, and Data Sources.

Oshima, H. T. (1991): Kuznets' Curve and Asian Income Distribution, in: Mizoguchi, T., et al. (Eds.), Making Economies More Efficient and More Equitable: Factors Determining Income Distribution, New York: Oxford University Press.

Paukert, F. (1973): Income Distribution of Different Levels of Development: A Survey of the Evidence, International Labour Review, August–September, 97–125.

Psacharopoulos, G., Morley, S., Fiszbein, A., Lee, H., Bill, W., Poverty and Income Distribution in Latin America: The Story of the 1980s, Washington: World Bank.

Randolph, S. M., Trzcinski, E. (1989): Relative Earnings Mobility in a Third World Country, in: World Development Vol.17, No.4, 513–524, April.

Ravallion, M. (1994): Poverty Comparisons, Chur, Switzerland: Harwood Academic Publishers.

Ravallion, M. (1995): Growth and Poverty: Evidence for the Developing World, Economics Letters, 411–417.

Ravallion, M. (1996): Data in Transition: Assessing Rural Living Standards in

Southern China, in: China Economic Review (7) 1, 1996, 23–56.

Ravallion, M., Chen, S. (1997): What Can New Survey Data Tell Us About Recent Changes in Distribution and Poverty?, in: World Bank Economic Review, Vol. 11, No. 2, 357–382.

Ravallion, M., Datt, G., van de Valle, D. (1991): Quantifying Absolute Poverty in the Developing World, in: Review of Income and Wealth, Series 37, Number 4, December.

Ray, D. (1998): Development Economics, Princeton: Princeton University Press.

Saposnik, R. (1981): Rank Dominance in Income Distributions, Public Choice.

Schultz, T. P. (1998): Inequality in the Distribution of Personal Income in the World: How Is It Changing and Why?, in: Journal of Population Economics, June, v11, n3, 307–344.

Scott, C. D., Litchfield, J. A. (1994): Inequality, Mobility and the Determinants of Income Among the Rural Poor in Chile, 1968–1986, London School of Economics, STICERD, Working Paper No. 53, March.

Sen, A. K. (1999): The Possibility of Social Choice, in: American Economic Review, 89:3, June, 349–378.

Shorrocks, A. F. (1983): Ranking Income Distributions, Economica.

Trzcinski, E., Randolph, S. (1991): Human Capital Investment and Relative Earnings Mobility: The Role of Education, Training, Migration, and Job Search, Economic Development and Cultural Change, 153–168.

United Nations, Human Development Report, annual.

World Bank (1997): Poverty and Income Distribution in a High-Growth Economy (Chile): 1987–1995, Report No. 16377-CH.

World Bank (1999): http://www.worldbank.org/poverty/data/trends/income.htm.

Chapter 3

Abraham, V. (2009): Employment Growth in Rural India: Distress-Driven?, in: Economic and Political Weekly, April 18, 97–104.

Ahmad, E., Drèze, J., Hills, J., Sen, A. (1991): Social Security in Developing Countries, Oxford: Clarendon.

Appleton, S., Song, L., Xia, Q. (2005): Has China Crossed the River? The Evolution of Wage Structure in Urban China during Reform and Retrenchment, in: Journal of Comparative Economics 33(4), 644–663.

Asian Development Bank (2005): Labor Markets in Asia: Promoting Full, Productive, and Decent Employment, in: Asian Development Bank, Key Indicators 2005, Manila: Asian Development Bank.

Banerjee, A., Duflo, E. (2007) The Economic Lives of the Poor, in: Journal of Economic Perspectives, 21(1), Winter, 141–167.

Banerjee, A., Duflo, E. (2008): What Is Middle Class about the Middle Classes around the World? in: Journal of Economic Perspectives 22(2), Spring, 3–28.

Bardhan, P. K. (2010): Awakening Giants, Feet of Clay, Princeton: Princeton University Press.

BBC News (1998): World: Asia-Pacific Global March against Child Labor Begins,

References

January 17, http://news.bbc.co.uk/2/hi/asia-pacifi c/48267.stm, accessed 2/2/09.

Bourguignon, F. (2005): Development Strategies for More and Better Jobs, presentation at the conference "Help Wanted: More and Better Jobs in a Globalized Economy," Washington, Carnegie Endowment for International Peace, April.

Charmes, J. (2009): Concepts, Measurement and Trends, in: de Laiglesia, J. R., Jütting, J. (Eds.), Is Informal Normal? Towards More and Better Jobs in Developing Countries, Paris: Organisation for Economic Co-operation and Development.

Chen, M., Hussmanns, R., Vanek, J. (2007): Measuring the Informal Economy: Concepts and Definitions, WIEGO (Women in Informal Employment: Globalizing and Organizing) Working Paper.

Chen, M., Vanek, J. (2005): Informal Employment: Rethinking Workforce Development, in: Avirgan, T., Bivens, L. J., Gammage, S., (Eds.), Good Jobs, Bad Jobs, No Jobs, Washington: Global Policy Network and Economic Policy Institute.

Chen, M., Vanek, J., Lund, F., Heintz, J., Jhabvala, R., Bonner, C. (2005): Progress of the World's Women 2005, New York: United Nations Development Fund for Women (UNIFEM).

Collins, D., Morduch, J., Rutherford, S., Ruthven, O. (2009): Portfolios of the Poor, Princeton: Princeton University Press.

Edmonds, E. (2008): Child Labor, in: Schultz, T. P, Strauss, J. (Eds.), Handbook of Development Economics, Vol. 4, Amsterdam: North Holland.

Felipe, J., Hasan, R. (2006): Labor Markets in Asia, Manila: Asian Development Bank.

Fields, G. S. (2007a): Employment in Low-Income Countries: Beyond Labor Market Segmentation, in: Paci, P., Serneels, P. (Eds.), Employment and Shared Growth, Washington: World Bank.

Foster, A., Rosenzweig, M. (2008): Economic Development and the Decline of Agricultural Employment, in: Schultz, T. P., Strauss, J. (Eds.), Handbook of Development Economics, Vol. 4, Amsterdam: North Holland.

Fox, M. L., Gaal, M., S. (2008): Working Out of Poverty: Job Creation and the Quality of Growth in Africa, Washington: World Bank.

Gertler, P., Shah, M., Bertozzi, S. (2005): Sex Sells, but Risky Sex Sells for More, in: Journal of Political Economy, 518–550.

Ghose, A. K., Majid, N., Ernst, C. (2008): The Global Employment Challenge, Geneva: International Labour Organisation.

Glinskaya, E., Lokshin, M. (2005): Wage Differentials in the Public and Private Sectors in India, Washington, World Bank Working Paper No. 3574.

Günther, I., Launov, A.: Informal Employment in Developing Countries: Opportunity or Last Resort? in: Journal of Development Economics, forthcoming.

Hamlin, K. (2008): Chinese Manufacturers Shun Low-Wage Inland for Vietnam, India, bloomberg.com, May 11, accessed 5/15/08.

Harriss-White, B. (2003): India Working, Cambridge: Cambridge University Press.

Hasan, R., Magsombol, R. (2005): Labor Markets in India: Some Findings from

NSS Data, Manila, Economics Research Department, Asian Development Bank.

Inter-American Development Bank, IDB (2003): Good Jobs Wanted, Washington: IDB.

International Labour Organisation (ILO) (1972): Employment, Incomes, and Equality: A Strategy for Increasing Productive Employment in Kenya, Geneva: ILO.

International Labour Organisation (ILO) (2006): The End of Child Labor: Within Reach, Geneva: ILO.

International Labour Organisation (ILO) (2007b): World Social Security Forum— Building a "Social Security Floor" Worldwide Where Growth Can Meet Equity, Geneva: ILO.

International Labour Organisation (ILO) (2007c): Working Time around the World: Trends in Working Hours, Laws and Policies in a Global Comparative Perspective, Geneva: ILO.

International Labour Organisation (ILO) (2009a): Global Employment Trends for Women, Geneva: ILO.

International Labour Organisation (ILO) (2009b): Stemming the Crisis: World Leaders Forge a Global Jobs Pact, in: World of Work , August, 4–9.

International Labour Organisation (ILO) (2011): Global Employment Trends, Geneva: ILO, January.

Jütting, J., de Laiglesia, J. R. (2009): Is Informal Normal?, Paris: Organization for Economic Cooperation and Development.

Kucera, D., Roncolato, L. (2008): Informal Employment: Two Contested Policy Issues, in: International Labour Review 147(4), 321–348.

Levy, S. (2008): Good Intentions, Bad Outcomes, Washington: Brookings Institution Press.

Luce, E. (2007): In Spite of the Gods, New York: Doubleday.

Maloney, W. F. (2004): Informality Revisited. World Development 32(7), 1159–1178.

Millennium Challenge Corporation (2008): Private Sector Initiatives Toolkit.

Narayan, D., Chambers, R., Shah, M. K., Petesch, P. (2000): Voices of the Poor: Crying Out for Change, New York: Oxford University Press.

Nattrass, N., Seekings, J. (2005): Class, Race, and Inequality in South Africa, New Haven: Yale University Press.

Peek, P. (2006): Labor Market Indicators, presentation at the Conference on Labor Markets and Growth, International Development Research Centre (Canada), Ottawa, November.

Rosenzweig, M. (1988): Labor Markets in Low Income Countries: Distortions, Mobility, and Migration, in: Chenery, H., Srinivasan, T. N. (Eds.), Handbook of Development Economics, Amsterdam: Elsevier.

Sen, B., Mujeri, M. K., Shahabuddin, Q. (2007): Explaining Pro-Poor Growth in Bangladesh: Puzzles, Evidence, and Implications, in: Besley, T., Cord, L. (Eds.), Delivering on the Promise of Pro-Poor Growth, New York: Palgrave Macmillan.

Smith, S. C. (2005): Ending Global Poverty, New York: Macmillan.

Squire, L. (1981): Employment Policy in Developing Countries: A Survey of Issues and Evidence, New York: Oxford University Press.

Stroll, E., Thornton, R. (2002): Do Large Employers Pay More in Developing Countries? The Case of Five African Countries, Working Paper No. 660, Bonn: IZA.

Tao, R. (2006): The Labor Market in the People's Republic of China: Development.

Thorbecke, E. (1973): The Employment Problem: A Critical Evaluation of Four ILO Comprehensive Country Reports, in: International Labor Review 107(5), 393–423.

Turnham, D. (1971): The Employment Problem in Less Developed Countries, Paris: Organization for Economic Cooperation and Development.

Turnham, D. (1993): Employment and Development: A New Review of Evidence, Paris: Organization for Economic Cooperation and Development.

United Nations (2007): Kenya: Bangaisha na Mzungus—Youth, Sex, and Tourism on the Kenyan Coast, http://www.irinnews.org/InDepthMain.aspx?InDepth Id=28&ReportId=69989&Country=Yes, accessed 2/2/09.

United States Bureau of Labor Statistics (2007): Hourly Compensation Costs for Production Workers in Manufacturing, April 30, ftp://ftp.bls.gov/pub/special. requests/ForeignLabor/indCountryTable.txt, accessed 1/18/10.

Wittenberg, M. (2002): Job Search in South Africa: A Nonparametric Analysis, in: South African Journal of Economics 70(8), December, 1163–1197.

World Bank (1993): The East Asian Miracle, Washington: World Bank.

World Bank (2005): Economic Growth in the 1990s: Learning from a Decade of Reform, Washington: World Bank.

World Bank (2007): Promoting Gender Equality and Women's Empowerment, ch. 3 of Global Monitoring Report 2007, Washington: World Bank.

Chapter 4

Annable Jr., J. E. (1972): Labor distribution in low income countries: A theoretical and empirical analysis, Unpublished paper, Massachusetts Institute of Technology, Cambridge, Mass.

Bhagwati, J., Srinivasan, T. N. (1974): On reanalysing the Harris-Todaro model: Policy rankings in the case of sector-specific sticky iivates, in: American Economic Review, June, 502–508.

Blaug, M., Layard, R., Woodhall, M. (1969): The causes of graduate unemployment in India, London: Penguin Books.

Bowles, S. (1970): Migration as investment: Empirical tests of the human investment approach to geographical mobiiity, in: Review of Economics and Statistics, November, 356–362.

Fields, G. S. (1972): A theory of education and labor markets in less developed countries, Unpublished doctoral dissertation, Ann Arbor: Department of economics, University of Michigan.

Fields, G. S. (1974a): The allocation of resources to education in less developed countries, in: Journal of Public Economics, May, 133–143.

Fields, G. S. (1974b): The private demand for education in relation to labor market conditions in less developed countries, Economic Journal, December.

Frank Jr., C. R. (1971): The problem of urban unemployment in Africa, in: Ridker,

R. G., Lubell, H. (Eds.), Employment and unemployment problems of the Near East and South Asia, London: Vikas Publication.

Gugler, J. (1968): The impact of labour migration on society and economy in sub-Saharan Africa: Empirical findings and theoretical considerations, African Social Research 6, December.

Harberger, A. C. (1971): On measuring the social opportunity cost of labour, in: International Labour Review, June, 559–579.

Harris, J. R., Todaro, M.P. (1970): Migration, unemployment and development: A two-sector analysis, in: American Economic Review, 126–142.

Johnson, G. E. (1971): The structure of rural-urban migration models, in: Eastern Africa Economic Review, June, 21–28.

Jolly, R. (1969): Rural-urban migration: Dimensions, causes, issues and policies, in: Jolly, R. (Ed.), Education in Africa: Research and action, Nairobi: East African Publishing House, 117–126.

Kemeny, J. J., Snell, J. L. (1960): Finite Markov chains, New York: Van Nostrand Reinhold.

Kemeny, J. J., Snell, J. L. (1962): Mathematical models in the social sciences, New York: Blaisdell.

Krueger, A. (1971): Turkish education and manpower development: Some impressions, in: Miller, D. R. (Ed.), Essays on labor force and employment in Turkey, 225–256.

Lopez-Toro, A. (1970): Migration and urban marginality in underdeveloped countries, in: Demografía y Economía 4(2), 192–209.

Mazumdar, D. (1973): The theory of urban underempioyment in less developed countries, mimeo, Washington: International Bank for Reconstruction and Development.

Sjaastad, L. A. (1962): The costs and returns of human migration, in: Journal of Political Economy, October, part 2, 80–93.

Skorov, G. (1969): Highlights of the symposium, in: Manpower aspects of educational planning (UNESCO, Paris).

Stiglitz, J. E. (1969): Rural-urban migcation, surplus labour, and the relationship between urban and rural wages, in: Eastern Africa Economic Review, December, 1–28.

Thurow, L. C. (1972): Education and economic equality, Public Interest, summer, 66–81.

Todaro, M. P. (1968): An analysis of industrialization employment and unemployment in less developed countries, Yale Economic Essay, fall.

Todaro, M. P. (1969): A model of labor migration and urban unemployment in less developed countries, in: American Economic Review, March, 138–148.

Todaro, M. P. (1971): Education and rural-urban migration: Theoretical constructs and empirical evidence from Kenya, Paper prepared for a conference on urban unemployment in Africa, Institute for Development Studies, University of Sussex.

Turnham, D. (1971): The employment problem in less developed countries, Paris: Development Centre for the Organisation for Economic Cooperation and Development.

Chapter 5

Anand, S., Joshi, V. (1979): Domestic distortions, income distribution and the theory of optimum subsidy, in: The Economic Journal, June, 336–352.

Banerjee, B. (1983): The role of the informal sector in the migration process: A test of probabilistic migration models and labour market segmentation for India, Oxford Economic Papers, 399–422.

Burdett, K., Mortensen, D. T. (1978): Labor supply under uncertainty, in: Ehrenberg, R. G. (Ed.), Research in labor economics, Vol. 2, Greenwich, CT: JAI Press, 109–157.

Fields, G. S. (1974): The private demand for education in relation to labor market conditions in less developed countries, in: The Economic Journal, Dec., 906–925.

Fields, G. S. (1975): Rural-urban migration, urban unemployment and under-employment, and job search activity in LDCs, in: Journal of Development Economics, June, 165–187.

Fields, G. S. (1976): Labor force migration, unemployment, and job turnover, in: Review of Economics and Statistics, Nov., 407–415.

Gramlich, E. M. (1976): Impact of minimum wages on other wages, employment and family incomes, in: Brookings Papers on Economic Activity 2, 409–461.

Hall, R. E. (1970): Why is the unemployment rate so high at full employment?, in: Brookings Papers on Economic Activity, 369–409.

Hanushek, E. A. (1983): Alternative models of earnings determination and labor market structures, in: Journal of Human Resources, 238–259.

Harberger, A. C. (1971): On measuring the social opportunity cost of labour, in: International Labour Review, June, 559–579.

Harris, J. R., Todaro, M. P. (1970): Migration, unemployment and development: A two-sector analysis, in: American Economic Review, March, 126–142.

Matilla, J. P. (1974): Job quitting and frictional unemployment, in: American Economic Review, March, 235–239.

McDonald, I. M., Solow, R. M. (1985): Wages and employment in a segmented labor market, in: Quarterly Journal of Economics, Nov., 1115–1141.

Merrick, T. (1976): Employment and earnings in the informal sector in Brazil: The case of Belo Horizonte, in: Journal of Developing Areas, April, 337–354.

Mincer, J. (1976): Unemployment effects of minimum wages. in: Journal of Political Economy, July/Aug., Part 2, 87–I04.

Squire, L. (1981): Employment policy in developing countries, New York: Oxford University Press.

Stiglitz, J. E. (1982): The structure of labor markets and shadow prices in L.D.C.'s, in: Sabot, R. H. (Ed.), Migration and the labor market in developing countries, Westview Press, Boulder, CO, 13–63.

Tobin, J. (1972): Inflation and unemployment, American Economic Review, March, 1–18.

Todaro, M. P. (1976): Internal migration in developing countries, Geneva: International Labor Office.

Chapter 6

Adelman, I., Taft Morris, C. (1973): Economic Growth and Social Equity in Developing Countries, Stanford: Stanford University Press.

Atkinson, A. B. (1970): On the Measurement of Inequality, Journal of Economic Theory, 11, 244–63.

Ayub, M. (1976): Income Inequality in a Growth-Theoretic Context: The Case of Pakistan, Ph.D. thesis, Yale University.

Bardhan, P. K. (1974): The Pattern of Income Distribution in India: A Review, in: Srinivasan, T. N., Bardhan, P. K. (Eds.), Poverty and Income Distribution in India, Calcutta: Statistical Publishing Society.

Berg, E. (1969): Wage Structure in Less Developed Countries, in: Smith, A. D. (Ed.), Wage Policy Issues in Economic Development, London: Macmillan.

Berry, R. A., Urrutia, M. (1976): Income Distribution in Colombia, New Haven: Yale University Press.

Bowman, M. J. (1973): Poverty in an Affluent Society, in: Chamberlain, N. W. (Ed.), Contemporary Economic Issues, Homewood, Ill: Richard D. Irwin, Inc.

Champernowne, D. G. (1974): A Comparison of Measures of Inequality of Income Distribution, in: Economic Journal, LXXXIV, Dec., 787–816.

Chenery, H. B., et al. (1974): Redistribution with Growth, New York: Oxford University Press.

Cline, W. R. (1975): Distribution and Development: A Survey of the Literature, in: Journal of Development Economics, I, Feb., 359–400.

Dalton, H. (1920): The Measurement of the Inequality of Incomes, in: Economic Journal, XXX (Sept.), 348–61.

Fei, J. C. H., Ranis, G. (1964): Development of the Labor Surplus Economy, Homewood, Ill: Irwin.

Fei, J. C. H., Ranis, G., Kuo, S. W. Y. (1978): Growth and the Family Distribution of Income by Factor Components, in: this Journal, XCII, Feb., 17–53.

Fields, G. S. (1977): Who Benefits from Economic Development? A Re-Examination of Brazilian Growth in the 1960's, in: American Economic Review, LXVII, Sept., 570–82.

Fields, G. S., Fei, J. C. H. (1978): On Inequality Comparisons, in: Econometrica, XLVI, March, 303–16.

Fishlow, A. (1972): Brazilian Size Distribution of Income, in: American Economic Review, LXII, May, 391–402.

Hirschman, A. O., Rothschild, M. (1973): The Changing Tolerance for Income Inequality in the Course of Economic Development, in: this Journal, LXXXVII, Nov., 544–66.

Jorgenson, D. (1961): Development of the Dual Economy, in: Economic Journal, LXXI, March, 309–37.

Kondor, Y. (1975): Value Judgements Implied by the Use of Various Measures of Income Inequality, in: Review of Income and Wealth, XXI, Oct., 309–21.

Kuznets, S. (1955): Economic Growth and Income Inequality, in: American Economic Review, XLV, March, 1–28.

Kuznets, S. (1963): Quantitative Aspects of the Economic Growth of Nations:

VIII: Distribution of Income by Size, in: Economic Development and Cultural Change, XI, Part II, Jan., 1–80.

Kuznets, S. (1966): Modern Economic Growth, New Haven: Yale University Press.

Langoni, C. (1972): Distribuicao da Renda e Desenvolvimento Economico do Brasil, in: Estudos Economicos, II, Oct., 5–88.

Lewis, W. A. (1954): Economic Development with Unlimited Supplies of Labor, The Manchester School, XXII, May, 139–91.

Little, I. M. D., Mirrlees, J. A. (1969): Manual of Industrial Prolect Analysis in Development Countries, Volume II: Social Cost Benefit Analysis, Paris: OECD.

Perlman, R. (1976): The Economics of Poverty, New York: McGraw-Hill.

Rawls, J. (1971): A Theory of Justice, Cambridge, Mass.: Harvard University Press.

Robinson, S. (1976): A Note on the U Hypothesis Relating Income Inequality and Economic Development, in: American Economic Review, LXVI, June, 437–40.

Rothschild, M., Stiglitz, J. E. (1973): Some Further Results on the Measurement of Inequality, in: Journal of Economic Theory, VIII, April, 188–204.

Sen, A. K. (1976a): Poverty: An Ordinal Approach to Measurement, in: Econometrica, XLIV, March, 219–31.

Sen, A. K. (1976b): Real National Income, in: Review of Economic Studies, XLIII(1), 19–39.

Sheshinski, E. (1972): Relation Between a Social Welfare Function and the Gini Index of Inequality, in: Journal of Economic Theory, IV, 98–99.

Stern, N. H. (1972): Optimum Development in a Dual Economy, in: Review of Economic Studies, XXXIX(2), April, 171–84.

Swamy, S. (1967): Structural Changes and the Distribution of Income by Size: The Case of India, in: Review of Income and Wealth, XIII, June, 155–74.

Szal, R. J., Robinson, S. (1977): Measuring Income Inequality, in: Frank, Jr., C. R., Webb, R. C. (Eds.), Income Distribution and Growth in the Less-Developed Countries, Washington: Brookings Institution.

Turnham, D. (1971): The Employment Problem in Less Developed Countries, Paris: Organization for Economic Cooperation and Development.

Weisskoff, R. (1970): Income Distribution and Economic Growth in Puerto Rico, Argentina and Mexico, in: Review of Income and Wealth, XVI, Dec., 303–32.

Chapter 8

Ahluwalia, M. S. (2007): Planning, in: Basu, K. (Ed.), The Oxford Companion to Economics in India. Oxford University Press, New Delhi.

Anand, G. (2011): India Graduates Millions, but Too Few Are Fit to Hire. Wall Street Journal, April, 5.

Arnal, E., Förster, M. (2010): Growth, Employment and Inequality in Brazil, China, India and South Africa: An Overview, in: Arnal, E., Förster, M. (Eds.), Tackling Inequalities in Brazil, China, India, and South Africa. OECD, Paris.

Asian Development Bank (2007): Key Indicators 2007, Asian Development Bank, Manila.

Banerjee, A., Duflo, E. (2011): Poor Economics, Public Affairs, New York.

Banerjee, A., Galiani, S., Levinsohn, J., McLaren, Z., Woolard, I. (2008): Why Has

Unemployment Risen in the New South Africa? in: Econ Transit 16(4): 715–740.

Bardhan, P. (2010): Awakening Giants: Feet of Clay. Princeton University Press, Princeton.

Besley, T., Burgess, R. (2004): Can Labor Regulation Hinder Economic Performance? Evidence from India. in: Q J Econ 119 (1): 91–134.

Bhorat, H., Leibbrandt, M., Maziya, M., van der Berg, S., Woolard, I. (2001): Fighting Poverty: Labor Markets and Inequality in South Africa, Cape Town: University of Cape Town Press.

Bhorat, H. (2012): What Are the Most Important Research Questions on the Economics of Growth and Labour Markets in Low-Income Countries? University of Cape Town, processed.

Cai, F., Du, Y. (2006): Changing nature of rural poverty in China and new policy orientation, in: Chin Econ 39(4).

Cai, F., Wang, M. (2010): Growth and structural changes in employment in transition China. in: J Comp Econ 38: 71–81.

Carrillo, J. (2010): The Maquila model in Mexico: industrial upgrading or downgrading? Presentation at Cornell University.

Chen, S., Ravallion, M. (2012): An Update to the World Bank's Estimates of Consumption Poverty in the Developing World, Washington: World Bank.

Cho, Y., Margolis, D., Newhouse, D., Robalino, D. (2012): Labor Markets in Middle and Low Income Countries: Trends and Implications for Social Protection and Labor Policies, World Bank Social Protection & Labor Discussion Paper No. 1207.

de Mel, S., McKenzie, D., Woodruff, C. (2008): Returns to capital in microenterprises: evidence from a field experiment. in: Q J Econ 123(4): 1329–1372.

Dollar, D., Glewwe, P., Agrawal, N. (2004): Economic Growth, Poverty, and Household Welfare in Vietnam, Washington: World Bank.

Duhigg, C., Bradsher, K. (2012): How the U.S. Lost Out on iPhone Work. The New York Times, January 21.

Easterly, W. (2006): The White Man's Burden, New York: Penguin Books.

ECLAC (United Nations Economic Commission for Latin America and the Caribbean) (2011): Social Panorama of Latin America, Santiago: ECLAC.

Fair Labor Association (2012): Independent Investigation of Apple Supplier. Report Highlights, Foxconn, Available online at www.fairlabor.org.

Fields, G. S. (1980): Poverty, Inequality, and Development, New York: Cambridge University Press.

Fields, G. S. (1984): Employment, Income Distribution and Economic Growth in Seven Small Open Economies, in: Econ J 94 (373): 74–83.

Fields, G. S. (1994): Changing labor market conditions and economic development in Hong Kong, the Republic of Korea, Singapore, and Taiwan, China, in: The World Bank Economic Review 8(3): 395–414.

Fields, G. S. (2001): Distribution and Development: A New look at the Developing World, Cambridge, MA and New York: MIT Press and Russell Sage Foundation.

Fields, G. S. (2012): Working Hard, Working Poor: A Global Journey, New York: Oxford University Press.

Fields, G. S., Bagg, W. S. (2003): Long-Term Economic Mobility and the Private

Sector in Developing Countries: New Evidence, in: Fields, G. S., Pfeffermann, G. (Eds.), Pathways out of Poverty, Boston: Kluwer.

Fields, G. S., Raju, D. (2007): Assessing Current and Changing Labor Market Conditions in Brazil, Report prepared for the World Bank, processed.

Fox, L., Gaal, M. S. (2008): Working Out of Poverty: Job Creation and the Quality of Growth in Africa, Washington: World Bank.

Freeman, R. B. (2010): Labor Regulations, Unions, and Social Protection in Developing Countries: Market Distortions or Efficient Institutions? in: Rodrik, D., Rosenzweig, M. (Eds.), Handbook of Development Economics, Volume 5., Amsterdam: Elsevier.

Ghose, A. (2011): Employment: The Faultline in India's Emerging Economy, Paper presented at the Workshop on Employment – Global and Country Perspectives. New York University, September, 2011.

Güder, G. (2006): Changing Labor Market Conditions and Economic Growth and Crisis in Turkey, Korea and Mexico. Unpublished Masters thesis, Cornell University.

Gutierrez, C., Paci, P., Ranzani, M. (2008): Making Work Pay in Nicaragua, Washington: World Bank.

Heal, G. (2008): When Principles Pay, New York: Columbia Business School.

Hoftijzer, M., Paci, P. (2008): Making Work Pay in Madagascar, Washington: World Bank.

International Labor Organization (ILO) (2008): World of Work Report 2008, Geneva: ILO.

International Labor Organization (ILO) (2012): Global Employment Trends, Geneva: ILO.

Karlan, D., Appel, J. (2011): More Than Good Intentions, New York: Dutton.

Kingdon, G., Knight, J. B. (2008): Unemployment: South Africa's Achilles Heel, in: Aron, J., Kahn, B., Kingdon, G. (Eds.), South African Economic Policy under Democracy, Oxford: Oxford University Press.

Kotwal, A., Ramaswami, B., Wadhwa, W. (2011): Economic Liberalization and Indian Economic Growth: What's the Evidence?, in: J Econ Lit 49(4): 1152–1199.

Leibbrandt, M., Woolard, I., McEwen, H., Koep, C. (2010): Better Employment to Reduce Inequality Further in South Africa, in: Arnal, E., Lin, J. Y. (2012), New Structural Economics, Washington: The World Bank.

McKenzie, D. J., Woodruff, C. (2006): Do Entry Costs Provide an Empirical Basis for Poverty Traps? Evidence from Mexican Microenterprises, in: Economic Development and Cultural Change 55: 3–42.

National Commission for Enterprises in the Unorganised Sector (2009): The Challenge of Employment in India: An Informal Economy Perspective, Delhi: Academic Foundation.

Paci, P., Sasin, M. (2008): Making Work Pay in Bangladesh, Washington: World Bank.

Psacharopoulos, G., Patrinos, H. (2004): Returns to investment in education: a further update. in: Educ Econ 12(2): 111–134.

Rangel, E. (2009): Have the Poor in Mexico Benefited from Economic Growth in

Mexico from 2000 to 2006? Unpublished Masters thesis, Cornell University.

Reddy, R. R. (2012): Poor Quality of Engineers in India, The Hindu.

Rodrik, D. (2007): One Economics, Many Recipes: Globalization, Institutions, and Economic Growth, Princeton: Princeton University Press.

Rosenzweig, M. R. (2012): Thinking Small: A Review of Poor Economics: A Radical Rethinking of the Way to Fight Global Poverty by Abhijit Banerjee and Esther Duflo, in: J Econ Lit 50(1): 115–127.

Sabel, C., Fernández-Arias, E., Hausmann, R., Rodríguez-Clare, A., Stein, E. (Eds.) (2012): Export Pioneers in Latin America, Washington and Cambridge: Inter-American Development Bank and Harvard University.

Sachs, J. (2005): The End of Poverty, New York: Penguin Books.

Schultz, T. P. (1988): Education Investments and Returns, in: Chenery, H., Srinivasan, T. N. (Eds.), Handbook of Development Economics, Rotterdam: North Holland.

Song, Y. (2012): Central Features of the Current Chinese Labor Market, Cornell University, processed.

Spielman, D. J., Pandya-Lorch, R. (2009): Millions Fed: Proven Successes in Agricultural Development, Washington: International Food Policy Research Institute.

Stiglitz, J. E. (2012): The Price of Inequality, New York: Norton.

Stiglitz, J. E., Charlton, A. (2005): Fair Trade for All, Oxford: Oxford University Press.

Tao, R. (2006): The Labor Market in the People's Republic of China: Development and Policy Challenges in Economic Transition, in: Felipe, J., Hasan, R. (Eds.), Labor Markets in Asia: issues and Perspectives, Manila: Asian Development Bank.

Tavernise, S. (2011): Percentage of Americans Living in Poverty Rises to Highest Level Since 1993, The New York Times.

United Nations (2011): Human Development Report 2011, New York: United Nations.

World Bank (2011): More and Better Jobs in South Asia, Washington: World Bank.

World Bank (2012): World Development Report 2012, Washington: World Bank.

Yang, D. T., Chen, V., W., Monarch R. (2010): Rising Wages: Has China Lost Its Global Labor Advantage? in: Pac Econ Rev 15 (4):482–504.

Yang, Y., Gu, Y. (2010): Registered Unemployment versus Surveyed Unemployment in China, in: Jianmin, L. (Ed.), Chinese Labor Market: Perspectives, Problems and Solutions, Nankai University Press.

Chapter 9

Atkinson, A. B. (1970): On the Measurement of Inequality, in: Journal of Economic Theory, 5, 244–263.

Champernowne, D. G. (1974): A Comparison of Measures of Inequality of Income Distribution, in: The Economic Journal, 84, 787–816.

Dalton, H. (1920): The Measurement of the Inequality of Incomes, in: Economic Journal, 30, 348–361.

Dasgupta, P., Sen, A., Starrett, D. (1973): Notes on the Measurement of Inequality, in: Journal of Economic Theory, 8, 180–187.

Hicks, J. R. (1939): Value and Capital. Oxford: The Clarendon Press.

Hirschman, A. (1973): The Changing Tolerance for Income Inequality in the Course of Economic Development, with a mathematical appendix by Michael Rothschild, in: Quarterly Journal of Economics, 87, 544–566.

Kondor, Y. (1975): Value Judgements Implied by the Use of Various Measures of Income Inequality, in: Review of Income and Wealth, 21, 309–321.

Kuznets, S. (1957): Quantitative Aspects of the Economic Growth of Nations, II: Industrial Distribution of National Product and Labor Force, in: Economic Development and Cultural Change, 5 (Supplement), 3–111.

Rothschild, M., Stiglitz, J. E. (1973): Some Further Results on the Measurement of Inequality, in: Journal of Economic Theory, 8, 188–204.

Sen, A. K. (1973): On Economic Inequality, New York: Norton.

Sen, A. K. (1976): Poverty: An Ordinal Approach to Measurement, in: Econometrica, 44, 219–231.

Szal, R., Robinson, S. (1975): Measuring Income Inequality, Princeton University and Brookings Institution, mimeo.

Theil, H. (1967): Economics and Information Theory, Chicago: Rand McNally.

Chapter 10

Amiel, Y., Cowell, F. (1992): Measurement of income inequality: experimental test by questionnaire, in: Journal of Public Economics, 47, 3–26.

Anand, S., Kanbur, R. (1993): The Kuznets process and the inequality development relationship, in: Journal of Development Economics, 40, 25–52.

Atkinson, A. B. (1970): On the measurement of inequality, in: Journal of Economic Theory, 2, 244–63.

Atkinson, A. B. (1983): Social Justice and Public Policy, Cambridge, MA: MIT Press.

Blackorby, C., Donaldson, D. (1977): Utility vs. equity: some plausible quasiorderings, in: Journal of Public Economics, 7, 365–81.

Blackorby, C. (1984): Ethically significant ordinal indexes of relative inequality, in: Advances in Econometrics, 3, 131–47.

Dalton, H. (1920): The measurement of the inequahty of incomes, in: Economic Journal, 3, 348–61.

Dasgupta, P., Sen, A., Starrett, D. (1973): Notes on the measurement of inequality, in: Journal of Economic Theory, 6, 180–7.

Ebert, U. (1987): Size and distribution of incomes as determinants of social welfare, in: Journal of Economic Theory, 41, 23–33.

Eichhorn, W., Gehrig, W. (1982): Measurement of inequality in economics, in: Korte, B. (Ed.), Modern Applied Mathematics, Amsterdam: North-Holland.

Fields, G. S. (1979): A welfare economic analysis of growth and distribution in the dual economy, in: Quarterly Journal of Economics, 93, 325–53.

Fields, G. S. (1987): Measuring inequality change in an economy with income growth, in: Journal of Development Economics, 26, 357–74.

Fields, G. S. (1993): Inequality in dual economy models, in: Economic Journal,

103, 1228–1235.

Fields, G. S., Fei, J. E. H. (1978): On inequality comparisons, in: Econometrica, 46, 303–16.

Foster, J. (1985): Inequality measurement, in: Peyton Young, H. (Ed.), Fair Allocation, Providence, RI: American Mathematical Society.

Kakwani, N. (1988): Income inequality, welfare and poverty in a developing economy with applications to Sri Lanka, in: Gaertner, W., Pattanaik, P. K. (Eds.), Distributive Justice and Inequality, New York: Springer-Verlag.

Knight, J. B. (1976): Explaining income distribution in less developed countries: a framework and an agenda, in: Bulletin of the Oxford Institute of Economics and Statistics, 58, 161–77.

Kolm, S. C. (1966): The optimal production of social justice, in: Guitton, H., Margolis, J. (Eds.), Public Economics, London: Macmillan.

Kolm, S. C. (1976): Unequal inequalities, in: Journal of Economic Theory, 12, 416–42.

Kuznets, S. (1955): Economic growth and income inequality, in: American Economic Review, 45, 1–28.

Kuznets, S. (1966): Modern Economic Growth, New Haven: Yale University Press.

Lambert, P. (1989): The Distribution and Redistribution of Income, Cambridge, MA: Blackwell.

Robinson, S. (1976): A note on the U hypothesis relating income inequality and economic development, in: American Economic Review, 66, 437–40.

Rothschild, M., Stiglitz, J. (1973): Equilibrium in competitive insurance markets: an essay on the economics of imperfect information, in: Quarterly Journal of Economics, 90, 629–50.

Sen, A. K. (1973): On Economic Inequality, Oxford: Oxford University Press 1982. Choice, Welfare and Measurement, Oxford: Basil Blackwell (forthcoming). Equality and Diversity.

Shorrocks, A., Foster, J. (1987): Transfer sensitive inequality measures, in: Review of Economic Studies, 54, 485–97.

Swamy, S. (1967): Structural changes and the distribution of income by size: the case of India, in: Review of Income and Wealth, 13, 155–74.

Temkin, L. S. (1986): Inequality, in: Philosophy and Public Affairs, 15, 99–121.

Chapter 11

Atkinson, A. B. (1983a): The Economics of Inequality, 2d ed., Oxford: Claredon.

Bhagwati, J. N. (1991): The World Trading System at Risk, Princeton: Princeton University Press.

Bhagwati, J. N., Srinivasan, T. N. (1983): Lectures on International Trade, Cambridge: MIT Press.

Blackburn, M. L. (1994): International Comparisons of Poverty, American Economic Association Papers and Proceedings 84(2), May, 371–374.

Council of Economic Advisers (1964): Economic Report of the President, Washington, DC: U.S. Government Printing Office.

Dandekar, V. M., Rath, N. (1971): Poverty in India, Pune: Indian School of Political

Economy.

Deaton, A. (1997): The Analysis of Household Surveys. A Microeconomic Approach to Development Policy, Washington, DC: World Bank.

Foster, J. E., Sen, A. K. (1997): On Economic Inequality After a Quarter Century, in: Sen, A. (Ed.), On Economic Inequality, 2d ed., Oxford: Claredon Paperbacks.

Ganuza, E., Morley, S., Taylor, L. (1998): Politicas Macroeconomicas en América Latina y el Caribe, 1980-1996, Mexico, D.F.: Fondo de Cultura Económica.

Lipton, M., Ravallion, M. (1995): Poverty and Policy, in: Behrman, J., Srinivasan, T. N. (Eds.), Handbook of Development Economics, Volume III, Amsterdam: Elsevier Science.

Minhas, B. S., Jain, L. R., Kansal, S. M., Saluja, M. R. (1987): On the Choice of Appropriate Consumer Price Indices and Data Sets for Estimating the Incidence of Poverty in India, The Indian Economic Review, January-June.

Orshansky, M. (1965): Counting the Poor: Another Look at the Poverty Profile, Social Security Bulletin, January.

Ravallion, M (1994): Poverty Comparisons, Chur, Switzerland: Harwood Academic Publishers.

Sen, A. K. (1997): From Income Inequality to Economic Inequality, Southern Economic Journal 64(2), 384-401.

Srinivasan, T. N., Bardhan, P. K. (1988): Introduction, in: Srinivasan, T. N., Bardhan, P. K. (Eds.), Rural Poverty in South Asia, New York: Columbia University Press.

Chapter 12

Anand, S., Kanbur, S. M. R. (1993b): The Kuznets Process and the Inequality-Development Relationship, Journal of Development Economics 40(1), 25-52.

Atkinson, A. B. (1970): On the Measurement of Inequality, Journal of Economic Theory.

Atkinson, A. B. (1983b): Social Justice and Public Policy, Cambridge: MIT Press.

Barros, R. P. d., Mendoça, R. S. P. d. (1995): The Evolution of Welfare, Poverty and Inequality in Brazil Over the Last Three Decades: 1960-1990, IPEA, March.

Bishop, J. A., Formby, J. P. (1994): A Dominance Evaluation of Distributions of Income and the Benefits of Economic Growth, in: Bergstrand, J. H., et al. (Eds.), The Changing Distribution of Income in an Open U.S. Economy, Amsterdam: Elsevier.

Buchanan, J., Tullock, G. (1962): The Calculus of Consent, Ann Arbor: University of Michigan Press.

Fields, G. S. (1979a): A Welfare Economic Approach to Growth and Distribution in the Dual Economy, Quarterly Journal of Economics, August.

Foster, J. E., Sen, A. K. (1997): On Economic Inequality After a Quarter Century, in: Sen, A. (Ed.), On Economic Inequality, 2d ed., Oxford: Claredon Paperbacks.

Hammond, P. (1989): Envy, in: Eatwell, J., Milgate, M., Newman, P., The New Palgrave: Social Economics, New York: Norton.

Kakwani, N. (1984): Welfare Rankings of Income Distribution, in: Basmann, R., Rhodes, G., Advances in Econometrics, Greenwich, CT: JAI Press.

Knight, J. B. (1976): Explaining Income Distribution in Less Developed Countries: A Framework and an Agenda, Bulletin of the Oxford Institute of Economics and Statistics, August.

Lambert, P. J. (1989): The Distribution and Redistribution of Income: A Mathematical Analysis, Oxford: Blackwell, Second edition published by University of Manchester Press, 1993.

Pyatt, G. (1989): Social Evaluation Criteria, in: Dagum, C., Zenga, M., Income and Wealth Distribution, Inequality and Poverty, Berlin: Springer-Verlag.

Sherman, R. (1976): A Note on the U Hypothesis Relating Income Inequality and Economic Development, American Economic Review, June, 437–440.

Sen, A. K. (1970): Collective Choice and Welfare, San Fransico: Holden-Day.

Sen, A. K. (1973): On Economic Inequality, New York: Oxford.

Shorrocks, A. F. (1983): Ranking Income Distributions, Economica 50, February, 3–17.

Welch, F. (1999): In Defense of Inequality, American Economic Review 89(2), May, 1–17.

Chapter 13

Atkinson, A. (1970): On the measurement of inequality, in: Journal of Economic Theory 2, 244–63.

Atkinson, A. (1980): The measurement of economic mobility, in: Eijgelshoen, P., van Gemerden, L. (Eds.), Inkomensverdeling en Openbare Financién, Utrecht: Het Spectrum.

Atkinson, A. B., Bourguignon, F., Morrisson, C. (1992): Empirical Studies of Earnings Mobility, London: Harwood Academic Publishers.

Bartholomew, D. (1982): Stochastic Models for Social Processes, London: Wiley.

Bound, J., Brown, C., Mathiowetz, N. (2001): Measurement error in survey data, in: Heckman, J., Leamer, E. (Eds.), Handbook of Econometrics, vol. 5, Amsterdam: North-Holland.

Buchinsky, M., Fields, G., Fougère, D., Kramarz, F. (2004): Francs or ranks? Earnings Mobility in France, 1967-1999. Mimeo. Paris: INSEE.

Chakravarty, S., Dutta, B., Weymark, J. (1985): Ethical indices of income mobility. Social Choice and Welfare 2, 1–21.

Chronic Poverty Research Centre (2004): The Chronic Poverty Report 2004–05, Manchester: Chronic Poverty Research Centre.

Cowell, F. (1985): Measures of distributional change: an axiomatic approach, in: Review of Economic Studies 52, 135–51.

D'Agostino, M., Dardanoni, V. (2005): The measurement of mobility: a class of distance indices, Paper presented to the Society for the Study of Economic Inequality, Palma de Mallorca, Spain, July.

Dardanoni, V. (1993): Measuring social mobility, in: Journal of Economic Theory 61, 372–94.

Deaton, A. (1997): The Analysis of Household Surveys, Baltimore, MD: Johns Hopkins University Press.

Duval Hernández, R. (2005): Dynamics of labor market earnings and sector of employment in urban Mexico, Doctoral dissertation, Cornell University.

Fields, G. (2001): Distribution and Development: A New Look at the Developing

World, Cambridge, MA: MIT Press and Russell Sage Foundation.

Fields, G. (2005): Does income mobility equalize longer-term incomes? New measures of an old concept, Mimeo, Cornell University.

Fields, G., Leary, J., Ok, E. (2002): Stochastic dominance in mobility analysis, in: Economics Letters 75, 333–9.

Fields, G., Ok, E. (1996): The meaning and measurement of income mobility, in: Journal of Economic Theory 71, 349–77.

Fields, G., Ok, E. (1999a): The measurement of income mobility: an introduction to the literature, in: Silber, J. (Ed.), Handbook on Income Inequality Measurement, Boston: Kluwer.

Fields, G., Ok, E. (1999b): Measuring movement of incomes, in: Economica 66, 455–72.

Foster, J., Sen, A. (1997): On Economic Inequality, expanded edition, Oxford: Oxford University Press.

Freije, S. (2001): Household income dynamics in Venezuela. Unpublished doctoral dissertation, Cornell University.

Gottschalk, P., Spolaore, E. (2002): On the evaluation of economic mobility, in: Review of Economic Studies 69, 191–208.

Jarvis, S., Jenkins, S. (1998): How much income mobility is there in Britain?, in: Economic Journal 108, 1–16.

Jenkins, S., Van Kerm, P. (2003): Trends in income inequality, pro-poor income growth, and income mobility, Discussion Paper No. 904, Bonn: IZA.

King, M. (1983): An index of inequality, with applications to horizontal equity and social mobility, in: Econometrica 51, 99–115.

Krugman, P. (1992): The rich, the right, and the facts, in: American Prospect 11, 19–31.

Maasoumi, E. (1998): On mobility, in: Giles, D., Ullah, A. (Eds.), Handbook of Applied Economic Statistics, New York: Marcel Dekker.

Markandya, A. (1982): Intergenerational exchange mobility and economic welfare, in: European Economic Review 17, 301–24.

Markandya, A. (1984): The welfare measurement of changes in economic mobility, in: Economica 51, 457–71.

OECD (Organisation for Economic Co-Operation and Development) (1996): Employment Outlook 1996, Paris: OECD.

OECD (1997): Employment Outlook 1997, Paris: OECD.

Ruiz-Castillo, J. (2004): The measurement of structural and exchange mobility, in: Journal of Economic Inequality 2, 219–28.

Sánchez Puerta, M. (2005): Earnings mobility in urban Argentina, Unpublished doctoral dissertation, Cornell University.

Schumpeter, J. (1955): Imperialism and Social Classes, New York: Meridian Books.

Sen, A. (1973): On Economic Inequality, New York: Norton.

Shorrocks, A. (1978a): Income inequality and income mobility, in: Journal of Economic Theory 19, 376–93.

Shorrocks, A. (1978b): The measurement of mobility, in: Econometrica 46, 1013–24.

Shorrocks, A. (1993): On the Hart measure of income mobility, in: Casson, M.,

Creedy, J. (Eds.), Industrial Concentration and Economic Inequality, London: Edward Elgar.

Slemrod, J. (1992): Taxation and inequality: a time-exposure perspective, in: Poterba, J. (Ed.), Tax Policy and the Economy, vol. 6, Cambridge, MA: MIT Press for the NBER.

Solon, G. (1999): Intergenerational mobility in the labor market, in: Ashenfelter, O., Card, D. (Ed.), Handbook of Labor Economics, vol. 3, Amsterdam: North-Holland.

Chapter 14

Acemoglu, D., Autor, D. H. (2011): Skills, tasks and technologies: Implications for employment and earnings, in: Ashenfelter, O., Card, D. E. (Eds.), Handbook of Labor Economics, vol. 4, 1043–1171, Amsterdam: Elsevier.

Antman, F., McKenzie, D. J. (2007): Earnings mobility and measurement error: A pseudo-panel approach, in: Econ. Dev. Cult. Chang. 56(1), 125–161.

Atkinson, A. B., Bourguignon, F. (Eds.): Handbook of Income Distribution, vol. 2. Elsevier, Amsterdam (2015).

Azariadis, C., Stachurski, J. (2005): Poverty Traps, in: Aghion, P., Durlauf, S. N. (Eds.), Handbook of Economic Growth, vol. 1A, 295–384, Amsterdam: Elsevier Science.

Baulch, B. (Ed.) (2011): Why Poverty Persists: Poverty Dynamics in Asia and Africa, Edward Elgar, Cheltenham.

Bound, J., Brown, C., Duncan, G. J., Rodgers, W. L. (1994): Evidence on the validity of cross-sectional and longitudinal labor market data reviewed, in: J. Labor Econ. 12(3), 345–368.

Bound, J., Brown, C., Mathiowetz, N. (2001): Measurement error in survey data, in: Heckman, J., Leamer, E. (Eds.), Handbook of Econometrics, vol. 5, 3705–3843, Amsterdam: Elsevier Science.

Cuesta, J., Ñopo, H., Pizzolitto, G. (2011): Using pseudo-panels to measure income mobility in Latin America, in: Rev. Income Wealth 57(2), 224–246.

Deaton, A. (1997): The Analysis of Household Surveys: A Microeconometric Approach to Development Policy, Baltimore: The Johns Hopkins University Press.

Duval Hernández, R. (2006): Dynamics of Labor Market Earnings and Sector of Employment in Urban Mexico, 1987–2002, Ph.D. dissertation, Cornell University.

Duval-Hernández, R., Fields, G. S., Jakubson, G. H. (2014): Changing Income Inequality and Panel Income Changes in Times of Economic Growth and Economic Decline, unpublished manuscript.

Fields, G. S., Duval-Hernández, R., Freije, S., Sánchez Puerta, M. L. (2007): Intragenerational income mobility in Latin America, in: Economía 7(2), 101–143.

Fields, G. S., Sánchez Puerta, M. L. (2010): Earnings mobility in times of growth and decline: Argentina from 1996 to 2003, in: World Dev. 38(9), 870–880.

Furceri, D. (2005): β and σ convergence: A mathematical relation of causality, in: Econ. Lett. 89, 212–215.

Gasparini, L., Lustig, N. (2011): The rise and fall of income inequality in Latin America, in: Ocampo, J. A., Ros, J. (Eds.), Oxford Handbook of Latin American Economics, Oxford: Oxford University Press.

Glewwe, P. (2010): How Much of Observed Economic Mobility is Measurement Error? IV Methods to Reduce Measurement Error Bias, with an Application to Vietnam, in: World Bank Econ Rev 26(2), 236–264.

Gottschalk, P. (1982): Earnings mobility: Permanent change or transitory fluctuations?, in: Rev. Econ. Stat. 64(3), 450–456.

Gottschalk, P., Huynh, M. (2010): Are earnings inequality and mobility overstated?, The impact of nonclassical measurement error, in: Rev. Econ. Stat. 92(2), 302–315.

Grimm, M. (2007): Removing the anonymity axiom in assessing pro-poor growth, in: J. Econ. Inequal. 5(2), 179–197.

Henry, A. (1978): Politics and the Professors, Washington, DC: Brookings Institution.

Jäntti, M., Jenkins, S. P. : Income Mobility, in: Atkinson, A. B., Bourguignon, F. (Eds.), Handbook of Income Distribution, vol. 2., Amsterdam: Elsevier (2015).

Krebs, T., Krishna, P., Maloney, W. F. (2012): Income Risk, Income Mobility and Welfare, IZA Discussion Paper No 7056.

Kuznets, S. (1955): Economic growth and income inequality, in: Am. Econ. Rev. XLV(March), 1–28.

Meade, J. E. (1976): The Just Economy, London: Allen and Unwin.

Merton, R. E. (1968): The Matthew effect in science, in: Science, 159.

Moffitt, R. A., Gottschalk, P. (2002): Trends in the transitory variance of earnings in the United States, in: Econ. J. 112 (March), C68–C73.

Palmisano, F., Peragine, V. (2014): The distributional incidence of growth: A social welfare approach, in: Rev. Income Wealth.

Ravallion, M. (2004): Pro-Poor Growth: A Primer, World Bank Policy Research Working Paper 3242.

Ravallion, M. (2009): A Comparative Perspective on Poverty Reduction in Brazil, China and India, World Bank Policy Research Working Paper 5080.

Sánchez Puerta, M. L. (2005): Earnings Mobility in Urban Argentina, Ph.D. dissertation, Cornell University.

Wodon, Q., Yitzhaki, S. (2006): Convergence forward and backward?, in: Econ. Lett. 92, 47–51.

Chapter 15

Arrow, K. J. (1968): Criteria for Social Investment', in: Bowman, M. J., et al. (Eds.), Redings in the Economics of Education, Paris: UNESCO, 869–880.

Balogh, T., Streeten, P. P. (1963): The Coefficient of Ignorance, Bulletin of the Oxford University Institute of Economics and Statistics, May, 99–107.

Becker, G. S. (1964): Human Capital, New York: Columbia University Press.

Berg, E. J. (1966): Major Issues of Wage Policies in Africa, in: Ross, A. M. (Ed.), Industrial Relations and Economic Development, London: MacMillan.

Blaug, M. (1967): A Cost-Benefit Approach to Educational Planning in Developing

Countries, International Bank for Reconstruction and Development, Report No. EC-157, December.

Bowen, W. G. (1968): Assessing the Economic Contribution of Education, in M. Blaugh, ed., Economics of Education 1, London: Penguin Books, 67–100.

Bowman, M. J. (1962): Converging Concerns of Economists and Educators, Comparative Education Review, October.

Cash, W. C. (1969): A Critique of Manpower Planning in Africa, Blaug, M. (Ed.), Economics of Education 2, London: Penguin Books, 98–122.

Fei, C. H., Ranis, G. (1964): Development of the Labor Surplus Economy Homewood, Illinois: IIwin.

Fields, G. S. (1971): The Educational System of Kenya: an Economist's View, University of Nairobi, Institute for Development Studies, Discussion Paper No. 103, April.

Fields, G. S. (1972): Private Rates of Return to Investment in Higher Levels of Education in Kenya, University of Michigan, Center for Research on Economic Development, Discussion Paper.

Hansen, W. L. (1963): Total and Private Rates of Return to Investment in Schooling, Journal of Political Economy, 128–141.

Lewis, W. A. (1968): Education and Economic Development, in: Bowman, M. J. (Ed.), Readings in the Economics of Education, Paris: UNESCO, 135–147.

Marshall, A. (1968): Principles of Economics, p. 216, quoted in: Report of the Meeting of Ministers of Education of Asian Member States Participating in the Karachi Plan, in: Bowman, M. J., et. al (Eds.), Readings in the Economics of Education, Paris: UNESCO, 148–150.

Merrett, S. (1966): The Rate of Return to Education, a Critique, Oxford Economic Papers, November, 289–303.

Moorthy, S. K., Sten, A. O. (1959): Accelerator Theory in Education, Indian Economic Review, February, 57–69.

Moris, J. (1967): Farmer Training as a Strategy of Rural Development, in: Sheffield, J. R. (Ed.), Education, Employment and Rural Development, Nairobi: East African Publishing House, 322–365.

Prest R., Turvey, R. (1965): Cost-Benefit Analysis: a Survey, Economic Journal, December.

Psacharopoulos, G. (1970): Estimating Shadow Rates of Return to Investment in Education, Journal of Human Resources, Winter, 34–50.

Psacharopoulos, G., Hinchliffe K. (1970): Rates of Return: International Comparison, London School of Economics, Higher Education Research Unit, mimeo.

Republic of Kenya (1969): Ministry of Education, Annual Report.

Thias, H. H., Carnoy, M. (1969): Cost-Benefit Analysis in Education : a Case Study on Kenya, IBRD, Report No. EC-173, November.

Weisbrod, B. A. (1962): Education and Investment in Human Capital, Journal of Political Economy, October, Part 2 (supplement), 106–123.

Wood, W. D., Campbell, H. F. (1969): Cost-Benefit Analysis and the Economics of Investment in Human Resources: an Annotated Bibliography, industrial Relations Centre, Queen's University.

References

Chapter 16

Anand, S., Vijay, J. (1979): Domestic distortions, income distribution and the theory of optimum subsidy, in: Economic Journal 89, 336–352, June.

Atkinson, A. B. (1987): On the measurement of poverty, in: Econometrica 55, 749–764, July.

Basu, K. (1997): Analytical Development Economics, Cambridge, MA: MIT Press.

Bell, C. (1991): Regional heterogeneity, migration, and shadow prices, in: Journal of Public Economics 46, 1–27, October.

Bhagwati, J. N., Srinivasan, T. N. (1974): On reanalyzing the Harris-Todaro model: policy rankings in the case of sector-specific sticky wages, in: American Economic Review 64, 502–508.

Bourguignon, F. (1990): Growth and inequality in the dual model of development: the role of demand factors, in: Review of Economic Studies 57, 215–228.

Calvo, G. A. (1978): Urban unemployment and wage determination in LDC's: trade unions in the Harris-Todaro model, in: International Economic Review 19, 65–81.

Chakravarty, S. R., Dutta, B. (1990): Migration and welfare, in: European Journal of Political Economy 6, 119–138.

Corden, M., Findlay, R. (1975): Urban unemployment, intersectoral capital mobility and development policy, in: Economica 42, 59–78, February.

Fields, G. S. (1975): Rural-urban migration, urban unemployment and underemployment, and job search activity in LDC's, in: Journal of Development Economics 2, 165–187, June.

Fields, G. S. (1989): On-the-job search in a labor market model: ex ante choices and ex post outcomes, in: Journal of Development Economics 30, 159–178, January.

Fields, G. S. (1997): Wage floors and unemployment: a two-sector analysis, in: Labour Economics 4, 85–92.

Foster, J. E., Shorrocks, A. F. (1988): Poverty orderings, in: Econometrica 56, 173–177.

Foster, J. E., Sen, A. K. (1997): On Economic Inequality After a Quarter Century., in: Sen, A. K. (Ed.), On Economic Inequality, Second edition, Oxford: Clarendon Paperbacks, 107–220.

Foster, J. E., Ok, E. A. (1999): Lorenz dominance and the variance of logarithms, in: Econometrica 67, 901–907, July.

Foster, J. E., Greer, J., Thorbecke, E. (1984): A class of decomposable poverty measures, in: Econometrica 52, 761–766.

Gupta, M. R. (1988): Migration, welfare, inequality and shadow wage, in: Oxford Economic Papers 40, 477–486.

Hadar, J., Russell, W. (1969): Rules for ordering uncertain prospects, in: American Economic Review 59, 25–34.

Harris, J. R., Todaro, M. P. (1970): Migration, unemployment and development: a two-sector analysis, in: American Economic Review 60, 126–142 (March).

Heady, C. J. (1981): Shadow wages and induced migration, in: Oxford Economic Papers 33, 108–121.

Khan, A. M. (1989): The Harris-Todaro Model, in: Eatwell, J., et al. (Eds.), The New Palgrave, London: MacMillan.

Lambert, P. J. (1993): The Distribution and Redistribution of Income, Second edition, Manchester: University of Manchester Press.

Marjit, S., Hamid, B. (2003): Possibility or impossibility of paradoxes in the small country Harris-Todaro framework: a unifying analysis, in: Journal of Development Economics 72, 379–385, October.

Moene, K. O. (1988): A reformulation of the Harris-Todaro mechanism with endogenous wages, in: Economics Letters 27, 387–390.

Moene, K. O. (1992): Poverty and landownership, in: American Economic Review 82, 52–64, March.

Rauch, J. R. (1993): Economic development, urban underemployment, and income inequality, in: Canadian Journal of Economics 26, 901–918, November.

Ravallion, M. (1994): Poverty Comparisons, Chur, Switzerland: Harwood Academic Publishers.

Sah, R. K., Stiglitz, J. E. (1985): The social cost of labor and project evaluation: a general approach (February), in: Journal of Public Economics 28, 135–163.

Saposnik, R. (1981): Rank dominance in income distributions, in: Public Choice 86, 147–151.

Sen, A. K. (1976): Poverty: an ordinal approach to measurement, in: Econometrica 44, 219–231.

Stiglitz, J. E. (1974): Alternative theories of wage determination and unemployment in LDCs: "The Labour Turnover Model," in: Quarterly Journal of Economics 88, 194–227, May.

Stiglitz, J. E. (1976): The efficiency wage hypothesis, surplus labour, and the distribution of income in LDCS, in: Oxford Economic Papers 28, 185–207, June.

Stiglitz, J. E. (1982): The Structure of Labor Markets and Shadow Prices in LDCs, in: Sabot, R. H. (Ed.), Migration and the Labor Market in Developing Countries, Boulder, CO: Westview Press, 13–63.

Temple, J. (1999): Income Distribution in the Harris-Todaro Model, Working Paper, Oxford University, March.

Temple, J. (2003): Growth and Wage Inequality in a Dual Economy, University of Bristol, August 21.

Todaro, M. P., Smith, S. C. (2003): Economic Development, Eighth edition, New York: Addison Wesley.

Index of Subjects

M

Index of Names

About the Author...

 ***Gary S. Fields*** is John P. Windmuller Professor of International and Comparative Labor and Professor of Economics at Cornell University, Program Coordinator of the IZA Program on Labor and Development, and a UNU-WIDER Non-Resident Senior Research Fellow. He has been an Ivy League teacher and professor for more than forty years. He teaches and conducts research in labor economics and development economics, and has published more than 150 books and articles.

Gary S. Fields received the 2014 IZA Prize in Labor Economics.

...and the Editor

Janneke Pieters is tenured Assistant Professor at Wageningen University, Netherlands. She is a IZA Research Fellow and EUDN Associate Member. From 2011 till 2014 Pieters has been Research Associate at the IZA and Deputy Program Director for IZA's and the United Kingdom Department of International Development's GLM|LIC programme. Also she did short term consultancies for the World Bank and the European Commission. She received her B.Sc. (2005), M.Sc. (2007) and Ph.D. (2011) at the University of Groningen, Netherlands.

Her main research interests are employment and development, women's economic empowerment as well as international trade. Janneke Pieters articles were published e.g. in the Journal of Human Resources, World Bank Economic Review and the IZA Journal of Labor and Development.

Printed and bound by CPI Group (UK) Ltd, Croydon, CR0 4YY